THE CACOPHONY OF POLITICS

A Nation Divided: Studies in the Civil War Era

orville vernon burton and elizabeth r. varon, *Editors*

THE CACOPHONY OF POLITICS

NORTHERN DEMOCRATS AND THE AMERICAN CIVIL WAR

J. MATTHEW GALLMAN

UNIVERSITY OF VIRGINIA PRESS
Charlottesville and London

University of Virginia Press

Printed in the United States of America on acid-free paper

First published 2021
1 3 5 7 9 8 6 4 2

Library of Congress Cataloging-in-Publication Data

Names: Gallman, J. Matthew (James Matthew), author.
Title: The cacophony of politics : Northern Democrats and the American Civil War / J. Matthew Gallman.
Description: Charlottesville : University of Virginia Press, 2021. | Series: A nation divided : studies in the Civil War era | Includes bibliographical references and index.
Identifiers: LCCN 2021018724 (print) | LCCN 2021018725 (ebook) | ISBN 9780813946566 (hardcover) | ISBN 9780813946573 (ebook)
Subjects: LCSH: Democratic Party (U.S.)—History—19th century. | Political parties—United States—History—19th century. | Opposition (Political science)—United States—History—19th century. | Politics and war—United States. | United States—Politics and government—1861–1865. | United States—History—Civil War, 1861–1865.
Classification: LCC E459 .G28 2021 (print) | LCC E459 (ebook) | DDC 324.2736/09034—dc23
LC record available at https://lccn.loc.gov/2021018724
LC ebook record available at https://lccn.loc.gov/2021018725

Cover art: Engraved envelope by F. K. Kimmel. (Schuyler Rumsey Philatelic Auctions)

To the nation's nurses, technicians,
orderlies, and medical staff

CONTENTS

ACKNOWLEDGMENTS

The idea for this book emerged at one of the national conferences, probably over adult beverages. I am pretty sure that Gary Gallagher first suggested the strange idea that I should write about Civil War politics. Many conversations followed.

I am very proud to say that over the years I have become increasingly adept at seeking smart advice, some portion of which I follow. In the earliest stages, Bill Blair and Mark E. Neely Jr. offered wonderful thoughts in long emails.

As the project matured from vague notions to concrete research, I profited immensely from three research fellowships and a grant from the University of Florida. I was pleased to return to the Huntington Library, where I mined the wonderful manuscript collections. Thanks to Olga Tsapina for her wise counsel, Steve Hindle for his intellectual generosity, and Carolyn Powell for her characteristic assistance. I visited the Kentucky Historical Society in search of material on Willie Waller and ended up finding a wealth of other sources as well. Patrick Lewis and Stephanie Lang were wonderful hosts and guides. While in Kentucky I enjoyed a marvelous excursion with LeeAnn Whites to Maysville and the Kentucky Gateway Museum. It was a particular pleasure to return to my old stomping grounds in Philadelphia as a fellow at the Library Company of Philadelphia and the Historical Society of Pennsylvania. Thanks to Jim Green for his warmth and wisdom, and special thanks to Cornelia King and Erika Piola. While in Philadelphia I spent good times talking history with Judy Giesberg and with John Hill. Thanks to Tara Craig of the Columbia Rare Book and Manuscript Library and to Brooks Tucker Swett, who photographed the Anna Mercer LaRoche journals.

Several colleagues took time to answer a quick email. Thanks to Matt Hulbert, Ryan Keating, Will Kurtz, Tim Wesley, Jack Furniss, Anne Marshall, Stephanie McCurry, Scott Hancock, Frank Towers, and Kid Wongsrichanalai, who all set aside their own work to answer a query or offer counsel. Thanks to Jennifer Weber for a fine book exhibit chat about Democrats. Dan Sutherland and Bob Sandow each read a chapter, improving my work and saving me from error.

Quite a few friends and colleagues plowed through the entire manuscript at some stage. Thanks to Jeff Adler, Gary Gallagher, Carrie Janney, Steve Maizlish, Louise Newman, Tom Pegram, Mark Simpson-Vos, Joan Waugh, and Jonathan

White, who all read the book and offered suggestions, large and small. Thanks especially to Liz Varon, who read the whole thing twice, including as an editor of the series, and to Vernon Burton, who stepped in with a detailed comment as series co-editor. And to the University of Virginia's Nadine Zimmerli, who commented on the entire manuscript. Thanks as well to two fine anonymous readers.

After many years of research and thought I began writing this book on a summer day while I was recovering from an unanticipated—and extended—visit to the cardiology wing at North Florida Regional Medical Center. It seemed to be a good idea to start writing since I was in for an extended recovery, and they would not let me drive. At that point I owed considerable debts to many nurses, medical technicians, and orderlies. (There were also considerable debts to many doctors.) Since that day I have accumulated more debts to nurses and technicians. As I finish this project, a bit more than two years later, I join the chorus of folks worldwide thanking many thousands of nurses and medical staff for their sacrifices. This book is dedicated to all of those amazing professionals.

TIMELINE OF KEY EPISODES

1860

November 6	Abraham Lincoln is elected president.

1861

March 4	The Senate passes the proposed Corwin Amendment.
March 4	Lincoln delivers his First Inaugural Address.
April 12	South Carolina guns fire on Fort Sumter.
April 19	Baltimoreans riot on Pratt Street.
May 25	John Merryman is arrested in Maryland.
May 31	Joseph Holt writes to the people of Kentucky.
June 3	Stephen Douglas dies in Chicago.
August 19	Pierce Butler is arrested in Philadelphia.

1862

March 6	Charles Biddle delivers "Alliance with the Negro" in Congress.
June 6	Sunset Cox asks Congress, "Is Ohio to be Africanized?"
July 8	George McClellan hands Harrison's Landing Letter to Lincoln.
July 17	Congress passes the State Militia Act.
September 3	Edward G. Ryan delivers his "Address" to Wisconsin Democrats.
September 22	Lincoln issues the Preliminary Emancipation Proclamation.
November 10	Draft rioting erupts in Port Washington, Wisconsin.

1863

January 1	Lincoln issues the Emancipation Proclamation.
January 14	Clement Vallandigham gives a fiery final address to Congress.
February 6	The Society for the Diffusion of Political Knowledge (SDPK) forms in New York City.
March 3	Congress passes the Enrollment Act.
April 12	Captain Matthew H. Jouett signs a pass for Lavendar Hale.
April 13	Ambrose Burnside issues General Order no. 38.
May 4	Mayor Francis Sherman gives his inaugural address in Chicago.
May 5	Clement Vallandigham is arrested in Ohio.

May 7	Willie Waller is arrested in Kentucky.
May	Angry crowds visit the *Philadelphia Age* office.
June 1	Burnside orders the *Chicago Times* shut down.
June 12	Abraham Lincoln writes to Erastus Corning and others.
July 1–3	The Battle of Gettysburg
July 4	Vicksburg falls to Union forces.
July 11	Draft riots break out in New York City.
October 3	Abraham Lincoln issues a Thanksgiving Proclamation.
October 12	George McClellan writes a letter endorsing George Woodward.
August	The SDPK issues Bishop John Henry Hopkins's *Bible View of Slavery.*
December 8	Lincoln issues the "Proclamation of Amnesty and Reconstruction."

1864

January 12	August Belmont hosts Democrats at his New York home.
March 4	Emma Webb speaks in Brooklyn.
April 5	Reverdy Johnson speaks for a constitution amendment.
April 24	New York fair-goers vote to give General Grant a sword.
May 18	Manton Marble gets arrested in New York City.
July 12	Congress passes the Wade-Davis bill on Reconstruction.
August 23	Lincoln shares the "Blind Memo" with his cabinet.
August 29	Democrats convene in Chicago and nominate George McClellan.
September 17	Robert C. Winthrop speaks for McClellan in New York City.
September 22	Republicans reportedly stage a "Miscegenation Ball" in New York City.
November 8	Abraham Lincoln wins reelection.

1865

January 31	Congress passes what becomes the 13th Amendment.
March 4	Lincoln delivers his Second Inaugural Address.
April 3	Richmond falls to Union forces.
April 14	John Wilkes Booth shoots Lincoln at Ford's Theater.
April 27	Edward Ingersoll is attacked at a Philadelphia train station.

1871

June 16	Clement Vallandigham shoots himself in Ohio.

1872

November 5	Ulysses S. Grant defeats Liberal Republican Horace Greeley.

THE CACOPHONY OF POLITICS

Introduction

This is a book about northern Democrats during the American Civil War. It looks at politicians and ordinary civilians from a variety of perspectives. Some sections focus on the actions and public statements of elected officials or powerful journalists. Others dive into the private correspondence of Democratic insiders, who I often call "wirepullers." Some portions consider the thoughts and behaviors of ordinary citizens, including those who wrote diaries or letters we can read and those whose political opinions are only reflected by their public actions. It is the story of a political party at war, and also of a diverse array of Americans scattered across the nation. It tells many stories, large and small, that combine to convey the North's cacophony of politics in the midst of wartime.

For just a moment, let us start in the middle, in the lingering winter of late 1862 into early 1863. It was a challenging time for the party of opposition in what had become a horribly bloody civil war. National events had set the stage for vocal dissent. In December 1862, Union troops under General Ambrose E. Burnside had sustained 12,500 casualties in the disastrous battle at Fredericksburg, Virginia.[1] Two weeks later, 13,000 men fell under General William Rosecrans at Stones River, Tennessee. Meanwhile, Union forces under Ulysses S. Grant were stalled in their prolonged efforts to capture the fortified city of Vicksburg, on the Mississippi River. Northern citizens read newspaper accounts of "despondency and desperation" among the men in blue. Meanwhile, northerners inclined to be critical had much to criticize in the Abraham Lincoln administration. Military and political exigencies had led to various assaults on free speech and civil liberties. On January 1, 1863, Lincoln issued his controversial Emancipation Proclamation, and in early March Congress passed the Enrollment Act, ushering in federal conscription to replace the already notorious state militia conscription.[2]

The northern Democrats, who stood as the party of opposition against Lincoln and his Republican administration, had some reason for political optimism. At the end of the previous year—a year and a half into the Civil War—Democratic candidates had fared quite well in state and congressional elections against the Republicans. But still the party faced serious problems. Its opponents had grown increasingly adept at portraying Democrats as a treasonous threat to the Union. Meanwhile, Democrats struggled to define themselves and their role as the opposition party in the middle of a civil war. It was not clear how they should proceed, or if they should act as a political opposition at all. The positions offered by party leaders and the rank and file were all over the place. Three examples for now:

In mid-1862 conservative Democrat Chauncey Burr launched *The Old Guard,* a strongly anti-administration and anti-Lincoln journal, which began appearing monthly the following January. A devoted racist and ardent defender of the Constitution, Burr supported the right of secession, hated abolition, and attacked the use of federal power to battle individual sovereign states.[3] He found the Civil War unconstitutional in its whole, as well as in its various constituent parts.[4] Viewing national events from this unbending perspective, Burr rejected the entire notion that so-called War Democrats—members of his party who had at least partially aligned with Lincoln in supporting the war—were Democrats at all in that they had abandoned the party's core ideological commitments. He sought to reclaim the key values of "loyalty" and "Union" for those Democrats who opposed the administration and the war. "To support the Constitution and the laws is true *loyalty,*" he insisted over and over again.[5] In response to Republican efforts to cast themselves as the party of the Union, Burr wrote, "The habit of speaking of some conservative men *as Union men* in distinction *from Democrats* is a mischievous mistake. Every true Democrat is a Union man."[6] In this formulation, War Democrats had abandoned both their party and the Union. The truly loyal patriot would not support Lincoln's war.

At the other end of the Democratic spectrum in early 1863, and halfway across the country, Scottish-born Robert Dale Owen shared little in common with Burr. The son of the great British reformer Robert Owen, Robert Dale Owen had built a considerable reform reputation of his own, both in and out of politics. Before the war, Owen had served as a Democrat in Congress and in the Indiana General Assembly before signing on for a stint as a diplomat. With the outbreak of fighting, Owen established himself as a loyal Indiana War Democrat, working under Republican governor Oliver Morton as a procurement agent. In 1863, not long after the Emancipation Proclamation went into effect, Owen penned a pamphlet entitled *Emancipation Is Peace* in response to Democrats who were calling for immediate peace, arguing that in fact "Emancipation is Peace." "We want peace," it began. "We desire to see an end to this war." But unlike those in his party who wished to see an immediate end to the fighting, and those who were unwilling to consider emancipation as an ultimate war aim and not merely a necessary war measure, Owen wove an argument for why military victory and the end of slavery constituted the only legitimate path into the future. He warned that the true danger would be a rush to peace that would not produce a lasting result. The Indiana Democrat opposed slavery on moral grounds and would go on to become a strong advocate for postwar freedmen, but in this short pamphlet Owen made a pragmatic case aimed at his Democratic brethren. The wisest path to permanent peace depended on a national acceptance of emancipation.[7]

Then there were William and Jane Standard of Illinois. Will had enlisted ahead of the draft, but he was an avowed antiwar Copperhead. And so was Jane. In early February 1863, completely disillusioned with his life as a citizen-soldier, Will wrote to his wife, trying out strategies for getting out of uniform. The beginning of Jane's response was characteristic and instructive: "Dear Will, you say you are very anxious to get out of that scrape. I don't doubt that at all, but Will, I don't think I am smart enough to plan for you in this case. If I was thare I think I could do something, if I was a man. you know I don't know much about things down there but I will tell you a little. It won't do any harm but don't take my advice if you don't think best."[8] Jane went on to propose that Will and some comrades attempt to be captured in hopes of being paroled. It was a risky idea, and one that Will did not pursue. But Jane left little doubt that she was certainly smart enough to work through these thorny topics with her husband, even while she was savvy enough to play down her own political acumen in these conversations.

Burr and Owen map out some of the myriad ways northern Democrats saw things differently in the middle of the Civil War. The Standards, whose political perspectives were quite distinct from the professionals, offer a window into how some private citizens mulled over wartime politics and navigated those conversations in their own worlds. These four Democrats do not appear here, in the first pages of this book, to illustrate particular categories of northern Democrats. They appear here to illustrate that Democratic politics during the Civil War was a messy affair, which this book hopes to unravel. In fact, one chief goal here is to demonstrate how fundamentally messy, and often inconsistent, Civil War partisan politics really were.

Now, a few words about words and titles.

For decades before the secession crisis, American politicians dedicated to one compromise or another—and particularly northern Democrats and

Whigs—applied the language of "The Union as It Is" to call for national unity amid regional tensions. It became a popular rallying cry for those in search of compromise. With the coming of the Civil War, some northern Democrats opposed to the war itself adopted the language of "The Union as It Was," a slogan that suggested looking backward to a nation before secession and talk of emancipation.[9] But in those months between the end of 1862 and early 1863, even such simple terms seemed contested. The Democratic Party did look backward, and yet its members struggled to frame a distinctive vision looking to the future.

On December 5, 1862, the 37th Congress was only a few days into its third and final session. On that day the House debated the "Objects of the War." Clement L. Vallandigham of Ohio, who a great political historian described as one of the "two most irritating Peace Democrats in the House," offered an amendment to a resolution that had been offered by Pennsylvania Republican Thaddeus Stevens (who surely was a candidate for the most irritating Republican).[10] Vallandigham offered six resolutions, the first of which declared, "That the Union as it was must be restored and maintained one and indivisible forever under the Constitution as it is." Illinois representative Owen Lovejoy objected, and the *Congressional Globe* reports that "the resolutions were withdrawn." Congressman Stevens had earlier offered a series of resolutions that began by declaring that "the Union must be and remain one and indivisible forever."

That congressional debate is entertaining to read, although hardly momentous. On December 16, when Vallandigham's resolutions again appeared before the House, Kentucky Democrat Charles A. Wickliffe offered a new resolution, "That all those who are opposed to the closing of this war upon the principle of preserving the Constitution as it is, and the restoration of the Union as it was formed by that Constitution, is an enemy of the country, and is unfit to hold any office of trust or profit." Even the meaning of "Union" and "Constitution" had become fraught in the midst of civil war.[11] All revered the Union, but some disagreed about what that reverence meant.

Early in the war, patriotic Democrats occasionally campaigned with the slogan "the Union as it was, the Constitution as it is," as a way of affirming that they were neither abolitionists nor secessionists but loyal defenders of the Union staunchly standing between radical extremes.[12] With time, some Ohio Democrats associated the slogan with Vallandigham and his vocal opposition to the Lincoln administration.[13] But in those early days the words allowed for multiple understandings. In February 1863 a Democratic newspaper in Iowa called on its readers to attend a mass rally to support the Union and the administration, in a grand display of Democrats and Republicans gathering together. The paper took pains to call on "Germans of every township" to come to support "the

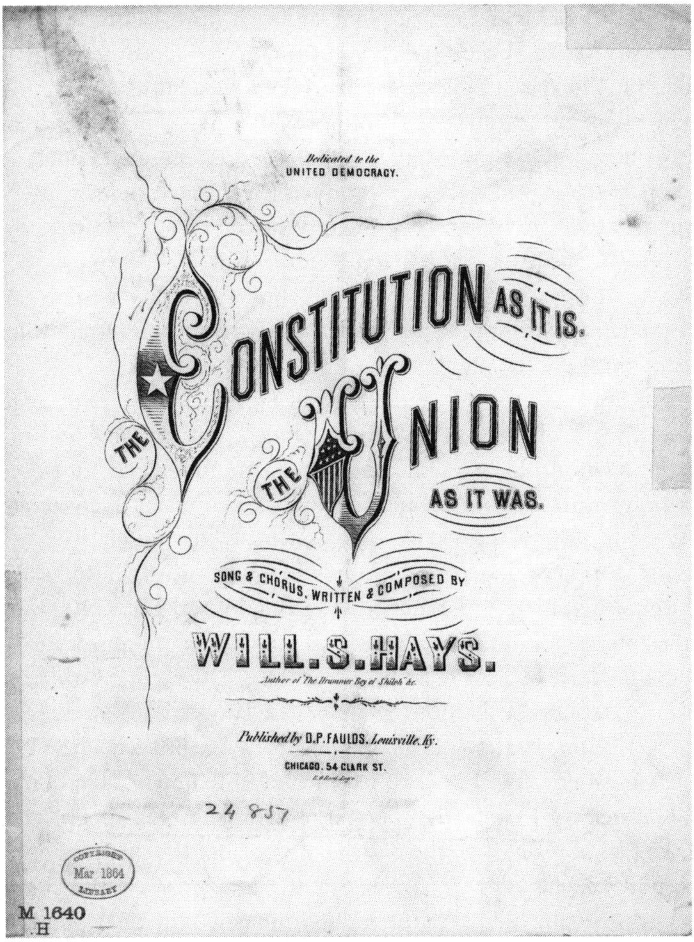

Song sheet: "The Constitution as It Is. The Union as It Was," Will. S. Hays, Louisville, 1863. In the mid-nineteenth century, Americans purchased a large number of "song sheets" as well as small volumes of songs. They commonly included both the music and lyrics so that consumers could entertain themselves. "The Union as It Was"—composed by Kentucky native William Shakespeare Hays in 1863—was a popular Democratic song, building on the party's slogan. (Library of Congress)

Constitution as it is—The Union as it was," promising that there would be oratory in their native language.[14]

Eventually the paired phrases "the Constitution as it is, the Union as it was" would be associated with the Peace wing of the Democratic Party, sometimes combined with a third phrase of varying words, calling for an entirely White future (generally presented in appalling language). But in late 1862 and early 1863, even words like "Union" and "Constitution" remained up for grabs, or at least subject to different meanings. In a marvelous illustration of wartime popular discourse, two New York bankers, both of whom had some minor reputation as philosophers and political thinkers, published dueling pamphlets on what "the Union as it was, and the Constitution as it is" really meant.[15] The language was certainly catchy. Kentucky song writer Will. S. Hayes published a six-stanza song on "The Constitution as It Is. The Union as it Was." The tune addressed Democrats "who ask for honest laws," but the lyrics called for northerners to support the Union and "the cause" until a day when "Abolition finds its grave" and "Secession sleeps beside."[16]

For four years of war, northerners—and especially Democrats—grappled with what they really meant by "Union" and "Constitution," and how they viewed the relationship between the past and the uncertain future. It was a conversation with varied voices, and the terms of discussion evolved over time.

The words "Northern Democrats" sounds straightforward, but it invites some clarification. First, there is the matter of geography and place. When we think about the antebellum decades and the war years it is commonplace to speak in terms of "the North" and "the South," and those geographic distinctions were familiar to Americans at the time. More precise language would describe a war between the United States and the Confederacy. In 1861 when the Civil War began, some Americans who remained in the United States—in border states such as Kentucky or Maryland—thought of themselves as southerners and also part of the Union. And, with the passage of time and the successes of the military and political efforts of the United States, "the North" expanded to include various territories, including Tennessee and the new state of West Virginia. In the process, the number of "northerners" grew even while their sense of geographic identity evolved more gradually. So, "northern Democrats" is a somewhat variable term—but precise enough for our purposes.

And those northerners lived in substantially different worlds, particularly when it came to matters of race and slavery. In the border states of the lower Union, Whites lived in slave societies where for many their economic and social worlds were built on the institution of slavery, and at least at the outset of the war many border-state Democrats felt politically committed to both the Union and to slavery. Most White voters in northern free states had little personal experience with African Americans, yet many had internalized massive prejudices. In 1860 barely 1.2 percent of residents in those free states were

African American (including those people who the census listed as of mixed race). New Jersey—with 25,336 African Americans—had the greatest share of Black residents with 3.8 percent. Michigan, Indiana, Illinois, Iowa, Minnesota, and Wisconsin each had populations that were under 1 percent Black in 1860. In fact, only 0.15 percent of the populations of Minnesota and Wisconsin were Black. More free Black men and women lived in cities than in the countryside, but even in metropolitan areas their numbers were small. New York City, the site of the war's worst racial violence in 1863, was fewer than 2 percent African American.[17]

Then there is the more complicated matter of defining Democrats. By 1860 the Democratic Party was the nation's oldest national political party. It enjoyed a full institutional structure, from local party organizations to state Democratic bodies to a Democratic National Committee. Democratic newspapers across the North supported the party's goals and distributed its messages. It was a large and varied political party, although substantially smaller and less varied after the southern states seceded. Democrats shared core ideological beliefs as well as broad institutional goals, and they felt strongly about the power of the party's longevity. They sought political power and hoped to win elections toward that goal, but the true insiders played a long game as well. In that context, the search for wartime Democrats is fairly simple: we are interested in the people who ran for office as Democrats; those who aided them in those elections; and members of the rank and file who attended party rallies, read partisan newspapers, and voted for Democratic candidates. Those people were northern Democrats. But they were not alone.

The very fact that the United States was in the middle of a civil war complicated how some understood partisan loyalties. A large portion of Democrats maintained their party identity throughout the conflict, even while they saw it as their roles as patriotic citizens to support the administration in time of war. And, to muddy things further, by mid-war—as Democrats struggled to define their party—the Republican Party had successfully redefined itself as the party of Union, and its advocates fought mightily to label political enemies of the administration as disloyal traitors. Democrats who weighed political concerns and military developments and concluded that they should side with the Lincoln administration on specific matters often did so without abandoning their party loyalty. These people, even if they cast their lot—and their votes—with Lincoln and his supporters, were still Democrats.

Other northerners may have endorsed Democratic ideals while their partisan affiliations do not find their way into the historic record. Foremost in this group were the North's White women who supported the Democratic Party. A substantial portion of northern women thought hard about politics, particularly in time of war. Many shared the partisan affiliations of their fathers or husbands, but that is a far cry from saying that Democratic women parroted the opinions expressed by the men in their lives. The correspondence between men and women, and the private journals of individual women, offer evidence of women and men differing about political issues large and small. And they also reveal a world where Democratic couples commonly debated those issues as political equals. Jane Standard could not vote, but her actions and written opinions speak to strongly held political convictions.

While a substantial portion of this book concerns parties and campaigns and elections, I argue that when we search for political activity we should move beyond partisan narratives. At crucial moments throughout the war, ordinary civilians who did not always articulate partisan points of view (at least that we can uncover today) did articulate—often in symbolic ways—positions on matters of public policy and power. Sometimes they broke things; sometimes they shot at people; often they acted as parts of unruly groups. Here I am thinking of rioters, draft evaders, deserters, members of secret societies, and unapologetic pro-secessionists. Their dissenting acts were political actions, if we think of politics as the ongoing public conversation about power and policy. These sometimes disruptive men and women appear in this book, even if I cannot say for certain that when they dissented they also self-identified with the Democratic Party.[18] This is part of a broader argument about what constituted politics in mid-nineteenth-century history.

In their political lives, these northern Democrats and their allies were a diverse lot. Some scholars have described them as belonging to two large camps: the War Democrats, who eventually aligned with the Lincoln administration even while dissenting on some points, and the Peace Democrats—sometimes called "Copperheads"—who came to oppose both the war and the political tyrants who ran it. This is no doubt a useful framework, but as is so often the case when we construct large categories of historic actors, the labels are liable to obscure more than they reveal. It is more accurate, if also more murky, to imagine these Democrats as falling along a fairly broad ideological spectrum, and one that was perpetually in motion. Certainly—as we shall see—some Democrats who had rallied to the war effort in April 1861, furious at the behavior of southern secessionists, lost their enthusiasm for the Republican administration as new measures (arbitrary arrests, conscription, emancipation, and so on) challenged their core assumptions about what a federal government should do, even in the midst of civil war. Others maintained their Democratic allegiance while serving loyally in Lincoln's administration or fighting valiantly on battlefields across the nation. And, as we consider the shifting identities of voters and politicians, it is also worth recalling that although the Democratic Party had a long national history, some men who voted for Democratic candidates in 1860 were ex-Whigs who found themselves without a viable party as the nation faced sectional division. Others had deep roots in the party of Andrew Jackson and the core ideas of Thomas Jefferson. For many, party politics at midcentury seemed perpetually in flux, even while other political actors claimed partisan loyalties that went back for generations.

But of course those Democrats—almost exclusively men of some substance—who engaged in these partisan discussions are only part of the war's complex political story. Men and women across the nation observed wartime events and came to deeply held conclusions, about the war but also about particular policies. Perhaps they attended parades or rallies, maybe they took part in riots or gathered in farmhouses as members of shadowy secret societies. Others read newspapers and pamphlets and came to their own political conclusions, without doing much at all to shape public discourse. These citizens found their way into the public record—either by attending a public gathering or by leaving behind some scraps of personal papers—as dissenters of one sort or another. In many cases their broader political identities remain in shadows. Did the Irish woman who tossed stones at the draft enroller in Milwaukee object to the war itself? Did she disagree with the Lincoln administration's constitutional arguments about conscription or emancipation? Or was she in her marrow a prowar patriot who was also convinced that in her corner of the universe the folks running the draft were a bunch of crooks? Often wartime dissenters made it clear that their affections were with the Democratic Party, and in other cases we only know that in a particular moment they were angry with how events were unfolding.

In sum, this is a book about those men and women who did not see eye to eye with Abraham Lincoln and the Republican Party, at least for part of the Civil War. Those northerners who voted for Democrats in 1860 constituted a substantial slice of the American electorate when the nation was divided by sectionalism. Four years later, after the horrors of a thousand battlefields, those voters who sided with the Democratic Party were still remarkably numerous, even while we can quibble about what they felt their votes meant. In our sweeping historic narrative, the forces of Union, and eventually of emancipation, pursued at the point of a bayonet won the day. And Abraham Lincoln and the Republican Party are rightly credited with that momentous victory. This book is about those northerners who agreed with some things but declined to throw in their lot with the party in power, even if they gave that party their votes at specific moments. Generally more ideologically conservative than members of Lincoln's party, these northern Democrats—whether or not they identified themselves as "War Democrats"—saw themselves as, in the words of one historian, "a bulwark against radical change."[19]

The nine chapters that follow fall into three parts. Part 1, spanning the first three chapters, considers the Democrats from the election of 1860 until the beginning of 1863. It was in these crucial years that the Democratic Party gradually adjusted to its position as the party of opposition in the midst of civil war, and as an enduring national party whose numbers had been gutted by southern secession. Part 2, chapters 4 and 5, changes gears considerably. Chapter 4 shifts from national politics and party developments to a series of case studies on how politics and political debates unfolded in individual communities and households, and how political conflicts played out in a regional context. Chapter 5 examines "politics in the streets," focusing largely on the northern community response to conscription in the war's final two years. Part 3, chapters 6 through 9, returns to the national chronology, beginning with crucial events in 1863. As Burr and Owen demonstrated, at mid-war the Democratic Party faced major challenges in determining its own identity and agreeing on the political position it should take toward emancipation, the war, and pathways to peace. Chapters 7 and 8 concentrate on the events leading up to the election of 1864 and some of the details of that campaign and its results. Chapter 9 looks at how Democrats, defeated in 1864, navigated their role as the party of opposition in the war's final months and beyond, including a few thoughts about the unusual election of 1872. The conclusion focuses on two clusters of questions: what the Democrats thought about their duty as citizens, and how the party considered race and emancipation as political problems.

A few words about structure. This book is partly synthesis, building on the insights of a wide array of great historians, and partly a close discussion of case studies.[20] Although I have learned an enormous amount from other historians, I am not attempting historiographic interventions here. I mention other scholars on occasion when they have made observations that I have borrowed, but I only rarely engage with interpretive disagreements.[21] While this book concentrates on only about four years of American history, and focuses on only a subset of northerners during those years, there is really an awful lot of institutional history one might mention, including governors, senators, congressmen, newspapers, editors, and the like. Many of those key political figures find their way into these pages, but others who played a considerable role in their states or in national politics are neglected.

Instead, I have opted for a broad chronology interspersed with illustrative episodes. Some of those concern a particular figure or event, others involve a discussion of an important speech or piece of writing. My goal has been to tell particular stories and to knit those moments together into a coherent whole. That process involves casting light on sometimes obscure individuals and moments in hopes that those episodes illustrate broader themes in useful ways. Along the way I have selected people and events from across the North, although I have not sought to present a complete geographical history any more than I have attempted a full coverage of people or events. I have jumped around geographically, hoping to illustrate the importance of "place" as well as chronology. Quite a few characters, such as Pennsylvania's Charles Biddle, Ohio's Clement Vallandigham, New York's Maria Lydig Daly, and General George McClellan, reappear at different moments. I have included a timeline of key episodes, which might prove useful to readers.[22]

Most historical monographs I have read, or have written, are organized around broad arguments presented as supporting a central thesis. In that structure the author commonly ends chapters by explaining how we are building toward that main point. This book is not quite like that. When all the dust settles *The Cacophony of Politics* forwards a series of core arguments that appear periodically through the text, followed by some other broad arguments that appear in the conclusion. I hope that each of the specific arguments contributes to our understanding of Civil War politics and the history of the Democrats. What follows considers those major observations, grouped into six core arguments.

1. Labels must be examined with care.

Historians who write about Civil War politics commonly divide northern Democrats into two camps: War Democrats and Copperheads. The first group supported the war, even while some continued to vote for Democratic candidates. The second group are understood as northerners who sought peace above all else. Some of them were, in the eyes of many, treasonous figures who did what they could to undermine the national cause. These broad terms are a useful shorthand, so long as we keep several things in mind.

The term "copperhead," which really only emerged in popular usage in late 1862, was commonly used as a term of derision. Some Democrats proudly claimed the title, but often the label was applied by partisan enemies, not always fairly.

Northerners who opposed the war did so for many different reasons, and their opinions often shifted over time. It is hard to see them all as opposed to the Union, even if they opposed the bloodshed.

Contemporaries conflated treason and political opposition and applied labels pretty casually.

In this book I use the term "Copperhead" on occasion to describe people who actively opposed the war but usually only when they accepted the label for themselves.

It is also worth noting that although contemporaries recognized the existence of the two political parties, in their own private writings they routinely applied other terms to themselves and their adversaries. And those labels are also instructive. Democrats routinely described themselves as "conservatives" and Republicans as "abolitionists" or "radicals." And in the hands of an author like Chauncey Burr, even the term "conservative" was contested. The labels are a useful window into how wartime individuals saw their political world. Democratic insiders, for instance, commonly wrote that Abraham Lincoln was really a "moderate" or even a "conservative" under the sway of radicals in his own party.

This is a good moment to say a bit more about some other key words. Although Burr had his own ideas about who deserved to be called "conservative," in more general ways the word had a meaning that most northerners would recognize. Conservative Americans generally resisted change or were at least skeptical of anything that smacked of revolutionary change. They revered the Constitution and questioned any measure that seemed to expand the language of that document. As the war began, they leaned toward the preservation of local and states' rights rather than efforts to expand centralized federal power. Northern Democrats commonly spoke of themselves as "conservatives," and they hoped to see conservative values in their political adversaries, including Abraham Lincoln. The word placed the individual on a recognized ideological spectrum.

In this volume I periodically describe individuals or publications as particularly "racist." In truth, this is the application of a modern understanding of a term to a historic moment. When it comes to thoughts about racial difference, it is fair to say that nearly all current readers would find the opinions of all Civil War–era Whites essentially racist in that they believed in fundamental differences between the races and the superiority of Whites over people of color. And nearly all Whites agreed with at least some laws and cultural traditions that treated the races differently, enforcing notions of Black inferiority. When I describe specific people or publications as unusually "racist," I mean to indicate that their writings were particularly appalling in the context of their historic moment, or that they were unusually active in repeatedly portraying their racial prejudices in print.

2. Politics was everywhere.

In the mid-nineteenth century, or at least in the middle of the Civil War, "politics" in the United States went well beyond formal party organizations and elections to encompass a wide range of debates about power and public policy. From that perspective, wartime northerners lived in a world thick with politics. I am not convinced that every citizen cared about all congressional or gubernatorial elections, but it is a good bet that when we expand our definitions to include political arrests, conscription, emancipation, and other controversial war measures, nearly all northerners—whether or not they voted—cared about politics and power. Throughout this book I explore politics as expressed in the streets and in private households and at the polls. My goal is to write a history that incorporates all of these voices and settings into one broad political culture.

And, as a corollary to this broad argument, a recurring theme in this book is that *northern women thought about politics,* talked about politics, and wrote about politics. Occasionally they cursed and threw things.

It is commonplace in formal political histories of the Civil War to play down the political roles of women. After all, they did not vote or hold office. Some scholars seem to have assumed that insofar as women thought about public life during the war, they funneled their actions into fundamentally apolitical voluntary activities. (Or, their voluntarism became a form of political speech.) Moreover, northern women who were most engaged in public advocacy, women's rights, and wartime politics—people such as Susan B Anthony, Elizabeth Cady Stanton, Mary Livermore, Anna E. Dickinson, and many others—consistently aligned themselves with the Republican Party, or certainly not with the Democrats.

While these observations are true, they miss the key political roles of Democratic women. From the outset of the war, women who were the wives, lovers, and daughters of Democrats framed their own opinions about political issues, and commonly went toe to toe with their loved ones about national events and debates closer to home. The Democratic men may have been even more conservative than Republicans when it came to the push for the political rights of White women, but in these private political conversations, mutual respect among women and men was generally the order of the day.

Another corollary to this larger argument: *politics mattered in the Union military.* Although I do not attempt to mine all the facets of this interesting subject, the North's citizen-soldiers—whether they were volunteers, substitutes, or draftees—saw themselves as political actors. The military had its byzantine quarrels about the behavior of Democratic and Republican officers.[23] When men in uniform heard tales of disloyalty on the home front, they responded with angry letters and petitions. In the crucial election of 1864, thanks to shifts in state laws and some manipulation of furloughs, soldiers became crucial voters.

3. Chronology mattered; timing mattered.

Although many northern voters who were Democrats in 1860 were still party members five years later, the crucial military and political events between late 1860 and April 1865 affected how northerners felt about the war and about the Lincoln administration. As events unfolded, both national political parties jockeyed over how to define themselves and present their case to voters. In all sorts of ways, the story of Civil War politics is a narrative in constant flux, often reflected in the changing labels participants applied to each other, and commonly affected by events on the battlefield.

As Chauncey Burr and Robert Dale Owen illustrated, the events surrounding the beginning of 1863 were crucial (thus explaining the timing of part 2). At the end of 1862, the state militia draft had triggered some disturbances, and the following year the United States would turn to a controversial federal draft, with more violence to follow. In the off-year elections in late 1862, the Democratic Party did quite well, but the Republican Party was braced to fight back. Not coincidentally, the term "Copperhead" had by early 1863 become a mainstay in partisan discourse. Finally, on January 1 the Emancipation Proclamation took effect. Democrats persistently struggled with what they believed and how they should proceed as a formal opposition party.

In understanding the ebbs and flows in partisan politics and angry dissent, the military is once again crucial. Events on the battlefield, and reports that filtered back to the home front, had a huge impact on politics at home. I spend considerable energy discussing how George McClellan pursued the presidency in 1864, but his political fate may have depended more on the actions of William Tecumseh Sherman and Sherman's men than on his own.

4. Location framed political beliefs and experiences.

Much like in modern electoral maps, the state of partisan politics before and during the Civil War varied enormously from place to place, with the nineteenth-century version of "red states" and "blue states" dotting those maps. Citizens in various states behaved differently when it came time to vote. The same holds true for the broad patterns of draft resistance and civil disobedience. Individual experiences depended on where one lived. On the other hand, Democrats and Republicans coexisted—happily or not—in all corners of the North, and nearly every congressional district experienced some level of resistance.

The chapters that follow attempt to pay attention to geographic differences, without becoming too bogged down in local details. Location—along with other variables—no doubt helped frame what Owen and Burr and the Standards thought and how they expressed it. Some patterns were key. Midwestern Democrats in the lower North watched events through particular lenses defined by the presence of slaves and the ongoing tensions caused by guerrilla warfare. Peace Democrats spoke their minds all over the North, but they clustered in states like New Jersey, Ohio, Connecticut, and New York. Larger cities, such as New York, Philadelphia, and Chicago, had their own complex community dynamics when it came to society and politics. Secret societies existed across the North, although such groups prospered in some locations more than others. Democrats voted in all northern states; at times this book gives more attention to places where their actions and opinions had the greatest impact on local debate, while occasionally neglecting Republican strongholds where local Democrats had opinions but limited influence on events.

5. Civil liberties is a multitiered topic.

The history of civil liberties in the North is a complex tale, but the main lines are well known in the literature. Among the many episodes described in this book, the reader will find discussions of the political arrests of John Merryman, Pierce Butler, and Clement Vallandigham; the suppression of the *New York World* and the *Chicago Times;* and other controversial episodes surrounding wartime civil liberties.

Democrats, not always unreasonably, saw their voices muted by governmental, judicial, and military forces, prompting anger in party circles. This book argues that in addition to military and governmental actions, there was another, more subtle assault on free speech. Immediately after the firing on Fort Sumter, patriotic civilians attacked Democratic newspapers, threatened accused prosecessionists, and silenced those who dared to celebrate the Confederate cause. Later, ministers who declined to use their pulpits for political statements faced angry congregants who wanted open displays of patriotism. Public speech and political dissent were commonly conditional, depending on the particular community or neighborhood. In Kentucky and Missouri, guerrillas roamed in some parts of each state, while angry federals counterattacked in other communities; noncombatants with opinions to share had to choose their spots carefully. New state laws enabled soldiers to cast absentee ballots in the field, but it seems likely that a healthy percentage of Democrats in Republican-dominated regiments wisely declined the privilege. Following the assassination of President Lincoln, angry mobs demanded displays of mourning and affirmations of patriotism from the silent. Like so much else, freedom of expression was conditional.

6. Race and ethnicity played a large role in wartime politics.

As we have seen, relatively few African Americans lived in the North before or during the Civil War, especially in those regions north of the slave-owning border states. Although it would be very difficult to measure, it seems a fair assumption that nearly all White northerners in 1860 harbored some level of racial prejudice, even those who were adamant abolitionists. But that having been said, it seems equally fair to assert that northerners who felt the most profound hostility toward, or fear of, Black Americans gravitated toward the Democratic Party. Certainly the most virulently racist Democratic newspapers, who knew their readership well, took pains to fill their pages with the dangers that free Blacks posed to White northern society.

Meanwhile, there is ample reason to believe that members of some immigrant groups—particularly Irish and German Catholics—opposed emancipation and resisted the war in large numbers. The most famous story, which we revisit in these pages, concerned the terrible draft riots in New York City in July 1863, where largely Irish mobs targeted free Blacks and African American institutions. Draft day proved to be the catalyst, but racial tensions over jobs provided the fuel.

But each of these crucial historical forces—both individually and combined—must be assessed with care. Wartime politics was notorious for racist messages and imagery, largely inherited from antebellum popular culture. Nonetheless race hatred was far from the sum total of Democratic appeals, particularly as articulated by more formal party spokesmen. And while conservative Catholic leaders commonly resisted emancipation, and immigrant workers fell pray to virulent racism, the New York story hardly covers the wartime experiences of a diverse body of workers. Irish Catholic immigrants in particular labored hard to defend their patriotism and civility in the wake of the July riots.

These attitudes about race quickly became intertwined with vituperative *public debates about slavery and emancipation.* For White slave owners in the Union's border states, the issues surrounding emancipation were particularly fraught. Abraham Lincoln's Emancipation Proclamation on January 1, 1863, only promised the freedom of enslaved people still held in the Confederate states. The fact that people in places such as Maryland and Kentucky owned slaves surely called into question their individual morality, but that did not mean they were stupid. Slaveholders in the border states recognized the march of progress was not in their favor. Here, again, the timing of events mattered tremendously as some staunch Unionists in those border states eventually shifted their political allegiances.

Only a tiny fraction of northern Democrats owned slaves. And it seems likely that most northern Democrats—whether or not they had ever encountered enslaved people—devoted little time to wrestling with slavery as a moral issue. But many still worried about emancipation. For some the concerns were really about race in their own communities. They feared that emancipation in the South would produce huge numbers of southern freedmen heading north, undermining their notions of a racially homogenous culture. And some political operatives became adept at stirring that pot, provoking hysterical concerns about "miscegenation" in their midst.

At the other end of an intellectual spectrum, leading Democrats—who in some cases saw themselves as sage constitutional scholars—questioned emancipation as a federal violation of states' rights. Even if some came to conclude that slavery was morally wrong, as well as bad for society, they still questioned whether the Lincoln administration had adopted a proper strategy to end the peculiar institution.

Finally, when events on the battlefield indicated that the war would soon be over, some Democrats worried that the administration would insist on emancipation as a condition of peace negotiations. For Democrats who were anxious for peace and essentially indifferent to slavery, any negotiation that required the Confederates to accept emancipation threatened an unacceptable delay before the war would end.

The book's conclusion wrestles with how Democrats considered race and emancipation as practical political concerns and as moral dilemmas.

These six broad arguments weave their way through the nine chapters that follow, leading to a conclusion that focuses on a few key concerns. From a purely political standpoint, the crucial moment in this book comes in chapter 8, when Abraham Lincoln defeats George McClellan in the presidential election of 1864. Lincoln won reelection rather easily in the Electoral College, perhaps leaving a sense that political events were essentially predetermined. But, as we shall see, that analysis ignores argument no. 3: *Chronology matters.* It is not hard to imagine an election with a different result had it occurred six months earlier or had events unfolded in different ways.

Moreover, in this election in the midst of the Civil War, despite important recent military successes, 45 percent of voters cast their votes against the president's reelection. That number merits contemplation. Perhaps some were entirely opposed to the war—those true Copperheads—but those voters were only a fraction of the total. Others felt a deep loyalty to the Democratic Party or an animus toward the administration in power.

As we shall see, politics was indeed a complicated matter.

I

Becoming an Organized Party

1

A Political Collapse

OF A PARTY AND A UNION

The story of the coming of the Civil War turns on the crucial election of 1860. For Democrats in the North, internal conflicts among themselves and with the powerful Democrats in the southern states produced a great divide, and politically disastrous results. Within months after that election, Democrats—and all northerners—wrestled with how to proceed in a nation dividing.

Northern Democrats, Stephen Douglas, and the Election of 1860

The political, economic, and ideological narrative that led the United States to civil war is a complex tale, told often by academic scholars and popular historians. This is not the place for a detailed revisiting of these events, but a few things are worth noting. Two are most central to this book. First, the events that led to the election of 1860 and its surprising (to some) results had everything to do with what happened over the next five years and beyond. And second, we cannot overstate the huge role the Democratic Party had played in national political life for many decades. By 1860 the Democrats were the only national party, with a strong presence in every state of the Union. Proud Democrats traced their ideological traditions to the likes of Thomas Jefferson and Andrew Jackson. They saw themselves as part of a grand tradition that transcended particular political debates and issues. By this point the Whig Party, the Democrats' ideological opponents, had crumbled under the weight of clashes over slavery, ethnicity, and region, giving way to the new Republican Party, which stood for many things, although most prominently for a conviction that slavery should not be allowed in the federal territories. And while the Republicans also stood proudly, with their short history, they only stood in the northern portion of the United States. Many Whigs had found ideological kin and political refuge in the new Republican Party, but it is perhaps noteworthy that as the Civil War unfolded, northern Democrats would claim the great Whig politicians Henry Clay and Daniel Webster as part of their ideological legacy, even though Democratic heroes such as Andrew Jackson would have loathed the notion. And while antebellum Democrats really did have a long and proud identity, wartime Democrats did their best to make their party stronger and their traditions loftier. But it would be tough going.

During the Civil War political debates and celebrated military clashes commonly occurred in the eastern states, but the most consequential military events and the most illuminating political clashes often unfolded further to the west. Such had been the case in the antebellum decades as well. Angry rhetoric periodically exploded in Washington, D.C., but the worst national fissures had their origins in places like Kansas. The narrative leading up to the war is complex.

If we begin the narrative with the election of 1860, the story goes something like this: In November 1860 the voters selected Abraham Lincoln—the Republican nominee—as president-elect. Lincoln, a lawyer from Illinois, was neither an obscure fellow nor was he the party's frontrunner. The Republican delegates who gathered in their convention in Chicago, after numerous votes and much manipulation, had opted for a fairly moderate choice in Lincoln rather than selecting a more well-known, and more radical, option. The Republicans also adopted a series of strategic decisions—in their platform and in how they campaigned—designed to be more appealing to voters in the lower free states, thus hoping to improve on their 1856 voting returns.[1]

Although Lincoln had some reputation in his home state and in the North, southern voters had reason to worry about his election. After all, he was the candidate of an exclusively regional party, founded on the commitment to stopping the expansion of slavery into the territories. Lincoln did not appear on ballots in nearly any of the southern slave states (with the exception of a few cities), and it was not unreasonable for a White southern man, whether or not he was himself a slave owner, to perceive the election as a revolutionary act against his core interests. Abraham Lincoln insisted that he had no intention of disrupting slavery in the states where it existed, but many southern Whites remained unconvinced. Upon learning of Lincoln's victory, the states in the Deep South almost immediately seceded, setting the stage for complicated machinations between the election and the infamous firing on Fort Sumter five months later. That, then, is the very quick version of the final months leading to the Civil War, as told through the lens of the new Republican Party.

If we widen our lens just a bit and consider events in the decade before Lincoln's election, the story grows more complex. In broad strokes, *that* narrative goes something like this: Sectional tensions grew throughout the 1850s, with much of the national focus concentrating on the fate of slavery in the territories. Slavery's most ardent defenders believed that individual slaves were property, and that that property could rightly be taken into any federal lands. The North's antislavery voters—not to be confused with those abolitionists who sought to end all slavery—wished to keep slavery from expanding into western lands that had not yet been organized into states. They felt the peculiar institution was bad for society and for economic development, and they were happy to restrict it to those states already dependent on slave production.

A long history preceded those thorny conflicts in the 1850s. The political story is important here, even while there are other stories to be told about the expansion of the federal territories, the changing economic viability of slavery in those territories, and the steady march of American settlers from the East to the West. The national Democratic Party stands at the center of that political narrative. The party's institutional history was already long in 1860, dating back to the contentious election of 1824 and the ultimate rise of Andrew Jackson as the party's iconic leader in 1828. The party's ideological roots ran even more deeply, with strong ties to Thomas Jefferson. From the emergence of Jackson to the mid-1850s, partisan politics had played out in the second party system, with the new Democratic Party dueling with the Whig Party. In many senses, the two parties believed in fundamentally similar things, and certainly some of their differences were cultural or geographic. But in broad strokes, the Whig Party favored a more activist government, with federal powers encouraging economic growth and expansion. Their Democratic adversaries preferred a more limited central government, with more reliance on local communities and less enthusiasm for rapid change. They proudly embraced the nation's republican traditions, but they leaned toward skepticism and worries about tyranny in their midst, as opposed to open optimism. In these core ways, the national Democratic Party had been more conservative than its Whig adversaries. Although their beliefs amounted to a party ideology, one historian has noted that in the years before the Civil War, "the Democrats had habits, instincts and traditions" including commitments to "states' rights, federal restraint, and an assertive Unionism."[2]

Then there was slavery, which had divided the nation geographically. Since 1820 the nation had accepted an uneasy compromise on the issue, where slave owners were allowed to bring enslaved people into territories below the 36'30" parallel, while those territories (from the original Louisiana Purchase) above that line remained free of slaves. In 1854 Congress jettisoned this compromise by passing the Kansas-Nebraska Act. This hugely significant piece of legislation opened up the possibility of slavery in the northern territories, providing that settlers in these territories voted to allow the introduction of slaves. Thus, the act embraced the ideologically appealing (if logistically incoherent) notion of "popular sovereignty." Rather than dictating to the western territories, the new law let the people (White men) on the ground decide for themselves. The political architect of the Kansas-Nebraska Act was Illinois Democratic senator Stephen A. Douglas. Douglas's motives were complex and probably had little to do with any strong opinion about the institution of slavery. He did feel that this measure would facilitate the more rapid settlement of the territories. In national political terms, Douglas loomed large over these debates. Quite a few northern Democrats found the Kansas bill too tough a pill to swallow. Half of the free-state Democrats in the House voted against it, and after its passage many bolted the party. Moving forward, Douglas enjoyed a huge position in national politics, but not all northern Democrats thought of him fondly.[3]

The slave issue presented major challenges to Democratic leaders who were desperate to maintain a national party despite core divisions over the peculiar institution. But while the Democrats struggled, the Whigs crumbled. Out of the partisan rubble, the Republican Party emerged in 1854 as a regional party dedicated—among other things—to keeping slavery out of the federal territories. The North's strongest antislavery voices became central to this new party. The Republicans soon absorbed some antislavery Democrats and a huge portion of the dissolved Whig Party.

The new Republican Party also became home to some of the most vehement northern nativists, thus encouraging Catholic immigrants to cast their lot with the Democratic Party. Other Whigs—particularly in those northern border states where slavery still thrived—joined the Democratic Party. By the mid-1850s the two parties divided over slavery, particularly since the Democrats maintained their powerful southern wing and generally maintained ideological—and constitutional—divisions about the proper role of the central government.

One hugely important antebellum Whig, Kentuckian Henry Clay, died in 1852 just before the Republican Party emerged. Clay, who had been Speaker of the House for three terms, had walked a fine line on race and slavery. A slaveholder himself, Clay described the peculiar institution as "a great evil" but one that was protected by the nation's legal institutions. Slavery would and should gradually disappear, Clay argued, but the radical abolitionists who had developed a powerful voice by the 1840s threatened to destabilize the nation with their urgency. To counter these radicals, Clay—a devout defender of the Union—posed arguments in the early 1840s about the dangers of rapid "amalgamation." Freed slaves would, he insisted, move out of the South where they would "enter into competition with the free laborer" before they were prepared, producing disastrous results for Blacks and Whites alike.[4] It was an argument that would resonate with wartime Democrats two decades later.

In 1858 Douglas faced Republican challenger Abraham Lincoln in a hotly contested battle for Douglas's senate seat. Douglas kept his seat, but in the campaign the two men staged a series of high-profile debates that elevated Lincoln's status and perhaps damaged Douglas's national political fortunes. Douglas was one of a handful of politicians in American history who seemed destined, at least in his own mind, to become president of the United States. His chance seemed to come in 1860, but unforeseen circumstances intervened. Although Douglas was the frontrunner for the Democratic nomination, his party remained divided. When the party delegates met in Charleston, South Carolina, in April 1860, the South's most adamant defenders of their slave system—known as the "fire-eaters"—pushed hard for a strong proslavery platform, despite the warnings from their northern brethren that such measures would cost the party northern votes. Unable to sway the northern representatives, about fifty Democratic delegates from seven southern states walked out of the convention, and the party left Charleston without a nominee. In June the bulk of the Democratic Party reconvened in Baltimore and nominated Douglas, but they did so without the support of most of the southern delegates. Those proslavery gentlemen nominated Vice President John C. Breckinridge of Kentucky as their standard-bearer. Meanwhile, some moderates in the North and the border states, seeing the handwriting on the wall, created the Constitutional Union Party and nominated John Bell on a platform that promised to avoid sectional conflict.

There is certainly much that can be said—and has been said—about all of these events. For now I will settle for three observations: First, it is quite reasonable to see the election of 1860 as a contest between one brand-new party, the upstart Republicans, and another party—the Democrats—that had a long political history. That is certainly how many northern Democrats saw things. But despite this core truth we should keep in mind that party allegiances were fairly fluid at midcentury. Many voters who would call themselves Democrats in 1860 had been loyal Whigs before that party crumbled in the mid-1850s. Certainly in places like Kentucky slave-owning Whigs found a more comfortable home in the Democratic Party, even though their ideological roots were elsewhere. The men whose names appeared as possible Republican nominees in early 1860 had histories in a bewildering array of political parties.[5] And, perhaps easiest to forget, as soon as the southern delegates walked out of the Democratic convention, that party's political dynamics changed tremendously, even if the name did not. Still, the fact remains that the leaders of the national Democratic Party—although now representing far fewer voters in a suddenly shrunken nation—saw themselves as part of a party with a long and distinguished lineage. They were conservative defenders of the nation and the Constitution.

Second, the events from April 1860 to April 1861 should remind us of a crucial political reality: in times of crisis voters commonly believe things that are not true. White southerners seemed to have an exaggerated sense of the depth of abolitionist sentiment in the northern states, leading them to pursue defensive measures to protect slavery that far exceeded the immediate dangers their institution actually faced in the South. These perceptions became even more overwhelming after Lincoln's election, as southern slaveholders became convinced that this revolutionary election constituted a threat to slavery in the South. President-elect Lincoln grew frustrated with these sentiments, calling on friends and foes alike to read his party's platform and his many speeches on the subject. His electoral victory, he insisted, meant that his party would push to keep slavery out of the territories, but he had no designs on ending slavery nationwide. They were not buying this.[6]

Third, and finally, while many voters and political actors proceeded on mistaken, and even foolish, assumptions about their adversaries, there were others who had a very clear-eyed view of the practical political dangers that lay ahead. For one class of northern Democrats, the political wirepullers and highly engaged partisans, the events from the Charleston convention to the election of 1860, and then the subsequent events from November 1860 to April 1861, constituted serious threats to national political stability and to the future of their party. Some of these men labored behind the scenes to redirect the course of events. It is these political insiders who begin our story.

Samuel L. M. Barlow and Democratic Insiders Respond

New York had long been the center of Democratic politics, dating to the heyday of Martin Van Buren. And for the political insider, no one symbolized the smoke-filled rooms shaping party politics more than Samuel L. M. Barlow. Barlow, a prominent lawyer who built his wealth from mining and railroad interests, seemed to know all the city's most powerful political players, as well as an impressive array of key men—especially Democrats—scattered across the country. He had had a hand in James Buchanan's nomination in 1856, and in 1864 he would serve as a major architect of George McClellan's presidential campaign.[7]

Long before the Charleston convention, Barlow's political informants warned that Douglas—despite his strong national reputation—would raise southern Democratic hackles.[8] In February fellow mining magnate Samuel Butterworth reported that the talk among future delegates leaned toward the Illinois senator, which "is damaging them very much with southern men."[9] But the following week, a wealthy railroad investor and Midwestern politician wrote from Indiana, assuring Barlow that key southerners had embraced Douglas, at least as their second choice.[10] As is so often the case with politicians who have been in the national limelight for many years, Douglas had his supporters but had also accumulated his share of political adversaries.

As events unfolded, it became clear that the party would not hold together through the convention process. Washington journalist William Montague Browne, whose personal sympathies lay with the South, wrote from Charleston that their worst fears had been realized and the party had crumbled.[11] Former New York governor Horatio Seymour watched the proceedings from Utica and seemed similarly philosophical about how things had unfolded, concluding that—after all—he had never felt very sanguine about the party's presidential chances in 1860.[12] A month later Butterworth wrote from Baltimore that "I consider a breakup inevitable," a prospect that he seemed to welcome.[13] Some Democrats who were used to playing the long game seemed willing to absorb this electoral loss while preparing for the future.

It is fair to describe Douglas as the candidate of most of the North's Democrats, whereas Breckinridge represented the southern—and more emphatically proslavery—wing of the party. But there were pockets in the North, most notably in Connecticut, New York, and Pennsylvania, where Breckinridge enjoyed some support and even some party infrastructure. For some northern Democrats, such as New Yorker Daniel S. Dickinson, the political calculus was clear: Douglas, as an outspoken advocate of popular sovereignty, would alienate the White South almost as much as Lincoln, threatening a division of the Union. Only Breckinridge promised a constitutionally pure protection of slavery, and thus the Union. Other northern voters were unabashedly proslavery—or at least had pro-southern economic interests—and easily rallied to Breckinridge and his southern brethren.[14] And many northern Democrats, including some of Barlow's key acquaintances, could not stomach the Illinois Democrat's candidacy under any circumstances. Indiana senator Jesse David Bright, who would soon be banished from the Senate and headed to the Confederacy, wrote to Barlow that he was backing Breckinridge.[15] Douglas Brown, who would also end up in the Confederacy, insisted that "I would rather run a separate ticket & be beaten than have anything to say to Douglas and his gang anywhere."[16] Samuel A. Bridges wrote to Lewis S. Coryell, a lower level Pennsylvania wirepuller, reporting that Democrats in Allentown shared this general distaste for Douglas: "Good democrats cannot support him, nor he who loves his Country and its constitution."[17]

Many of these insiders understood that the party split was an almost inevitable response to the party convention, especially once most northern Democrats had cast their lot with Douglas. After the dueling Democratic conventions had settled on Douglas and Breckinridge as separate candidates, Democrats began talking about how best to proceed. For some pragmatists the answer was to construct some sort of "fusion ticket"—especially in key states like Pennsylvania, New Jersey, and New York—where Douglas and Breckinridge and their followers would be aligned together, at least to salvage the party's chances in local and state elections. In Massachusetts, Democratic talk of a fusion ticket went nowhere. The powerful *Boston Pilot,* the official publication of the Catholic diocese and the voice of the city's Irish immigrants, fully aligned with Douglas, dismissed those calling for working with Breckinridge as "traitors." The Boston *Courier* argued that the best strategy would be to support the Constitutional Union ticket of John Bell and local Democrat Edward Everett.[18] Connecticut Democrats, divided between Douglas and Breckinridge, had no better luck. State party leader Thomas Hart Seymour, a man of distinct southern leanings, initially supported Breckinridge; even when he saw the handwriting on the wall he could not bring himself to officially endorse Douglas in the name of party fusion.[19]

In mid-September John Slidell wrote to Barlow that Pennsylvania might be lost to Lincoln, but "New York may be the better ground if there be an honest fusion which is more than I can hope."[20] One correspondent from Rome, New York, reported on the state's fusion plans, with the same electors to be affiliated with both Douglas and Breckinridge.[21] Two weeks later James Tophan Brady sent Barlow a note summarizing the state's ultimate fusion plan. Douglas, he reported, had agreed to give up several electors to Breckinridge as well as other considerations in the name of their ultimate fusion.[22] But James Asheton Bayard, a conservative Democratic senator from Delaware and one of Barlow's most politically astute correspondents, wrote from Wilmington a few weeks later, asking Barlow what he thought about the chances of the "Union ticket succeeding in New York." As Bayard saw things, the Empire State had become a crucial bulwark against Lincoln's candidacy, because his Pennsylvania neighbors—and particularly the Philadelphia businessmen he knew—appeared blind to the dangers of a Republican victory.[23] Worried about upstate voters going Republican, Democrats in New York City—a party stronghold—staged a mass meeting at Cooper Union, where they declared themselves "the white man's party" and a bulwark against abolitionist Republicans.[24]

With the Pennsylvania state elections approaching, outgoing president James Buchanan—who despised Douglas—wrote to Coryell, his old friend in Bucks County, expressing confidence that Breckinridge would carry the entire South, with the possible exception of Virginia. Thus, Buchanan commented, "never was there a period in our history when so much of good or of evil depended upon the result of the election in the Keystone State."[25] But Democratic humorist Benjamin Penhallow Shillabar worried that in Philadelphia, "people are crazy for the rail splitter."[26] When Republicans carried Pennsylvania in the gubernatorial election, Bridges wrote to Coryell from Allentown, reflecting the thoughts of many northern Democrats: "I look now to N York now to give the death blow to Lincoln. If that fails, we are gone, and sad will be our fate."[27]

In Chicago ex-Whig turned Douglas Democrat Henry Waller watched these events with interest. Waller—who only recently had been a Kentucky politician—feared that Lincoln might pull out the election, with dire consequences, but he told his wife, Sarah, that "I hope he will be defeated. I think he will be. The fusion in New York, I think secures it." Sarah, writing from the family home in Kentucky, expressed much more optimism about the future. Even if Lincoln were to be elected, she felt sure that the South would not secede. Henry and Sarah continued to spar about politics, with Henry remaining more pessimistic about Douglas's chances and the nation's fate. On October 7 Henry looked ahead and declared that "if the Pennsylvania & Indiana state elections go against him next Tuesday, his doom is sealed," but Sarah stood her ground, insisting that the consequences of a Lincoln election were not so dire as her husband insisted.[28]

When the presidential votes were counted, where the Democrats succeeded in maintaining fusion tickets they did quite well, although not well enough to stop Lincoln and the Republicans. In New York the fusion ticket won 46.4 percent of the popular vote, and in New Jersey fusion voters gave 51.9 percent of the vote to Democrats, earning three of the state's seven electoral votes. In Pennsylvania a fusion ticket of Breckinridge-Douglas earned 37.5 percent of the vote, while Douglas won 3.5 percent of the votes on his own.[29] Across the northern free states, Douglas received about 41 percent of the vote and slightly more in the non-seceding states.[30] Nationwide, the Democratic Party's various candidates won 47.6 percent of all 1860 votes and 44.7 percent of the votes in the North's non-seceding states, slave or free. These totals were remarkably similar to the party's 1856 returns.[31] But thanks to the Democrats' internal divisions and the power of the Electoral College, the Republicans won a pretty substantial victory. If we imagine Democratic insiders as card-players in well-appointed club rooms across the North, the men who hoped to pull out the election had done their best with a bad hand after Charleston. Those northern wirepullers who had seen the handwriting on the wall now braced for the southern response to Lincoln's election.

Pursuits of Compromise

Almost immediately after learning that the nation had elected a "black Republican" as president of the United States, conversations in the Deep South turned to secession. After all, the Republican Party was an unapologetically regional party, and Lincoln's election over the divided Democrats seemed a direct threat to southern slavery.[32]

For a short time the United States faced two crucial questions: How many of the southern states would leave the Union? And how should the federal government respond to their actions, and to their complaints? The North's Democrats found themselves cast in the role of observers, as southerners debated their future. President-elect Lincoln cautiously tried to reassure some correspondents, and the hugely unpopular President James Buchanan faced the rising crisis. Samuel Barlow's many correspondents watched with interest.

On the eve of the election, wealthy Democrat Henry Douglas Bacon concluded a long business letter from St. Louis, "before I get answer the back of the Union or the [N—r] will be broken. God grant the latter!" A week later, with Lincoln elected, Bacon adopted a philosophical tone. "You have worked industriously to defeat Lincoln, but have failed," Bacon wrote. "There could be no doubt but that you love the Union, & now your influence should be given with the same unwavering patriotism to lead your friends to give Lincoln's administration a fair trial." While southern fire-eaters were already talking about how the Republicans would use their power to destroy slavery, Bacon—taking the Republican platform more seriously—declared, "I am confident nothing will be done to interfere with the constitutional rights of the slave states."[33] In the weeks to come, Bacon repeatedly tried to reassure Barlow that the Lincoln administration would behave judiciously, and that "in some way this Negro question must be settled," and perhaps Lincoln was the man to steer the nation to a wise conclusion. Only a week before the election Barlow had confided to Bayard that he had some hopes that Lincoln, if elected, "would be conservative," but he still did not share Bacon's sanguinity about the president elect.[34] This discussion would tantalize moderate northern Democrats for the next four years. On the one hand, Lincoln and his administration would seem to be architects of all sorts of measures that outraged the sensibilities of Constitution-minded Democrats. On the other hand, some Democrats persisted in suspecting that the president himself was a rather conservative potential ally under the sway of radical abolitionists in his circle.

Others disagreed. Journalist Browne, whose sympathies lay more squarely with the southern states, sent Barlow long letters discussing national politics and expressing his belief that Buchanan was not the man to handle the crisis.[35] In Browne's eyes, the very fact of Lincoln's election gave the South every right to secede, regardless of the institution of slavery. "My intimate conviction is that were I a citizen of a Southern State I should suffer anything rather than submit to Lincoln's election," he wrote. Moreover, Browne felt that a peaceful separation might be best for the South economically, even though secession would likely harm the federal Union.[36]

While Browne concentrated on the constitutional right to secede, anticipating an argument that would persist in the party for the next four years, Senator Bayard wrote from Delaware engaging the question of slavery. The border-state Democrat blamed the emerging crisis on the "spirit of fanaticism" in the Northeast, where "the masses" had come to conclude that slavery was a "sin," but one that would gradually disappear. In fact, Bayard argued, "in the Cotton States it must be a permanent institution," and sensible men should be practical about it. Looking to the nation's uncertain future, Bayard worried that "it will be difficult to elect men to a Convention who will deal with the question practically."[37] Time and again throughout the war, Democratic politicians would return to "practical" political arguments, skirting talk of the morality of slavery.

In mid-December—shortly before the South Carolina secession vote—Philadelphians gathered for a grand "Union Meeting" to call for reconciliation with the South. A reporter for the city's *Sunday Dispatch,* an independent Democratic paper, found much to mock in the somber event. After all, he noted, the southerners were acting precisely as they had promised to act when they walked out of the Democratic convention in Charleston. The current situation was predictable months before. Talk of abandoning personal liberty laws and guaranteeing the enforcement of the Fugitive Slave Act, which promised the federal government's assistance in returning runaways, were all well and good, and could likely pass the Pennsylvania legislature. But such measures would be too little too late. Now, the author asked, with events developing as might have been expected, were the political victors really willing to reopen the slave trade to placate angry slaveholders? Would they be willing to open all the territories to slavery? These were the concessions the "conservative citizens of the South" now demanded. The *Dispatch* editorial concluded that the lofty talk of the "Union Meeting" failed to address the core questions that divided the nation. Only serious talk of serious national compromises over slavery could save the day. But such conversations seemed unlikely.[38]

While Bayard and many of Barlow's northern colleagues were contemplating measures that might forestall the secession crisis, and anxious northerners held meetings calling for modest appeasement, southern slaveholders were holding conventions to leave the Union. Not surprisingly, South Carolina was the first to go; on December 20 a state convention voted 169–0 to secede. By early February Mississippi, Florida, Alabama, Georgia, Louisiana, and Texas had followed suit. In the North, observers had a range of reactions. President Buchanan declared that secession was unconstitutional but proved entirely ineffectual in imposing his convictions on the rebellious southerners. Others debated options from capitulation to compromise to various forms of coercion.[39] In early December Barlow revealed to railroad executive George B. McClellan that some New Yorkers were discussing plans to break off from the "fanatics" in the Northeast.[40]

In the months after South Carolina seceded, political insiders within the Democratic Party divided, with some content to let the southern states go in peace while many others discussed strategies for restoring the Union. Barlow wrote to Louisiana senator Judah P. Benjamin, who would soon leave the Senate to join Jefferson Davis's cabinet. Benjamin, responding on December 9, had little reason for optimism. Nothing would change "the naked fact that the Union is dissolved," he wrote. "The solitary gleam of hope," he added, "is that after secession, the conservative sentiment of the masses of the middle states will induce the call of state conventions and a tender to the South of the reconstruction of the government on such a basis as will tender it perfectly secure for the future."[41] Democrat John B. Cochrane, writing from Washington, agreed that perhaps the answer lay in some sort of public gathering. "If Republicans and Democrats can unite in a demonstration," he wrote, "their convention may do much good here."[42] Bayard also felt that a serious gathering of the various states might solve the nation's ills.[43]

On December 18, just days before the South Carolina vote became official, the Senate named a bipartisan Committee of 13 to examine strategies for compromise. The most active committee member was Kentucky senator John J. Crittenden. A one-time member of the Know Nothing Party, and then the Whig Party, in 1860 Crittenden helped lead the Constitutional Union Party in Kentucky.

With the nation crumbling, the proud Kentuckian—a loyal heir to Kentucky's Whig leader Henry Clay—crafted a series of possible compromises to entice the South back into the Union. Most did not win the support of the Committee of 13, but Crittenden's proposed constitutional amendment promising that slavery would remain protected below the 36'30'' line, in U.S. territories and also in those territories "hereafter acquired," earned substantial support.[44]

Crittenden's compromise, and various other proposals that floated through popular discussions, became the subject of Democratic discussions across the North. Browne read newspaper accounts of the nation's challenges and reminded Barlow that events were precisely as Barlow had predicted if the Republicans won in 1860.[45] In early 1861 Bacon reported an enthusiastic rally in St. Louis supporting the Crittenden Compromise. A few days later he wrote from Springfield, Illinois, describing a meeting of Democrats intent on preserving the Union.[46] But on January 17 Benjamin contacted Barlow just before he left for the Confederacy, offering the opinion that Crittenden's compromise had no chance of success so long as Republicans refused to endorse it.[47] A month later Bacon seemed similarly disgusted with the country's political leadership, blaming radicals in both the North and the South for the nation's travails.[48]

In New York City leading conservative Democrats cast around for solutions. In mid-December a group of the city's wealthy and powerful gathered at Pine Street to discuss ways to appease the South and promise them protections for slavery. The following month the city's mayor, Fernando Wood, who enjoyed tremendous popularity among Irish Catholic voters, floated an audacious plan calling for the city to secede from the state and maintain trading relationships with the Confederacy. The idea did not go over well.[49]

Barlow's correspondents shared substantial political acumen and little optimism for the future. Meanwhile, across the nation Democrats clung to hopes for compromise even while specific proposals crumbled under the weight of partisan conflict. In the final days of the year one correspondent wrote from Buffalo to Isaac Sherman, reporting that "there is much anxiety here about the political situation, & I think some disposition among Republicans to be content with the Crittenden plan for a settlement."[50] In the first week of January a Philadelphia engraver recorded in his diary that he had signed a petition to Congress supporting the Crittenden Compromise.[51] Across the Keystone State Democratic newspapers and party leaders embraced Crittenden's plan as a "just and honorable remedy for our present threatening problems." Pennsylvania senator William Bigler, a Democratic member of the Committee of 13, became an outspoken advocate of his colleague's plan as the best way to save the Union.

Correspondence from his Democratic constituents poured in supporting the proposed compromise.[52]

As winter wore on, the secession crisis took a toll on the northern economy, forcing thousands of laborers out of work. In Philadelphia unemployed workers held nonpartisan rallies supporting Crittenden's plan or any other compromise that might restore the Union. On January 26, six thousand "mechanics and workingmen" gathered at Independence Hall in a snowstorm to defend the Union, passing a series of resolutions supporting the Crittenden Compromise and other possible accommodations. Meanwhile, other workers rallied in the state capital calling for conciliation with the Confederacy.[53]

On February 21 and 22, Philadelphians hosted three important national events, each of which unfolded on the city's historic streets and squares. Much of the popular attention focused on Abraham Lincoln's visit on his whistle-stop tour of the North's major cities. The president-elect arrived in Philadelphia on the 21st and on the following day spoke at Independence Hall to an enthusiastic crowd. Meanwhile, on the 22nd, Philadelphians staged a variety of traditional martial events honoring George Washington's birthday. After Lincoln left the city, Mayor Alexander Henry hosted the central annual event in Independence Hall, where Constitutional Unionist Joseph R. Ingersoll read Washington's Farewell Address. Later in the day military veterans gathered at Mechanic's Hall for patriotic addresses and martial airs. The afternoon concluded with traditional parading and more speeches. The two sets of events, overlapping in time and space, invited contemplation of the nation's founding as well as the terrible challenges that the president-elect faced.[54]

Meanwhile, segments of Philadelphia's workingmen staged two public events of their own. Shortly after Lincoln spoke at Independence Hall, representatives of the city's industrial unions gathered at Third and Chestnut for their Washington's Birthday parade. These workers marched to National Hall where a multistate gathering of labor representatives was meeting to discuss national affairs. The Workingmen's Convention had been meeting all day in the city. In the morning their leaders gathered at Wetherill Hall, in a meeting chaired by a Kentuckian. The assembled workingmen passed resolutions urging Americans—and especially laborers—to "lay aside all their party freedom" and pursue regional reconciliation at any cost. These skilled artisans, representing thirty-four states, agreed to meet next in Louisville in July.[55]

Less than two months before the nation would erupt in warfare, the North's organized workingmen, a large portion with strong Democratic leanings, had aligned squarely with compromise and reconciliation, even while declaring their unbending loyalty to the Union. Of course these prewar parades and meetings only involved a segment of northern workers, focusing on larger urban manufacturing establishments and the skilled trades. In two years the political terrain would shift, as many northern workers—and particularly miners and unskilled immigrant laborers—responded angrily to conscription and many turned their backs on the northern war effort.

Events had moved at a bewildering pace in the ten months since Democrats met in Charleston. In the chain of events that brought the nation to that moment in February when president-elect Abraham Lincoln visited Philadelphia's Independence Hall, we can identify all sorts of political constituents who had a hand in how things unfolded. At one level this is a story of national politicians and elections. Democratic delegates made the fateful decisions in April 1860 that resulted in a divided party, perhaps making everything to come more or less inevitable. Republican delegates wrestled with alternatives before settling on the lanky Illinois lawyer. From conventions to election, an assortment of Democratic political wirepullers, often acting at the local and state level, attempted to at least partially undo what had been done by negotiating fragile fusion tickets in key states. In the 1860 election itself, individual voters spoke for themselves. It seems likely that most northern voters went to the polls recognizing that this was an unusually important election but still not anticipating the implications of a Republican victory. Once the results were in and the Deep South seceded, the political discussions in the North shifted abruptly, with both leaders and members of the rank and file—especially among Democrats—seeking some sort of path to compromise and reconciliation. The gathering of skilled artisans in Philadelphia is instructive. Their statements were not about political partisanship. They wanted no part of a dissolved Union and a possible war. In the years to come northern workers in various guises would return to the streets to share strongly held political beliefs and hostilities, only occasionally aligning with the established party structure.

Looking ahead, it is easy to identify points where the two parties differed as the nation fought a destructive civil war. In certain core convictions Democrats and Republicans already were deeply at odds in 1860. Republicans, heirs to the Free Soil Party as well as portions of the old Whig Party, had coalesced around their shared hostility to the expansion of slavery into the federal territories in the West. Some in the party held to more radical abolitionist beliefs, while others—including the newly elected president—were best described as moderately antislavery. In addition to their beliefs about the peculiar institution, which only existed in a few border states in the remaining United States, Republicans—following Whig traditions—saw the possibility for an expanded federal role in encouraging growth and shaping the economy.

In ideological terms, the victorious Republicans arrayed from radical to moderate on most of the key issues of the day. In contrast, the North's Democrats, which also included refugees from the Whig Party, saw themselves as ranging from moderate to conservative. Some had an economic dependence on slavery, and others had seemed perfectly happy to accommodate their southern brethren, but many northern Democrats saw slavery as a bad labor system, even if they questioned the notion of federal intervention in its future. More generally, on the eve of the Civil War the Democrats described themselves as fairly conservative. They revered the Constitution and many recoiled at what they saw as puritanical moralizing in the new Republican Party. As the Catholic *New York Freeman's Journal* put it: "It is a mistake to say that the fundamental idea of the Republican Party is opposition to African slavery. . . . The fundamental idea of that party is the claim to the right to determine by political legislation questions that, among a free people, do not belong in politics."[56]

With the coming of war they would speak out against revolutionary changes and federal measures that seemed to run counter to core conservative principles. No doubt nearly all harbored fundamentally racist views, and most had been perfectly willing to support the southern defense of slavery. But northern Democrats in the free states probably thought relatively little about race or slavery in the months leading to war. Stephen Douglas, the choice of most northern Democrats in 1860, had sought a practical political solution to the national dilemma. "Popular Sovereignty" had a distinct appeal for those who, like Douglas, appeared untroubled by slavery's large moral issues and who wished for a political solution that would enable the nation to move forward. Now they would have to adjust to a new political role in a completely transformed political reality. They would maintain their conservative stance on constitutional issues and their fundamentally pragmatic approach to the politics of slavery.

The Bread Pill

In the early hours of March 4, 1861, the day Abraham Lincoln was to be inaugurated, the U.S. Senate did a rather extraordinary thing: they passed a new constitutional amendment. It read, "No amendment shall be made to the Constitution which will authorize or give to Congress the power to abolish or interfere, within any state, with the domestic institutions thereof, including that of persons held to labor or service by the laws of said state."[57] Although the final language omitted the use of the word "slavery," the point of this amendment—which was slated to be the 13th Amendment to the U.S. Constitution—was clear. The authors were promising that going forward, Congress, as the nation's federal legislative body, would not—and could not—touch the institution of slavery.

The story behind this crucial amendment is long and the product of much debate in both houses of Congress.[58] This first 13th Amendment originated with the House's Committee of 33, that body's counterpart to the Senate's Committee of 13. The Committee of 33, headed by Ohio Republican Thomas Corwin, debated various measures that might please the North and appease the South, heading off armed conflict. It soon became apparent that the much-heralded Crittenden Compromise, which would protect slavery below the 36'30" line, had no chance of success. Northern Republicans, flush with electoral success and committed to blocking the expansion of the peculiar institution, would not support such a measure. And they had the votes.

In the end, after much internal wrangling, Corwin and his committee endorsed a proposed constitutional amendment assuring the South that slavery would remain safe in their home states. But Corwin, an ex-Whig with some hope of building bridges across these great divides, watched the debates with chagrin. Shortly after submitting the House's version of the amendment, Corwin wrote to Abraham Lincoln, "I cannot comprehend the madness of the time. Southern men are theoretically crazy. Extreme northern men are practical fools. The latter are really quite as mad as the former."[59] Still, the amendment moved to the Senate's Committee of 13, where New York's William Henry Seward took charge of steering it forward, with Illinois Democrat Stephen Douglas playing a large role. The members of the upper chamber had their own debates, culminating in slightly altered language proposed by Seward. That version, which became the final amendment, returned to the House in late February.

Here things became even more complicated. The House approved the new language by a vote of 120 to 61, nearly reaching the two-thirds margin required to approve an amendment. But then when Corwin pushed forward for a vote on the amendment itself on February 27, it won with only a 120–71 vote, far short of the requisite two-thirds needed. The following day, with the congressional session on the verge of ending and congressmen facing enormous pressure from many fronts, the House voted a second time and it passed 133 to 65. This margin included support from all Democrats in the House as well as all the opposition members who remained from the Upper South. House Republicans voted against the amendment by a vote of 63 to 46. But those 46 Republicans were enough to win the day.[60]

From there the amendment returned to the Senate for final congressional ratification. Once again, the vote required a two-thirds majority before it would be sent to the states. In the Senate, Stephen Douglas took on a familiar role, attempting to steer through a compromise that would please at least a portion of both parties. But this time he had all the Democrats on his side and had to help win over some Republicans. The debate went on through the night, and at 5:20 on the morning of the 4th the Senate passed what became known as "the original 13th amendment" by a vote of 24 to 12. Once again, 12 of 20 Republicans opposed the amendment, but the remaining eight were just enough.

What should we make of this flurry of activity? On the face of it, the original 13th Amendment is remarkable. In early 1861 each house of Congress voted by a two-thirds margin to change the Constitution and stipulate that the nation would not interfere with slavery where it existed. As the historian Daniel Crofts points out, "The other thirteenth amendment runs contrary to uplifting national theology."[61] It is difficult to paint the American Civil War as a grand conflict to emancipate southern slaves when Congress was willing to pass an amendment promising to leave slavery alone. Of course, we know that the war did not really begin as a war to end slavery. It was a war to preserve the Union.[62] But still, the amendment—which Crofts notes has been oddly forgotten—runs counter to what we would like to believe. Where is the uplift when the North seemed willing to go so far to appease the Confederacy?

On the other hand, the original 13th Amendment made perfect sense, and it was the fight to get it passed that seems odd. Corwin was absolutely right in throwing his hands up at the madness all around him. For Democrats, the conversation was quite simple. The party valued Union at almost all costs, and this amendment hardly seemed to be a cost at all. Ohio congressman Samuel S. "Sunset" Cox, who would be a thorn in the administration's side for four years of war, put the matter succinctly on the House floor. Southerners, he insisted, were excessively worried about "slave insurrections and abolition," and they had convinced themselves that Lincoln had been "elected on a principle of hostility to the social systems of the South." Those southerners were wildly mistaken, but the challenge was to calm them down and convince the secessionists they had badly misread things.[63] Faced with such profound confusion, North Carolina's John Gilmer recommended that "the South is deranged and only needs a few bread pills, to cure their madness." Gilmer, who remained in Congress, referred to a popular placebo of the time. Douglas soon embraced the metaphor, suggesting that the amendment would be the perfect "bread pill" to soothe angry southerners.[64]

The point was clear. Only a handful of Republicans—and no Democrats—believed that slavery was unconstitutional, or that the federal government had any right to interfere with the internal workings of sovereign states. Lincoln, as he wrote to Gilmer and Georgia's Alexander Stephens and anyone else who would listen, insisted that he and his administration had no intention of touching slavery in the southern states. The Republican Party was only committed to stopping the expansion of the peculiar institution into federal territories. If this amendment would somehow appease the South, that was apparently okay with him. It was certainly fine with President Buchanan. So, in the early morning hours of March 4, 1861, Congress approved an amendment protecting the future of slavery in the United States. Some Republicans refused to go along with the measure, but for some of those, that reflected their refusal to placate the southern radicals. A larger majority of elected representatives agreed on the constitutional limits on what they could do. What harm could there be in passing a bread pill?

Later that day, Abraham Lincoln stood on the steps of the yet unfinished Capitol to deliver his First Inaugural Address. The Union was fully dissolved and the Confederacy in place. The nation teetered on the brink of war. The new president addressed those southerners who had left the Union and those in the border states who remained uncertain. "We are not enemies, but friends," he insisted. "We must not be enemies." As president, he would not "interfere with the institution of slavery in the states where it exists."[65] Surely the northern Democrats approved of those sentiments, even while they had serious doubts about the new president and his upstart political party. But much remained to be decided, and the role of the North's Democrats moving forward seemed perilously unclear.

2

Stumbling into War

In the half-year after Abraham Lincoln visited Philadelphia, the nation went to war. This required the United States to confront a host of structural, legal, and ideological questions. Three seemed paramount: What would the border states do? How should the nation treat dissenters? And how would Democrats who opposed Lincoln and his party respond to the national crisis? All three questions found Democrats at the center of the storm, even while the party enjoyed little power.

Whereas many in the South understood Lincoln's 1860 victory as making secession—at least by some states—inevitable, northerners from both parties felt betrayed as they watched the departure of southern states. White southerners had abandoned the Union, rather than waiting to see how events would unfold. But this anger at secession was followed almost immediately by calls for compromise and conciliation. Here there was a bit of a partisan divide. Abraham Lincoln felt that electoral victory meant something, and he was loath to unring that bell. His fellow Republicans agreed with him, and some would have been happy to see the slave states out of the Union under any circumstance. But for others, especially the North's moderate Democrats, the threat posed by secession and possible war called for emergency measures, even if that meant offering added inducements to the seceded states. In many corners of the Union, compromise remained the rallying cry of the day, as evidenced by the last-minute passage of the Corwin amendment by both houses.

South Carolina's Guns Fire on Fort Sumter

All this changed abruptly on April 12, 1861, when South Carolina guns fired on the U.S. troops garrisoned at Fort Sumter, on a small island in Charleston

Harbor. After a thirty-four-hour bombardment, Colonel Robert Anderson surrendered the fort. On April 15 President Lincoln called for the enlistment of 75,000 men for ninety days. War had begun. The fall of Fort Sumter came at the end of a complex series of events and decisions, and the bombardment itself did not produce any deaths. It is no exaggeration to see the fall of Fort Sumter as a pivotal moment, particularly in popular discourse in both the Union and the Confederacy. It surely changed life for many northern Democrats.

New York Democrat Maria Lydig Daly, the wife of prominent judge Charles Patrick Daly and one of the North's great diarists, wrote that "the attack upon Fort Sumter has united all the North as one man against the South. Party is forgotten." In this newly united society, Daly added, "every man must do his best to sustain the government, whoever or whatever the President may be."[1] Pundits who had been lukewarm about a looming conflict became vigorous, even bloodthirsty, patriots. The printed response in the Evansville, Indiana, *Daily Journal* was typical: "Whatever a Democrat or a Bell man may think of the issues which were discussed so warmly in the recent campaign, they, in common with the Republican, have but now one common opinion; that is, the Union must be preserved, the Constitution maintained in its purity, and the laws enforced."[2]

Democrat Stephen Douglas made it clear what he thought of partisan politics in time of national crisis. "There are but two parties," he declared, "the party of patriots and the party of traitors." Lest there be any confusion, the Illinois senator added that Democrats "belong to the first."[3] With these words Douglas marked out a perspective that most in his party shared. In Massachusetts, where Republicans had fared particularly well in 1860, leading conservative Democrats called for shutting down partisan conflict for the duration of the war. Benjamin F. Hallett and Caleb Cushing declined to attend the party's state convention in 1861, although fellow Massachusetts Democrats did nominate a slate of candidates.[4] In the years to come Douglas's declaration would define one end of a spectrum within the Democratic Party, as some leaders persistently sought to play down party conflict in time of war. But eventually the partisan questions would reemerge, as Democrats wrestled with how to be patriots while also being the party of opposition.

For the time being, unanimity—or close to it—was the order of the day. The other side of that coin was that this upsurge of popular enthusiasm tended to silence dissent, particularly on the streets. Jacob D. Cox, who would go on to be a Union general, recalled that "in New York, wildly excited crowds marched the streets demanding that the suspected or the lukewarm" display the flag. "He that is not for us is against us, was the deep, instinctive feeling," he wrote.[5] New York's *Journal of Commerce,* with its pro-southern sympathies, made an easy target. The crowd visited the newspaper office and demanded the display of the American flag, and newspapers across the North noted the episode. Other papers reported that a New York mob chased James Gordon Bennett Sr. the editor of the *New York Herald,* down the street until his workers managed to acquire and display a flag.[6] Diarist George Templeton Strong described angry visits by mobs to a host of New York's Democratic papers, including the *Express, Day-Book,* and *Daily News.* For the first few days after the fall of Fort Sumter, Democratic newspapers—and especially those with known southern sympathies—had to tread very carefully in the face of popular threats. New York's flamboyant Democratic mayor Fernando Wood, who only weeks earlier discussed the city's possible secession, issued a proclamation calling on the citizens to maintain order and respect property. Like Douglas, Wood announced that there is "no party now." Still, the mayor's brother, Benjamin Wood, resisted pressures to fly the flag outside the window of the *Daily News,* his Democratic newspaper.[7]

Less than a hundred miles to the southwest, Philadelphians reacted to Sumter's fall and Lincoln's call for troops with similar enthusiasm. But perhaps because the City of Brotherly Love was further south and had more substantial cultural and economic ties with the South, tense encounters in the streets and public squares seemed more frequent and threatening in those early days. Once news of the bombardment arrived, crowds of Philadelphians packed the city streets, congregating around newspaper office bulletin boards to read the latest reports. On April 14 a mob gathered after two men on Third Street were heard speaking up for secession. Fortunately for them, the local police marched them off to jail before blood was shed. On the same day the Philadelphia *North American* reported that one man in the crowd "ventured to justify the Charlestonians, when his hat was smashed down over his eyes, and a dozen boots left impressions upon his person" before he was dragged to safety.[8]

The following day one Democratic businessman told a reporter that "I voted for Breckinridge, and oppose the politics of the present administration, but to maintain the government I will part with all I have" and enlist in the Union Army if the cause required it. The reporter for the *North American* noted that if there were pro-secessionists in the crowd, they "cloaked their valor under discretion." He overheard one local Democrat who was heading to the railroad depot to head south to bring his family from Florida. Although the man owned a large cotton plantation and felt confident that he and his relatives would be safe in the hands of White southerners, he worried that unfolding events would lead to a Black insurrection and unspeakable "horrors."[9]

Late on the morning of the 15th a handful of men visited the Chestnut Street offices of *The Palmetto Flag,* a modest advertising sheet that had been linked with pro-secession activities. The mob grew quickly, but the police arrived—accompanied by Mayor Alexander Henry—and managed to ease the tensions. The crucial moment came when Mayor Henry appeared at a window waving an American flag. Before the crowd dispersed, they found another target in the person of a well-dressed young lawyer with ties to South Carolina radicals. Rioters ripped his coat and enjoyed sport with his hat until the young man slunk away, leaving his hat in the gutter. In the afternoon the crowd wandered the streets, demanding displays of the flag at newspaper offices and other buildings. One Chestnut Street hotel nearly faced an attack when they accidentally flew their flag upside down.[10]

Philadelphia's residents—both Democrat and Republican—recognized that the local surge in patriotism also suppressed dissent and threatened order. The same day Katherine Brinley Wharton, a strong patriot, recorded in her journal that "there has been quite a mob in Ches[nut] St today to tear down an obnoxious printing office," and that the mob went to the homes of prominent Democrats demanding flag displays.[11] Philadelphia diarist Sidney George Fisher was a conservative curmudgeon who had a wide assortment of Democratic friends and relatives, including people who would become harsh critics of the war and the Lincoln administration. In the 1860 election Fisher did not favor the Democratic candidates, but he could not bring himself to vote for Abraham Lincoln. On April 15 Fisher "went to town" and "found the city in a state of dangerous excitement. . . . Several well-known persons, who had openly expressed secession opinions had been assaulted in the streets." A few days later Fisher returned to the city with his wife, Elizabeth, happy to learn that the streets were mostly peaceful, with flags decorating homes and public buildings. But the overall tranquility came at a price. Suspected secessionists had to be protected in their homes "from insult by the mob," he noted, and "it is at the risk of any man's life that he utters publicly a sentiment in favor of secession or the South." Looking to the future, Fisher noted that local Democrats had been "zealous in support of the government," but the party still "chafes at defeat" and was poised to strike back at the hated Republican Party when an opening came. As if to underscore his predictions, Fisher ended his outing by visiting Democrat Charles Ingersoll, whose "opinions are most extravagant & absurd," and his father, whose declarations were "still more violent."[12] From where Fisher sat, Philadelphians enjoyed a calm after days of disorder, but tensions seethed under the surface.

Philadelphia's more ardent Democrats eyed local events with particular concern. A young Democratic engraver who lived close to the most distressing action wrote on the 16th that "yesterday was a reign of terror. Black Rep ruffians mobbed the Argus office, the only Dem paper, the house of Gen. Patterson, chased Rob Tyler with a rope to hang him! Etc etc!!" The following day the agitated Democrat added, "The reign of terror still in the ascendant, notwithstanding the rain. The mob visited Josiah Randall & W.B. Reed. The mayor came, told them he was determined to stop further mobs by force if necessary & then blood will be on their hands."[13]

Sarah Butler Wister, the twenty-five-year-old daughter of English actress Fanny Kemble and pro-southern Philadelphian Pierce Butler, recorded long entries in her journal on national and local events. By the evening of the 15th Wister reported "the most tremendous excitement" as mobs gathered in the streets, "swearing revenge on all disunionists or disaffected." Wister noted that a few local Democrats left town, and others took care to fly the flag, but the mob "committed no outrages, beyond knocking down a few persons in the crowd. Which will always happen, almost accidentally."[14]

In the first days after the fall of Fort Sumter, newspapers across the country ran particularly long columns summarizing events in Philadelphia, suggesting that the Pennsylvania city was the most inflamed by the events in April. The attacks on New York's *Journal of Commerce* and the harassment of the *Herald*'s Bennett also appeared in short newspaper squibs. Other reports underscored that in those heady days northern pro-Confederates were wise to keep their mouths shut in the streets, even if they grumbled in the safety of their own parlors. In Albany, New York, a man attended a Union gathering and offered a defense of the South, at which point a mob of enthusiasts ran him out of the room.[15] A Columbus, Ohio, crowd gave a suspected secessionist the same treatment.[16] Democratic congressman Clement Vallandigham already had a pro-southern reputation when the shooting started. A Washington mob visited the congressman's house, prompting him to flee the capital.[17]

In Baltimore tensions ran high and would soon break out into serious mob violence. In the immediate aftermath of the bombardment of Fort Sumter, the national press picked up on one strange story about a Baltimore man who was accosted by a mob for wearing a secessionist cockade in his hat. This tale of the man with the cockade appeared again and again in different forms across the country, although those same newspapers failed to mention any other Baltimore disturbances.[18] Pro-Union enthusiasm essentially silenced dissent for a time. As an Evansville paper noted, "Secession sympathizers will be as 'scarce as hen's teeth' in thirty days."[19] But not indefinitely.

Those immediate days after the Charleston guns fired on Fort Sumter mapped out some crucial patterns in public behavior in the North. Even where communities had engaged in vigorous debate in the previous months, the outbreak of war imposed a sort of public unanimity in many places. Tempers ran high. Crowds identified institutions—usually newspapers and journals—associated with the South, or merely with the Democratic Party, and demanded shows of patriotism. Philadelphia, with its politically divided population, including prominent conservative Democrats with southern ties, seemed to experience particular threats to social order. New York City, a Democratic stronghold, witnessed its own flurries of activity but seemingly less outright violence. But across the North in April 1861 it was private individuals moving as parts of large crowds who threatened civil liberties, not instruments of the state.

The Pratt Street Riots

When Abraham Lincoln called for volunteers to put down the rebellion, excited men flocked to recruiting stations, quickly overwhelming the resources available to arm and equip them. Some of the first state militia volunteers in uniform came from Pennsylvania, where they boarded a train in Harrisburg, headed south. On April 18 the Pennsylvanians arrived in Baltimore, and a substantial portion rode by cars across the city to Camden Station, where they would board their southbound train for Washington. As the volunteers traversed the city streets they were accosted by a large body of southern sympathizers who hurled rocks and bricks at the soldiers. The Pennsylvanians managed to get out of the city, aided by the Baltimore police, but the next day things grew more violent.

On April 19 members of the newly formed 6th Massachusetts Militia arrived in Maryland's Charm City, having traveled through New York and Philadelphia. By the time the Massachusetts troops reached Baltimore, they were accompanied by a thousand unarmed Pennsylvania recruits. Baltimore ordinances did not allow locomotives to travel across the city, so through travelers routinely arrived in one station and departed from another. The men of the 6th Massachusetts reached President's Street Station, where their thirty-five cars were detached from the locomotive and drawn by horses along tracks to Camden Station, about a mile and a half to the west. Once again, a large Baltimore mob accosted the Massachusetts volunteers. The first six companies made it safely to Camden Station, but the mob closed in on the car carrying Company K, pummeling it with rocks and bricks, while a few men in the crowd fired guns into the car. The officers eventually ordered the men to return fire from inside their car, but before they reached the station they discovered that the mob had blocked their progress by tearing up tracks and blockading the streets. They had no choice but to abandon the cars. The men of Company K fought their way on foot for the remaining quarter mile. With the cars useless, the remaining 228 Massachusetts soldiers battled their way on foot from President's Station to Camden Station, with angry Baltimoreans raining bricks on their heads and firing into their ranks. By the time the 6th Massachusetts had gotten out of Baltimore, four soldiers and twelve civilians were dead, and several dozen soldiers—and untold citizens—were bleeding. The unarmed Pennsylvania soldiers managed to board cars to return to Philadelphia without further violence.[20]

With the combined weight of political tensions in the public square and reports of rioting in Baltimore, officeholders charged with policing their cities worried about incessant talk of subterranean plots threatening the peace. On April 22, only days after the Baltimore riots, two railroad men wrote to Philadelphia's Mayor Alexander Henry asking for "a strong force of police armed to watch [ ] Ferry Bridge for a few nights." About a week later a representative from the Army Clothing and Equipage Office sent the mayor an urgent note about a crowd threatening the U.S. arsenal on the Schuylkill River. A month after the fall of Fort Sumter, the mayor of Newport, Rhode Island, dropped Henry a note passing on a rumor about activities "in your city, N. W. corner of Arch and 13th streets, which is suspected to be occupied by Southern spies, who are strong and influential."[21]

Even before armies met in the field, blood had been shed and authorities braced for much more.

Ex Parte Merryman

From a military and political perspective, the first goal of the Lincoln administration would be to control those vital border states, particularly Maryland, Tennessee, Kentucky, and Missouri.[22] Meanwhile, local and federal forces charged with protecting order wrestled with strategies for controlling the streets and—on occasion—limiting public speech. In the first weeks of the war Marylander John

Merryman became a crucial figure in what would become an ongoing political and legal debate.

Immediately following Baltimore's Pratt Street riots, Baltimoreans—acting with the general consent of the city's political and police leadership—set about destroying railroad bridges and telegraph lines in hopes of keeping more federal troops out of their city. Word of the riot outraged northerners, but for a time President Lincoln adopted a conciliatory tone toward Baltimore. He hoped to soothe tensions and keep the crucial border state in the Union. As one step toward conciliation, Lincoln ordered a detachment of Pennsylvania soldiers stationed in Baltimore County, north of the city, to be returned to their home state. As these men marched north, members of the pro-secessionist Baltimore County Horse Guards followed their path, destroying bridges and generally doing their best to inhibit future visits from the Union military. John Merryman, a slaveholder and ardent secessionist, owned a substantial body of land north of Baltimore, not far from where the Pennsylvania troops had been stationed. As a first lieutenant in the Horse Guards, Merryman commanded the troops who followed the Pennsylvanians, destroying property along the way. From Merryman's perspective, he was following orders and acting to preserve Baltimore from further violence. After all, Merryman had received his commission to the Horse Guards in February from Maryland governor Thomas Hicks. But Merryman and his men had confronted watchmen and other officials charged with protecting the property the Horse Guards sought to destroy. It was a military action, but arguably a treasonous one.

Meanwhile, the political battle for the control of Maryland unfolded. Governor Hicks, an ex-Whig who had been elected as a member of the Know Nothing Party, called for the state legislature to convene in Annapolis; a few days later he changed the location to Frederick, hoping to help ensure a pro-Union vote. Lincoln faced the real possibility that the Marylanders would vote to leave the Union, turning a political debate into a military clash. His challenge was to calm the waters long enough for a pro-Union vote in the state. On April 17 the president took a large step in suspending the privilege of the writ of habeas corpus in portions of Maryland, thus enabling federal forces to incarcerate treasonous pro-secessionists without charging them. The president gave his commanders authorization to expand the suspension as needed along the line from Philadelphia to Washington. Meanwhile, all eyes were on the state legislators. On May 7 leading Democrat Reverdy Johnson spoke to the delegates at Frederick, calling on them to vote against secession. Given the state's precarious geographic position, Johnson worried that Maryland faced "immediate and total ruin" if the state abandoned the Union. After considerable back and forth with the Lincoln administration, the Maryland legislature adjourned without voting to secede. The state would remain in Union hands, even if many Marylanders ended up fighting for the Confederacy.

Once the federal government exercised some control over Maryland, it shifted focus toward asserting power over the state's most contested areas. Less than two weeks later, on May 25, Union officers arrested Merryman and placed him in Baltimore's Fort McHenry. There is some reason to believe that the decision to select Merryman for arrest was because his Unionist neighbors had grown thoroughly sick of him and were more fond of other officers in the Horse Guards. In any case, it was Merryman who ended up in shackles, and an impressive list of locals lined up to testify to his treason. The wealthy Merryman enjoyed strong representation; his lawyers promptly petitioned in federal court for a writ of habeas corpus, which would require that he be brought forward and charged. That federal case ended up on Chief Justice Roger Taney's desk, whose circuit court included Maryland. Taney, a Maryland Democrat and chief author of the infamous *Dred Scott* decision protecting the institution of slavery, promptly issued a writ on May 26, ordering General George Cadwalader—the newly appointed commanding officer at Fort McHenry—to bring Merryman before the court. But this posed problems for the commander. Two thousand spectators gathered at Judge Taney's courtroom at the appointed hour, and 150 armed men prepared for any disturbances to come. Rather than presenting Merryman to the court, General Cadwalader sent a note through a subordinate. Citing Lincoln's suspension of the writ of habeas corpus, Cadwalader refused to obey Taney's instructions.

This put the ball squarely in the court of the chief justice, who was surprised and furious at Cadwalader's actions. The judge placed Cadwalader in contempt of court and turned to the issues at hand. With no prisoner in his court, Taney could not rule on the merits of the case. Instead, Taney wrote an opinion on the broader issues, denying the president's right to suspend the writ, arguing that that constitutional power rested with Congress. And, moreover, Taney ruled that a civilian should not have been arrested by military officers where civil courts were available.

Faced with this challenge from the eminent jurist, Lincoln turned to his attorney general, Edward Bates, and Reverdy Johnson for opinions. Bates, an ex-Whig from Missouri who had pursued the Republican nomination in 1860, wrote a long paper on the writ, concluding that in times of "great and dangerous insurrection, the President has the lawful discretionary power to arrest and hold in custody, persons known to have criminal intercourse with the insurgents." Johnson, a Democrat and one of his state's great legal minds, agreed with Bates. Responding to Taney's argument, Johnson concluded that although the Constitution did presume Congress would be the branch to suspend the writ of habeas corpus, the president could claim such authority in the midst of a national crisis, and—moreover—the president, as commander in chief, could order his military to act when the crisis required it. Backed by the counsel of Bates and Johnson, Lincoln declined to follow Taney's order, instead keeping Merryman in jail and maintaining the limited suspension of the writ of habeas corpus.[23]

The issues surrounding the suspension of the writ of habeas corpus, and broader debates concerning the suppression of civil liberties, would continue to tear at the fabric of northern society for the next four years. In those early days of the war, more than 850 civilians faced arrest without specific charges in areas where the writ had been suspended.[24] Often the terms of discussion turned on whether the federal government was acting in occupied or contested territory, or whether federal or state forces were attempting to silence dissent in the heart of the Union.[25] In the days after the Baltimore riots, perhaps Merryman, acting as an ardent secessionist, quite literally committed treason in leading his men across the Maryland countryside. In the years to come the Union would routinely limit civil liberties in territory conquered by the federal military. But what about dissent far from the seat of war? Interested parties could certainly debate when, if ever, governmental forces should silence Democratic critics who were not actively threatening the Union Army. With General Cadwalader and Judge Taney at loggerheads, Merryman remained in Fort McHenry, where the judge ordered home-cooked meals delivered to his cell. In July, when the initial firestorm had passed, Merryman was released without trial.

Watching from the capital, Senator James Asheton Bayard wrote to his friend Samuel Barlow of his concerns about "the gross illegality of the admin in subordinating the civil to the military power." "I allude more particularly to its actions in Maryland in superseding the police commissioners," he wrote, "and afterwards, arresting and confining them without the semblance of a charge—to the monstrous outrage of continuing the impressment of those gentlemen—after having a subservient grand jury in session which was unable to find the slightest grounds for indictment, and their removal out of the state and entire separation from their friends and families."[26] Bayard, a Wilmington Democrat, was most concerned about the constitutional issues surrounding these arrests and incarcerations. Merryman's arrest and its aftermath had laid out the terms of debate, but the battles over civil liberties in wartime would fester for years.

Joseph Holt and Kentucky Unionism

While in the east all eyes seemed to be on the violence in Baltimore, the political fate of Maryland, and the constitutional fate of civil liberties, some of the nation's most complex political conversations unfolded in another border state: Kentucky. The Bluegrass State faced particular challenges shaped by culture, politics, and geography, placing the state's Democrats in sometimes precarious positions.

Among the northernmost slaveholding states, Kentucky sat in a geographically tenuous place, with free states Indiana, Illinois, and Ohio on its northern border, and the crucial slaveholding border states of Missouri to the west, Tennessee to the south, and Virginia to the east. The 1860 census counted 1,155,684 Kentucky residents, roughly 1 in 5 of whom were enslaved. Nearly a quarter of white Kentucky families owned slaves. More than 200,000 Kentuckians were born outside of the state; most of those had family ties with the South. The state was economically and culturally dependent on the institution of slavery.

In the decades before secession, voters in Kentucky had commonly aligned with the Whig Party of their native son Henry Clay. In 1859, after the demise of the Whigs, Kentuckians elected Democrat Beriah Magoffin as governor and returned Democratic majorities in both branches of the state legislature. In the 1860 election 45 percent of the state's voters selected John Bell and the Constitutional Union Party, or four times the share Bell garnered nationwide. Bell's candidacy stood primarily as a failed bulwark against regional division. That peace-loving appeal found a receptive audience in Kentucky. The rest of the state's 1860 voters—both long-term Democrats and recent Whigs—turned to the two national Democratic candidates. Thirty-six percent selected Kentuckian John C. Breckinridge, who represented the southern wing of the party. The remaining 18 percent voted for Douglas of Illinois. Kentucky-born Abraham Lincoln won fewer than 1 percent of the state's votes.

With the secession of the Deep South, and then the gradual emergence of military conflict, Kentucky was an overwhelmingly Democratic, slave-owning state but deeply divided on how the state should proceed. A vocal minority sought to cast the state's lot with the Confederacy. Governor Magoffin, supported by a special session of the state legislature, advocated for a strategy of "armed neutrality," where the state would do its best to stay out of the fighting while encouraging paths to compromise. On January 17, 1861, Robert J. Breckinridge delivered a powerful speech rejecting neutrality and urging his state to remain in the Union. Meanwhile, Kentucky congressman John J. Crittenden emerged as a leading architect of possible compromise. And, as a measure of the state's larger commitments, in early April Kentucky voted to ratify the proposed 13th Amendment.

It was in this uncertain political situation that Joshua Speed—one of Abraham Lincoln's oldest and closest friends—turned to fellow Kentuckian Democrat Joseph Holt for assistance. The popular and powerful Holt had spent the final two months of the Buchanan administration as secretary of war, and he would go on to be Lincoln's judge advocate general. Speed urged the staunch Unionist to weigh in on his state's vital debate.[27]

On May 31, 1861, just days after Chief Justice Taney delivered his oral opinion on *ex parte* Merryman in Maryland, Holt authored a long public letter addressed to Speed. Holt's letter, which soon appeared as a fifteen-page pamphlet, offered the case for the Union in the strongest possible terms. In the abstract, Holt argued, the state could attempt a position of neutrality in the emerging conflict, but as soon as neutrality meant stopping the movements of federal troops into the state, the policy would run counter to the state's obligation to remain loyal to the federal government. Holt, not unlike Maryland's Reverdy Johnson, devoted much of his attention to making a pragmatic case for union. To side with the Confederacy would be both costly and dangerous, yielding an unclear future and the loss of crucial protections. Meanwhile, he insisted, despite fears and rhetoric to the contrary, the federal government remained the best guarantor of continuing slavery in Kentucky. Although there were strong-willed abolitionists in the North, Holt pointed out that the Supreme Court had weighed in in favor of slavery in the territories, and the Fugitive Slave Act remained a strong defense of the state's peculiar institution. If Kentucky left the Union—and thus federal protection—the state would be a northern island inviting slaves to flee across the Ohio River into free territory. In sum, Kentucky would be foolish to "[abandon] her present honored and secured position" in the United States.[28]

Holt's letter to Speed quickly attracted a broad audience, as Louisville publishers printed and distributed thirty thousand copies.[29] Although hardly a piece of eloquent prose or soaring rhetoric, Holt's words struck a chord among Kentucky readers as well as interested parties nationwide. Some of these people felt moved to write to Holt.[30]

Louisville resident John H. Heywood wrote "that my eyes filled with tears once and again during the perusal of your letter." Joseph T. Halloway, a Republican from neighboring Ohio, had a similar reaction, reporting that "tears were running down my face, and the hart heaving with immotion" as he read the pamphlet. L. R. Webb sent a short note from Peoria, Illinois, telling Holt how

"I have read with tearful eyes and a thrilling heart." A Madison, New Jersey, man described still more "tearful eyes" as he read the letter and contemplated his "strong patriotic affection . . . in this day of our Country's crisis." Something in these powerful issues, if not Holt's prose, brought these men to tears.

A Pennsylvania man who did not reveal his party but announced a great hostility to abolitionism told Holt that "I fully believe that your letter will accomplish a greater work in demolishing the sophistry of secession arguments, from the Southern side, than any other production that this wonderful crisis has called forth." A Detroit Democrat praised the letter and reported that it had been republished in full in the local Democratic press; a Pennsylvania man was pleased to find the letter reprinted in a Pittsburgh paper.

Female readers also weighed in, ignoring gender conventions about writing to unfamiliar men. "A Clergyman's Wife" read Holt's letter and sent him a long response, hoping that he would "pardon the liberty I have taken, dear sir, in addressing you as a stranger & a female." A Louisville woman also chose anonymity while adopting a similarly apologetic tone, but in this case the author was less pleased with Holt's offering, accusing him of adopting a stance that would encourage bloody conflict, when he might have followed a more conciliatory path.

This stack of personal notes in response to a printed public letter suggest various things. Certainly ordinary citizens, including people with no apparent ties to Kentucky, recognized that the stakes were high and Kentucky's future of great importance. Holt's letter also captured the particular concerns of many Kentucky Democrats. An active rejection of secession in favor of the Union seemed the safest and most practical path, and he made the case that it was the route most likely to protect slavery. Armed neutrality really made little sense in the long run, and although a vocal minority of radical Kentuckians called for immediate secession, moderate Democrats—and loyal ex-Whigs—found a powerful advocate in Joseph Holt.

Kentucky diarist Ellen Wallace's response to events was typical. After Lincoln's election Wallace worried about "the distracted state of the country," fearing that "the whole country is fearfully agitated and apparently on the eve of Civil War." Following the fall of Fort Sumter she recorded that "Virginia seceded from the Union tonight. Kentucky it is feared will soon follow. She has all to lose and nothing to gain by such a course but ruin."[31] Henry Haviland was traveling on business in Cincinnati when Fort Sumter fell. The worried Kentucky entrepreneur wrote to his fiancée, Sue Scrogin, "the people are not divided in Covington, Newport, & Cincinnati. They are all for Union but are fearful that Ky will Secede. It is the interest of Cincinnati that Ky should stay in the Union—It is the general opinion there that if Ky goes out that Civil War will be inevitable, then Ky & Ohio would be friends no longer & the result would be Cincinnati must & would be forever ruined." Echoing the comments from eastern cities, Haviland noted that in both Cincinnati and across the river in Covington, Kentucky, the popular message was the same: "If you are for the secession, keep it to thy Self, so they say."[32]

Despite Holt's strong plea for unconditional Unionism, Governor Magoffin maintained his emphasis on "aggressive neutrality," with a state militia ready to repel those who threatened the state's borders. Things came to a political head in mid-June when voters gathered to select representatives for the special session of Congress called by Abraham Lincoln. With Kentucky's Southern Rights Party members boycotting the proceedings, the Union Party elected nine of ten congressional winners. Once again Lincoln had opted to tread lightly when faced with challenging border-state politics. He did his best to acknowledge Magoffin's goal of neutrality, but in his July 4 message to the Special Session the president made it clear that he would not countenance "armed neutrality" that suggests "no obligation to maintain the Union." In subsequent communications with Magoffin, Lincoln reassured the governor that he had no interest in disturbing Kentucky's preferred neutrality, so long as he could also do his duty to the nation.[33]

Late in July Wallace wrote that "the nutrality of Ky at this time is I fear only like the omenous calm before a great storm."[34] A week later sixteen-year-old Confederate volunteer J. T. Barlow, of Paris, Kentucky, wrote to his sister from camp in Tennessee. Barlow was a loyal Rebel, but he told Lucy that "I admire the way Ky is holding her neutrality." He went on to note that Kentucky "has now several thousand of Lincoln soldiers encamped upon her soil and I think if the [authorities] of the state allows them to remain Ky will yet be a dark and bloody ground." Before long any semblance of Kentucky neutrality collapsed under the weight of federal troop movements across the state.[35]

Before the end of the year Kentucky slaveholders who had favored Union began to worry about their peculiar institution. Lincoln's first annual message in early December spoke to the provisions in the First Confiscation Act and suggested the possibility that some states might choose to free slaves and offer slaveholders compensation.[36] Although the president tried to keep his language modest and quite cautious, Kentuckians eyed even this speech—and surrounding conversations—with concern. Despite Holt's predictions, they worried that the decision to stay with the Union might in fact cost them their slaves. Wallace, who owned slaves with her husband, recorded an unusually long entry: "This day President Lincoln message has been received and filled the hearts of all loyal citizens with disappointment, shame and indignation, arming and emancipating the slaves seems to be in contemplation, or the extermination of slavery by force."[37]

Kentucky's talk of "armed neutrality" did not last long, as the state's politicians succumbed to common sense in early September, after Confederate troops occupied Columbus in the western corner of the state, and forces soon arrived to address the threat.[38] It would be quite awhile before Kentucky slaves would be freed by law, but for the months to come Kentucky Democrats who saw themselves as conservative Unionists worried about what would become of slavery in their state, despite Holt's confident words. On the national map, it seemed that the Bluegrass State was safely secured in the Union column. But many Kentucky Democrats privately—and sometimes not so privately—supported the Confederate cause. And for some of those slaveholding Kentuckians, the devotion to Union seemed conditional and not quite absolute.

Democrats Mourn Stephen Douglas

On June 3, 1861, Stephen Douglas died in Chicago. Within days the controversial politician became recast as a great lion of the Democratic Party, as opposed to as a blindly ambitious man who wanted desperately to be president. No doubt public opinion reflected the nation's changing fortunes over the previous half-year and was not merely a gracious response to the recently departed. After all, Douglas ran for president in a moment when only a sliver of northerners really anticipated how events would unfold if Lincoln won the election of 1860. Now they were in the early stages of war. Douglas's candidacy suddenly seemed more appealing.

Soon after his death, the senator's friends arranged a ceremony in his honor at Washington's Smithsonian Institution. They turned to Pennsylvania's John W. Forney to deliver the eulogy. At the time Forney was serving his second stint as the clerk of the U.S. House of Representatives. He had also edited several Democratic newspapers, most recently the independent Philadelphia *Press,* founded in 1857. A crucial supporter of Buchanan in 1856 and a long-term ally of Douglas, Forney had broken with Buchanan over the debate over the admission of Kansas as a slave state, when the president put his finger on the scale backing the proslavery forces in the state. In 1860 Forney was a strong Douglas

Patriotic envelope: "Stephen A. Douglass [*sic*]. Patriot." The Civil War witnessed an explosion in the production of "patriotic envelopes." These envelopes, which featured various images and slogan, were commonly purchased to send letters to soldiers at the front, although they soon became collectors' items as well. This wartime envelope shows Stephen A. Douglas, who died a few months after the war began. Although the fiery Democrat Douglas had run for president in 1860 in opposition to the Republican Abraham Lincoln, here he is remembered simply as a "patriot." (Library of Congress)

backer, clashing further with Buchanan. A month after Douglas's death Forney would become the secretary of the U.S. Senate while continuing to edit the *Press.* He was an interesting choice to eulogize the departed senator.[39]

Despite the somber occasion, Forney did not shy away from harsh political commentary. Douglas was, Forney recalled, a man "who regarded the Democratic party as incapable of error." But that party failed him when Buchanan fell under the sway of southerners in adopting "the path of depravity" by supporting the Lecompton Constitution in Kansas, and then—much worse—when hundreds of thousands of his fellow Democrats supported a candidate (Breckinridge) whose object was to tear the nation asunder. Douglas, Forney insisted, "was preeminently and always a national man" who consistently sought to protect the true interests of southerners, even traveling to the South in hopes of derailing secession. It was no wonder that upon hearing of Douglas's death, President Lincoln—Douglas's adversary in two momentous elections—ordered the army to "crepe their colors in mourning" and federal government offices to close for the day. With the nation divided and anxiously awaiting events on the battlefield,

Forney's eulogy, which was published as a twenty-four-page pamphlet, managed to portray Douglas as a great patriot and nationalist and as an ideological ally of Lincoln, while the previous Democratic president (Buchanan) and Buchanan's 1860 choice (Breckinridge) became symbols of a nation torn asunder.[40]

A few days after Forney spoke in Washington, the Philadelphia *Sunday Dispatch,* an independent Democratic weekly, offered its own retrospective on Douglas's life and career, unfiltered by sentiment. "Although we believed that the salvation of the Democratic Party in 1860 depended upon the unconditional nomination and support of Stephen A. Douglas," the paper pronounced, "we were never very enthusiastic admirers of the man." The paper praised Douglas for standing up to Buchanan's silliness in Kansas, but it could not forget the senator's overwhelming ambition, which elevated the "Kansas difficulties" to a national stage. Even when Douglas had good political instincts, his own ambitions had helped produce the chaotic moment the nation found itself facing.[41]

Douglas had attracted a broad national following, particularly in the Midwest. But by 1860 he had accumulated an entire decade of controversial baggage. As a presidential candidate, Douglas earned support from many—but far from all—northern Democrats, but he failed to attract substantial support from southerners, even while northerners blamed him for paving the way for the expansion of slavery. While Douglas the candidate was a lightning-rod attracting hostile responses, after the senator died he became a symbol of another sort, reminding northern Democrats that their party leaders had once stood for the Constitution and nation. In that sense Douglas was perhaps more useful to the Democrats in death, as a voice of nationalism as opposed to as a man consumed with ambition. His memory became a valuable marker as Democrats wrestled with how to be both loyal patriots and members of an opposition party in the midst of a civil war.

Pierce Butler and Philadelphia Democrats

In those first weeks after the fall of Fort Sumter, political dissent in northeastern cities played out in a way that seemed to reflect urban geography itself. Baltimore secessionists felt outraged at the appearance of federal troops in their city, almost imposing a Unionist loyalty on a state that had yet to make its own decisions. The presence of the 6th Massachusetts outraged civilians on the streets, but it was the particular intricacies of the city's geography that turned them into targets, riding in horse-drawn cars from one station to another.

In Philadelphia the story of dissent and disorder was quite different but no less shaped by the city's location and geography. Although Philadelphia's physical dimensions had been quite large since county and city boundaries unified in 1854, the heart of the metropolis was still fairly contained, and residents tended to live and work in small neighborhoods. This was the case for Philadelphia's conservative Democrats, and particularly those who attracted the mob's attention in the first weeks of the war. *The Palmetto Flag,* a rather unimportant publication until it became the target of rioters, had its modest offices on the 300 block of Chestnut Street (roughly two blocks from Independence Hall). The *Evening Journal,* which would face its own legal troubles in a few years, was around the corner on Third Street. The *Christian Observer* was on Fourth Street, just below Chestnut. The conservative *Philadelphia Age* would begin publication in two years, at Fifth and Chestnut. These Democratic newspapers, including several that would see popular attacks, operated in the same community as several of the city's more moderate pro-Union papers. The *Public Ledger* was on the same block as *The Palmetto Flag,* Forney's *Press* only a block away. All of these newspaper offices were just a few minutes walk from each other.

A block south of Chestnut Street, the stately homes and offices on Walnut Street included many of the city's most prominent lawyers. In those violent days in April, the mob visited the Walnut Street home of Josiah Randall, just west of Washington Square, and the offices of prominent Democrat lawyer William Bradford Reed a few blocks west at 905 Walnut. The outspoken Democrat Charles Ingersoll, who Sidney George Fisher visited on April 18, lived on the 500 block of Walnut, near his law office; Edward Ingersoll's offices were around the corner. Leading Democrats George Wharton and Peter McCall had their law offices on Fourth Street below Walnut, barely two blocks south of *The Palmetto Flag.* The city's Central Democratic Club opened its doors in January 1863, at 524 Walnut Street. Each of these individuals played a role in April 1861, if only as the targets of mob violence, and most cropped up in the years to come.

When Sarah Butler Wister recorded the events following the bombardment of Fort Sumter, she concluded with a rather odd thought: "How thankful I am for father's absence." She had good reason. If any Philadelphian could be said to have a foot in both worlds as war began, it was Pierce Butler. Butler, who was in his mid-fifties, had been born in Philadelphia and was the heir to substantial southern plantations in South Carolina and Georgia and claimed ownership of a large number of slaves. He had married the celebrated actress Fanny Kemble in 1834, but the pair eventually divorced as Kemble grew increasingly hostile to Butler's slaveholding. In the years before the Civil War, Butler responded to economic hardships by selling much of his southern property and auctioning off a huge group of enslaved men, women, and children. With the outbreak of war Butler still had a financial and cultural stake in the South.[42] And he had a law office at 424 Walnut Street.

Sidney George Fisher knew both Butler and Kemble and preferred the latter. "She," he wrote, "is a woman of genius & of noble impulses. . . . Too much will & vitality & force of character, however, to be happy in domestic life, more especially with such a man as Butler, her inferior far in all intellectual endowments, but her equal in fierceness & strength of character."[43] Shortly after Lincoln's election, Butler dropped by Fisher's home during a Christmas visit from his holdings on the Georgia Sea Islands. Butler declared that Georgians were unanimous in their enthusiasm for secession, and that "he came here only to buy arms and intends to return immediately and join the army." "What madness," Fisher wrote, "yet one cannot help admiring the knightly spirit these southern men are displaying."[44]

Butler had grown estranged from many in the Fisher clan, who had taken Fanny Kemble's side in the couple's acrimonious divorce. But in a March entry Fisher offered a perfect illustration of the social and geographic complexities that shaped their corner of Philadelphia society. On that day he visited Joshua Fisher, a cousin, and his South Carolina–born wife, Eliza. Both Joshua (generally known as "Fisher") and Eliza had been "loud in their denunciations of Butler" and had cut off all ties with him. But the previous year Fisher and Eliza had confronted a social quandary as they prepared a gala party and wished to invite Butler's daughter Fanny. This required that they also invite Pierce, who showed up and managed to make "himself acceptable to Mrs. Fisher." Now, with secession in place and war in the wind, Eliza Fisher wanted to make a final visit to her family in South Carolina. Pierce Butler gallantly volunteered to escort Mrs. Fisher on his way to his Georgia plantation. Sidney did not miss the irony in national secession being the vehicle for personal reconciliation. And thus when war broke out Pierce Butler was out of harm's way in Georgia, as his daughter Sarah was pleased to note.[45]

Shortly after Fort Sumter, Butler was on his way back toward Philadelphia. Sarah Butler Wister was in contact with her sister, Fanny, and learned that there was no more "talk of him joining the Confederate army."[46] That spring Wister's diary, like the journal kept by Sidney George Fisher (who was twice her age), illustrated the ways in which national events had muddled their sometimes insular elite social world. Entries describing visits, social gatherings, and the latest correspondence routinely reported on discussions of the national crisis. On

May 16 Wister read reports of the arrest in Baltimore of Maryland millionaire Ross Winans "for furnishing bullets &c to the secessionists." A few weeks earlier "some miserable little merchant" in Philadelphia "had been sending arms to the South & barely escaped the indignation of the crowd." But now, Wister wrote, "things have gone much further; the treason laws are enforced," and Winans was both a millionaire and an elected official, as opposed to a "little merchant" chased down by a mob.[47] The differences she noted were certainly a matter of scale: Winans was a very big fish. But they were also a matter of shifting law and enforcement. Mobs had given way to federal officials, acting under changed rules of evidence, producing arrests rather than public assaults. On August 3 Pierce Butler arrived in Philadelphia.[48]

Soon after her father came home, Sarah left town for a visit to Atlantic City. When Sarah returned she discovered that U.S. marshals had arrested her father, on the orders of Secretary of War Simon Cameron. Before carting the prisoner off, the marshals searched his room, hoping to discover evidence that he had a "commission from the Southern Confederacy."[49] They then took the prisoner by train to New York's Fort Lafayette. That evening Sidney and Elizabeth Fisher dined at the family's estate at Brookwood with various guests, where the Butler arrest dominated conversation. Sidney wrote that Butler had been accused of treason for corresponding with southern secessionists. The diarist doubted that Butler was guilty of this charge, but he acknowledged that the accused had spoken openly of his southern sympathies, and "in such times as these that alone is sufficient to justify his arrest." In fact, Fisher admitted that he thought it was just as well that Butler had been arrested, for it would leave him safely out of trouble in Fort Lafayette.[50] Philadelphian Emma Biddle wrote to her husband, Congressman Charles Biddle, on the same day, describing the arrest and adding that "nobody seems to know what he has been arrested for. He has just returned from the South, after having had a great deal of trouble to get here, and has, I believe, been very prudent."[51]

Once in Fort Lafayette, Butler set about trying to clear his name, turning to the considerable expertise of Philadelphia Democrats in the legal community. On the 20th Sarah Wister went to see her "Uncle George" to discuss the case. "Uncle George" was General George Cadwalader, who had been the commander who refused Justice Taney's order to free John Merryman. Cadwalader told her that he had spoken with Butler in Camden, New Jersey, before he set off to New York, and her father had assured Cadwalader that the seized correspondence contained nothing compromising, although it did illustrate his prosecessionist feelings.[52] Anxious to do something, Sarah consulted with various locals and accumulated letters of support. She finally wrote directly to Abraham Lincoln, seeking permission to visit her father. She worried that most of her father's friends "were either democrats or Republicans of no political weight," limiting his negotiating options. Finally, on September 3 Sarah received word that she had permission to visit her father.[53]

As his daughter lobbied for his future from home, Butler sat in Fort Lafayette, living a life that was—as Fisher had predicted—not uncomfortable. It soon became clear that the case against Butler was weak. The correspondence confiscated from his home yielded no evidence of treason. While he waited in prison, Butler relied on Cadwalader to defend his interests while turning to other Philadelphia Democrats to help keep his bills paid and his finances afloat. The charge of treason seemed almost secondary. "I think that my arrest must have been caused by false information lodged at Washn by some person residing in Philadelphia," he wrote. "I would give not a little to know who they are." Butler added an "addendum," listing a diverse array of ten firearms, ranging from two dueling guns and two derringer pistols to a shotgun and a "ducking gun," that he had shipped to the South. This was his answer to what he claimed were spurious charges that he had been purchasing guns for the Confederacy. Instead, as he explained, "my desire was to establish a little armory in the house there in case of any disturbance among the negroes." In short, Butler insisted that he was not sending guns south to aid the Confederacy, he was arming his own plantation to suppress his slaves. (Apparently neither Butler nor Fisher felt moved to point out that the previous December Butler had bragged of his plans to help arm the Confederacy.)[54]

Meanwhile, Charles Henry Fisher—the wealthiest member of the Fisher clan—pursued other strategies, unbeknownst to Butler. On September 12 he wrote directly to Lincoln, explaining that Butler had been imprisoned for three weeks despite the fact that after the search of his effects "nothing was found throwing the slightest suspicion upon him." Fisher attested to Butler's honesty and explained that his client was in an awkward position because he still held a sizeable plantation in Georgia and therefore "must act with great caution to preserve his estate." The following day Fisher wrote to Cameron, enclosing his letter to the president and explaining that, given "my known friendly relations with you," it was wisest to write directly to Lincoln. Cameron responded that he knew nothing of Butler's case, but "relying upon your statement" he was happy to order the prisoner's release. He enclosed a copy of the order he had sent to the commander of Fort Lafayette.

The problem was that Cameron's order was contingent on Butler signing the normal loyalty oath expected of political prisoners. Fisher explained that Butler worried that by signing an "Oath of Allegiance" he would be putting his Georgia property, and that of other family members, at risk. Would it not be possible to grant Butler parole with "good Bonds to secure it being kept," without the formality of a signed oath? On the same day, September 16, Fisher and Cadwalader sent a telegram to Philadelphia congressman W. H. Kelley in Washington, informing him that a courier would be bringing him a letter, and he should pick it up at Willard's Hotel the next day. That letter explained the situation to Kelley, an abolitionist Republican, and asked him to see Cameron about the matter.[55]

Two days later Fisher wrote Cameron yet again, putting more pressure on the secretary of war. He reminded Cameron that Butler had two daughters who were "both strong Northern women," including "one who is married to one of the staunchest of our party." Moreover, since Butler had been arrested on Cameron's order, and Cameron now agreed that he was innocent, it seemed appropriate to release him "on a proper parole and bond." Fisher added that Butler knew nothing of these negotiations and would prefer a public trial to being forced to sign an oath. A few days later Cameron appended a two-sentence endorsement to this letter, noting Butler's fear that he could be damaged by a formal oath of allegiance, and thus "I would let him go if he would promise to remain."[56] Upon the receipt of Cameron's endorsement, Secretary of State William Seward issued a brief order to the commander at Fort Hamilton (where Butler was being moved) ordering him to release Butler on a written pledge following the agreed upon language. Butler complied, and on September 24 the federal officials released Butler after he signed a declaration that he would remain loyal to the Union and not visit South Carolina "without a passport from the Secretary of State."[57]

In the end, Pierce Butler's arrest and incarceration was both unremarkable and instructive. Unlike John Merryman, Butler had not actually done anything to damage the federal cause or aid the Confederacy. He had not written a hostile editorial or pamphlet, nor had he delivered a public speech about the war. His greatest sin seemed to be that he was vocally pro-southern in his private speech. And yet he became a political prisoner six months into the war. Perhaps he had accepted a commission in the Confederacy and then thought better of it, but the U.S. marshals were unable to turn up any evidence of that fact. Like many pro-southerners in the North, Butler spent time in prison until he affirmed that he was not going to take up arms against the United States.[58]

Butler's story is most interesting as a window into a world of Philadelphia Democrats, tied together by family, geography, wealth, and party while in many cases quite divided on the war itself. Butler's arrest sent shockwaves through this social world, even while many no doubt felt the blustery patrician had brought the troubles on himself. George Cadwalader and Charles Henry Fisher worked diligently to win Butler's freedom, although neither shared his southern sympathies. Meanwhile, these powerful Democrats managed to command the assistance of other party members. Much as Butler had managed to mend fences with Eliza and Joshua Fisher by being gracious at a social event, the southerner and proud slave owner seemed to be accepted as part of a community, largely because of intertwined ties of family and wealth.

John Merryman and Pierce Butler both spent time in prison early in the war, as northern authorities were struggling to navigate the larger legal world of civil liberties. Their stories are about both law and privilege, and also about partisan politics. The North's Democrats responded to the outbreak of war with predictable confusion, reflecting their diverse perspectives and positions in life. Some, like Merryman and Butler, actively—or at least vocally—supported the secessionists, prompting public outrage and eventually federal measures to limit their voices. Other Democrats, such as Kentucky's Joseph Holt and Maryland's Reverdy Johnson, remained firmly allied with the United States and the Lincoln administration, while they adopted carefully constructed pragmatic arguments about how to proceed, pushing their border states to remain in the Union. Immediately after the war broke out, Stephen Douglas had declared that war was no time for partisan disputes, and upon the senator's death, John Forney—with his own strong ties with Washington—chose to recall the "Little Giant" as a great nationalist who had done battle against the party's sectional forces. In later years the party would add Henry Clay, who was no Democrat, to the Democrats' pantheon of nationalist leaders.

In the short run, most of the party's leading figures rallied around the flag, even while questioning the early signs of an increasingly powerful central government. It would take time before the fundamentally pragmatic impulses of the party's political leadership settled on some notion of how they should proceed as the opposition party—loyal or otherwise—in time of war.

3

The Opposition's War

POLICY AND POLITICS

From the fall of 1861 until the following winter, the United States made the gradual transition from fighting an "improvised war" to an "organized war."[1] *In the meantime, the Democratic Party developed the structural tools and political strategies of an opposition party in time of war. In the process, the party honed messages about race and slavery in a reconfigured political climate, ending 1862 with electoral gains.*

Congress Goes to War

Political historian James A. Rawley once observed that "greatness was thrust upon the Thirty-Seventh Congress."[2] Certainly these elected representatives faced unexpected challenges. After decades of regional conflicts fought out in the halls of Congress, the men of the 37th Congress went to work in a Washington, D.C., empty of nearly all the most powerful southern voices, who had abandoned their seats to join the Confederacy. The new Congress took over in a political environment where the presidential branch was controlled by the first Republican president. Lincoln represented a new party with a substantial domestic agenda that had nothing to do with war or even slavery. And the nation had just entered a civil war.

On July 4, 1861, the president called Congress into special session. Although three months after the fall of Fort Sumter, Lincoln's hands were tied by the timing of state congressional elections. By the time the 37th Congress convened in special session, the president had already implemented a blockade of the seceding states, and he had taken important measures to assemble an enormous army of volunteers. And, as we have seen, the president had issued proclamations suspending the writ of habeas corpus in portions of the country and laying the groundwork for arming and equipping the federal army. When they arrived in July, most members of Congress lined up to support the administration as it prepared for war. That summer party affiliations sometimes became garbled, but the core truth was that the secession of the southern states had completely reconfigured partisan lines in Congress. In the 36th Congress, Democrats held 38 of 66 Senate seats and 100 of 237 seats in the House.[3] When Congress convened in July for that special session, 106 Republicans, 42 Democrats, and 28 "Unionists" took their seats in the House, and 31 Republicans, 10 Democrats, and 7 Unionists sat in the Senate. In these early days a large portion of the elected Democrats who remained seemed content to support the nation as it went to war, even while they had reservations about the new party in power.[4]

But that was not universally the case. Kentucky senator John C. Breckinridge, who had worked valiantly for some sort of compromise short of war, found himself in a peculiar spot. In March 1861 the Kentucky legislature named the ex–vice president and recent presidential candidate to a seat in the U.S. Senate. In July, despite having clear sympathies with the Confederacy, Breckinridge attended the special session, still hoping that his home state would remain out of the conflict. But when events demonstrated that that dream was not to come true, the senator left Washington before facing a charge of treason. On December 4 the Senate formally expelled Breckinridge from their ranks. Before the end of the year Breckinridge had accepted a commission in the Confederate Army.[5] Indiana's Democratic senator Jesse Bright had supported Breckinridge for president and shared his affection for the Confederacy. In January the Senate debated Bright's expulsion. Delaware's James Asheton Bayard defended Bright, insisting that the Republicans sought to oust the Indiana senator for his strong anti-abolitionist rhetoric, for which he "is therefore to be accounted disloyal!"[6] But it was a hard sell. Henry Douglas Bacon attended several days of the debate and described the proceedings to New York's Samuel Barlow: "I believe there are many loyal men who doubt the propriety of the war, but I have yet to know the man to whom I could accord the profession of loyal sentiment, who as late as March 1st 1861, could have written 'Jefferson Davis, President of the C.S.A.'" The senator's colleagues agreed, and on February 5, 1862, voted to expel Bright from their ranks.[7]

As the Senate was debating the removal of their Indiana colleague, they were also turning their attention to Benjamin Stark, who had been appointed to replace Oregon's Senator Edward D. Baker, a heroic casualty at Ball's Bluff. Baker had been a close friend to President Lincoln and a loyal Republican, but Oregon's Democratic governor—John Whiteaker—put forward Stark's name.

Stark—like Bright—had supported Breckinridge in 1860. Maine senator William Pitt Fessenden led a fight to refuse Stark's credentials, arguing that in Oregon he was generally known as an avowed secessionist. Stark officially took his seat replacing Baker on February 27, 1862, although he remained at the center of Senate conflict about his alleged disloyalty.[8]

When Congress reconvened in December 1861 many of the crucial membership issues had been settled, but other big questions stood before the administration and Congress. Some of the core issues involved a continuation of the key tests of a nation at war. They would have to wrestle with how the nation would pay for this growing conflict, and how the new volunteer armies would be raised and outfitted. Other issues strayed into more explicitly partisan concerns, as the new Congress—dominated by Republicans—turned their attention to questions concerning slavery. And, finally, the 37th Congress took on legislation that followed the antebellum goals of northern Republicans, and in some cases the Whigs who came before.

In the first months of the new year, congressional Republicans floated a long list of measures that had something to do with the future of slavery. A bill passed in March prohibited federal officers from returning fugitive slaves to their purported masters. A month later Congress took a huge step in abolishing slavery in Washington, D.C., providing for compensation for each slave owner. Using the District of Columbia as their laboratory, Congress passed further legislation creating schools for Black children and allowing African Americans to testify in D.C. courts. Most importantly, on July 17 Congress passed the Second Confiscation Act, which allowed for the confiscation of Confederate property, including slaves. Even where this new legislation had only a modest impact, northern Democrats had every reason to conclude that their Republican colleagues were pursuing a broader agenda that could easily end in emancipation.[9]

Meanwhile, legislative conversations about funding the war became intertwined with debates about federal economic policies. In February 1862 Congress passed the Legal Tender Act, authorizing the issue of $150 million in treasury notes, establishing a mechanism for funding the conflict while also provoking serious constitutional debate. The 37th Congress went on to pass the National Bank Act, the Homestead Act, the Morrill Act, the Pacific Railroad Act, and the Internal Revenue Act. Collectively this flurry of legislation enacted large portions of the Republican economic agenda.

In ideological terms, the two parties and their elected representatives fell along a spectrum largely defined, among other things, by the proper role of the federal government, where the new Republican Party generally imagined a more active role for the government and the more conservative Democrats questioned excessive federal powers. Before long, these core disagreements would define key differences between the wartime parties. But in practice, during those early months the most important divisions in the 37th Congress did not fall along simple partisan lines, although certainly Democrats expressed disapproval on multiple fronts. Roll call analysis indicates that on many economic issues the Republicans divided regionally, with westerners commonly voting as a bloc against their eastern colleagues. On other key issues, including the early measures addressing slavery, Republicans divided along ideological lines, with radical Republicans emerging as a crucial voting bloc, sometimes running up against the restraining voices of more moderate party members.[10] Later in the war the debates in Congress would take on a more explicit partisan cast, and northern Democrats would battle mightily to expand their voice.

In September 1861 James Buchanan—only months removed from the presidency—observed events from his Pennsylvania estate of Wheatland. "I trust that the Democratic party every where may adopt strong resolutions," he wrote to Pennsylvania Democrat Lewis S. Coryell. "I favor a vigorous prosecution of the war to restore the Union. This is the course of expediency & what is of infinitely more importance, it is the course of our highest duty to our Country. In that point there should be no division. . . . The Union must be restored & preserved if this be possible."[11]

At the end of March 1862, barely a month after he had been sworn in, Stark sent Barlow a valuable assessment of the inner workings of the 37th Congress. "It is quite apparent that every day the radical element is losing ground," Stark reported, "and yet from some quarter or other there is an influence at work which prevents the conservative element in Congress from crystalizing. If we could but render the profoundly democratic element entirely homogeneous the task would not be a difficult one to draw towards it the conservative men of the Republican Party who can now manifest a very strong affinity for those of us who confine opposition to the Administration within reasonable and constitutional limits." It is telling that Stark placed his colleagues along an ideological spectrum, rather than a purely partisan one. He seemed convinced that there was a powerful "conservative" element in Congress, including members of the Republican Party, who would gladly coalesce as a single bloc so long as they were asked to support "reasonable and constitutional" measures. On the other hand, certain Democrats felt so committed to their patriotic loyalty that "'a rigorous prosecution of the war' is more of a party shibboleth than it is with the conservative Republicans." These unbending patriots, who sounded very much like President Buchanan, were nearly as bad as all but the most "ultra" Republicans, Stark concluded. Looking to the political future, Stark argued that there was "growing evidence on the part of the democracy everywhere to perpetuate its organizations, and to present its accustomed front of opposition to the party in power, leaving the responsibility of war measures for the preservation of the Union where they profoundly belong, with the Administration." In sum, Stark—anticipating party debates of a year and more later—envisioned a Democratic Party that would accept its rightful role as the conservative opposition party, pushing against the Republican administration while joining forces with those true "conservatives" who were part of the party of Lincoln.[12]

Stark's perspective on the political spectrum in early 1862 came from an Oregon Democrat whose loyalties seemed conflicted, even though he privately insisted that he supported the United States.[13] A few months earlier St. Louis Democrat and wealthy railroad man Henry Douglas Bacon had sent a long letter to Abraham Lincoln, volunteering his thoughts on the war and politics, and especially on the future of slavery. Bacon explained that he wrote to express "my gratification to you for the Conservative course which has thus far characterized your management of the Government" and to offer a "few reflections & suggestions in relation to the course to be pursued with the slaves found in the rebellious districts & which may come within the jurisdiction of our advancing armies." As Bacon saw things, the national debate fell into three main groups: First, "the radical ultra politician of the Country disregarding Constitutional obligations, & the grave question of what is to be done with the slave if emancipated urge immediate, unconditional emancipation." A second, more moderate group "are continually asking themselves the question 'Why should slave property of the rebel be regarded in a different light from any other?'" The third and largest group, as Bacon saw it, was unwilling to see any permanent disruption in slavery. This group included most of the politicians from the key border states of Kentucky, Missouri, and Maryland. In essence, Bacon's assessment of national politics mirrored the debates that had preceded the passage of the original 13th Amendment.[14]

Taken together, the comments from Stark and Bacon—who were really at different ends of the Democratic spectrum—suggest a shared understanding of politics falling along an ideological spectrum, from true "conservatives" to radical "ultras." Both men, and many of their Democratic colleagues, held out some hope that Lincoln and more moderate Republicans would adopt an appropriately "conservative" path in the face of constitutional challenges. This perception of Lincoln as an essentially conservative man under the thumb of more radical Republicans would reoccur in Democratic circles throughout the war. And as Bacon correctly understood, the fate of slavery would define the political fault lines in the months to come, and those lines would have much to do with both geography and ideology.[15]

Charles J. Biddle and the "Alliance with the Negro"

In March 1862 first-term congressman Charles J. Biddle stood before his colleagues to object to proposals promising to accelerate the freeing of slaves and suggesting the worrisome prospect of arming Black men in the Union cause. Biddle, a Pennsylvanian, described himself as "temperate" on the issues surrounding slavery. "I have never been blind to the disadvantages and evils of slavery, I have not been indifferent to their alleviation by constitutional means," he explained, "yet I have ever regarded the intemperate and aggressive policy of the political anti-slavery party to be as sterile of benefit to the negro as it has been disastrous to the peace, the prosperity, and the unity of our country."[16]

Biddle was, in his marrow, a conservative fellow, uninterested in destabilizing the peculiar institution even while resisting any charge that he was an "advocate of slavery." As the son of Nicholas Biddle and the nephew of a conservative congressman, Biddle came by his "temperate" ideology naturally. A clear-headed Unionist Democrat, in his youth Biddle had enjoyed a distinguished military career in the Mexican American War, before returning home to a lawyer's life in Philadelphia. With the outbreak of the Civil War Biddle joined the Pennsylvania Reserves, eventually becoming a colonel in the 42nd Pennsylvania Volunteers. In July 1861 Biddle joined the 37th Congress as the representative from Pennsylvania's 2nd District.

Although Biddle proved to be politically astute, he was far from a career politician. He only ran for the congressional seat to replace Republican Edward J. Morris, who had accepted an ambassadorship. And he did so after an informed pundit assured him that "there is not the least chance in my opinion for the election of a Democrat."[17] Biddle's twenty months in Congress offer a useful window into wartime politics in Washington, the relationship between one congressman and his constituents, and between that man and his wife. Several things stand out.

Whenever he was in Washington, Biddle exchanged regular, chatty letters with his wife, Emma. These missives suggest that war had done little to change

Washington culture, beyond removing most of the southern representatives and reducing the total number of Democrats substantially.[18] Like many representatives who traveled to the capital without their families, Biddle lived in boardinghouses with other congressmen. His letters home are full of small dinners, pleasant gatherings, and occasional soirees with men of all parties. On one illuminating occasion, Illinois Republican William Kellogg stopped to chat, and Charles shared the highlights with Emma. "'Biddle, I like you for three things,'" Kellogg declared. "'When you want to be heard you make yourself heard; and you seem to know how to do what you want to do; and you come of an old Whig Stock.' I told him I reciprocated his good opinion—he is a Republican, but one of the most rational, and, as you see, has a good opinion of your husband."[19] For a man with strong Democratic leanings, and no reticence about sharing his opinions, it is striking how often these dinners were packed with Republicans and Union Party members, rather than fellow Democrats.[20] In February 1863, for instance, Biddle dined at the home of Massachusetts congressman and former justice Benjamin Thomas, in a lively group that included Rhode Island's Republican senator Samuel Arnold, Ohio Republican congressman Valentine Horton, and Union congressmen Horace Maynard of Tennessee and Richard Harrison of Ohio.[21]

When Charles went off to the capital, Emma always stayed home with their large brood of children, either in their Philadelphia home or at Andalusia, the Biddle family estate on the Delaware River. Charles's letters revealed an occasional interest in gender dynamics in Washington society, always noting the women present at various social gatherings and often reporting on what they had to say. His comments combined traditional assumptions about the public roles of women with a broader appreciation of women as political actors. At Thomas's dinner, Charles felt annoyed that the wives stayed at the table too late, inhibiting familiar political talk among the men, but then he noted that Thomas's wife and daughter—frequent visitors to the House—could hold their own in serious political discussions. In late 1861 he received a letter from Sarah J. Hale, the celebrated editor of *Godey's Ladies Book.* Hale had written seeking legislation appropriating "public lands for a school for female teachers." Biddle seemed impressed with Hale and could not resist adding to Emma that "I would have you to know that she pays me some very pretty compliments in her letter."[22]

However Biddle viewed the women he encountered in D.C., the best window into gender roles comes from his extensive correspondence with Emma. Emma's letters were often full of details about their boys, who seemed to take turns suffering bloody injuries. But Emma was also deeply engaged in Charles's political life, commenting on his published speeches and other ventures onto the public record. Charles, in turn, filled his notes with details about congressional debates, pending legislation, and the politicians he encountered. He was also acutely aware of the fact that Emma, especially when she was in Philadelphia, essentially represented him among his constituents. In January 1863 Charles sent a word of caution just as Congress contemplated measures to enlist Black troops. "Dear wife," he wrote, "your country is going to the bow wows, but you need not mention this publicly. Indeed I do not want you ever to pretend to give my views on political or military matters; for as my eyesight is bad I have not been able to communicate to you fully, in my letters. So say nothing of them, until I have opportunity to consult you about them."[23] On the one hand, in this letter Charles seems to be attempting to silence his wife, who often reported on having political chats with friends and neighbors. But as the note continued, Charles revealed that he was particularly anxious that Emma have a full understanding of his beliefs on these thorny issues, an understanding that would have to wait until they could talk politics in person.

This relationship between the congressman and his constituents is nowhere better illustrated than in Biddle's March 1862 congressional speech on "The Alliance with the Negro." In this address, which quickly appeared as a published pamphlet, Biddle articulated the true northern conservative's position on slavery, and particularly on talk of freeing enslaved men and women and perhaps arming Black men. Positioning himself as a Pennsylvania conservative and not a strong partisan, Biddle explained that as a representative of a state that bordered slavery, he preferred to adopt a "temperate" approach to the issues surrounding slavery, whereas some of his colleagues found the topic had "the same effect that a red rag has on a bull." Most specifically, Biddle took issue with statements by Republican senator Charles Sumner endorsing the arming of Black men. The congressman, revealing his fundamental perceptions of race, saw this as complete folly: "Of the slave you cannot make a soldier; you may make an assassin." Far better, he insisted, to trust the White federal armies to win the war without provoking such a racial revolution.

His Democratic Party, Biddle reminded his colleagues, had formed as "the people's protest against the concentration of power in the Federal government." The nation should respect its own civil laws and not task the Union Army with freeing slaves, except when they were explicitly assisting the enemy, or with arming freedmen. Better for these people to be laboring in the fields, rather than following federal armies on the move, he insisted. Biddle closed by acknowledging that some listeners would label him "'an advocate of slavery,'" but he insisted that he was in fact "a northern man with northern principles," standing up for the rule of law and resisting revolutionary measures at the hands of an overzealous federal government.[24]

In "The Alliance with the Negro," Biddle—echoing the comments by Henry Douglas Bacon to Abraham Lincoln—presented himself as a clear-headed conservative, far removed from angry partisan rhetoric. A year later, after delivering a similar speech, Biddle responded to a congratulatory note from prominent Philadelphian Charles Stillé by explaining that he began with the simple—and too often neglected—starting point: "the actual existence of war." And thus policy should focus on "an early and desirable peace." The problem was that his colleagues across the aisle saw the war as an opportunity to destroy slavery as well.[25]

The published pamphlet found an appreciative audience in Pennsylvania, illustrating the importance of such publications in shaping wartime discourse. As was commonly the case, Emma Biddle acted as her husband's advocate, distributing copies of his speech to inquiring women and men. Meanwhile, Biddle's own correspondence includes dozens of letters from friends and strangers praising the speech or seeking printed copies.[26] One Philadelphia man observed, "Had such conservative principles been promulgated by every free state man, our free republican Constitutional Union would this day be bound together with belts far stronger."[27] One-time Democratic congressman Joseph Reed Ingersoll praised the speech and added the prescient observation, "We are given to understand here that there are two parties in Washington—McClellan and Anti McClellan—and that the Anti is Abolition in different shapes."[28]

Biddle, in his private correspondence and his public utterances, embodied a sort of ideological conservatism that remained largely removed from the partisan rancor which surrounded him. His letters to Emma never adopted the angry rhetoric or vicious labels that others employed. He did, however, reveal a consistent worldview that joined most congressional Democrats in objecting to the administration on an array of issues, from rights of habeas corpus to compensated emancipation to the arming of Black men. Although the label would have meant nothing to him this early in the war, Biddle was a true "War Democrat." He supported the cause but never abandoned his party. After twenty months in Congress, Biddle lost his bid for reelection and returned to his Philadelphia law practice. But he would not abandon party politics for good.

While Democrats in Congress gradually adjusted to life as a minority party in opposition, nationally a new conservative leader emerged.

George B. McClellan: The Young Napoleon

Readers who are only slightly familiar with the main lines of the Civil War drama recognize that George B. McClellan played a crucial role in two of the war's most important acts. As a West Point–trained military leader, McClellan commanded the Army of the Potomac until the winter of 1862. In the process he frequently tangled with Abraham Lincoln and his cabinet, and McClellan left behind letters—many written to his wife, Ellen—that revealed him to have an overzealous ego and a sometimes vicious pen. In the Union's grand military narrative, McClellan often fares poorly at the hands of historians, especially when compared with Ulysses S. Grant. Two years after he lost his command, after a lengthy hiatus partially out of the public eye, McClellan returned to center stage as the Democratic Party's nominee for president in 1864. Once again history did not treat the man they called "the Young Napoleon" very kindly, casting him as the foil to Lincoln's victorious reelection campaign.

For the North's more knowledgeable businessmen and committed Democrats, George McClellan did not emerge on the national scene out of nowhere. Following a brilliant academic career at West Point and distinguished service during the war with Mexico, McClellan caught the attention of some of the nation's military and business leaders. In 1855 Secretary of War Jefferson Davis—much taken with the young officer—named McClellan, not yet thirty years old, to a three-man commission to study military developments in Europe. Two years later, having finished the grand tour, McClellan left government service, eventually accepting a position as chief engineer of the Illinois Central Railroad. That appointment, which launched McClellan into a short and highly successful career as a railroad man, owed much to his friend New York financier Samuel Barlow. Barlow and McClellan had known each other for two years and remained close long after McClellan left the railroad business. In fact, it would be Barlow who served as the general's most influential political advisor when he sought the presidency nearly a decade later.[29]

Long before the election of 1860, McClellan had established himself as a young man to be reckoned with. Barlow's cronies in the railroad world knew all about him. Many, but not all, admired his considerable talents. In mid-1860 Barlow helped arrange for McClellan—recently married—to leave the Illinois Central Railroad to become the superintendent of the eastern division of the Ohio and Mississippi Railroad, at double his previous salary. Barlow wrote to Henry Douglas Bacon in St. Louis, briefing him on plans that were bound

Carte de visite: Major General George B. and Ellen Mary Marcy McClellan. George McClellan served as an immensely popular, and sometimes controversial, general in the U.S. military. In 1864 he was the Democratic Party's nominee for the presidency. McClellan was one of the most frequently photographed people of his age. Here he is shown with his wife, Ellen McClellan. (Library of Congress)

to displease his old friend. Bacon replied with a testy letter, pointing out that "I have never been a man worshipped in my life, nor am I disposed to disparage the gifts which the Almighty has bestowed upon me." Bacon added that McClellan had exaggerated his role on the Illinois Central, and Bacon insisted that he was really more qualified to run the railroad. Barlow demurred. McClellan seemed to get along well with his superiors, and he enjoyed his marriage and his newfound income, but the line's financial challenges and his regular clashes with his subordinates led him to threaten resignation, even as the national ills were soon to change his professional path.[30]

McClellan had been raised as a conservative Whig, following the lead of his father, Philadelphia doctor George McClellan. In the years prior to the Civil War young McClellan had cast his lot with the Democratic Party and counted prominent Democrats from both the North and the South, such as Stephen Douglas, John J. Crittenden, Jefferson Davis, John C. Breckinridge, and of course Samuel Barlow, as his friends and supporters. As director of the Illinois Central, McClellan had several encounters with lawyer Abraham Lincoln and came away unimpressed, opinions that only grew as Lincoln gravitated toward the Republican Party. McClellan was happy to support Douglas in the state's 1858 senatorial campaign; he maintained his friendship with the Illinois senator until Douglas's death in 1861.[31]

Once sectional conflict turned to war, McClellan—like many of his West Point brethren—returned to uniform. In the next year and a half he gave no indication that he aspired to political office but nor was he reticent about sharing his opinions about public policy and his distaste for Lincoln's Republican Party. Northern civilians followed military leaders with enthusiasm, purchasing photographs of favored generals and routinely debating who should be leading the nation's armies in the field. McClellan was a popular choice in these discussions. He was handsome, youthful, vigorous, charismatic, and clearly talented. Northern Democrats—perhaps particularly those in the Northeast—saw in McClellan a conservative shining light and were quick to embrace him.

As a young commander, McClellan took on the task of rebuilding—and in fact naming—the Union's Army of the Potomac, when he replaced General Irvin McDowell following the disastrous First Battle of Bull Run. McClellan proved adept at his new task, winning the enthusiastic support of his men. In mid-September the young officers orchestrated the arrest of suspected disloyalists in the Maryland legislature, blocking the state's possible secession. On November 1, 1861, following the retirement of General Winfield Scott, Lincoln named McClellan as his new general in chief. When the president expressed some reservation about giving his young general a second major role to go with his command of the Army of the Potomac, the general whose men called him "Little Mac" pronounced, "I can do it all."[32]

As he prepared to lead his army into the field, McClellan wrote frankly to Barlow. "Help me to dodge the [n—r]," he implored. "I am fighting to preserve the integrity of the Union & the power of the Govt—on no other issue. To gain that end we cannot afford to raise up the negro question—it must be incidental & subsidiary."[33] The following month James Asheton Bayard, responding to an offer from Barlow, said he would be happy to meet McClellan and "hear his views on the struggle, since McC has power to bend things in good directions."[34]

Throughout much of the winter the general and his commander in chief bickered continually, if sometimes politely. Lincoln wanted his army to move on the enemy at Richmond, and McClellan kept finding good reasons for delay while he persistently overestimated the Confederate forces in his front. He finally devised a complex plan to move his men by ship to the coast southeast of the Confederate capital, where he would move his army up the peninsula toward his quarry. Whatever the merits of McClellan's plan, the president chafed at the lack of progress, finally ordering McClellan to move by February 22, 1862. When that deadline came and went, Lincoln took the extreme step of removing McClellan from his role as general in chief of the Union Army, leaving him with his command of the Army of the Potomac. Military historians have read Lincoln's decision as one of frustration about military affairs, but some contemporaries saw it as a partisan decision. A few weeks later Bacon told Barlow that in his view, "the Abolitionists & Stanton have at last induced the President to strip McClellan of his Department."[35]

That spring McClellan finally launched what became his Peninsula Campaign against Richmond. On June 1 General Robert E. Lee replaced the badly wounded Confederate general Joseph E. Johnston. For over a month the two armies battled southeast of Richmond. Finally, on July 8, Lincoln visited the Army of the Potomac at Harrison's Landing, Virginia, on the northern bank of the James River. The president was pleased with the men he saw and impressed at how they responded to their commander, but in the weeks to come the president seemed to cool on his young general. By the end of the month Lincoln had ordered McClellan and the Army of the Potomac to return to Washington.[36]

Even with his demotion and his army's retreat from Virginia, northern Democrats continued to see McClellan as something of a savior, both of their party and of the nation. Emma Biddle regularly invoked McClellan's name in discussing the national crisis with her congressman husband.[37] Newly elected Democratic congressman John D. Stiles wrote to fellow Pennsylvania politician Lewis Coryell that "McClellan has not and will not resign in my judgment—as he is the only man left fit for the position he occupies."[38] In Philadelphia, diarist engraver John L. Smith made several brief notations expressing his confidence in McClellan.[39] The press responded to McClellan's failed campaign with characteristic partisanship. The Democratic *New York World* called the administration's treatment of McClellan "a suicidal policy," to be blamed on radical abolitionists in Congress and the "incompetent civilian" Secretary of War Edwin Stanton.[40]

Despite the popular enthusiasm for McClellan on the home front, it is not at all clear that he had political aspirations in the summer of 1862. But he did have strong political opinions. After Lincoln reviewed the troops at Harrison's Landing, he boarded the steamer *Ariel,* bound for the North. Before the president left, McClellan handed him a formal letter dated July 7. In his "Harrison's Landing Letter," McClellan volunteered his thoughts on the state of the conflict, acknowledging that he was going well beyond the scope of his official duties. McClellan stressed that the national situation was "critical," and "our cause must never be abandoned." To that end he suggested the administration should settle on a "civilian and military policy" up to the tremendous task of winning the Civil War. McClellan stressed that the nation should not attempt to subjugate civilian populations but should be at war "against armed forces and political organizations." Specifically, McClellan advised against the confiscation of lands, "forcible abolition of slavery," or military arrests "except in places where active hostilities exist." In speaking specifically of policies toward slavery, McClellan supported the protection of "contrabands" who had run from Confederate masters and the compensated freeing of slaves for labor required by the military. He acknowledged that military necessity might even require the emancipation of slaves in an entire state, such as Missouri or West Virginia, so long as the nation followed a policy both "constitutional and conservative." Leaning on his familiarity with the North's fighting men, McClellan warned that any declaration of radical policies about slavery "will rapidly disintegrate our present Armies."

Having shared his thoughts on these big policy issues, the thirty-five-year-old McClellan turned his attention to broader strategic concerns. First, he suggested that the government concentrate its forces in large armies, rather than wasting men in smaller expeditions or occupation posts. Those armies should focus on attacking the enemy. The Confederacy would crumble politically once its military had fallen. He concluded by noting that these military policies would require a "Commander in Chief of the Army" prepared to direct all the nation's military forces in the field. Such a commander would have enormous power, and although McClellan insisted that he did "not ask that place for myself," he would be willing to take any role the president assigned to him. McClellan's extraordinary letter left no doubt that he felt he was just the man to command the nation's entire war effort.[41]

These final passages, read today in the context of McClellan's fraught relationship with Lincoln and the further tensions to come, feeds the narrative that the general was an almost bizarre egomaniac, convinced that the wisest military strategy to save the nation would be to give him supreme power over the entire Union war effort. There is truth to that charge, although given the fawning praise Little Mac received from so many quarters, he came by his self-esteem honestly. But the fact that McClellan essentially volunteered to take on such a massive role (befitting his "I can do it all" announcement of the previous year) should not obscure the significance of the first page of his letter. In those crucial passages, McClellan laid out a conservative approach to fighting this terrible war. He mentioned the Constitution repeatedly and made it clear that although military necessity made certain measures—including occasional compensated emancipation and limited military arrests—necessary, the administration should be constrained by the rule of law while only making war on opposing armies. Although not the typical stuff of messages from commanders in the field, McClellan's defenders point out that Lincoln had welcomed his general's thoughts and they were not particularly unusual.

In the future the Harrison's Landing Letter would become an important illustration of McClellan's political beliefs as a candidate for president. He wanted to win the war but without abandoning core conservative principles. And he was no abolitionist, even while he supported selective emancipation for military reasons.[42] Privately, McClellan's men spoke more bluntly. In May Brigadier General Fitz John Porter—a key McClellan advisor—wrote to the *New York World*'s Manton Marble, explaining that the army's "conservative course" in Virginia was designed to "win the respect of the people," while the North's radical abolitionists would "be looked upon with contempt."[43]

Although Lincoln and McClellan did not see eye to eye on the constitutional issues surrounding the Union's war effort, the general remained in uniform even after his Peninsula Campaign failed. In August—as McClellan and his men slowly set off for Washington—Robert E. Lee's Army of Northern Virginia moved on General John Pope's men outside of the capital, defeating Pope's Army of Virginia at the Second Battle of Bull Run. Many of the president's advisors questioned McClellan's actions leading up to Pope's defeat, but faced with few alternatives Lincoln gave McClellan command of the forces surrounding Washington. Two days later Lee launched an invasion into Maryland.

Emerging Political Tensions

As the Civil War moved into its second year, and the Army of the Potomac stalled on the Virginia Peninsula, partisan conflicts expanded. Both parties looked ahead to the 1862 elections, establishing political arguments while mapping out a complex ideological spectrum across the major parties. Democratic voices—both in Washington and across the nation—grew emboldened in articulating objections to administration policies, even as Congress addressed the war's expanding challenges.

Well before Abraham Lincoln's Emancipation Proclamation sent shockwaves through political discourse, Democrats had grown increasingly vocal about the Republicans' broader agenda on race and slavery. Charles Biddle's speech on the "Alliance with the Negro" earned some enthusiastic response in March. That June Ohio Democrat Samuel S. Cox gave a much less moderate address in Congress, questioning the direction the nation was taking toward race and slavery. The congressman, known as "Sunset" Cox, delivered a stinging attack on legislation that had already been passed, as well as measures that were under discussion. As he noted, the Senate had already approved transformative measures allowing Blacks to deliver the mail and abolishing slavery in the nation's capital, and various measures calling for compensated emancipation and outright confiscation had begun to circulate. Cox called his speech "Emancipation and Its Results—Is Ohio to Be Africanized?" and took as his point of departure the argument that the eventual result of widespread emancipation would be a huge burden on his state of Ohio while also subjecting freed slaves to starvation and other deprivations. It was an argument that resonated with Henry Clay's warnings of two decades before. Would White soldiers from Ohio continue to fight if the result would be "the flight and movement of the black race by millions northward to their own State?" he asked. Cox went on to frame the issue in more explicitly partisan terms, noting "the murmurs of discontent which come to us from Army and people to the alliance between Republicans and abolitionists." As Cox saw it, even the relatively modest early measures to promote selective emancipation and civil rights, which more moderate Democrats could accept, were laying the foundation for disastrous national results, which would be laid at the feet of the Republican Party.[44]

Cox, like Biddle before him, had laid out an argument against emancipation and racial change by arguing two core points. First, he claimed that federal legislation aimed at removing barriers to Black rights elsewhere would eventually damage the lives of Whites in his home state. Second, he—again like Biddle—questioned whether such measures might effectively undermine the Union's military effort. Both Democrats steered clear of central moral arguments, nor did they frame their concerns along legal or constitutional lines. These were conservative objections to the march of change put to receptive audiences on largely pragmatic terms.

For the North's leading Irish Catholics, talk of emancipation provoked dismay from ardent Unionists. New York's Archbishop John Hughes had been a strong advocate for the Union cause from the beginning of the conflict while rejecting abolitionism as a war aim. Although stopping short of embracing the morality of slavery, the Catholic leader had insisted that "we despise in the name of all Catholics the 'Idea' of making this war subservient to the philanthropic nonsense of abolitionism." Patrick Donahue—the conservative editor of the Irish Catholic *Boston Pilot*—shared Hughes's convictions. Donahue and his readers would support the patriotic war, but "the war is not for emancipation" or any such violation of the Constitution. Irish and German Catholic editors across the country disagreed over the proper approach to slavery, although the bulk of Catholic editors and leaders—generally an ideologically conservative group—lined up in favor of the war but against the revolutionary forces that emancipation would unleash. The North's immigrant Catholics—largely Democrats—took pride in their martial spirit in the name of the Union but most persistently balked at emancipation.[45]

As elected politicians across the Democratic spectrum developed rhetorical strategies for pushing back against efforts to promote emancipation and civil rights, the nation's Democratic newspapers—and especially those that would become associated with opposition to the war—perfected their own strategies for turning racial prejudice into political convictions, commonly targeting the white working class. Like Sunset Cox, these editors concentrated on the purported economic threat posed by Black emancipation and mobility. In the midst of the New York gubernatorial campaign, the *New York World* endorsed Horatio Seymour, the Democratic candidate, with an appeal to racism, declaring that "a vote for Seymour is a vote to protect our white laborers." Worse, the *World* claimed that the radicals were encouraging slave insurrections, which would flood northern cities with Black labor.[46] With time, these antiwar editors would become increasingly adept at appealing to the racist fears of their readers.

Of more immediate concern to some Democrats, on July 17 Congress passed the State Militia Act of 1862, giving the president authority to call up the militia for nine months and laying the groundwork for the federal government's first conscription (the Confederacy had been conscripting men for several months by this time). The Lincoln administration had already called for 300,000 three-year volunteers, but in early August it called for an additional 300,000 nine-month men to be rounded up following the rules laid out by the State Militia Act. As with all Civil War drafts in the United States, the overall goal was to encourage vigorous local recruiting, so that communities would not be subjected to a draft. In the case of the 1862 militia draft the details were byzantine. The short version is that each community already had a quota—based on population—to fill its share of the 300,000 three-year volunteers. For each recruit *beyond* that quota, the community's quota of nine-month conscripts would be reduced by four (because each three-year volunteer was deemed the equal to four nine-month recruits).

Considered from the perspective of 1865, the Militia Act looks surprisingly unsophisticated. In 1863 the United States would turn to a federal draft, administered by the provost marshal general. In the remaining years of the war, the federal government would administer four large federal drafts, yielding huge numbers of recruits and conscripts.[47] But in the fall of 1862 the State Militia Act was a huge step. In one sense the latest legislation fit snugly into an emerging pattern where the administration and the Republican-dominated Congress had been expanding their power in the midst of civil war. Observers who called for a strictly conservative approach to constitutional authority had another reason to question the direction of public policy. Constitutional scholars who doubted Congress's economic agenda or the use of arbitrary arrests and the limitations on free speech to further the war effort now had a new front upon which to fight the legal battle. But the Militia Act, and the specter of state conscription enforced by federal mandate, invited an entirely separate series of objections. And, meanwhile, the Militia Act also set the stage for the future use of Black troops, inviting yet another chorus of outrage. Suddenly the Democratic opposition had an assortment of new arguments to make to voters.

Edward G. Ryan and the "Address to the People of the Democracy of Wisconsin"

The situation in Wisconsin was both highly distinctive and also typical of national politics in early September, only weeks before the president would issue his Preliminary Emancipation Proclamation. In 1860 Wisconsin voters had aligned solidly behind Lincoln and the Republican Party, with the state casting 86,110 votes for the eventual president. Nearly all of the remaining Wisconsin voters supported Stephen Douglas (65,021). Barely a thousand citizens cast ballots for Breckinridge (889) or Bell (151). As in much of the country, many of those Wisconsin Democrats who had voted against Lincoln initially rallied 'round the flag after the firing on Fort Sumter, enthusiastically supporting the war. But this patriotic consensus did not survive a year and a half of controversies and disappointments.

Several factors conspired to make Wisconsin Democrats particularly susceptible to criticisms of the administration. For starters, the first year of war took a toll on the Upper Midwest economy, as the state's farmers lost access to the Mississippi River. Although still a solidly Republican state, Wisconsinites questioned whether the East Coast monied interests in their party enjoyed too much control over national economic policy. Moreover, as the United States turned to the state militia draft, the state's large immigrant population grew more vociferous in doubting both the need for conscription and the processes that shaped local drafts. In 1860 roughly a third of the state's residents were foreign born, with over half of these German immigrants, largely Catholic.[48]

When the state's Democratic leaders convened for their state convention in Milwaukee in September, their mood had grown more partisan and less unquestioningly patriotic. Edward G. Ryan, the principal author of the convention's "Address to the People," illustrates this evolution. Like many of his peers, the Irish-born Ryan had backed Douglas in 1860 but supported Lincoln and the war effort after the South seceded. But by the fall of the war's second year, Ryan—who trained as a lawyer in New York—took exception to the administration's constitutional interpretations in the name of war. Rather like George McClellan, Ryan questioned a war that sacrificed the civil liberties of individual citizens, and he doubted the legal foundations underlying the state militia draft. When the Democrats met in Milwaukee they asked the Irish lawyer to author what amounted to their party platform. The assembled Democrats adopted the "Address to the People by the Democracy of Wisconsin"—soon to be known simply as "Ryan's Address"—on September 3 and published it in a short pamphlet. Democratic newspapers across the state reprinted the entire address.[49]

Ryan's Address adopts an almost scholarly tone for what amounts to a political manifesto. The starting point was that the Democratic Party had a long history of defending the Constitution, and that in the midst of civil war those in power had lost track of the fact that "the administration is not the government." In the name of pursuing civil war, they had set aside constitutional guarantees protecting freedom of speech and other liberties. The address blamed the nation's current dilemmas on the seceding states for having abandoned the nation, but it also recognized that the 1860 victory of a "sectional party" constituted a "defeat of the spirit of the Constitution."

Ryan then turned to an extended discussion of slavery, as a historical and constitutional concern. In perhaps the address's most striking claim, Ryan argued that "the democracy has no apology to make for southern slavery. We regard it as a great social evil. But we regard it as a misfortune, and not a crime." Insofar as slavery constituted a crime, that crime had been committed generations earlier when enslaved people were brought to the American colonies. The continuing "misfortune" that slavery represented might be regrettable, but from a purely constitutional perspective the core issues had already been adjudicated. Contemporary problems had emerged because radical abolitionists insisted on viewing slavery as an "abstraction" rather than as a constitutional problem with a very long history.

In surveying the sources of the current conflict, the Milwaukee Democrats took aim at both the "revolutionary" forces within the Republican Party and those sectional voices that managed to divide the Democratic Party in 1860. In this narrative, those Democrats who had supported Stephen Douglas (echoing John Forney's speech honoring the deceased senator) backed a "true statesman" in a moment of revolutionary division. Ryan did not blame Abraham Lincoln for this state of affairs. Lincoln was personally a "patriot," whose election was perfectly constitutional, even if unfortunate. Moreover, as president, Lincoln had adopted the correct path in defending the Union in what amounted to a "defensive war . . . of self preservation." The problem was that in prosecuting this war, the administration had run afoul of constitutional limits, and it was up to the Democrats to defend the nation's core values. Thus, the address closed where it had begun, enumerating constitutional transgressions, including the suspension of the writ of habeas corpus in loyal states, the ongoing challenges to freedom of the press, and the legal niceties surrounding the meaning of treason in wartime. More troublesome still, Congress had acted to emancipate slaves in the District of Columbia and had entertained debates about compensated emancipation and similar measures attacking the peculiar institution.

Having laid out the case for the Democratic Party's crucial role in protecting the Constitution against excess and usurpation, Ryan's Address took an interesting turn in adding, "We believe that the executive acts of which we complain were done rather in inadvertence by subordinate officers, than in the deliberate purpose of subverting the constitution, or with the sanction of the President." That is, the array of affronts to the Constitution provoked by the Civil War owed more to human error and the failure of rigorous analysis than to any malicious agenda to expand the power of the executive branch. These challenges to the Constitution on multiple fronts were the fault of overzealous subordinates, or radicals in Congress, and not at all the fault of Abraham Lincoln, who remained in Ryan's eyes a patriotic defender of Union.[50]

Ryan's Address is a useful benchmark for Wisconsin's Democratic discourse in early September 1862. It is also a window into the state of partisan criticism of the administration nationwide. For the historic moment, Ryan's language was certainly tough on the Republican administration, posing sweeping constitutional challenges to how Lincoln's men interpreted their war powers. But rather like the private writings of other Democrats, Ryan's Address seemed to hint at the possibility that the president himself might be a conservative kindred spirit, led astray by others. In the end, Ryan's Address laid out an agenda for Democrats moving forward. First, the party stood as the defender of the Constitution against illegal usurpers. Second, slavery—as a constitutional issue—had already been decided, and as a practical matter it was really a local concern. This lawyerly approach differed from the tack taken by Biddle and Cox, who focused on the implications for emancipation for the folks back home. And, finally, as the loyal opposition, the party should take aim at radicals in the Republican Party while attempting to claim the president as an ideological kindred spirit.

Wisconsin Democrat and prominent constitutional lawyer Matthew H. Carpenter published a lengthy rebuttal, defending the war and critiquing Ryan's constitutional analysis.[51] Both Ryan and Carpenter had been Douglas Democrats in 1860, but less than two years later the two lawyers were moving in opposite directions, and they continued to do so. By the following July, Ryan—who had been so cautious toward Lincoln in his address—was calling the president "a weak, insufficient, unfortunate man" advised by "fools" and "knaves."[52] Meanwhile, Carpenter would embrace wartime emancipation, and after the war he became a Republican senator from Wisconsin.[53] The weeks and months after Ryan's Address witnessed an important rise in partisan tensions and dramatic clashes within the Democratic Party nationally, as the nation prepared to go to the polls and the country absorbed the implications of Abraham Lincoln's Preliminary Emancipation Proclamation. In Wisconsin, roughly a year after the Democratic Party released Ryan's Address, a group calling themselves "the Loyal Democracy," led by Carpenter, met at Janesville and issued a statement denouncing Ryan and his 1862 speech.[54] Democrats in Wisconsin, far removed from the seat of war, had begun to fight out the party conflicts that would leave the party of Stephen Douglas once again riven by 1864.

The 1862 Elections

Not long after Ryan wrote his address to the Democrats of Wisconsin, the military and political landscape changed dramatically. On September 17, 1862, the Army of the Potomac, under the command of General George McClellan, and the Army of Northern Virginia, under General Robert E. Lee, squared off in the bloodiest single day of the Civil War on the banks of Antietam Creek near Sharpsburg, Maryland. In the aftermath of the battle, Lee and his men crossed the Potomac River and headed south. General McClellan celebrated what he thought was a grand victory. Shortly after Antietam, as the nation was still trying to work out the battle's real significance, journalist T. J. Barnett sent Samuel Barlow an extraordinary letter. "McClellan is the acknowledged man," Barnett wrote. "Unless I much mistake me, henceforth he will have a party that shall bestride these Lilliputians." Barnett went on to acknowledge that "I hardly know McClellan—I do not believe him to be a prodigy, but I respect him as the greatest man these times has produced—great in soul, self-reliant, & true to truths as the needle to the pole."[55] But despite Barnett's early optimism, the die had been cast. In less than two months Abraham Lincoln would remove McClellan from command. It would be quite some time before the talented general would try to impose his substantial will on the North.

Five days after the battle, and before he had removed his popular commander, the president decided to issue the Preliminary Emancipation Proclamation, using the occasion of this victory to announce it in preliminary form. The document, issued on September 22, declared that as of January 1, 1863, the Union military would be an army of liberation. Using his powers as commander in chief, Lincoln explained that slaves in the Confederate states assisted the enemy's war effort, and thus as of the first of the year all enslaved people in states—or portions of states—still in rebellion would be free. In practice, that meant that slaves who successfully ran to Union lines would be treated as free men and women, and where the invading armies encountered enslaved people, the military would ensure their freedom. Lincoln cast the Preliminary Emancipation Proclamation in careful and even conservative terms. From a constitutional standpoint, he presented it as a war measure, thus enhancing the argument that the chief executive was acting within his prescribed powers. And from a political perspective, Lincoln took pains to ensure that slave owners in the loyal states would not have to give up their slaves, although he once again encouraged them to consider compensated emancipation.

Northern Democrats recognized the Emancipation Proclamation as a huge step, and one that would likely lead to universal emancipation. It certainly added an important piece to partisan political debate. As northern states turned to state and congressional elections, emancipation became a central point of debate, joining conscription, political arrests and habeas corpus, and Congress's diverse economic legislation in a political environment that had become increasingly torn.[56] For the nation's Irish Catholic immigrants, rising objections to the administration's policies—including emancipation—became intertwined with angry defenses against nativist charges that they were insufficiently loyal to the cause. Many Irish leaders proudly embraced dual loyalties, both to the nation of their birth and to their adopted homeland. But their patriotism did not mean they embraced the Republican policy agenda.[57]

As Wisconsin Democrats were dividing over their political agendas, and the Army of the Potomac was chasing Robert E. Lee across the Maryland countryside, politically engaged Democrats in New York and Philadelphia watched events through multiple lenses. Men and women in these urban communities gossiped about—and railed against—stories of political arrests among the more vocal in their communities. Meanwhile, savvy political wirepullers made plans for the elections to come. In all sorts of ways, the weeks after Lincoln's Preliminary Emancipation Proclamation suggested things had shifted.

Democratic newspapers across the North connected talk of emancipation with popular fears of freed Blacks storming the northern countryside, taking jobs from White workers and threatening White racial hegemony. The *Cincinnati Enquirer* reminded readers of Henry Clay's warnings, predicting that "if the four millions of slaves at the South are set free, they will swarm over the North and West in immense numbers."[58] Emancipation may have raised conservative questions about constitutional issues, but the partisan appeal concentrated on economic threats closer to home.

A substantial flow of political correspondence found its way to Samuel Barlow's desk in New York. On September 18, 1862, Horatio Seymour informed Barlow that he had accepted the nomination for New York governor.[59] A few days later Samuel Butterworth sent a jubilant letter, declaring that the Emancipation Proclamation would be the death knell for the Republican Party.[60] William Steel wrote to a friend from Illinois, reporting that the preliminary proclamation "meets the hearty disapproval of the faithful. Should it prove anything but a paper-bullet, there will be resistance throughout the Northwest."[61] Soon a new "Constitutional League" emerged in New York, with Barlow published as one of its directors, promising to pursue "the overthrow of the abolition and disunion element at the ensuing elections, and the establishment in the minds of the People of a sincere love for the Union, the Constitution, and the Laws."[62]

New York's Democrats were hardly unanimous about the upcoming elections. Seymour, who some saw as dangerously hostile to the Union, received mixed reviews from party loyalists. George William Curtis, one-time Democratic mayor of Buffalo, confided in Isaac Sherman that "the election of Seymour would be not only disgraceful to the State, but dangerous to the country," although he thought a Seymour victory unlikely.[63] Seymour saw himself as a dedicated conservative who believed that in Lincoln he might find a partner in battling the North's most dangerous radical elements. He backed the Union and the war effort but—like his fellow Democrats—objected to the administration's support of emancipation and affronts to civil liberties. Yet Seymour, along with many of his closest Democratic colleagues, clung to the notion that Abraham Lincoln was fundamentally a conservative, manipulated by radicals in his own party. In the end Seymour managed to win the state election, returning to the office of New York governor for a second time.[64]

In Philadelphia, with its close-knit community of elite conservatives, Democrat Charles Ingersoll took his turn in the political limelight. In late March Ingersoll penned *A Letter to a Friend in a Slave State,* which appeared as a bound fifty-eight-page pamphlet. Writing to this hypothetical southern friend, Ingersoll sought to "explain to you some of the views of persons in this State who regard conciliation as our only available resort." He began with an extended discussion of the realities of civil war. It would, he argued, be extremely difficult for the Union to conquer the Confederate states under the best of circumstances. Then, anticipating the direction of northern politics, Ingersoll noted that "emancipation is a word which sounds to virtue, for who can doubt that slavery is a blight to any region in which it is tolerated?" but in reality the North would never wish to absorb 4 million emancipated Black laborers into their society. Once again, a conservative northern Democrat claimed that northerners would not welcome freedmen in their midst. In truth, Ingersoll concluded, "had the South known that war was to follow, secession would not have been resorted to," and "had the North known secession was to be the consequence, they would not have tolerated the slavery agitation." On balance, he concluded, the fault really lay with the North and its radical agitators. The answer was for Democrats to regain control of the government at the polls: "If they do, the back of abolition is broken, and the process of regeneration will be commenced."[65]

Ingersoll's long pamphlet did not go unnoticed. Although perhaps not quite treasonous, *A Letter to a Friend* was certainly sympathetic to the enemy. Philadelphia's Martin Russell Thayer, who would serve as a Republican congressman in the 38th Congress, published a response that May. Although he praised some of Ingersoll's arguments, Thayer deemed the pamphlet "ill-timed and unpatriotic." Given the dangers the nation faced, Ingersoll must decide at long last "on which side of the great struggle do you stand?"[66] On April 26 Ingersoll dropped by Sidney George Fisher's home, bearing a copy of his pamphlet. The next day the diarist described it as "a strange mixture of extravagant ideas and good sense" before embarking on a lengthy entry on the pamphlet.[67] A few days later,

Sidney's wife and Ingersoll's sister, Elizabeth, wrote that she had read Charles's latest as well as a pamphlet by Edward Ingersoll: "They are both on our present troubles; neither of them good." She added, rather generously, that at least "Charles' is pleasant reading."[68]

On August 23, with the war going poorly and the nation preparing for elections, the Philadelphia Democrats staged a mass meeting in Independence Square, chaired by ex-mayor Peter McCall. Charles Ingersoll was one of the featured speakers, and far and away the most controversial. He accused the Lincoln administration of corruption and assailed the recent call for more men, accompanied by the state militia draft. Moreover, he declared that the entire war "[has been] to free the [n—r]."[69] Two days later the provost marshal arrested Ingersoll for speech that aided the enemy and discouraged enlistment.[70] Forney's *Press* spoke for moderate Philadelphians in declaring that "when conservative men utter such sentiments as these, in the name of Democracy, no one need be surprised that they be received with indignation and punished with arrest." But despite outrage in some quarters, the *Press* reporter noted that Ingersoll's speech was met with enthusiastic cheers from its Democratic audience.[71]

Sidney Fisher, Ingersoll's brother-in-law, heard from various sources that the Democratic meeting was not well attended, and that most of the resolutions and speeches—while partisan—were "not extravagant in their tone," with the notable exception of Charles's, which was "extremely violent." Still, Fisher felt that Ingersoll's arrest was a mistake. According to Fisher, the Ingersolls generally laughed off the whole affair, but the combative Charles intended to pursue a writ of habeas corpus, despite the fact that the federal government had suspended the writ. Underscoring the almost small-town nature of Philadelphia's Democratic community, Fisher ran into Ingersoll outside of McCall's office, where they proceeded to go and discuss strategy. And as he left the office, Fisher ran into Pierce Butler, who was thrilled that Ingersoll intended to fight. Ingersoll managed to get Democratic judge John Cadwalader to issue a writ of habeas corpus, which the marshal initially opted to ignore.[72]

Anna Mercer LaRoche, the enthusiastic daughter of prominent Democrat Rene LaRoche, wrote that "the Administration wish to compromise with Mr Ingersol—If Mr I will give up his Habeas Corpus bill he will be discharged. We hope for the sake of our state that he will not give it up."[73] The administration really had no interest in keeping Ingersoll as a political prisoner or fighting a battle over habeas corpus, and Secretary of War Stanton ordered his release before the marshals could move him to prison. The whole affair illuminated the range of issues that would frame the upcoming elections while also illustrating the more extreme Democratic position in the city. Ingersoll, not the least bit chastened, continued to share his opinions both privately and in public settings. On one occasion he reputedly challenged Republican congressman William Kelley to a duel when the latter called him a traitor. (This was the same Congressman Kelley who Butler's lawyers had turned to for assistance when their client was in jail.) The wry Fisher privately noted that his brother-in-law could not possibly have duels with everyone who shared such opinions.[74]

It is typical for the party in power to lose ground in off-year elections. On the other hand, voters commonly rally around the flag when the nation is at war, unless that war has dragged on too long, has commanded too great a cost, or is simply unpopular. In early October T. J. Barrett reported to Barlow from Washington, "It is thought here that the Republicans will be largely victorious over the Democrats in all the elections, & that the people & army will hail the Emancipation policy, as a military necessity forced on the Govt by the South, because of their obstinacy, especially of their attempts at invasion."[75] This Republican confidence turned out to be misplaced.

In the 1862 elections the Republican Party lost twenty-eight seats in Congress. And a case can be made that some Democratic seats shifted from moderates to more harsh critics of the administration. The bulk of the party's gains came from the North's southern states, including New Jersey, Pennsylvania, Ohio, Indiana, and Illinois. Eight of the twenty-five congressional seats from Pennsylvania were held by Democrats at the start of 1862. That fall Philadelphia's Charles Biddle lost his seat to a Republican, but overall the party picked up four seats in a twenty-four-man congressional delegation, and the state elected Democrat Charles R. Buckalew to replace Republican senator David Wilmot. In the 37th Congress, all three congressional representatives from Wisconsin were Republicans. Democrats won three of the state's six seats in the new congress. Democrats also won the governorships of New York and New Jersey, and carried the state legislatures of New Jersey, Illinois, and Indiana. To phrase the same points in a slightly different way, in 1860 Abraham Lincoln had carried politically crucial northern states: New York, Pennsylvania, Ohio, Indiana, and his home state of Illinois. Now all five states had Democratic majorities in their congressional delegations.[76]

Democrats nationwide celebrated their victories. In mid-October William Steel wrote from Joliet, Illinois, to a friend in Pennsylvania that "the Democratic victories this week, in Penna, Ohio, and Indiana are very cheering." He only hoped that his home state would follow suit. A few weeks later Steel was ebullient. "To say that we are 'full of glory' here is not saying too much," he wrote. "Abolitionism received a deadly blow throughout Illinois day before yesterday. We shall now have nine Congressmen instead of four; we will have a majority in both branches of State Legislature, and hence a Democratic successor in U.S. Senate for Douglas."[77] McClellan was similarly cheered by the early returns, writing to Barlow in mid-October.[78] In November a Boston correspondent wrote to Barlow: "I congratulate you on the splendid result of the election in your state. When I contrast the returns from yours and mine I am almost tempted to emigrate there."[79] David H. Armstrong checked in from St. Louis, congratulating Barlow "on the success of the only true Constitutional Party in your state—daylight is breaking."[80] This national network of politically engaged Democrats watched state returns with rapt attention, casting those elections as a fight against abolitionism and for the Constitution. They did not seem to see these votes as for or against the war itself. But certainly other observers, particularly in the Midwest, saw things differently.

The election returns, and particularly the specter of Democratic-controlled statehouses in Indiana and Illinois, took Republicans by surprise. Empowered Democrats in both states passed measures shifting state militia control from the governors to the legislatures, and radical new measures called for negotiated peace. Not all of their citizens were pleased. In a particularly dramatic series of responses, several Illinois regiments turned to politics, passing resolutions the following year denouncing the Democrats in their own state legislature who had talked openly of compromise and armistice with the Confederacy. The governments of both Indiana and Illinois would be roiled with partisan controversy for the remainder of the war.[81]

These elections, coming as they did a year and a half after the outbreak of war, no doubt reflected many forces. Frustrating military progress certainly took its toll. As Lincoln later acknowledged, "the ill-success of the war" hurt the Republican Party's electoral chances.[82] Northern Democrats of various stripes had reason to object to political arrests and other attacks on civil liberties, and in some quarters the turn to conscription had already sparked outrage. But in policy terms, they felt that the key determining factor was Lincoln's Preliminary Emancipation Proclamation. While many northerners embraced the proclamation on moral or practical terms, it gave Democrats quite a bit of ammunition in partisan conflicts. After all, with his proclamation Lincoln had effectively shifted the federal war aims, even while arguing that emancipation was out of military necessity. And the issue provided an opening for the raw racist rhetoric of men like Charles Ingersoll and Sunset Cox, as well as the somewhat more modest sounding language of a George McClellan or Charles Biddle. Emancipation—as both a constitutional issue and a supposedly terrifying threat to home and hearth—might help Democrats gain votes.

The political historian Mark E. Neely Jr. points out that these observations are really only half the equation. Yes, emancipation energized Democrats, and the timing of Lincoln's preliminary announcement surely undercut Republican political aspirations in 1862. But Neely argues that in those 1862 elections the Republican Party failed to rise to the challenge of "electioneering," largely because the president offered the party no political leadership. To put it differently, hostility to emancipation was a fine rallying cry for angry Democrats, but it also could have brought enthusiastic Republicans to the polls in greater numbers. "For the first time in his long political life," Neely notes, "Lincoln did nothing about winning an upcoming election." This may have been a matter of miscalculation: surely Republicans would embrace emancipation as a war aim. And it also reflected concerns about "the propriety of party competition in times of war."[83]

Concentrating on Horatio Seymour's successful New York gubernatorial campaign in 1862, historian Jack Furniss offers a powerful counterargument, emphasizing not so much Democratic anger at the Lincoln administration but rather Seymour's positive—fundamentally conservative—message. Furniss notes that Seymour argued for the legitimacy of loyal opposition in wartime, and for the patriotic coherence of a position calling for peace and honorable compromise. Moreover, Seymour presented a clear conservative rebuttal to the Lincoln administration, stressing constitutional limitations on federal power, even in time of war. In this framework, the northern Democrats—at least in New York—succeeded in mounting a convincing conservative response to the Republicans, rather than appealing to voter anger or racism.[84]

Whatever the precise cause, the political result in the final months of 1862 was that the Democratic Party was better organized and more energized as a partisan body, while various evidence suggests that the Republicans were disorganized and not prepared for electoral conflict in the midst of a civil war. The state by state numbers tell a stark tale. In 1862 Republican votes in Illinois dropped more than 30 percent from the 1860 level. In Ohio the decline was nearly 22 percent, in Pennsylvania 19.5 percent, and in New York 18.4 percent. Part of these declines in turnout can be explained by the off-year elections, but Neely notes that voting turnout for off-year elections in the nineteenth century was generally about 13 percent below the previous presidential election. Republican turnout in the vast majority of northern states dropped by much greater numbers.

Of course the voting numbers can accommodate various interpretations, all of which might have some truth. Lincoln placed some of the blame on the absence of Republican soldiers who were away at war, while Democrats—he claimed—stayed home in greater numbers where they could vote. It is also possible that some Republican voters chose not to vote because they were unhappy with the administration or the progress of the war or particular policy issues. The fact remains that the Democrats made substantial electoral gains in the second half of 1862, giving them a greater voice in Washington and in national political debates. And much of these gains were owing to substantial declines in Republican turnout. Neely's argument that the party—and its leader—failed to treat the elections as normal occasions for aggressive electioneering seems persuasive. Meanwhile, the Democrats made a more rapid transition to an organized opposition party in the midst of war. In any case, the Republicans would not make that mistake again.[85]

While the 1862 elections showed a Democratic opposition in resurgence, it also illustrated fissures in the nation's oldest party. In New York City, a longtime Democratic stronghold, Charles and Maria Daly, Douglas Democrats and strong advocates of the Union, absorbed the election returns with interest. Maria noted that after the huge election two years ago, "radicals have ruined themselves and abolitionism." She was not thrilled with Seymour's victory, wishing instead for "someone who exerted himself for the war," but Daly also viewed things through a decidedly local lens. Specifically, she regretted the successes of "those two scamps, Fernando Wood and his foolish, unprincipled brother [Benjamin] for Congress." Although Democrats, Daly found the Wood brothers—who would go on to become leading critics of the war—to be crooked products of New York politics. With time, these splits between Democrats would become destructive.[86]

Clement Vallandigham and "The Great Civil War in America"

While his fellow congressional Democrats fared well in the midterm elections, Ohio's fiery Clement L. Vallandigham lost his seat. Perhaps the most outspoken critic of the war among elected officials, Vallandigham did not go gently back to Ohio. Instead, he took advantage of his final months in Congress to deliver several major addresses, sharing his thoughts on the war and outraging many of his colleagues. He gave the most substantial of these on January 14, 1863, only weeks after the Emancipation Proclamation took effect.

Vallandigham took the opportunity to restate his many objections to the war, and particularly to what he saw as the constitutional violations produced by the Lincoln administration in the name of war. "I have denounced, from the

Carte de visite: Representative Clement L. Vallandighan of Ohio, c. 1860. A Democratic congressman from Ohio, Vallandigham became one of the most persistent—sometimes outrageous—critics of Abraham Lincoln and the war effort. In May 1863 federal forces arrested the Copperhead leader for speech they deemed treasonous. (Library of Congress)

beginning, the usurpations and the infractions, one and all," he wrote, "of law and Constitution, by the President and those under him; their repeated and persistent arbitrary arrests, the suspension of *habeas corpus,* the violation of freedom of the mails, of the private house, of the press and of speech, and all the other multiplied wrongs and outrages upon public liberty and private right, which have made this country one of the worst despotisms on earth for the past twenty months." The Ohio congressman freely acknowledged that slavery was the root cause of the war, but he blamed abolitionist fanatics who had pushed southern slaveholders into a corner, producing secession and war. And it was that war, he insisted, that was the nation's true horror, producing destruction, debt, and "the enslavement of the white race" to taxes and federal excesses. Turning to his western constituents, Vallandigham argued that after twenty months of war, "the people there begin, at last, to comprehend, that domestic slavery in the South is a question; not of morals, or religion, or humanity, but a form of labor, perfectly compatible with the dignity of free white labor in the same community."[87]

Vallandigham soon returned to Ohio, where he would remain an important—and highly controversial—figure in public debate. He would also soon become the most important national symbol of the "Peace Democrats," who their Republican opponents came to call "Copperheads." In the meantime, Democrats closer to the political mainstream worked on perfecting tools to bring their message to voters.

Bishop John Henry Hopkins, Pamphleteering, and the Public Debate on Slavery

As the war approached the end of its second year, and the 37th Congress gaveled to a close, the Democratic Party had made important strides in building its identity as the opposition party in time of war. The party had established an important political presence in Washington and across much of the North. Meanwhile, Democratic editors articulated an array of dissenting opinions on the war and on public policy. Most importantly, twenty months of events had provided the basis for loyal opposition along multiple axes. This partisan dissent coalesced among northern Democrats, but the party was far from unanimous on any crucial issue. Powerful Democrats had cast their lot with the Lincoln administration, generally supporting not only the war but the core tools the government had adopted in the name of war. But others remained staunchly loyal to the democracy, and they grew increasingly open with their objections to how the war was being fought. It would be a mistake to look at the northern Democrats in early 1863 as settling into some coherent binary, where some supported the war while others opposed the conflict, even hoping for Confederate victory. It is more accurate to imagine northern Democrats—and especially party leaders—as falling along a spectrum of convictions, some of which were defined by region as much as party.

In the first months of 1863 the Democratic Party as an institution made additional strides on two fronts. First, they improved on their means of popular communication, with the emergence of the Society for the Diffusion of Political Knowledge. Second, as the Emancipation Proclamation became national policy, Democrats worked on defining approaches to slavery and abolition that would reach a wide political audience. The story of Bishop John Henry Hopkins provides a useful perspective on these two intertwined threads.

The Democratic Party faced a complex problem articulating a position on the institution of slavery. Individual opinions varied tremendously, but some broad observations are worth making. In the decade before the Civil War, the Democratic Party had struggled to maintain a cohesive national party organization when the southern wing of the party was devoted to protecting their peculiar institution. Secession divided the party, and only a minority of northern Democrats—including men and women with familial ties with the South—actively supported the southern "slaveocracy." In 1861 the vast majority of northerners, both Republicans and Democrats, even many of those who also embraced abolitionism, believed that Whites were racially superior to African Americans. Most northerners had little personal experience with Black Americans, either free or enslaved. But those who were most committed to ending the institution of slavery, or at least stopping its spread into the federal territories, gravitated to the Republican Party. Conversely, those northerners who felt the greatest hostility to non-Whites were likely to vote Democratic, many supporting Breckinridge in 1860. They were, in many senses, truly the "White man's party."

Prior to the outbreak of war, most northerners understood the politics of slavery to be concentrated in debates over slavery in the territories. But once the nation was at war, the issues surrounding slavery expanded tremendously. Some Union military commanders moved the debate by pushing to free runaway slaves as "contrabands" of war. Border-state slave owners who remained loyal to the Union worried that they would lose their own slaves. Meanwhile, politics in Washington shifted with the removal of southern congressmen, tilting the balance of power toward Republicans who pushed for various emancipation and civil rights measures. In this shifting political world, politicians argued over military necessity, constitutional propriety, and—of course—moral imperatives. Some cast themselves as conservative defenders of the Constitution; others turned to practical arguments designed to appeal to the racial fears of White voters. Democratic politicians, especially those who were happy to steer clear of the core debates, were anxious to find intellectual cover.

John Henry Hopkins, bishop of the Protestant Episcopal Church in Vermont, was just the person to provide that ideological support. In 1851 the bishop had traveled to Buffalo to lecture on "Slavery: Its Religious Sanction, Its Political Dangers and the Best Mode of Doing It Away." Hopkins would repeat versions of his lecture repeatedly over the next decade, and it was reprinted in New

York as a pamphlet. In his 1851 address the bishop relied on biblical analysis to build his case, starting with Noah's curse of Canaan in the Old Testament, and continuing by arguing that slavery had been widely present in biblical times yet never sanctioned by Jesus or his disciples. But whereas there was no biblical teaching against slavery, Hopkins still believed that the institution was immoral and a blight on society, and that measures should be taken to abolish the institution. The answer, he concluded, was to pursue a form of compensated emancipation followed by colonization in Liberia. This 1851 version of his ideas fit rather comfortably with opinions professed at the time by moderate Republicans, including Abraham Lincoln.

By the eve of the Civil War the Dublin-born bishop had a substantial national reputation. Not long after Lincoln's election, with slavery threatening to divide the nation, a group of New Yorkers approached Hopkins about publishing his thoughts on the institution. Hopkins responded with a public letter in late 1860, offering his latest sense of "The Bible View of Slavery." His New York associates published the bishop's thoughts as a twelve-page pamphlet. In this new manifesto Bishop Hopkins shifted some of his beliefs, but his core argument that the Bible endorsed slavery remained, and now that claim became central to his overall analysis. Hopkins rejected political arguments about the immorality of slavery and denied that most southerners were in fact cruel to their chattel. And, responding to the challenges of the moment, the bishop claimed that the southern states had the constitutional right to secede.[88]

Hopkins's 1861 pamphlet drew some popular attention, including substantial commentary from the southern press who appreciated his biblical defense of slavery.[89] The pamphlet enjoyed successful distribution in the North. In the months and years to come politically engaged northerners would become far more adept at distributing pamphlets and targeting receptive audiences. Thus, for instance, Joseph Holt's open letter to Joshua Speed in May 1861 won a large readership when a Kentucky press reprinted and distributed the letter. Other early pamphlets, not unlike the bishop's public letter, originated as sermons by clergy—often supporting the Union—that became publications when supporters pitched in to spread the message. Other pamphleteers, like the outspoken Ingersoll brothers, took to the presses to publish and distribute their perspectives on the state of national affairs or articulating complex constitutional arguments about secession or civil liberties.

Into this wartime battle for the public mind, new publication societies aimed to shape public opinion. Those societies organized and funded by the Union

No. 8.

PAPERS FROM THE SOCIETY

FOR THE

Diffusion of Political Knowledge.

PRESIDENT, PROF. S. F. B. MORSE,
SECRETARY, WM. McMURRAY,
TREASURER, LORING ANDREWS,

OFFICE OF THE SOCIETY,
No. 13 PARK ROW, NEW-YORK.
C. MASON, COR. SEC'Y,
To whom all communications may be addressed

READ—DISCUSS—DIFFUSE.

BIBLE VIEW OF SLAVERY.

THE word "slave" occurs but twice in our English Bible, but the term "servant," commonly employed by our translators, has the meaning of slave in the Hebrew and the Greek originals, as a general rule, where it stands alone. We read, however, in many places, of "hired servants," and of "bondmen and bondmaids." The first were not slaves, but the others were; the distinction being precisely the same which exists in our own day. Slavery, therefore, may be defined as *servitude for life, descending to the offspring*. And this kind of bondage appears to have existed as an established institution in all the ages of our world, by the universal evidence of history, whether sacred or profane.

This understood, I shall not oppose the prevalent idea that slavery is an evil in itself. A *physical* evil it may be, but this does not satisfy the judgment of its more zealous adversaries, since they contend that it is a *moral* evil—a positive *sin* to hold a human being in bondage, under any circumstances whatever, unless as a punishment inflicted on crimes, for the safety of the community.

Here, therefore, lies the true aspect of the controversy. And it is evident that it can only be settled by the Bible. For every Christian is bound to assent to the rule of the inspired Apostle, that "sin is the transgression of the law," namely, the law laid down in the Scriptures by the authority of God—the supreme "Lawgiver, who is able to save and to destroy." From his Word there can be no appeal. No rebellion can be so atrocious in his sight as that which dares to rise against his

117

Pamphlet: John Henry Hopkins, *Bible View of Slavery.* By mid-war northerners had become inundated with private printed political pamphlets aimed at diverse audiences. The Society for the Diffusion of Political Knowledge emerged as the leading organization publishing and distributing Democratic pamphlets. In this pamphlet, published as the society's eighth number, Bishop John Henry Hopkins made the case that slavery was compatible with the Bible. This image shows the front page of the sixteen-page pamphlet. (Library of Congress)

Leagues—close cousins to the Republican Party—had a major numerical advantage on northern Democrats. The Loyal Publication Society run out of New York City and Philadelphia's Board of Publication, sponsored by the local Union League, dominated this public discourse. The Pennsylvania group published over 4 million copies of over 100 different publications; the Loyal Publication Society distributed an estimated 900,000 copies of 90 different pamphlets. These societies developed extensive distribution networks and a sort of "brand name" that readers quickly came to recognize. As products of pro-Union bodies, rather than explicitly partisan Republican organizations, these pamphlets also had the appeal that they were essentially patriotic and pro-war, and could deny party agendas, even when the messages smacked of partisanship.[90]

On February 6, 1863, barely a month after the Emancipation Proclamation went into effect, leading New York Democrats met at Delmonico's restaurant "to consult on the best means of diffusing correct political knowledge." A week later they reconvened and formed the Society for the Diffusion of Political Knowledge (SDPK) and named inventor—and avid racist—Samuel Morse as president. In his opening address Morse noted that "we have been charged with disloyalty," when in fact the society proposed to distribute information on the Constitution and on the protection of individual liberty in the face of "fanaticism." The following day New Yorkers who supported the administration and the war effort countered by forming the Loyal Publication Society. A new front of the Civil War had opened in earnest.[91]

The SDPK adopted the slogan, "When a party in power violates the Constitution and disregards States-Rights, plain men will read pamphlets," which appeared on many of its publications. As their second number, the society reprinted Indiana senator David Turpie's February 7, 1863, speech delivered on the floor of the Senate. Turpie, who had only recently arrived in the Senate replacing the banished Jessie Bright, wasted no time in making his mark. The senator rose to challenge legislation allowing for compensated emancipation in Missouri, a border state where slavery remained legal. Central to Turpie's argument, and no doubt the reason the society chose to highlight the speech, was the claim that Republicans in places like his home state of Indiana had recast themselves as the "Union Party" and used that cover to brand Democrats as traitors while pursuing their "radical" antislavery agenda. Turpie was having none of the "no party now" rhetoric that some Union Party members adopted. He and his fellow Democrats proposed to stand up for constitutional ideals in the face of a radical Republican agenda disguised as the party of patriotism.[92]

The SDPK produced about two dozen pamphlets in 1863 and 1864. Some (like Turpie's speech) were reprinted from other sources, while others were unique publications published by the society. In late 1864 the society's energies shifted to the production of numbered campaign pamphlets supporting George McClellan and the Democratic Party. Overall, the output of the SDPK was substantial, although dwarfed by the chief Union League publication operations. The story behind one key SDPK pamphlet offers a window into the inner workings of Democratic politics mid-war.

On January 16, 1863—two days after Vallandigham delivered his salvo in Congress—Bishop Hopkins wrote to Philadelphia lawyer and one-time Democratic mayor Peter McCall, reminding him that they had met a few months earlier. The bishop briefed McCall on his December 1860 public letter on "The Bible View of Slavery" and offered to pass along a copy.[93] Hopkins sent the 1861 pamphlet to McCall, who was impressed with its message. In May Charles Mason, the SDPK's New York–based recording secretary, wrote to McCall about Hopkins's letter, praising the biblical argument and his comments on "the commercial & social consequences involved in the question of emancipation."[94] The two savvy Democrats recognized that the bishop's biblical endorsement of slavery could be politically invaluable to contemporary debates. McCall and his Pennsylvania colleagues were particularly anxious to line up support from the Vermont cleric to provide George Woodward, the party's candidate for governor, some spiritual assistance for his apparent proslavery positions. Mason, who had an editor's knack and an entrepreneur's soul, had the idea that the bishop could upgrade his 1860 pamphlet to meet contemporary conditions, and that the Pennsylvanians could start their own branch of the SDPK, with Hopkins's pamphlet as their first number. Those plans did not quite unfold as he had in mind. Mason met with Bishop Hopkins, who declined to revise his earlier remarks, and although the recording secretary hectored McCall with a long string of letters, he never managed to get the sort of statewide funding from Pennsylvania for the separate pamphlet series he had in mind.[95] But he came close.

On April 15 six leading Philadelphia Democrats—including Biddle and McCall—wrote to Bishop Hopkins asking him to share his thoughts on the institution of slavery, with an eye toward making his views public. Their intentions were unambiguously political. "We believe that false teachings upon the subject have had a great deal to do with the bringing on of the unhappy strife between two sections of our common country," they wrote. The bishop responded two weeks later, enclosing a version of his 1861 pamphlet for their use.

The Philadelphians quickly produced a pamphlet with Hopkins's text preceded by copies of their correspondence.[96]

Shortly thereafter the SDPK published Hopkins's *Bible View of Slavery* as its eighth pamphlet.[97] This new iteration of Hopkins's pamphlet did not differ much from the 1861 version, except to exclude his earlier defense of secession. In Hopkins's eyes the core issues remained unchanged. He was concerned with slavery as a spiritual and moral problem, but in aligning with the Philadelphians the bishop was handing over his words to a political operation intent on winning elections.[98] In the end of August Mason was thrilled to tell McCall that SDPK no. 8 "outran every tract on our list. Thousands of it in a day go west." "In nearly every state our publications are regarded by the *daily & weekly editors as supplementing the press for the ends of the Democratic party,*" he declared.[99]

The bishop's *Bible View of Slavery* provided Democratic politicians with a scriptural argument for resisting emancipation in mid-1863, and between the Philadelphia pamphlet and the SDPK version, Hopkins's words found an expanded audience. Whereas Hopkins had written his original public letter in hopes of maintaining cohesion among his coreligionists, North and South, as secession threatened to divide churches even as it divided the nation, the pamphlet versions of *Bible View of Slavery* that circulated in 1863 had an explicitly partisan purpose. Pennsylvania Democrats had an election to win, and the SDPK wished to bring useful arguments about slavery and emancipation to Democratic editors and politicians nationwide.

In December 1863, with George Woodward's gubernatorial race lost months before, conservative Philadelphian Sidney George Fisher finally picked up Bishop Hopkins's pamphlet and recorded a few thoughts in his diary.[100] Fisher noted that *Bible View of Slavery* had been originally published in 1861 and only recently "republished here by a committee of the Democratic Party to influence the election." A frequent consumer—and occasional author—of political pamphlets, Fisher found Hopkins's work "written with skill, but full of fallacies, sophistries & misstatements" to the point that he questioned whether it was the product of "honest convictions." Whatever its origins, Fisher understood *Bible View of Slavery*—in this new iteration—to have an intended political purpose.[101]

Hopkins and his pamphlet became a major source of conflict in Philadelphia, as religious and lay figures objected to both his arguments and the explicitly partisan way that *Bible View of Slavery* was used. In September 1863, only weeks before the state gubernatorial election, Bishop Alonzo Potter, the Episcopal bishop of the Diocese of Pennsylvania, wrote a short and passionate critique of Hopkins's views on slavery and the politicians who had returned his pamphlet to the public eye. Summarizing these concerns, Potter concluded that "the Bishop and Clergy of Pennsylvania felt constrained to enter against it the following Protest." The two-paragraph protest that followed was signed by Potter and 165 other men.[102]

Stung by the frontal assault from the Pennsylvania clerics, Bishop Hopkins published a lengthy rebuttal in the *Philadelphia Age* and then responded in greater detail with yet another pamphlet, defending both his scriptural analysis and his own intentions in aligning with the Philadelphia Democrats.[103] But the damage was done. Not only had the bishop been tarred with the brush of partisan politics, but his biblical ideas had received much greater distribution and, in the process, far more scrutiny. Finally, in April 1864 Hopkins wrote to Peter McCall, who had remained a friend and correspondent. "I have given up all intentions of visiting Philadelphia for the present, as the position in which Bishop Potter and his clergy have placed me would make it unpleasant on all sides," he reported. "So long as our national troubles continue, and very probably to the end of my life, I must calculate on being intensely unpopular with a vast number of my former friends and trust that I shall bear my lot in this respect with equanimity as the price that must be paid for an honest effort to discharge my duty in times like these." In Hopkins's view, his public statements had been part of his responsibility to the Episcopal Church nationally, including those southern clergy who had departed with the Confederacy. The following January Hopkins rose to presiding bishop of the entire church, a position he maintained until his death three years later. Immediately following the Civil War he played a central role in reuniting the national church, bringing the departed southerners back into the fold. *Bible View of Slavery,* which he had been so anxious to see published in 1861 and perhaps too willing to have reprinted and distributed two years later, remained a black mark on a long career.[104]

The story of Bishop Hopkins's *Bible View of Slavery* illustrates many of the themes surrounding wartime pamphleteering. In this highly literate society, independent groups and large publication societies targeted pamphlets for particular groups, strategized about markets, issued rebuttals of opponents' pamphlets, and generally engaged in a war of words. These pamphlets circulated alongside newspaper editorials and political quarterlies, piling up on tables in drawing rooms and fashionable clubs and becoming the stuff of endless talk over meals and after-dinner drinks.[105] For Morse and the SDPK, Hopkins's biblical endorsement of slavery remained useful, even while many readers found the bishop's opinions appalling. Meanwhile, the society engaged on much broader terrain, fighting out a host of constitutional and political issues against their adversaries. The societies evinced no particular interest in biblical analysis, they only sought a bit of political help on a contentious issue.

Clement Vallandigham's January 1863 speech laid down important markers for the rest of the war. Northerners who objected to the war in its entirety found a voice in Vallandigham, who came to be known as an advocate for peace, or perhaps a Copperhead. For some, the Emancipation Proclamation represented an administration run amuck, imposing social revolution on the nation at the expense of the Constitution. Other northerners would seek to split the difference, disapproving of federal measures to end slavery while rejecting the Peace Democrats as fundamentally disloyal in time of war.

Even in Vallandigham's home state of Ohio, where many eventually gravitated to the Peace Democrats, the state's Democrats were hardly of one mind. Consider the Evans family of Huntington Township, just across the Ohio River from Kentucky. Andrew Evans, the family patriarch, ran a prosperous farm in southern Ohio where he and his family had been Democrats for generations. His son, Samuel, had enlisted with the 70th Ohio Volunteers early in 1862. In early February 1863 Sam wrote to his father from Tennessee, sharing his disgust with the claim that the conflict had become an "abolitionist war" thanks to Lincoln's proclamation. Sam, who saw himself as a good Douglas Democrat, was not swallowing this. "Who were the men who approved of the 'Emancipation Proclamation,'" he asked. "Gen. McClellan, Gen. Halleck, Burnsides and other Democrats of what I would call the 'Right Stripe.' So far as I am concerned about the matter, it suits me in a good many points of view." Good patriotic Democrats approved of the proclamation as a military necessity. In the same letter Sam, writing from his perspective as a soldier, pointed out that men like Vallandigham and other opposition leaders, "give the Rebels courage."[106]

Samuel Evans was hardly alone in seeing Vallandigham's message as an affront to the ideals of the Union fighting man. While the Emancipation Proclamation prompted some soldiers to turn on the administration and even desert from the army, many men in blue took umbrage at the rising antiwar rhetoric. In the first months of 1863 dozens—if not hundreds—of Union regiments passed resolutions denouncing northern Copperheads. No doubt some of these political statements from military camps came from die-hard Republicans, or enlisted men passively following the dictates of their more rabid officers, but other signees were loyal Democrats echoing Sam's conviction that partisan dissent gave comfort to the enemy.[107]

By the early months of 1863 the Democratic Party stood divided, and many struggled with how their opposition party should move forward. Conscription and emancipation had fueled angry dissent, and disappointments on the battlefield encouraged war weariness on the home front and in the field. Politics boiled over in familiar partisan settings, and also in households and communities. Let us step back from the political and institutional developments that had shaped the national Democratic Party and the overall direction of partisan political discourse as of the start of that year and consider wartime political life more broadly, as it was experienced in households, communities, and on the streets.

II

Politics in Communities; Politics in the Streets

4

Politics Is Personal/Politics Is Local

For the United States the Civil War was a war about Union, and eventually about abolition. Debates were over large national issues. But it was also a war experienced in communities and in families. By mid-war Democrats—and Republicans—had begun to feel the strains.

In the state and local campaigns of 1862, Democrats had done fairly well. But as the nation moved into 1863 the party members were hardly of one mind about the war and about how they should proceed as the opposition party. In December 1862 General Ambrose Burnside and the Army of the Potomac squared off against Robert E. Lee's Army of Northern Virginia, suffering well over twelve thousand casualties in a bloody defeat. By early 1863 the twin concerns of conscription and emancipation roiled political life on the home front. As is always the case in times of war, military and political concerns found their way into diverse households and communities.

This chapter considers an array of individual families and communities, seeking some sense of how politics—and Democrats—navigated these times. We start in the East and move westward, with some emphasis on families in the border states. The story of Democrats on the border has its own distinct political narrative, partially shaped by the presence of slavery and partially by the powerful hand of the government. In the border states political developments—and personal responses—must be understood in the context of federal military policies. Here the crucial figure at the center of the story is none other than General Burnside, who had been assigned to command the Department of the Ohio, and who used his authority to enforce some federal control over this contentious terrain. Politics in Chicago becomes a valuable case study as the nation attempted to unravel what it meant to be a "Copperhead" at mid-war.

Two themes emerge in this chapter. First, in a political culture where White men enjoyed nearly all of the available economic, political, and legal power, women were consistently engaged in political discussions in their own households as well as in broader public venues. And, second, time and again the major national political disputes unfolded in distinctive ways in different communities. Politics was indeed local as well as national, and invariably personal and familial.

Democratic Women and Politics: Philadelphia Families

There is no denying that White men dominated many aspects of wartime politics and political debate. But that is not to say that women were absent from wartime public discourse. Some women authored editorials and political pamphlets; a handful took to the platform to speak on partisan politics. Women attended partisan lectures and appeared in public when events drew spontaneous crowds into the streets. Thousands of women threw themselves into wartime voluntarism or paid employment. And, as we shall see in the following chapter, women regularly took part in civil disobedience.[1]

While there is substantial evidence of some women entering the public arena in various guises, northern women also became engrossed in the war's military and political debates in their private lives and conversations.

In the East, Democratic women and men disagreed on issues both large and small. Fifty-one-year-old Philadelphia diarist Sidney George Fisher observed how the emerging secession crisis affected relationships between conservative men and women in his elite universe. Sally Ingersoll, the wife of rabidly partisan pro-secessionist Henry Ingersoll, was "adopting all of her husband's opinions," Fisher wrote. The patronizing Fisher added that he spoke with Mrs. Ingersoll with care, because "she knows nothing whatever of the subject." Fisher concluded that "one of the evils of civil dissensions is that they produce discord between families & friends," but in truth he was observing that Philadelphia's Democratic women had their own minds and their own opinions.[2]

The war posed particular political and social challenges for Elizabeth Ingersoll Fisher, Sidney George Fisher's wife. Sidney—in an interesting contrast to his views on Sally Ingersoll—wrote that "Bet" "has her convictions & can think & is a good deal excited by the outrages of the South." Sidney and Bet lived in a household thick with political talk, and they frequently entertained conservative visitors who divided on the war. Although Ingersoll's brothers had become major voices of the party's most conservative wing, Elizabeth refused to share their politics even when sharing a dining table.[3] But when news that their father was sick reached the Ingersolls, Elizabeth found herself spending more time with Charles and Edward, despite their differences. In early January 1863, with the nation dividing over emancipation and conscription, Elizabeth wrote that "George went to town and came home gloomy about public affairs," adding that "he is less cheerful on that subject than I am now." And with her brother Charles jailed for his politics, there seemed little reason to be cheerful. "It is always darkest before dawn but when is darkest? Dark as it had been, it gets darker," she wrote in the same entry. In this corner of Philadelphia's elite conservative community, the personal and political had become hopelessly intertwined.[4]

Charles and Emma Biddle, who had been married for years and had a substantial brood of young children, lived a comfortable life with their core roles divided by gender. Charles had been a soldier and then early in the war became a congressman from Pennsylvania.[5] Emma split her time between their Philadelphia home and the Biddle estate outside of the city, and she devoted a portion of her letters to reports on the health and activities of their children. But Emma paid close attention to national politics and to her husband's political career.[6]

The Fishers and Biddles moved in conservative Philadelphia circles, where they knew many of the city's leading Democrats—both those who supported the war and those who bitterly opposed it. Since Charles Biddle held political office, Emma served as his supporter and sounding board, but she also had her own mind when it came to political events. Elizabeth Fisher shared her husband's general political sensibilities, but she navigated a political culture where her own brothers often acted as the city's most divisive political lightning rods.

Sarah Butler Wister, the twenty-five-year-old daughter of Pierce Butler and Fanny Kemble Butler, observed the start of the Civil War from her home in Philadelphia, where she also socialized with the city's elite conservatives, including many who shared her personal ties with the South. Just a week after the fall of Fort Sumter, Wister entertained "a succession of visitors," nearly all women. With each new caller the conversation quickly turned to politics, often combining talk of how events had affected their personal lives as well as the nation's future. Two cousins regaled Wister with tales of their boardinghouse, where several pro-secessionist southern visitors were stuck in town. Another visitor admitted that she would never take up arms against the South, even while her husband was off drilling with a New Jersey company. Wister reported that a Mrs. Harry Ingersoll—whose husband was a prominent and notoriously silent man—was so chatty that her talk became "almost comic," declaring that "we cannot help feeling with the South" even while Harry "was doing everything he can in the cause of the Union." In these conversations among women, politics took center stage.[7]

Anna Mercer LaRoche was the daughter of prominent doctor and leading Philadelphia Democrat Rene LaRoche. Throughout the war the young diarist maintained a strong interest in politics and a deep commitment to the party. On February 28, 1863, she attended a Democratic meeting where her father appeared on the platform. It was an exciting occasion, with the speakers calling for peace and reconciliation, among much enthusiasm. "We are of the obnoxious party," LaRoche wrote, "against the war & find times hard for us." In the months to come LaRoche followed her father's public career with enthusiasm, noting when he toasted Clement Vallandigham at the Democratic Club, and then later objected when fellow Democrats cheered Jefferson Davis, explaining that he did not want it to appear that "Democrats are Secesh." Still, in May when news of Stonewall Jackson's death reached Philadelphia, LaRoche wrote that "we felt as if it were the death of a friend."[8]

A momentous personal event occurred in May 1864: Anna LaRoche met Dr. Mott Francis at a party in New York. At the time she was not so sure that that was a good thing. "I like Dr. Mott's face so much he is so bright," she wrote in her diary, "but I did not wish to be introduced to him as he is such a republican—but at last Amelia caught me in a corner & introduced him to me." Ten days later LaRoche ran into Dr. Francis on her way home from Brooklyn and recorded a similar reaction: "Met Dr. Mott . . . he looked very bright & handsome I thought—with his bright blue eyes and pretty mouth—but I have taken a great dislike to him of his politics & will not be won over." The following day the doctor and a friend came to dinner and he sat beside her, "so I had to talk with him." The two discussed Napoleon, and Anna concluded that "I like him ever so much & I do not wish to as he is a republican." In just a few weeks Anna had met Mott three times, and each time she seemed drawn to the man and repulsed by his politics.[9]

LaRoche returned to her life in Philadelphia, which included attending more Democratic events. In early November she revisited New York and ran into Mott Francis again. The following June—after a lengthy hiatus from her diary—LaRoche wrote a hurried entry, summarizing a half year of events. In brief, during her November visit LaRoche had renewed her acquaintance with Francis, including socializing with his family and seeing him every day. On November 25 the two were engaged, and they married on February 7, 1865. From the close of 1864, LaRoche's diary entries grew less frequent and far less political.[10]

LaRoche's account of their whirlwind romance omits any discussion of politics, although it might be significant that they became engaged after Lincoln had won reelection and the war seemed to be nearing an end. Once she was married to Mott, Anna's diary stopped mentioning political events. If the rabid Democrat and loyal Republican bickered over politics, Anna chose to omit such conversations from her journal. After the war the couple toured the South, visiting a host of Confederate sites. But LaRoche's less frequent entries never noted conversations about the war or politics.[11] It is hard to avoid the conclusion that the couple had carved out a happy relationship by not discussing partisan politics, even while continuing to hold to different ideologies.

An Angry Copperhead and His Patriotic Fiancée

Gideon Winan Allen and his love, Annie Cox, offer another window into a young wartime couple differing over politics. Both lived in Madison, Wisconsin, at the outset of the war, but in 1862 Gideon set off for Ann Arbor, Michigan, to attend law school. From that point the couple—who would soon become engaged—corresponded enthusiastically, if not always fondly.[12]

Their challenge was that Cox was a "devout abolitionist" whereas Allen was not merely a Democrat but an outspoken Copperhead.[13] Winan, as he was known to his friends, grew up in a Whig household in Connecticut, and his father—who became a Republican—became dismayed at his son's contrary politics. Annie grew up in Wisconsin in a humble household, and with substantial academic ambitions. The couple seemed to be perfectly matched in many ways and curiously at odds in others. Annie was devoutly religious; Winan did not believe in God. Annie saw herself as a staunch patriot, loyal to the Union, to emancipation, and to the administration. Winan embraced the Democratic creed of "the Union as it was." He disliked the war and the policies that supported it, and he shared his strong beliefs at every opportunity. In early 1863, in the aftermath of the Emancipation Proclamation, Winan declared that "a large majority" of the Democratic Party actually "hate slavery; yet for the sake of the union we are willing to let it remain, and leave the government as our fathers made it." Annie disagreed. She insisted that Winan's "party encourage [slavery's] existence and extension," despite his claims. And so it went in letter after letter.[14]

In June 1863 Winan returned to Madison for awhile, and the two became engaged and seemed to solidify their relationship. But when he returned to Ann Arbor, Winan—like many of his ideological kinsmen in 1863—grew increasingly vocal in his hostility to the war. Annie disliked his opinions and worried about the implications of his angry public pronouncements on campus. She feared that her betrothed was tottering on the edge of treason. Their letters grew more harsh, so that in December and again in January Winan wrote that "we must not talk politics anymore."[15] This resolution seemed to work for a short while, but when Winan got his degree and moved to Sturgeon Bay, Wisconsin, he could not resist engaging in public debates about the upcoming election. And Annie admonished him about both his religious shortcomings and his loud political pronouncements. Sturgeon Bay—and Winan—managed to dodge the final draft in March 1865, and shortly thereafter the two wed and peace came.

The Allen-Cox correspondence is entertaining to read about, although it must have been troubling to live through. On at least one occasion the passionate relationship seems to have crumbled under the weight of the couple's profound disagreements, only to be reestablished some time later. Like Anna and Mott, it may be that the end of the Civil War helped calm the waters between Annie and Winan. But whereas the Philadelphia Copperhead does not appear to have really talked politics with the New York Republican during the war, the two Midwesterners resolved to face their differences in their conversations and correspondence. From the outset the couple agreed to discuss those disputes openly, and as equals. The historian who has examined the Allen-Cox relationship makes a key observation. Within the walls of their personal relationship, familiar power dynamics framed by gender did not appear. Instead, from the outset "he did not use her gender to discount her perspective or her right to express them."[16] For this young couple, like many other wartime pairs, women framed and articulated their own political opinions. Sometimes they were wildly at odds with their husbands or loved ones, and in other cases the disagreements were a matter of nuance. But disagree they did.

Slavery and Loyalty: Kentucky Families

In 1860, as the nation lurched toward war, Kentuckians Susan Scrogin and Henry Haviland were gradually finding their way toward love. In December Sue wrote to Henry, who was off on business in Harrison County, describing her recent visit to Lexington. "I think the Secession movement in the South is more talked of than anything else," she wrote. "Are you for union or disunion," Sue asked. "The Ladies you know are all for *Union* especially as this is the Close of Leap Year; and then for disunion the next 4 years." Scrogin was no fan of the incoming administration. Her father was a slave owner whose response to the crisis had been to sell his slaves and make plans to relocate to California.[17] The following month Henry proposed to Sue, while he laid the groundwork for a future in trade if the nation divided. The two exchanged regular letters, often with extended discussions of national events. After the fall of Fort Sumter, Henry supported the Union while hoping that Kentucky would embrace neutrality.[18] Neither had any enthusiasm for the Lincoln administration, but Sue—who wrote of "Lincoln and his northern horde of tyrants"—generally seemed more passionate about politics.[19]

Just over a month after Joseph Holt's public plea for Kentucky to reject neutrality and align with the Union, Henry wrote to Sue, pointing out that he was more sanguine about the future than she seemed to be, even while he rejected Holt's counsel. "I certainly differ with you as to Ky," he wrote in early July 1861, "for her conditions fare better than any state in the South, or North either. . . . It certainly is now the policy of Ky to maintain her neutral position. It is now advocated by all parties in this and adjoining counties. Secession now would ruin everything in Ky." In these first weeks after secession, Sue reported that she and her family had talked of moving South, largely because they feared that they would lose control over their remaining slaves.[20] As 1861 came to a close, Sue grew increasingly concerned about the future of slavery in Kentucky, even as her fiancé saw the war as presenting economic possibilities.[21]

Events in 1862 gave Kentucky slaveholders increasing reason to worry about their economic futures and the larger future of the state's peculiar institution. Although in May 1861 Holt had argued that the federal government constituted the strongest buffer against unwanted emancipation, by the end of 1862 white Kentuckians had every reason to believe that things had changed. It was true that Abraham Lincoln's Emancipation Proclamation, which was issued in preliminary form in September, expressly limited federal emancipation to those Confederate states still in rebellion, but July's Second Confiscation Act had opened the door for Black enlistment, and it seemed only a matter of time before Kentucky slaves would win their freedom one way or another. Meanwhile, tensions between Unionists and pro-Confederates, commonly supported by armed federal forces or guerrillas, tore at the fabric of border-state society.[22] And in contested areas across the state federal officials grew more brazen in limiting public dissent. On July 26, 1862, on the eve of state elections, officials—recognizing the political power of the clergy—arrested preachers across the state who they suspected of disloyalty.[23]

At the outset of the war Kentuckian Ellen Wallace supported the Union and hoped that her state would not secede, but as the months passed Wallace became increasingly disillusioned with the administration and worried about the future of Kentucky's slave institution, including the roughly thirty enslaved people who Ellen and her husband, Albert, held on their plantation in Christian County, in southwestern Kentucky.[24] In December 1861 Wallace—who had recently turned forty-one—wrote of the popular "shame and indignation" at talk of "arming and emancipating the slaves." The following September, upon learning of the Preliminary Emancipation Proclamation, Wallace turned to hyperbolic extremes, writing, "Lincoln's proclamation emancipating all the slaves is justly creating great indignation. The consequences of it are too awful to contemplate. The blood of women, children and helpless aged will flow in torrents if its carried into effect. The vile wretch ought to suffer all the torments that could be inflicted on him, body and soul. Then to place innocent women and helpless infants at the mercy of black monsters who would walk in human shape." By 1863 Wallace's diary included regular angry entries about local enslaved men enlisting in the Union Army or simply running to freedom. But throughout the war, despite her passionate hatred of Abraham Lincoln and her admiration of Robert E. Lee and of the individual Confederate soldiers who passed through her county, Wallace continued to insist that she supported the Union war effort against the Confederacy.[25]

On the other side of Kentucky, Henry and Sarah Waller observed the coming of the Civil War from a different perspective, despite sharing various traits with the Wallaces. The Wallers lived on a farm they called "Auvergne" outside the town of Maysville, on the Ohio River. Both Bell (as she was called) and Henry came from prominent Kentucky families, a background that would prove useful in the years to come. Henry was a lawyer by trade and a farmer by avocation, but for much of the 1850s he was really a politician. For nearly a decade he served as a Whig representative to the state legislature. When the Whig Party collapsed, Henry—like many other Kentucky Whigs—became a Stephen Douglas Democrat, supporting the Illinois politician in his successful 1858 senatorial campaign against Abraham Lincoln and his failed presidential bid two years later. In the meantime, the Wallers had decided to relocate to Chicago, where Henry would join his brothers in real estate investment while continuing his law practice.[26]

In 1860 the Wallers owned ten slaves, placing them among the quarter of white Kentucky families dependent on slavery.[27] But as Abraham Lincoln was elected and the nation braced for secession and war, Henry and Sarah were already in the process of liquidating their Kentucky possessions—including selling their slave men and women—to move to Illinois. The couple watched national political developments from different states, sharing periodic thoughts on the future. In September Henry wrote from Chicago, worrying that "the election of Lincoln, however, may ruin us all; as I verily believe we shall have a rupture, and with it a convulsion, which will be very disastrous." Still, the Democrat remained somewhat sanguine, adding that "I hope he will be defeated. I think he will be." The following week Bell replied from Auvergne, expressing much more confidence about the future: "You mentioned in your letter of the 28th that you feared sectional strife if Lincoln was elected. There is not the least danger at this time of the Souths seceding. She is almost destitute of food, and she will not go to war, with famine at her door and she cannot buy food, save from her sister states." Until the eve of the election the two continued their conversation by mail, with Henry counting on a Lincoln loss and Bell insisting that the South would not secede regardless of the outcome.[28] Although both Wallers turned out to be equally poor prognosticators, their correspondence reveals a partnership between a husband and wife where both thought seriously and independently about national politics and respected the other's opinions.

The following October Henry traveled to Washington in search of business opportunities. His letters to Bell reveal their ongoing focus on political events, while also underscoring Henry's ties with the centers of political power. While in the capital, Henry sought a business meeting with Montgomery Blair, the postmaster general and prominent Kentucky conservative. Blair was unavailable, but Henry did enjoy a productive meeting with Illinois Republican Isaac Arnold. A few days later he visited with Mary Todd Lincoln before heading to New York for more business meetings.[29]

In January 1863 the Wallers were once again apart, sharing regular letters. But now Bell was living in Chicago, getting that house in order, while Henry was back in Kentucky working on liquidating their property. Several of their letters refer to the future of "Emily" in this transition. It appears (from context) that Emily was an enslaved widow who had been with the family for many years. In early January Emily was staying in Lexington. Sarah urged Henry to see her but to not "make her any promises" he could not fulfill, but she argued that he should tell Emily they would do their best for her if she came to Chicago. "Of course we will have to pay her something," she added. A few days later Sarah added that "Mother" liked the idea of Emily living with them in Chicago, and that Emily had expressed interest in living with some portion of the family. That May Henry wrote from Cincinnati, reporting that he had seen Emily in Lexington, where she was staying with the McFarlanes. They promised to send her along to Chicago in a few weeks, and Mr. McFarlane offered to pay for Emily's hire for a final year. These letters, especially those exchanged in January 1863, provide an illustration of how the personal and political interacted in Kentucky. In the weeks after Lincoln issued the Emancipation Proclamation, many white Kentuckians were up in arms about the impending loss of their slave property, even though the proclamation technically did not apply to states that had not left the Union. But for Henry and Bell Waller, who were well on their way to leaving Kentucky for good, their ties to slavery had nearly ended. Instead, they found themselves discussing the post-emancipation future of one enslaved woman, seemingly untroubled by the larger moral issues associated with the peculiar institution they had embraced and now abandoned.[30]

As Bell Waller became more fully grounded in Chicago, she eased into a new public role as a conduit to Confederate prisoners of war held at Chicago's Camp Douglas. The Wallers remained unbending in their support for the Union and their opposition to the Confederacy, but they still had ties with southerners, including many who had sided with the Confederacy. In March 1862 Henry's niece wrote about a relative held in Camp Douglas. The Wallers contacted the Union authorities at the Department of Missouri in St. Louis, and they soon received an order signed by General Henry Halleck giving Sarah Waller permission to visit Confederate prisoners of war at Camp Douglas "for benevolent purposes."[31] For the next several years Bell maintained an interest in the goings-on in Camp Douglas. She visited the camp every few days, bringing the prisoners articles of clothing and various "delicacies" sent from family members in the South. Sarah's letters include regular correspondence from people in the Confederacy—especially women related to prisoners—who quickly learned that she was a valuable person to contact. Before long Sarah was directing a cohort of volunteers who raised money and brought items to the prisoners.[32] After the war Sarah Waller was commemorated in various publications as a true "heroine of the Confederacy" for her work in Camp Douglas. But although southerners celebrated her actions, Waller's wartime labors were with the approval—and supervision—of federal officials, and there is no suggestion that she supported the Confederate cause, even while she devoted her energies to helping Confederate prisoners.

By selling their slaves and liquidating their Kentucky estate, the Wallers managed to create a new identity in Chicago while maintaining their cultural and familial ties to Kentucky. But before long the realities of civil war would undermine the new world they had created.

William Standard Goes to War; Jane Standard Runs the Farm

When we consider the men who fought in the Union Army, it is useful to recognize—and then muddy—a host of assumptions about enlisted soldiers. It is easy to assume that Union volunteers were more enthusiastic about the war than their peers who stayed at home, and thus they must have been overwhelmingly Republican and antislavery. And that assumption is not entirely wrong. Many Republican men jumped at the chance to go to war against the Confederacy. And a good portion of them recognized that they were striking a blow against the "slaveocracy," particularly after Lincoln issued the Emancipation Proclamation. We should also consider that these Union recruits often left behind wives and children who were forced to struggle on without the presence of these men in their daily lives, and without the economic support that civilian men provided to their families. This narrative too builds on clear facts. When married men and fathers went to war, they left behind giant voids in the emotional and material lives of those left behind. Women on farms had to adjust the work they personally accomplished, as well as what they expected of their children. Wives in towns and cities often turned to war-related work, accepting low wages paid by contractors who could exploit women desperate for an income.[33]

Each of these familiar narratives are grounded in lots of evidence. But the broader history complicates both stories. Although Civil War soldiers certainly followed personal ideology, more so than soldiers in most wars, the best predictor of military participation was probably age.[34] In most communities younger men enlisted at far greater rates than their older neighbors. It is true that tens of thousands of volunteers left behind wives and children (these were huge armies after all), but the more typical recruit went to war as an unmarried man.[35] It is also true that Republicans embraced the war with particular fervor, but a large portion of northern Democrats supported the Union and the war, and many of them ended up in blue uniforms. Moreover, as the war dragged on, soldiers, both Republicans and Democrats, took advantage of their right to grumble about the administration. In sum, Union soldiers were a diverse lot, befitting their large numbers and geographic breadth. Most volunteers, but certainly not all, were fairly young men. The vast majority supported the Union, although many were Democrats and not all were enthusiastic about all Republican policies.[36]

And then there was William Standard of Fulton County, Illinois. Standard was certainly no typical Union volunteer, yet he served in the 103rd Illinois Volunteer Infantry Regiment for nearly three years. For his entire time in uniform, Standard corresponded with his wife, Jane, providing a window into both life on the home front and in uniform. This correspondence is particularly valuable because both Standards were outspoken Democrats. They are also of interest because Standard was forty years old in August 1862 when he enlisted; Jane was about six years younger.[37]

William Standard enlisted as a first sergeant in Company A of the 103rd on August 9, 1862, only a few weeks after Congress passed the Militia Act of 1862 and shortly before the administration assigned a draft quota to the state of Illinois. Standard may have followed any number of motivations when he enlisted. Historian Timothy Mason Roberts notes that the Standards—who owned farmland in Fulton County—were in a precarious financial situation by that fall. Roberts also speculates that Standard might have acted to avoid the dishonor of being drafted.[38] Or perhaps Standard calculated that a volunteer would have greater control over his military position than a conscript. In any case, the new recruit clearly did not enlist to strike a blow against slavery. His letters home reveal persistent disdain for emancipation and a fervent racism.[39]

From very shortly after his enlistment William discovered that he was no fan of soldiering. Soldiers' letters are commonly full of complaints about life in uniform, but William's correspondence is noteworthy for his various schemes to improve his lot. In September 1862, shortly after the men were officially mustered into service, Jane wrote telling William that there was unlikely to be any draft and that he should pursue an honorable discharge and come home. That winter William repeatedly wrote of his hopes for a quick end to the war and his conviction that his fellow soldiers would vote for compromise and peace. In December he wrote from Mississippi that he had requested a transfer to a clerical position, but he revealed that his ultimate hope was to get out of the military altogether and return home. William recognized that desertion was a poor option, because then he would not be able to return home. By February Mary's letters had grown increasingly morose, and William seemed more and more hostile to Lincoln and desperate to find a way to get home. Unfortunately, his health was too good to receive a medical discharge, so William and Jane wrote more openly about strategies for desertion.[40]

As the couple's letters grew increasingly focused on how William might get home, the gender dynamics between them emerged into sharp relief. In February William acknowledged that Jane had been right in urging him to take his chances with conscription, rather than enlisting. As the couple became more desperate, William sought Jane's advice on how to proceed. Jane, in turn, cloaked her opinions in a self-deprecating mask. "I am sorry I am not smart enough to tell you what is going on in the way of Politics," she wrote in early February, before sharing opinions that seemed every bit as sophisticated as William's. "I think that all the democrats wants the war stopped some way or other. The republicans wants the rebellion put down if it cost evry man woman and child life but they stay at home and talk big." A few weeks later Jane wrote, "If I was thare I think I could do something, if I was a man." As she did often in her letters, Jane apologized for not being "smart enough" and then went on to offer explicit advice on how William might successfully pull off a safe capture and parole.

The two continued in this pattern for weeks, with William turning to his wife for counsel and Jane nudging Will while insisting that she was ignorant of all such affairs. In early March Jane reported that she had been discussing things with local Democrats and had learned that parole papers could be purchased for fifty cents, if only Will could accomplish the transaction.[41] With time—as each new scheme seemed unmanageable—the Standards abandoned their talk of William getting out of the military altogether, shifting to strategies for getting a legal furlough. In the meantime, the couple—like many other farm couples—settled into correspondence about farm business. Here again Jane adopted a deferential tone, but Will became increasingly open in trusting her to make their joint business decisions. In all of these ways the Standards—although not "typical" in so many senses—are a superb illustration of what happened when the war separated couples. Although the two played out their own version of gendered theater, it is clear that William and Jane were political and economic partners, working out how to move forward in situations not of their choosing.

But the Standards were also Democrats who had strong beliefs and prejudices that shaped their behavior. Jane, despite her persistent claims that politics were beyond her ken, routinely commented on partisan goings-on in and around Fulton County. Meanwhile, William viewed national events and his own personal experiences through a highly partisan lens. Unlike couples who differed on politics, Jane and Will were commonly on the same page. They both hated Lincoln and Republican radicals. They were both hostile to emancipation. Time and again Will insisted that the men he knew—those Illinois volunteers—would have happily voted to secure some sort of compromise and end the war.

In late 1863 Standard and his regiment moved to the Southeast, joining Union troops in Alabama. Largely because of their location, William could no longer contemplate desertion, and more so than in the previous months the 103rd saw some real military action. Along the way Standard insisted that he was doing his duty even while he disliked the war and hated life in uniform. Will finally received the much-coveted furlough and went home, but it was not long before he was back in the Southeast and missing his family, and Jane was at home missing her husband. "I think I am the most unhappy man alive," William wrote from Mississippi in September.[42]

In January William—despite his devout racism—wrote to Jane asking for her advice on pursuing a command in the United States Colored Troops. Like many white men who sought transfers to these troops, William was thinking about personal advancement and certainly not racial justice. The following month William reported that he had been recommended to the "contraband service," but it seems that he never made the transfer.[43] Instead, William stayed with his regiment until the end of the war.

While William remained in uniform, he lost none of his hostility toward his commander in chief. In March 1864, as conversations turned to the next presidential election, he told Jane: "You know that I always told you that old Abraham Lincoln was an abolitionist but you would not believe me. I think just as I always did. I am a Democrat still, but not one in favor of secession. I am not in favor of the re-election of old Abe to the Presidency for four more years, no, not by any means. I am in for a good Democrat for that office."[44] Meanwhile, Jane kept William abreast of politics at home, prompting her husband to lash out at the Republicans who were "too cowardly to go to war." William also had little patience for those Democrats who supported the conflict, declaring that "the War Democrats and the Republicans all piss through the same quill."[45] As the nation moved toward a crucial presidential election, the Standards seemed remarkably consistent in their conviction that the war was an unnecessary conflict that should end with compromise, administered by Democratic leadership.

Ambrose Burnside and General Orders No. 38

While the Wallers, Standards, and Wallaces—and many other Democratic families—were first discussing how the Civil War would change their lives, General Ambrose Burnside was busily commanding Union troops in Virginia and then in North Carolina. Soon he would be in command of a huge swath of the Midwest. The Indiana-born Burnside had graduated from the United States Military Academy in 1847 in time to be stationed in Mexico but too late to see fighting there. Like many of his peers, Burnside eventually resigned his commission in the peacetime military. For a time he worked for the Illinois Central Railroad, under George McClellan, where they became friends. In 1858 he ran as a Democrat in an unsuccessful campaign for Congress from Rhode Island. Like McClellan and Charles Biddle and a host of others, Burnside returned to uniform when the Civil War began. In March 1862 Burnside was promoted to major general and transferred to the Army of the Potomac, where he famously commanded the 11th Corps on the left flank of the Union line at the Battle of

Antietam. Although he hardly covered himself with glory in that terrible battle, after Abraham Lincoln relieved George McClellan, Burnside found himself in command of the Army of the Potomac on November 7. Barely a month later Burnside led his men in the disastrous Battle of Fredericksburg. By early January 1863 Lincoln had replaced Burnside with Joe Hooker, who would have no greater success against the Army of Northern Virginia.

Rather than accept Burnside's resignation, Lincoln reassigned his experienced general to command the Department of the Ohio, which included Ohio, Indiana, Illinois, and portions of Kentucky and Tennessee. In this new command Burnside was in no danger of mismanaging large numbers of Union troops, but he did enter a world of complex politics and partisan tensions. In parts of Kentucky, pro-Confederate guerrillas roamed free, encouraging pro-southern dissenters while terrifying Unionist households. Across the state, slave owners worried about the future of their cherished institution, and their economic holdings, even if they remained loyal to the federal government. By mid-1862 Brigadier General Jeremiah T. Boyle had established himself as a de facto military governor in the state, applying sometimes ham-handed strategies to suppress dissent among editors and politicians alike.[46] To the north and west, antiwar Democrats maintained a steady drumbeat of criticism against the administration. In June 1862 Indiana's Governor Oliver P. Morton sent the War Department and the president a rather hysterical letter warning of a "secret political organization" in his state, and of a host of rapidly disloyal newspapers in Indiana, Ohio, and Illinois. He wanted them to send him "at least 10,000 stand of good arms" with which he would arm a local militia to protect the state. Morton's claims were exaggerated, but it seems his concern was heartfelt.[47]

By early 1863 popular objections to the suppression of civil liberties had become comingled with rising hostility to emancipation and conscription. Even civilians who had previously rejected secession and supported the war had begun to chafe at the measures applied to ensure stability and support the war effort. Burnside's Department of the Ohio faced a host of challenges, calling for a delicate hand. Atop the list of Burnside's headaches was the irascible, and intensely popular, Clement Vallandigham. In February Vallandigham had delivered his final salvo in Congress and headed home to Ohio.[48]

On April 13 Burnside issued his General Orders No. 38, intent on laying out to residents of the Department of the Ohio precisely what sort of behavior would put them in front of a military tribunal, charged with treason. "The habit of declaring sympathy for the enemy will not be allowed in this department," the new order declared. "Persons committing such offenses will be at once arrested with a view of being tried . . . or sent beyond our lines into the lines of their friends. It must be understood that treason, expressed or implied, will not be tolerated in this department." And while some offenders would face banishment, others—Burnside warned—would be subject to execution for treason. Burnside's idea was that such tough language would calm the most disruptive opposition rhetoric, allowing him to bring order to his new command.[49] That notion did not last long.

On May 1, just over two weeks after Burnside issued his General Order, a crowd of fifteen thousand Democrats gathered at Mount Vernon, Ohio, to hear an assortment of party luminaries, including Vallandigham and Ohio congressman George H. Pendleton. In eighteen months Pendleton would be the vice-presidential candidate on his party's ticket. In four days Vallandigham would be in jail.

When Vallandigham took his place at the speaker's podium he turned to familiar themes. The war was unnecessary and cruel, and Lincoln was intentionally prolonging the conflict in order to impose emancipation on an unwilling

Political cartoon: "A Rare Old Game of 'Shuttlecock.'" After Ohio congressman Clement L. Vallandigham was charged with treasonous speech, federal authorities sought to banish the Copperhead to the Confederacy. Jefferson Davis and the Confederacy had other ideas. This cartoon, which appeared in *Frank Leslie's Illustrated Newspaper* on June 20, 1863, shows the two presidents playing a vigorous game of shuttlecock, with Vallandigham at its center. (Library of Congress)

population. As he spoke, two men of the 115th Ohio, dressed in civilian garb, took notes. Their task was to catch the ex-congressman in treasonous talk. But Vallandigham deftly steered clear of such language, instead stressing that his supporters should make their views known at the ballot box by supporting his bid for the governorship. But while a reasonable observer might have concluded that the Mount Vernon gathering was little more than good old-fashioned political speech, albeit strongly hostile to the administration, Burnside believed otherwise. In the early morning hours of May 5 a military contingent, following Burnside's orders, went to the Vallandigham home to arrest the notorious Democrat. Vallandigham made their task as difficult as possible, refusing to open the doors or surrender to the authorities until they had broken into his home and then into his bedroom. But before long he was off to military confinement in Cincinnati. There Vallandigham stood trial before a military commission. He declared his innocence and challenged the military court's jurisdiction in a state where civil courts still functioned, but to no avail. The

Song sheet: Vallandigham Polka and Schottische. This five-page song sheet includes the music to a polka and a schottische celebrating the Ohio Copperhead Clement L. Vallandigham. Composed by R. Linter, the sheet was published in Cincinnati and St. Louis in 1863. (Library of Congress)

commission sentenced Vallandigham to military prison for the duration of the war. He was soon released and banished to the Confederacy.[50]

Ambrose Burnside and Chicago Politics

As in other corners of the Union, the federal forces in the Department of the Ohio worried about Democratic newspapers publishing hostile editorials, undermining what they saw as legitimate military objectives. For Burnside, the press presented every bit as big a challenge as the loquacious Vallandigham. And the greatest annoyances came from Wilbur Storey and his *Chicago Times.*[51]

Throughout the Civil War, the *Times* stood as the most powerful Democratic voice in the Midwest, persistently challenging the administration on matters large and small. After the war Brigadier General James Oakes—the provost marshal general for Illinois—recalled the paper with undisguised bitterness. Like many of his colleagues charged with enforcing the draft, Oakes felt that ordinary citizens had been led astray by antiwar newspapermen. His postwar report did not mince words: "And chief among these instigators of insurrection and treason, the foul and damnable reservoir which supplied the lesser sewers with political filth, falsehood and treason, has been the 'Chicago Times'—a newspaper which would not have need to change its course an atom, if its place of publication had been Richmond or Charleston, instead of Chicago."[52] In his own recollections, Burnside wrote that soon after taking over his new post he realized that local "newspapers were full of treasonous expressions."[53] If silencing politicians like Vallandigham was high on his agenda, suppressing antiwar newspapers was not far behind.

In many ways the arrest of Vallandigham and the shutting down of the *Chicago Times* followed similar trajectories. In Burnside's eyes both Vallandigham and Storey were guilty of undermining morale among civilians and soldiers, thus encouraging desertion and damaging the war effort. Storey had filled the pages of his paper with unhappy letters from soldiers in the field and angry editorials attacking conscription, while maintaining a steady stream of hostile commentary on Blacks and emancipation. In the weeks after Burnside arrived at his Cincinnati headquarters, Storey's editorials peppered his audience with anti-administration rhetoric. After Vallandigham's arrest, the *Times* led the public outcry against the government's suppression of political speech. Finally, on June 1 Burnside ordered the *Times* shut down because of its "disloyal and incendiary statements."[54]

News of Burnside's actions reached Lincoln almost immediately. Much like Vallandigham's capture, the president understood this new measure in both constitutional and political terms. He directed Secretary of War Edwin Stanton to remind General Burnside that while military matters fell under the general's command, matters dealing with civil liberties and civilian arrests called for presidential consultation. But Stanton sent his message by mail rather than telegraph, so for a few days Burnside was unaware of Lincoln's displeasure, leaving him to his own devices.

In those few days Storey opted to defy the general and publish his newspaper, provoking the local military commander to occupy the *Times* offices and seize the latest issues. Once again Burnside's actions in the name of national military concerns led to angry local protests and civil disturbances, and Storey did his best to stoke those flames with special handbills and public appearances. A group of local businessmen and politicians met and appealed to Lincoln to end the suppression of the *Times* before the divided city suffered greater political tension. Meanwhile, Lincoln received a second telegram from Springfield, signed by a leading Illinois jurist and by William Herndon, the president's one-time law partner, urging him to rescind the order on constitutional grounds. In short, the weight of political and legal pressure on Lincoln seemed to match his initial thoughts on Burnside's actions. On the 4th Lincoln wrote to Stanton and instructed him to order Burnside to rescind the order. But soon the balance of political evidence began to shift, as leading Republicans—including the editor of the *Chicago Tribune*—spoke in favor of keeping the *Times* out of business. Lincoln, recognizing the complex local politics, sent a second message indicating that he was happy to let the suppression order sit, at least for awhile, until he had a clearer sense of how things would play out. But Burnside—in an ongoing illustration of the limitations of wartime communications—received Lincoln's second telegram after he had already removed the suspension, making it too late to shut the paper back down.[55]

The arrest of Vallandigham and the suppression of the *Chicago Times* both quickly became national stories, fitting a Democratic narrative that the Lincoln administration was guilty of unrestrained tyranny in the name of the war. Or, conversely, both episodes demonstrated that Lincoln was more concerned with practical politics than with constitutional purity. But however observers read the events, they were part of a vigorous national debate about free speech and civil liberties. Burnside and the federal officers in the Department of the Ohio might have been forgiven for viewing these events through a more local lens. After all, although Vallandigham was banished to the Confederacy, that status did not last long. He eventually found his way to Canada, where he ran for governor of Ohio from Windsor, Ontario. And there is no reason to conclude that the temporary suppression of the *Times* left an enduring impact on the paper, its editor, or the city of Chicago.

Francis Sherman Runs for Mayor of Chicago

All the national attention on the *Times* occurred as the city fought out its own partisan battles, with Mayor Francis Sherman at the heart of the conflicts. Sherman, a Chicago brickmaker by trade and the owner of one of the city's leading hotels, had a long history in local politics. He had served a term as the city's fifth mayor in the early 1840s and as alderman of the 1st Ward before that. In 1856 Sherman lost another bid for the mayor's office, running as a Democrat who opposed the extension of slavery. The city's first wartime mayor had been Republican Julian Rumsey, elected for a one-year term on April 1, 1861, only weeks before the fall of Fort Sumter. The following April, immediately after news of the disastrous Battle of Shiloh, Chicago once again selected Sherman as mayor, defeating the Republicans' nominee. The weather was poor on election day, and voter turnout was low. The city's Democrats profited from working-class support combined with concerns about slow progress on the battlefield and increasing talk of abolition. In that 1862 contest Sherman proved adept at appealing to Republican voters in addition to local Democrats. In November the ambitious Sherman ran for Congress as a prowar candidate on a "non-partisan ticket," losing a close election while earning a five-hundred-vote margin within the city limits.[56]

By early 1863 when Burnside took over operations in Cincinnati, politics in Chicago—three hundred miles to the northwest—had become increasingly polarized. The city's major newspapers, the *Times* and the *Tribune,* defined two ends of a bitter political spectrum. A historian of Chicago's wartime experience has called the *Times* "the official organ" of Mayor Sherman. Certainly editor Storey aligned himself enthusiastically with the Democratic mayor, even if Sherman tried to distance himself from Storey's more radical stances. Meanwhile, the *Tribune* supported the national Republican administration and missed no opportunity to lambast the mayor or the *Times.* Whatever the labels, Sherman enjoyed support from the *Times,* and the *Tribune* entertained its readers with long columns attacking Sherman as a Copperhead and worse.

When Burnside suppressed the *Times,* his actions took on national significance as part of a larger conversation about freedom of the press and civil liberties, but locally those steps triggered a partisan morality play. Joseph Medill, the popular co-publisher of the *Tribune,* initially endorsed the suppression of the opposition paper. Local Republicans expended their political capital calling on the Lincoln administration to keep the Democratic paper out of business. Meanwhile, Mayor Sherman chaired the bipartisan public meeting of businessmen and politicians that called on the president to rescind the suppression of the *Times* in the name of public harmony.

Burnside's actions at the *Times* occurred immediately following the city's 1863 mayoral election. Barely a week after the general issued his General Orders no. 38, Mayor Sherman stood for reelection against Union candidate Thomas Bryan. Despite Sherman's pursuit of a broader audience, the *Tribune* told its readers that the mayor was the treasonous representative of the Copperheads and little more than a "tool" of the *Times.* On election day the paper called on voters to treat the election like a major fight on the battlefield. "We don't say that every man who proposes to vote for Sherman is disloyal," the *Tribune* explained, "but we do say that all the disloyal voters in this city will vote for him."[57]

Sherman won reelection by the slimmest of margins. Published accounts reported that the Democrat defeated his Union Party rival by a mere 115 votes, 10,209 to 10,094.[58] The *Ottawa* (Illinois) *Free Trader* put the contest in a broader context, noting that Chicago had long been an abolitionist stronghold, electing Republicans to office, and that in the previous year Sherman had managed to win in a low-turnout election by appealing to Republicans as well as Democrats. But in this election the Republicans fought hard under the banner of the "Union" Party while growing more open in claiming their opponents were traitorous Copperheads. And yet Sherman managed to squeak by, while the Democratic Party swept most of the city's key offices and fourteen of the twenty-three seats on the council.[59]

Both the close election and the Democratic victory attracted modest national attention. The *New York Tribune* noted that a year earlier Sherman had won with a margin of about a thousand votes, but now—despite all the patronage advantages he enjoyed—the mayor's margin had dropped to barely over a hundred votes, suggesting that Chicago was moving back toward the Republicans. Closer to home, Chicago's *Tribune* persisted in calling the mayor a Copperhead and claimed that the Democratic victory was largely owing to the dishonesty of Chicago Democrats in power, who claimed to be loyal to the Union and in favor of the war effort when in fact they were "disloyal" enemies of the nation. These scoundrels had managed to fool the city's true Unionist Democrats while manipulating the large numbers of immigrants pouring into the city into believing Sherman would block conscription. "A bad day's work has been done," the *Tribune* declared. "The city has been dishonored." Later in the same issue the Medill paper, never at a loss for hyperbole, called it "a disgraceful and mortifying defeat, viewed in any light."[60]

On May 4 Mayor Sherman delivered his inaugural address before the largely Democratic Common Council. He devoted the bulk of his short address to the sort of municipal issues that occupied the minds of all midcentury mayors, before turning his attention to the state of national affairs. Sherman insisted that he hoped for a peaceful end of the war and a return of "national authority everywhere throughout the land," like any good patriotic American. In fact, he would not have raised these obvious sentiments "were it not for the persistent efforts made by my opponents, both before and since the election, to create the impression . . . that my election was to be considered as giving aid and comfort to the rebellion." Sherman declared that any suggestion that he or his followers favored the Confederacy was no more than partisan dishonesty. "I am a democrat," he declared, "devoted to the success of democratic principles, because those principles make the constitution the sole and unchangeable test of all political operations." This devotion to the Constitution meant that he and his supporters rejected the rebellion as a violation of the nation's laws. Sherman closed this discussion by affirming that

> while thus faithful in their duty to their government, the democracy are not the less faithful to themselves and their fellow-citizens. While they are lavish in all things needed or asked by the government to put down the rebellion against the laws and constitution, they are not the less opposed to, and by all lawful means will resist, the employment of the power and means placed by the people in the hands of the Executive to put down those engaged in rebellion, for the illegal and wanton oppression and destruction of the true and faithful people of the northern States who are not engaged in rebellion.

The *Chicago Tribune* quoted extensively from this section of Sherman's speech, accusing the mayor of libeling Abraham Lincoln with his words.[61] That night Burnside's men would arrest Clement Vallandigham at his home, and less than a month later federal troops would shut down the *Chicago Times*.

Mayor Sherman is an interesting figure for the historian in search of Civil War Democrats, and that 1863 mayoral election an illuminating moment. After all, the notorious *Chicago Times* embraced the mayor with enthusiasm, certainly inviting the conclusion that Sherman should be aligned with both the *Times* and the Vallandigham wing of the party. And the *Tribune,* one of the nation's most prominent Republican newspapers, pounded away at the mayor as a treasonous Copperhead, even while pointing out that the mayor and his closest followers sometimes cleverly disguised their true intentions beneath the rhetoric of prowar patriotism. Sherman managed to navigate his way through Chicago's stormy political waters, winning the support of War Democrats and moderate Republicans while also picking up votes from Chicago immigrants who opposed the war, or at least conscription. When it came to the crucial issues of the day, Sherman had long opposed the expansion of slavery while also objecting to radical abolitionism. He often sounded like a classic Douglas Democrat. And, as his 1863 address indicated, although he insisted that he supported the war, he joined his fellow Democrats in objecting to federal measures that he found unconstitutional.

As was so often the case, Sherman's political role became entangled with family ties in complicated—and in his case quite public—ways. Sherman, like many other northern Democrats tarred with the brush of treason, had a son who served in the Union Army. In 1863 Francis T. Sherman was a thirty-eight-year-old colonel in the 88th Illinois, known as the Board of Trade Regiment, recruited out of Chicago. A longtime Democrat, Colonel Sherman continued to claim his party affiliation in 1863, even while he grew increasingly outraged at people at home who seemed to be undermining the war effort. On February 18—as the mayor was preparing for his contentious reelection campaign—Colonel Sherman sent his father a long letter, attacking those partisan actors in Illinois who provided aid and comfort to the southern traitors. His letter did not explicitly criticize his father's politics, or even mention Democrats by name, but he made it clear that voters should throw such people out of office, and he promised that the men in his regiment—if they could vote—would do just that.[62] This was a private letter from son to father, but a few days earlier the younger Sherman had sent an even longer letter on the same themes to his friend Frederick Tuttle of the Chicago Mercantile Association. The Tuttle letter, written from Stones River, appeared on the front page of the *Chicago Tribune,* apparently with the colonel's approval. Here again Sherman lambasted the "damnable sentiments of party" and warned, "Let the disunionists of the North take heed."

Sherman's letter to Tuttle, like his missive to his father, did not explicitly name the Democratic Party or offer any unflattering assessments of his father the mayor. He merely attacked those people back home who were failing to support the war and in so doing were providing comfort to the enemy. But surely the colonel understood that sharing such a letter with the *Tribune* at that particular moment would embarrass his father and energize the mayor's opponents. In fact, the Republican newspaper ran a lengthy editorial about the letter, praising Sherman's patriotic words and noting that he was the mayor's son. "The Colonel himself was, and we suppose is, a Democrat," the Medill paper noted, leaving the reader to see the contrast between father and son.[63]

A few weeks later the colonel began a letter to his parents by noting, "It seems that my letter to Mr. Tuttle has made a great stir in the Chicago world. Well, let it." He explained that he wrote his letter "as a Democrat, [and] a loyal citizen," and he denied rumors that he had become an abolitionist. A week later, in a slightly more conciliatory letter to his father, Colonel Sherman once again noted the "considerable excitement" his letter had created in Chicago. But he pointed out that that he had not mentioned any party by name, and there was nothing in the letter that any loyal Democrat—including his father—would reject. In the next few weeks Colonel Sherman, who displayed an impressive passion for lengthy letters thick with political outrage, told his father that "I claim to be as good a Democrat as ever I was," but he could not accept the party's attacks on the commander in chief. With the mayoral election approaching, Sherman had hoped that his father would focus more on his "love of country" rather than partisan battling. After his father won reelection, Colonel Sherman sent a short note congratulating him while adding that he did not feel the same enthusiasm for some other Democratic victors. On May 7 he assured his father, "I am as good a Democrat as ever."[64]

The letters from Francis T. Sherman to his father bring together a host of themes that defined Democratic politics in the first months of 1863. First, they offer a distinctive version of the familiar story that the Civil War divided households, and the more specific story that geographic location often shaped such disputes. In the most remarkable instances, family members divided between support for the Union and the Confederacy, even enlisting in competing armies.[65] The differences between the Shermans were less dramatic, but clearly father and son were not on the same page about the war and politics. And even if their core opinions were more similar than different, we can only surmise that Mayor Sherman was not pleased to see his son's letter on the front page of the *Chicago Tribune.* This was a generational family dispute played out on the pages of Chicago's leading newspapers. As family drama, it made for a good story.

A second theme, which has far broader implications, is what the story of the Shermans, father and son, and the larger Chicago political climate in 1863, tells us about wartime Democrats locally and nationally. Mayor Sherman's 1863 inaugural address is central here. Having won a hotly contested election, and having endured endless assaults on his patriotism and his character, Sherman took the opportunity to assert his support for the Civil War and his overall patriotism, but as a committed Democrat Sherman refused to back off from his party's ideological critique of the administration and particularly its understanding of constitutional law. It was a partisan statement, but Sherman insisted that he spoke as a loyal citizen and not an enemy of his nation. Moreover, as a candidate in a city divided right down the middle, Sherman had to appeal to Democrats across a broad spectrum while also luring some Republican voters—perhaps drawn to his business focus—into the fold. The letters from Colonel Sherman add another layer to this discussion of what it meant to be a Democrat. Both Shermans called themselves Democrats, and they seemed to accept that they belonged to the same party. Certainly neither was pro-secession or in favor of the institution of slavery. Yet Colonel Sherman felt that the war required a level of loyalty to Lincoln and the administration that the mayor of Chicago did not accept. We might call Mayor Sherman a War Democrat, but his enemies made much of labeling him a Copperhead. In the meantime, despite his enthusiastic support for Lincoln and his clashes with his father, Colonel Sherman insisted that he too was a Democrat. This divide, played out in one Chicago family, portended the party's dilemma a year later.

Let us shift back to Kentucky, about 350 miles southeast of Chicago, and consider how the geographic and political and familial played out on different terrain.

What Is the Case of "Willie Waller"?

By early 1863, as Ambrose Burnside was taking over command of the Department of the Ohio, Henry and Sarah (Bell) Waller were busy relocating to Chicago. But even as they were leaving Kentucky behind, Burnside's General Orders no. 38 would soon turn their lives upside down.[66] Sometime in the first week of May, Colonel William H. Wadsworth, a Unionist Democratic member of the 37th Congress and the commander of the local Home Guards, got wind of a rebel plan to assemble recruits in and around Maysville, Kentucky. More than two dozen raw recruits intended to meet at the fairground east of town in the early hours of the morning of May 7. They would then head to another rendezvous spot in Mason County, where they would join ranks with more young men before heading off into the heart of the Confederacy. It was an audacious plan. Kentucky remained in the United States, even though many of its residents sided with the Confederacy. In military terms Maysville was unambiguously within the Union lines, and the local population was generally loyal to the United States. Even if these recruits were committed to the rebel cause and able to keep a secret, no doubt other locals knew of the rendezvous, and someone told Colonel Wadsworth.

With this intelligence in hand, Wadsworth set out with a half-dozen men, arriving at the fairgrounds around three in the morning. When the Home Guard men struck, the Confederate recruits scattered into the night. Most reports said that Wadsworth had encountered twenty-five to thirty men, but when the chaos settled down Wadsworth had a dozen men and boys in custody, along with a cache of rebel mail. The captured documents revealed that a coterie of Maysville citizens had cast their lot with the Confederacy. The arrests showed that some of Maysville's sons had done the same. One contemporary report identified William Waller as their commander. At the very least, Waller was one of the few who actively tried to resist when the Home Guard struck.

Henry and Bell Waller thought that their son had stumbled into a bad place through no real fault of his own. Others told a different story. Maysville's own *Dollar Weekly Bulletin* reported that Willie was a resident of Chicago who had been actively engaged in recruiting Confederate troops. In 1866, as part of his bid for a presidential pardon, Waller would affirm that at some point in 1863 he had journeyed from Kentucky to Virginia, where he had enlisted in the Confederacy. But the Wallers knew nothing about that, and he was content to let that impression remain. In the immediate aftermath of Willie Waller's arrest, he seemed—at least to his parents—to have been a wayward son who had blundered into an awkward situation.

Willie Waller's arrest began a long, complex, and ultimately sad tale. In terms of wartime politics, the story illustrates some key themes. Henry and Bell Waller were slaveholders but also staunch prowar Kentucky Democrats. They both came from established families with considerable connections. As events unfolded, it became a story about White elites and Kentucky kinship, confronting the realities of federal power and the impulse to suppress treason. With Willie imprisoned, husband and wife worked together to pull any strings they could imagine, soliciting advice on the intricacies of military justice as well as letters of support from a host of the state's luminaries, including John Crittenden, Joshua Bell, and Lincoln confidants Joshua and James Speed. Early on, local politics seemed to intervene in Willie's favor. Henry went to Maysville, where he acquired a stack of supporting letters from various locals who were willing to attest that Willie was a fine young fellow, even if they knew nothing of the actions that led to his arrest. Wadsworth, who had arrested the boys, initially promised to put in a good word with Burnside, but in the end the colonel failed to appear in court or put anything in writing. Wadsworth was up for reelection to Congress, and he apparently calculated that silence and a broken promise was politically expedient.

Henry and Bell's furious efforts to get Willie released before trial failed, so their son faced a general court-martial. The court concluded that he had indeed been a Confederate officer recruiting men behind Union lines (not an unreasonable assessment). The good news was that although the court—following official guidelines—ordered Waller's execution, they also recommended clemency, putting the ball back in Burnside's court. At this point the Wallers' extensive networking seemed to begin bearing fruit.

On June 8, with Willie's fate in Burnside's hands, Harrison Blanton—another of Henry's powerful Kentucky friends—wrote from Frankfort to Postmaster General Montgomery Blair about young Willie Waller. He reminded Blair—a powerful Kentucky conservative as well as a member of Lincoln's cabinet—that they had met, although they were hardly even acquaintances. Still, Blanton felt it appropriate to write because Willie was the grandson of William S. Waller, who had been a friend of Blair's famous father, Francis Preston Blair Sr. Blanton explained that Willie had been arrested and was facing capital punishment. Much like the letters from the Speed brothers before him, Blanton did not claim to know much at all about the case, but he opined that "so far as I can learn it appears to me that the sentence against him is one of more severity than is required to vindicate the rights and security of the Union." Despite knowing little of the case, Blanton was blunt: "May I therefore ask your aid and that of your Father to aid me to obtain from the President, a mitigation of young William S. Wallers sentence from Capital punishment to confinement in some military prison during the war[?]" And lest there be any confusion about the nature of this appeal, Blanton went on to praise Willie's father and his mother, *and* he added an extended discussion of both of his grandmothers, concluding that "two more superior women cannot be found in the Country." "Surely the President," upon contemplating the situation, would not rob these women of their grandson, "a mere child." This is how the author appealed to one of the most powerful men in the state of Kentucky, in the name of a twenty-five-year-old man who had been caught in U.S. territory recruiting troops for the enemy. Do not, he argued, disappoint these two "superior" Kentucky women.[67]

Blanton's letter apparently did the trick. On June 11 Blair passed the note on to the president of the United States. Blair explained that "the young man referred to is Kinsman of my brothers on his mothers side & of my fathers on his fathers side & as Mr Blanton says must be very young." For those reasons, Blair said, "I hope you will order his execution to be suspended till the case can be looked into." In short, Blair asked Lincoln to step in largely because Willie Waller's family tree was deeply intertwined with his own.[68]

On the 26th the president sent a one-sentence telegram to his commander of the Ohio District, asking, "What is the case of 'Willie Waller' at Maysville, Kentucky?" Burnside telegrammed the following day, seeking presidential permission to commute young Waller's sentence. Lincoln's response was concise: "Let the sentence be commuted as Gen. Burnside recommends. The name is Willie Waller. A. LINCOLN."[69] It is not entirely clear what had happened here. Did Lincoln really look into the events surrounding Willie Waller's arrest and conviction and come to this conclusion? Or, more likely, did he follow the advice offered by Blair, who was really following the request of Blanton? Meanwhile, Burnside seemed happy to follow the recommendation offered by the men of the general court-martial. Perhaps he was still smarting at the public reactions to his arrest of Vallandigham.

Waller and his comrades were sent to the Ohio prisoner of war camp on Johnson's Island, where they were to be held in irons during their incarceration. This prompted another extended process of appeals, where Waller's supporters sought to get the young man freed as part of a prisoner of war exchange. The problem was that although Waller was treated as a Confederate soldier, he had been arrested and charged as a spy. Although the Wallers managed to get more notes to the president's attention, it proved a tough argument. Federal officials responsible for prisoner exchanges were loath to treat Confederates charged with spying in Kentucky the same as soldiers captured on the field of battle. By the time they agreed to exchange Waller, the young man was physically damaged and would not survive another decade.[70] In the end, Willie Waller's fate had much more to do with where he was from, and who his parents knew, than anything he—or they—thought about the war or politics. Although in their particulars the stories were wildly different, Waller's story shared key components in common with Pierce Butler's drama half a continent away. Butler, like Waller, had run afoul of federal forces and the Union war effort and found himself incarcerated. In the ensuing private campaigns to get both men released, prominent Democrats in their personal orbits relied on powerful connections and individual endorsements to sway powerful figures to their side.[71] And perhaps the Wallers' wartime story should call to mind the far less dangerous, and equally public, disagreement between Francis Sherman and his son. In both cases, fathers and sons disagreed about what it meant to be a citizen—and a Democrat—in the midst of a civil war.

Lavender and Jonathan Hale

On April 12, 1864, Captain Matthew H. Jouett of the 3rd Kentucky Cavalry signed a form permitting a Mr. Lavender Hale—an African American man, aged twenty-three—to travel "North of the Ohio River into free territory." In a war thick with confusing, ideologically incoherent, and often disturbing moments of racial legislation, this short form illustrates some of the most strange. At this moment, almost precisely three years after the start of the Civil War and a year until its close, enslaved people in Kentucky were in a peculiar legal place. They lived in a state that remained in the Union, and thus the Emancipation Proclamation—which had been in effect for fifteen months—did not apply to them. On the other hand, if the military commission appointed by the Western District of Kentucky concluded that once enslaved men and women encountered in Kentucky had been the property of rebels, or had been captured by the Union Army, they could rule that those freed people were free to journey across the Ohio River into a world where slavery was illegal. (That is, the government could free people who had been enslaved by the enemy but not people who had been enslaved by loyal Kentuckians.) But this little form was probably not so simple. Since 1863 state officials had taken to (illegally) reenslaving fugitive slaves who had run from the Confederate states, thus raising the stakes for documentation for African Americans in the state. This form, signed by Captain Jouett, apparently declared that Lavender Hale was a legally enslaved man in the state of Kentucky who had permission to cross the Ohio River into free territory.[72]

It was a confusing moment in history, particularly for enslaved Americans. It is impossible to know what Lavender Hale might have thought about this form that bore his name, but it seems pretty clear that his status was more perplexing still.

Jonathan Davis Hale grew up in New Hampshire, where he was a doctor. At some point in the antebellum decades Jonathan and his new wife, Pheroba, moved to eastern Tennessee; Jonathan became the proprietor of a lumber mill. The transplanted New Englanders started a family there, and they embraced their adopted culture enough to acquire several slaves. When Tennessee voters turned out in 1860, they voted much like their Kentucky neighbors to the north. More than 47 percent—or a few percentage points more than Kentucky—of Tennessee voters opted for John Bell, the Constitutional Union Party candidate, who seemed to offer the greatest buffer against rising sectional conflict. Many of these Bell voters, particularly in East Tennessee, had been members of the Whig Party before the demise of the Whigs. Nearly 45 percent of Tennesseans selected John C. Breckinridge, the proslavery Democratic candidate. In contrast, only 7.7 percent selected northern Democrat Stephen Douglas, or fewer than half the share the Illinois Democrat won in Kentucky. Abraham Lincoln, the Republican nominee, was not even an option on Tennessee ballots, an omission that probably bothered few voters.

A few days before the Confederates fired on Fort Sumter, one of Hale's friends wrote from Texas, declaring that "God knows I abominate abolitionism as much as any man living—. . . but this haughty and dictatorial spirit manifested by the secession party in the South is no less destructive of liberty."[73] We cannot know, but it seems a fair conclusion that Hale would have seen political events similarly. He was a prosperous slaveholder in a border state, with no love of secession or of abolition. It seems likely that he—like Henry Waller—had been a Douglas Democrat in 1860. During the first wave of southern secession, Tennessee—rather like Kentucky—resisted talk of leaving the Union; some even adopted the rhetoric of armed neutrality. But Governor Isham G. Harris favored joining the Confederacy, and in early June the Breckinridge Democrat successfully—and rather unscrupulously—navigated his state to voting for secession.[74]

For the next four years Tennessee was the scene of military conflict between established armies as well as ongoing clashes between roaming bands of guerrillas and partisan groups. Although the state joined the Confederacy early in the war, a substantial portion of citizens, especially in eastern Tennessee, remained loyal Unionists.[75] Early in the conflict Hale and his family fled their home in eastern Tennessee, recognizing that it was a dangerous place for a vocal Unionist. Hale spent his war as a prowar Democrat.[76]

In his mid-forties when the war began, Jonathan Hale was not a likely candidate for the Union volunteers. Instead Hale, like a handful of other Tennessee men, offered his services to the Union Army in helping hunt down guerrillas in their midst.[77] His wartime efforts are associated with the effort to track down the notorious Champ Ferguson. Ferguson, a Kentucky farmer in his early forties when the war began, came from a large family of Unionists. By one account all nine of his brothers sided with the Union cause. But Champ became a vicious guerrilla, nominally fighting for the Confederate cause. In the words of historian Daniel Sutherland, "Ferguson held no political views, only grudges." By the time he was captured and executed shortly after the war, Ferguson was credited with fifty-three murders.[78] Hale took particular interest in tracking Ferguson down.

By late 1862 Jonathan and Pheroba Hale were in adjoining states. Pheroba was a refugee in Covington, Kentucky, just across the Ohio River from Cincinnati; Jonathan was with the Union Army, based near Gallatin, Tennessee.[79]

Near the close of 1862 an anxious Pheroba wrote from Covington asking, "aint you in rather a dangers place the papers report rebels all around you I wish this wretched war was at an end I am getting heartily tired of it." Jonathan tried to reassure her, reporting, "I don't go outside the lines I am in no great danger unless we have a battle."[80] In a few notes Jonathan suggested that perhaps "Lav" could travel to be with him. Pheroba had her doubts, finally replying that "I think if you want Lav with you it would be safest to come home to get him. They have got so very particular here about negroes passing that I think it would be doubtful whether he could get to you."[81] Despite Pheroba's suggestion that her husband venture to Kentucky to escort Lav back to Murfreesboro, a few weeks later Jonathan sent a complicated letter offering instructions on how both Lav and "Jonny" were to travel from Covington to Louisville, and then on to Nashville, and finally to meet him in Murfreesboro. They were to bring a Henry rifle and two hundred cartridges, and at each stage they were to be met by Union officers. According to Jonathan's directions, Jonny should accompany Lav in the journey and then return home to Covington by the easiest route.[82]

The letters between Pheroba and Jonathan Hale left many details unclear to later readers, at least as the correspondence unfolded. Eventually their letters revealed that Jonny (Jonathan Jr.) was their son and Lav (Lavender) was an enslaved young man and apparently Jonny's close friend. Jonny traveled with Lav to Murfreesboro to ensure the Black man's safe passage, before returning to his mother in Kentucky. After mid-February Jonathan's letters included news about Lav and messages from him directed at both "[n—rs] & white folks" in Covington. In one such note Jonathan reported that "he is well & says tell them there are secesh negroes here."[83] In other letters Jonathan described how Lav had been busy working on reading and writing. In June Jonathan wrote that Jonny was with him, so he must have made the return journey at some point, but poor health forced him back to Covington.[84] An August letter from Pheroba included a message for Lav: "Tell Lav we are glad to hear of his doing so well but not any surprised as he was always better than most negroes tell him they say here the contrabands are not very well satisfied."[85] A few days later Jonathan wrote that Lav was in nearby Shelbyville and had not seen him in several days, but "I feel like I can trust him anywhere." Jonathan added, "Tell the negroes Lav often talks about them & would be glad to come home though he gets on well with me."[86]

From 1863 into 1864 Jonathan Hale's letters to Pheroba were full of his efforts to aid the Union military in hunting down Confederate guerrillas. Both still shared a particular antipathy for, almost an obsession with, Champ Ferguson. Jonathan's decision to bring Lavender to be with him in Tennessee was not simply because he wanted a personal slave to attend to his daily needs. In fact, Lavender joined Jonathan tracking rebel guerrillas. Many decades after the war the elderly Jonathan Hale penned some fond, distinctly paternalistic memories about his young slave. As Hale recalled him, Lavender had been "a man as black as night, with a flat nose, large nostrils, and though not considered a 'scholarly person,' remembered places, faces, names, rout[e]s, and how to go along crooked routs in the darkest night."[87] Lav, like many African Americans in the border states, had served the Union Army as a skilled tracker.[88]

Hale was in his marrow a Unionist, and his war was a thoroughly national war. Although he did not don a uniform, he was clearly a valued member of the United States' military operations. But Hale's war was distinctly local and highly personal. During much of the Civil War, and for decades afterward, Hale's true enemies were those men and women who took up arms against the nation and against their own neighbors. Hale saw these adversaries not as legitimate enemy combatants but as thieves, murderers, and traitors. And he saw those neighbors who protected these villains as complicit in criminal acts against his family and property, as well as against the nation.[89]

If the Hales were prototypical northern Democrats before and during the war, these one-time New Englanders were also unapologetic slave owners. Lavender Hale's role in their lives says something about the many faces of wartime slavery. The researcher, plowing through the Hales' wartime correspondence with no prior sense of who the characters were, looked in vain for any clues about who "Jonny" and "Lav" were, until Pheroba wrote worrying about Lav traveling as a Black man. Prior to that letter it seemed that the boys were siblings and sons of the Hales. Once Lav was in Tennessee with Jonathan, his race was clear in many letters, and Hale's letters revealed remarkable paternalism about Lav and his relationships with African Americans (almost surely all enslaved) back in Covington. And in at least one letter, Jonathan reported that he had not seen Lav for several days, presumably because he was on assignment tracking guerrillas elsewhere.

These events bring us to the April 1864 form affirming that Lavender Hale had permission to travel across the Ohio River into free territory. Despite appearances, the form did not declare Lavender free, perhaps as a loyal guerrilla hunter. The form has a space for noting that the bearer "was a slave of ____."

But Jouett scratched out the word "was" and changed it to "is." Despite his unusual freedoms, Lavender Hale remained legally a slave of Jonathan Hale.

A month after Captain Jouett signed the form, Pheroba wrote to Jonathan from Covington, reporting that "Johnny & Lav are cutting some wood." In August 1864 Pheroba told Jonathan that she expected that both Jonny and Lav would be drafted in the next conscription. A month later Jonny and Lav were back with Jonathan, perhaps to avoid conscription in Kentucky. In November Pheroba told her husband that "the negroes are at work, I believe the[y] are perfectly satisfied & will stay at home all the negroes who influence them are gone & they get rather bad news from them over the river." And she added a note to Lav: "Tell Lav the [n—rs] were glad to hear from him they want to know how large he feels since he has gone out recruiting."[90]

These letters from Pheroba indicate that months after the official form was signed, Lav was laboring in Covington, Kentucky, and then a few months later he was back in Tennessee with Jonathan, perhaps again tracking guerrillas. In that final letter Pheroba revealed that Lav had been "out recruiting" for the Union Army. In February 1865, with the war nearly over and the 13th Amendment ending slavery passed by both houses of Congress, Pheroba wrote from Covington that the "negroes" were generally working away from home, and Lavender—who was now with her—seemed generally satisfied with things. In June, two months after Appomattox, Pheroba sent Jonathan an extraordinary letter from Covington: "Lav will I think raise quite a good crop he will try at any rate, is going to cutting clover this week. . . . I don't care to go to our old place particular but if you think best—why go of course—but the [n—rs] say they wont go South any more. I for one wont care except for Lav should like to have him with me but he too seems to dread going South." With the war over and emancipation on the horizon, Pheroba still seemed to presume that Lav would remain a part of their household. Two weeks later Pheroba again wrote about relocating, confident that "the negroes will all come" wherever they went.[91] But at this point Lavender Hale disappears from the record, until Jonathan wrote his retrospective essay fondly recalling Lav's work as a guerrilla hunter during the war.

Jonathan Hale, Pheroba Hale, and Lavender Hale provide valuable windows into the worlds of wartime Unionists and slaves in Kentucky and Tennessee. Jonathan Hale was a loyal Democrat, even if he was more devoted to hunting down guerrillas. Pheroba Hale lived the life of a politically involved refugee in Covington, Kentucky, and a clear partner to her husband in all things. Lavender Hale served the Union Army as a guerrilla hunter, probably working alongside the much older Jonathan Hale. But when Lav was not in Tennessee, tracking down his nation's enemies, he lived in Covington among other enslaved men and women. Pheroba and Jonathan Hale seemed remarkably paternalistic toward Lav, even by the standards of paternalistic slave owners. After the war they apparently honestly believed that Lav, and the other enslaved men and women in their household, would choose to remain with them after emancipation. Somewhere along the line it seems that Lavender Hale went his own way. But we cannot know what forces actually motivated his decisions. Lavender, rather like "Emily"—who had been a part of the Waller household—had lived in a border state with strong Unionist Democratic slaveholders who had kept them enslaved as a war raged. Both the Hales and the Wallers gave every indication that they believed they cared deeply about the futures of these two African Americans. The record is silent about what Emily and Lav thought.

Maria Lydig Daly and New York Society

Let us conclude our tour of northern Democrats back on the East Coast with New York diarist Maria Lydig Daly. Daly was the wealthy heir to a New York fortune and the wife of prominent Democratic jurist Charles Daly. The two lived a few blocks north of Washington Square and a few blocks east of Fifth Avenue, where they welcomed a steady stream of visitors. Daly, the author of one of the North's most prominent published wartime diaries, met a wide assortment of military, political, and artistic luminaries, including the wives of Abraham Lincoln, George McClellan, Ambrose Burnside, and Ulysses S. Grant. Both Dalys were loyal to the Democratic Party and to the Union, frequently expressing distaste for the Republican administration while recoiling at the excesses of the city's antiwar Democrats. Daly's journal entries add additional layers to the themes in this chapter in multiple ways.[92]

First, although Charles and Maria Daly had distinctly different public and private roles, Daly's diary suggests a couple who talked about politics and national events, particularly in the midst of the Civil War. Charles had been a major figure in the city's public life for quite some time, and on multiple occasions he spoke at Democratic gatherings, often with Maria in the audience. Maria shared the same political principles and privately urged Charles to consider higher elective office.

Second, although the Dalys thought about national political issues—objecting to the Lincoln administration on multiple fronts—Maria's diary demonstrates how those political sensibilities were refracted through distinctly local concerns.

The Democratic Party had done well in the 1862 elections, particularly in both New York City and in the state elections, but Maria found Horatio Seymour too openly anti-administration for her tastes, and she clearly despised the Copperhead forces that had come to dominate the city's machine politics. They were proud Democrats even when not on board with some in the local party.

Finally, as a diarist (as opposed to a correspondent), Daly offered valuable insights about women and political discussions. Daly repeatedly illustrated the key point that women discussed politics with each other and with men. On November 21, shortly after the elections, Daly visited with several local women and talked politics at length. At her first stop the friends exchanged thoughts about Seymour and his Republican opponent James Wadsworth. Later that day she visited another woman who declared that Fernando Wood was "a rogue, a thief, whom we were only too glad to get rid of as mayor." Both conversations took on partisan aspects, as Daly found herself defending some Democrats while disavowing others, and each woman seemed to give as good as she got. But in January Daly revealed her other side, recording her "amus[ement]" at "the political views of the ladies" she encountered in a round of visits. "Such vapid, inconsistent, violent expressions!" she exclaimed. Daly reported that General Wadsworth's daughter "declared herself a dreadful abolitionist" and Republican, "and in the same breath" announced that she "hated the blacks" and found Lincoln to be "a miserable creature" and his "stupidity and vulgarity unendurable."[93] New York's elite Democratic women, like their counterparts in Philadelphia, took their politics seriously and defended their perspectives ardently.

Although opinions varied wildly, by the middle of the Civil War women and men found themselves absorbed by talk of elections and military campaigns, whether they were in living rooms in Philadelphia or New York, or in farmhouses in Kentucky or Tennessee or Illinois, or writing to loved ones at the front. Politics was, indeed, everywhere.

The next chapter expands on these conversations about political discourse shaped by local circumstances, by considering the multitude of ways in which northerners who objected to the war or to war measures took their arguments to the streets.

5

Politics in the Streets

Throughout the Civil War, expressions of political dissent—and efforts to control or suppress that dissent—took a host of forms. Elected officials and leading Democrats delivered speeches, authored pamphlets and editorials, and presented party opinions along a wide ideological spectrum. Other Democrats and critics of the war turned to the streets and the countryside to articulate their dissent.

Much of the wartime political commentary that scholars dissect comes to us in the form of the published word: speeches, editorials, pamphlets, sermons, and public letters.[1] These printed sources, although the written opinions of only a minority of citizens, became the fodder for thousands of conversations in homes, saloons, fire stations, sewing circles, social clubs, and wherever people gathered. Civil War–era Americans, and especially northerners, read widely and routinely took part in literate discussions of contemporary events.[2] But public discourse on wartime matters was never restricted to the written word. In the immediate aftermath of the firing on Fort Sumter, angry mobs formed across the North (and South), demanding displays of loyalty at the homes of suspected secessionists and at the offices of pro-southern newspapers. Political tensions rose to the surface in various communities, provoking occasional violence that ranged from angry fistfights in saloons to skirmishes between government officials and quasi-organized resisters to full-scale riots. The key here is that political debate and dissent took many forms, and periodically tumbled into the streets or remote countryside.[3]

In the first two years of the war, northerners—and especially the anonymous and otherwise politically inarticulate—found ample opportunities to express dissent, aimed at individuals, organizations, and occasionally the federal government. Scholars who have studied civil liberties in the wartime North generally focus on arbitrary arrests and the government's suppression of newspapers and other publications. This is a sensible way to frame the question, but it is worth keeping in mind that in many communities the greater threat to free speech came at the hands of angry civilians, rather than instruments of the state. With the almost simultaneous emergence of federal conscription legislation and serious talk about emancipation and the arming of Black men, politics in the streets became increasingly part of public life as the war approached its third year.

It should come as no surprise that civilians grew particularly restive when the government passed conscription legislation in the name of the war effort. The United States had a long history of turning to able-bodied men for military service. The colonies all had a tradition of militia service, with men expected to turn out for militia training. In times of emergency the colonial governments could call out the local militia. During the American Revolution the Continental Congress called on the new states to draft men into uniform, with mixed results. During the War of 1812 federal efforts at instituting a national draft failed to win popular support.

Given the massive scale of the American Civil War, it was really only a matter of time before both the United States and the Confederacy adopted some form of conscription. The Confederacy—which had seceded from the Union amid cries of states' rights—turned to a national conscription first, passing a draft law about a year into the war. The United States was not far behind. From the standpoint of political dissent, we might say that the most virulent—and violent—objections to wartime conscription flowed from three sources: First, many critics questioned the constitutionality of conscription, particularly when mandated by the federal government and not state authorities. The notion of requiring independent citizens to march far from home to fight a distant foe struck many as an outrage against their individual and states' rights. Second, and obviously related, critics of conscription commonly rejected the cause—or at least aspects of the cause—that they were being called on to serve. Objections to the draft became intertwined with hostility to emancipation. Why, northerners asked, should my sons be required to fight to free slaves? Finally, as with most military conscriptions, ordinary citizens questioned how the drafts were implemented. Part of those objections revolved around the conviction that the draft laws had effectively produced "a rich man's war and a poor man's fight." Northern men of means could pay commutation fees in early drafts, and they could always hire willing substitutes in order to avoid going to war.[4] While the rules themselves sparked controversy, objections to the drafts often turned on rumors that the figures in charge of administering conscription laws were corrupt or politically biased. Rumors claimed that Democrats were not given a fair shake, and that immigrants often suffered from raw deals at the hands of government officials. In sum, a portion of northerners found conscription unconstitutional in the abstract and outrageous in practice.[5]

Port Washington Erupts

As we have seen, the Militia Act, passed by Congress in July 1862, laid the complicated groundwork for a state militia draft to fill quotas announced by the federal government, while also setting the stage for the use of African Americans as laborers and perhaps soldiers. Both the specter of conscription and the looming possibility of federal emancipation became important subjects for Democrats in the elections that year and popular themes for the party's most radical newspapers. Before long, disputes about conscription prompted a scattering of violence. Let us return to Wisconsin, and Edward G. Ryan's address to the state Democrats, as a window into the connections between public discourse and politics in the streets.

Two months after Wisconsin Democrats published Ryan's Address, the state's Republican governor Edward Salomon braced for the state militia draft. Among the many possible trouble spots was Ozaukee County, nestled on Lake Michigan, north of Milwaukee. A largely agricultural county, half of Ozaukee's fifteen thousand residents were born in either Luxembourg or Germany and generally aligned with the Democratic Party.[6] The county had been given a quota of 575 men, reflecting their inauspicious recruiting record. Governor Salomon, attempting to avoid partisan tensions, put the county's draft in the hands of a Democrat, William Pors. But the choice of Pors, an active Freemason, raised more tensions than it soothed, especially among local Luxembourgers. When draft day arrived on November 10, things quickly went off the rails in the county seat of Port Washington. Mobs of angry citizens, spurred on by ample alcohol, packed the streets. Contemporary accounts reported women holding up signs declaring "no Draft," while drunk men roamed the streets armed with rocks "and other missiles." When Commissioner Pors arrived at the courthouse, a large crowd of angry—and drunk—protestors awaited him. The crowd attacked Pors on the courthouse steps, forcing the bleeding commissioner to take refuge in the basement before supportive citizens slipped him out of town. Several hundred Luxembourgers—both men and women—continued to roam the streets, attacking Pors's home as well as the houses of various political enemies. Finally the governor ordered the 28th Wisconsin Volunteers into Port Washington to settle things down. The troops, under the direction of a newly appointed provost marshal, arrested 131 rioters, including—according to the *Milwaukee Daily Sentinel*—several "bitter and vindictive" women. Nearly all the arrested were from Luxembourg.[7]

Rather like Ryan's Address, the Port Washington draft riot was both quite distinctive to the place and in other senses emblematic of broader national political tensions. The riot was the state's largest violent episode in response to the state militia draft, although Wisconsin also saw rioting in Milwaukee and West Bend.[8] The appearance of angry citizens on the streets harkened back to April 1861, with rioters accosting targeted homes and individuals while milling about in public space. But of course those episodes involved people claiming to be patriots intimidating supposed secessionists. Port Washington's street displays targeted officers of the state, and the federal military stepped in to put down the disorder. In that sense late 1862 looked much more like the sort of politics in the streets the following summer. Over the next several years the northern states would witness a variety of violent episodes triggered by conscription but enhanced by hostility to emancipation and the general progress of the war. Each would have its own local character even while reflecting national debates.

District Provost Marshals Report on Conscription Violence

Events in 1863 combined to raise public tensions, generating many more occasions of political disputes spilling out into public disorder. Lincoln's Emancipation Proclamation provoked hostile responses in many quarters. For some, the chief concern was constitutional and strategic: should the Union's military be actively freeing enslaved people in the Confederate states? Others worried about the broader implications of a war of emancipation destabilizing race relations in the North. And loyal Unionists in the slave-owning border states recognized that the freeing of their own slaves might not be far behind.

That spring, political tensions threatened to explode in the northern states after the United States passed the federal Enrollment Act on March 3, 1863. This legislation replaced the more limited state militia drafts of the previous year. Over the next two years the Union would hold four major drafts, administered by the provost marshal general's office. The specific rules changed over time, but the key characteristics remained consistent. The federal government would announce a draft day and the number of new recruits needed. That number would be apportioned by population to the congressional districts in each state. In preparation for the draft, enrollment officers—working with the provost marshals—would assemble lists of eligible men. Meanwhile, civilians in each community would work to recruit volunteers, who would be counted against the upcoming draft quota. On draft day, each district held its own public drawing, with the goal of assembling enough eligible men to meet the remaining quota. Drafted men were then subject to inspection, assessing whether they should be excused from service for medical disabilities or other characteristics. In the first 1863 draft, men who were "held to service" had the option of paying a three-hundred-dollar commutation fee, rather than entering the military. The U.S. government removed this option (except for conscientious objectors) after the first draft, but in each draft men who were held to service could hire a substitute to serve in their place.[9]

The Enrollment Act was not necessarily intended to fill the ranks with draftees or substitutes. The goal was to sign up new recruits. By allowing time between the announced conscription and the actual days of the drawings, the law gave each community the opportunity to fill quotas and avoid a draft. And by dividing the draft quotas by congressional districts (larger cities would have multiple drafts in different districts), the system shifted the focus toward local organizing, bounty fundraising, and recruiting. The numbers for the four federal drafts tell the tale. The four call-ups yielded 46,000 conscripts who ended up serving in uniform and another 118,000 men who furnished substitutes. The Enrollment Act and the provost marshal general's office proved very successful at filling the ranks, but the conscripts and substitutes amounted to fewer than 13 percent of the men who entered the Union Army.

The rules allowing for the hiring of substitutes and the initial paying of commutation fees smacked of bias. Wealthy draftees had an easy path to avoid service, and many took advantage of those options. But if judged as an entire system, the North's process of recruiting volunteers and conscripting draftees proved surprisingly equitable. When compared with occupational distributions in the federal census, the men in the Union Army were remarkably representative of the overall population. This is largely because the vast majority of Union volunteers were neither conscripts nor substitutes. It is probably also the case that the poor young man who had been drafted had as many options to avoid service—by "failing to report" to the examiners or by running off once called to service—as the wealthier man. In fact, age, much more so than class, determined who would end up in uniform.[10]

The North's federal drafts fell under the auspices of Provost Marshal General James B. Fry, who was charged with running a huge federal bureaucracy.

Despite many complaints about the Enrollment Act itself, and about its implementation in various localities, Fry—a Democrat—earned generally high marks from northern observers. In August 1863 John Hay, Lincoln's personal secretary, shared his thoughts with Irish-born humorist Charles Graham Halpine, a month after New York City had erupted in draft riots. Despite concerns about "a partisan enrollment," Hay assured Halpine that "neither the President nor Stanton interfere with the details of that business," and "Fry is as sound a Democrat . . . & certainly would favor no frauds against his own side. He is a splendid fellow, full of energy and will," Hay added, "but no Republican by any possibility."[11] Once again, like Secretary of War Edwin M. Stanton and Judge Advocate General Joseph Holt, Lincoln had turned to a Democrat for an important administrative position.

Shortly after the end of the Civil War, Fry instructed his district provost marshals to prepare reports on their wartime experiences, and their recommendations for the future, should the nation face a similar challenge. The request came as a series of empirical questions, inviting each district provost marshal to summarize the core numbers in his district, as well as general challenges they faced trying to do their jobs. Each state provost marshal submitted an overview for the state, and the individual district provost marshals prepared detailed handwritten reports. These postwar reports, which amount to roughly five thousand handwritten pages, are a valuable window into wartime draft resistance as understood by federal military bureaucrats doing their jobs at the local level.[12]

The state acting provost marshals general, and their district provost marshals, varied tremendously on what they had to say and the number of words they took to say it. Their reports indicate that the drafts went fairly smoothly in many districts, usually with some local deserters and occasional pockets of resistance. Examined collectively, they tell us quite a bit about popular hostility to the draft system, and about how federal officials explained the resistance they met. Although the federal draft unfolded in four separate stanzas, the postwar reports rarely followed that narrative. Instead, they considered the chronology from enrollment to drafting to examination to being held to service, with the four drafts commonly becoming melded into a single narrative.

The reports offer evidence on various big questions about the Civil War draft. The district provost marshals had much to say about the allocation of resources and various policy questions, speaking directly to Fry's concerns for the future should the nation ever return to conscription. But they also offer the marshals' thoughts on the motivations and behavior of local citizens who resisted their efforts, at least as those actions were understood by state and local provost marshals. Three themes are of particular interest: Why did civilians resist the draft? Did they resist with the assistance of organized societies? And what unfolded when resistance turned to violence? (Who was involved? What happened? How did the federal forces respond?) The individual reports tell very specific tales, often unique to a particular town or corner of a county. The reports make one thing quite clear: although dissent, and particularly organized violence, appeared in some regions more than others, aggressive dissent happened across the nation. The marshals told their tales in different ways, with varying levels of detail, but one observation is nearly universal: most provost marshals could point to specific trouble spots in their districts, even when their overall report celebrated calm and efficiency.[13]

These reports tell us something about political opinion and speech, enacted through public disorder, but they are not the equivalent of the letters and diaries in the previous chapter. In the case of the provost marshal reports or later printed accounts of draft riots, we do not have the words selected by the political participants. Instead, we have brief summaries of their actions, and occasionally their words, as presented by federal officials or reporters. Those reports are valuable in telling us what they believe happened and where events occurred. And the marshals' reports sometimes offer thoughts about what they believed motivated resistance. But unlike those correspondents whose letters survive in some archive, we learn of the actions and opinions of these civilians only as filtered through the eyes of men with their own memories and agendas.[14]

In many cases the district provost marshals blamed particular immigrant groups as the source of antidraft protests, reflecting some combination of ethnic tensions and class antagonism. The report for Ohio's 18th District, which included Cleveland, noted that violent resistance to draft enrollers "generally occurred in localities with a large Irish population."[15] The marshal for St. Paul, Minnesota, reported that "the records show a large percent of deserters to be Irish, German (low) and Canadian French, and nearly all of them of the Roman Catholic faith."[16] The report for Pittsburgh claimed that Irish conscripts were particularly likely to present false birth certificates.[17] Captain J. H. Bean's report on the 1st District of Wisconsin, including Milwaukee, offered a detailed tour of the city's ethnic wards. Draft enrollers faced resistance in the 2nd, 6th, and 9th Wards from largely German populations, while the 3rd Ward was full of violent Irish immigrants, and other wards also had large numbers of foreigners who were "bitterly hostile to the Government in its efforts to prosecute the war."[18] The reports for Wisconsin's 4th and 5th Districts—which witnessed disorder in

1862—also noted the prominent role of "foreigners" in resisting the draft.[19] In Yonkers, New York, with its substantial immigrant population, the provost marshal reached out to a local Catholic priest for assistance in enrolling names, but with no success. In the end he reported that his office had enjoyed general success, except for a "large floating population, composed mostly of foreigners."[20]

Various marshals reported resistance from workers clustering in particular occupations. In the mining districts of eastern Pennsylvania, organized violence against draft enrollers became a persistent problem, with the provost marshals generally pointing their fingers at Irish miners. The marshal for the 11th District wrote that "among the foreign population in the mining districts, an enrolling officer's life was in greater danger than in the front of battle."[21] In the western counties of the state, marshals reported the same concerns. The marshal for Blair County, in the 17th District, insisted that most locals were "law abiding" citizens, but that the local coal and ore miners were "foreigners of every nationality" who demonstrated little interest in "the genius of our institutions and hostile to any measure having for its object their improvement and perpetuation." That is, they did not wish to be drafted.[22] The marshal for Harrisburg, Pennsylvania, expressed particular disgust with bounty brokers and substitutes, adding that "most of them were foreigners of the vagabond class."[23]

The provost marshals in California and surrounding western districts pointed out that miners were an independent lot and particularly resistant to government interference.[24] On the other side of the country, the marshal for Vermont's 1st District claimed difficulties with Irish workers from the quarries in West Rutland. The men tended to give false addresses, their employers offered no assistance, and those workers who were drafted were liable to run off.[25] In Story City, Iowa, Irish railroad workers threatened draft enrollers with violence when they came seeking names. But the district provost marshal would have none of their antics, sending in an armed posse that made twenty-two arrests and successfully got their list of names.[26]

Quite a few of the reports that blamed immigrant workers for resisting the draft added harsh comments about the angry immigrant women they encountered. In July 1863 Portsmouth, New Hampshire, witnessed a series of episodes as working-class residents congregated in the streets to resist the draft, tossing rocks and threatening greater violence. As the district provost marshal recounted the episode, the military finally threatened to fire on the crowd, which led most of the rioters to disperse, "leaving only small knots of drunken sailors and Irish men and women" in the streets.[27] The marshal for Ohio's 4th District was pleased to report that the region had survived the war with "no difficulties

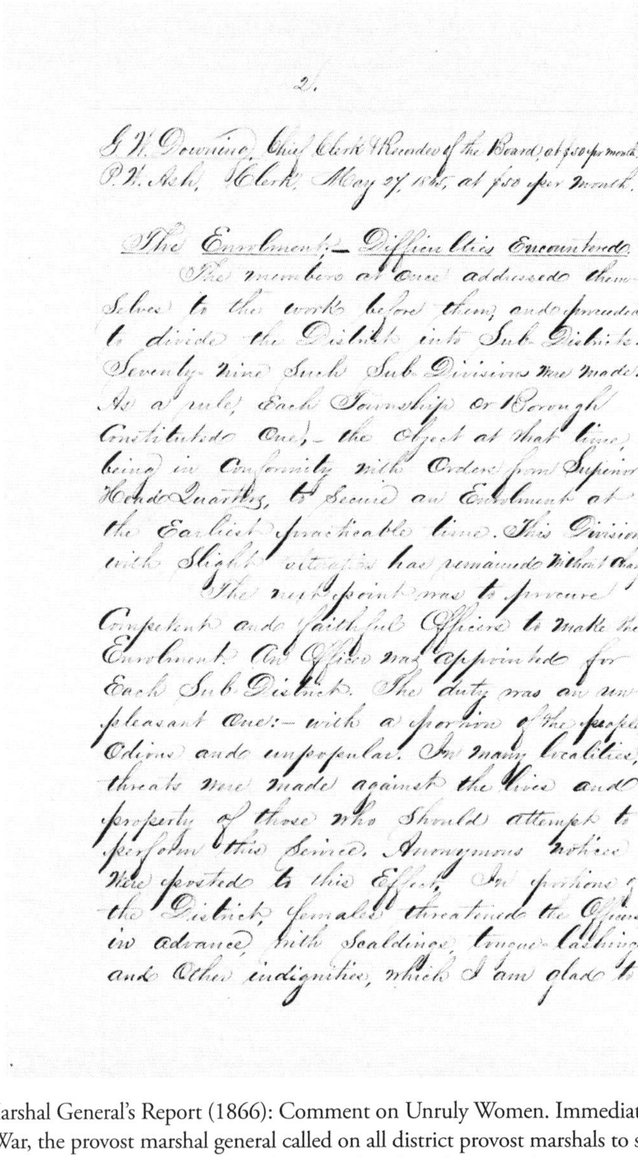

2.

G. W. Downing, Chief Clerk & Recorder of the Board, at $50 per month.
P. W. Ash, Clerk, May 27, 1865, at $50 per month.

The Enrolment.— Difficulties Encountered.

The members at once addressed themselves to the work before them, and proceeded to divide the District into Sub Districts. Seventy-nine such Sub Divisions were made. As a rule, Each Township or Borough Constituted One,— the Object at that time being in Conformity with Orders from Superior Head Quarters, to Secure an Enrolment at the Earliest practicable time. This Division with Slight alterations has remained without change.

The next point was to procure Competent and faithful Officers to make the Enrolment. An Officer was appointed for Each Sub District. The duty was an unpleasant One:— with a portion of the people Odious and unpopular. In many localities, threats were made against the lives and property of those who should attempt to perform this Service. Anonymous notices were posted to this Effect. In portions of the District, females threatened the Officers in advance, with Scoldings, tongue-lashings and Other indignities, which I am glad to

Provost Marshal General's Report (1866): Comment on Unruly Women. Immediately after the Civil War, the provost marshal general called on all district provost marshals to submit summaries of how wartime conscription functioned in their districts. This is a page from the report by Captain E. L. Christman, the provost marshal for Pennsylvania's 7th District. The text includes this passage about women engaging in angry political speech: "In many localities, threats were made against the lives and property of those who should attempt to perform this service. Anonymous notices were posted to this effect. In portions of the District, females threatened the officers, in advance, with scoldings, tongue lashings, and other indignities, which I am glad to say, were not generally carried out." (National Archives) encountered except opprobrious epithets, which were plenty in some portions of the District, especially from the ladies."[28] In West Chester, Pennsylvania, the general hostility to the draft made it a challenge to even line up willing draft enrollers. As the district marshal reported, "In portions of the District, females threatened the officers, in advance, with scoldings, tongue lashings, and other indignities, which I am glad to say, were not generally carried out."[29] And, as was repeatedly the case, the Wisconsin marshals submitted some of the most colorful accounts. In Milwaukee's 3rd Ward, known for angry Irish immigrants, the marshal reported that "the officers were set upon and beaten by infuriated house-wives."[30] And in several Milwaukee districts, enrollers faced serious violence, "principally from the Irish and German women, who pelted them with stones &c, and endeavored to scald them."[31] Although conscription endangered men, and most of the violent resistance fell to those men who were subject to the draft, the reports suggest that working-class women routinely engaged in aggressive political discourse in the North's city streets.

The 1866 reports frequently noted the significant roles of immigrants and workers (and working-class women) in resisting the draft enrollment and the drafts themselves, and in developing a range of strategies to encourage desertion and avoid the provost marshals. And the reports reflect a larger truth about the broader tendency of immigrant groups—and particularly Catholic immigrants—to resist both emancipation and conscription. But that having been said, such pointed remarks about immigrants only appeared in a minority of the reports. No doubt most northerners who objected to conscription, including those who attacked draft enrollers or ran when their names were called, were native-born Americans. It is also worth keeping in mind that although recently arrived immigrants were welcome to enlist or to sign on as substitutes, aliens—which at the outbreak of the war included immigrants who had been in the country for five years or fewer—were exempt from the draft.[32] Still, the tales of resisting immigrants tell a particular story about political resistance.

Even while the reports noted the resistance the marshals faced from newcomers, the reports singling out immigrant groups did not necessarily indulge in the worst ethnic stereotypes. The district provost marshals did not appear to blame draft resistance on inherent traits associated with ethnicity or religion. That is, the reports from these federal employees did not criticize the immigrant opposition as a failure of patriotism or an absence of bravery or martial spirit. They did see these newcomers as particularly susceptible to political manipulation. The district provost marshals, and their statewide superiors, consistently blamed grassroots draft resistance on working-class ignorance and the nefarious actions of editors and political leaders who conned them into believing that the draft was corrupt and enforced unequally. The marshals' implied argument was that American citizenship required a level of critical thought, and absent that political engagement naïve newcomers were potential pawns of cynical politicians. In these narratives, newspaper editors and disloyal politicians became the true villains. The examples are numerous.

In Maine's 4th District the provost marshal singled out Bangor as a center of disloyal activity and placed much of the blame on the *Bangor Democrat,* "an organ as base as it has been energetic." In a complex indictment of political developments, the local provost marshal explained that "the leaders of this opposition, many of whom had heretofore occupied honorable and influential position in the state, by means of this base and unscrupulous press, by private and public meetings, and with the aid of the foreign population, whom they universally control, by steady and persistent opposition sought to neutralize the effects of the Government for the suppression of the rebellion." That is, local Democratic leaders, spurred on by the disloyal press and supported by local immigrants, threatened the government.[33] To the south, the marshal in Portsmouth, New Hampshire, a city that had witnessed substantial violence involving local immigrants, concluded, "This attitude of hostility to the government was in a great degree instigated and encouraged by the treasonable utterances of prominent public men, and newspapers published within the District."[34]

In Pennsylvania's 11th District, where immigrants in the mining districts presented a constant threat to federal officers, the district provost marshal singled out the editor of Wayne County's *Hawley Free Press* as an ex-deserter and energetic voice of disloyalty.[35] The state's 19th District, which included Clearfield County, was the largest district in Pennsylvania and the site of some of the war's most notorious resistance. Many forces contributed to the local conflicts, but the marshal underscored the role of the "disloyal and traitorous press" in generated divisions.[36] Bucks County observers pointed their fingers at local politicians and the disloyal press for stirring up anti-administration sentiment.[37] The marshal in Elizabeth, New Jersey, came to the same conclusions. Grassroots objection to the draft, the report concluded, "arose mainly from the opposition to the 'Conscription' Act by the disloyal portion of the Press, leading the poor, and ignorant portion of the community to suppose that only they would suffer by the enforcement of the laws."[38]

In the Midwest, where draft resistance cropped up with disturbing regularity, the district marshal in Indiana's 10th District blamed "the opposition press" for teaching civilians to resist the draft, while his colleague in Lafayette, Indiana, reported that "the people were urged by the disloyal portion of the press . . . to resist the enrollment of this 'Tyrannical Administration.'"[39] In Milwaukee, the provost marshal attacked the German newspaper *Der Milwaukee See-Bote,* which "manifested the most intense disloyalty."[40] As we have seen, Chicago's notorious Copperhead newspaper the *Chicago Times* drew substantial attention from the state's provost marshal general, Brigadier General James Oakes, who wrote bitterly about the *Times* as "the foul and damnable reservoir which supplied the lesser sewers with political filth, falsehood and treason."[41]

The district marshals also blamed inflammatory newspapers and treasonous politicians for misleading poorly educated workers, and especially recent immigrants, into distrusting their government and undermining the efforts of the provost marshals' office to assemble enrollment lists and enforce the draft. Many of the reports seemed to suggest that the daily efforts of the provost marshals were inhibited by the failure of information, with ill-educated men and women lacking the facts to behave like informed citizens. They were, instead, being manipulated by political agitators with their own destructive goals. Sometimes the troublemakers were familiar instigators, but often the reports expressed disappointment at respected men leading the political resistance. As the district marshal in Hartford, Connecticut, described things, the July 1863 draft faced resistance, "not only by men of no character and position in this community, but by more men prominent politically, socially and officially, in various parts of the district."[42] Or, as the district marshal for the 2nd District in Illinois explained, "It is believed much of the resistance to the enrollment, and many of the arrests therefor except perhaps in internally disloyal districts might have been avoided by the proper explanations to the masses, or their leaders of the time object, extent, scope, and purpose of the enrollment." In short, many problems were owing to bad information, rather than poor character or disloyal intent.[43]

Of course this widely agreed upon narrative, shared by district provost marshals across the nation, must be read with care. Essentially what the reports commonly said was that opposition political leaders—editors, journalists, politicians—convinced the rank and file that the draft was both improper as a policy measure and dishonest in its implementation. The provost marshals disagreed with these assessments and blamed their political opponents, who came from various corners of the Democratic Party, for making their jobs more difficult and more dangerous. After all, if members of the opposition elite convinced citizens and voters that they should oppose the draft, they were not necessarily engaged in dishonest or nefarious behavior, unless they also encouraged active draft avoidance. The most vocal critics might have been guilty of treason in stirring up anti-conscription sentiments, particularly when those people who became stirred up turned to violence. But in most cases the local story was really that some northern civilians concluded that the draft was unfair and perhaps that they did not wish to go to war.

The district reports reveal a wealth of isolated moments where resistance of one sort or another turned to violence, producing casualties, both marshals and civilians. In Iowa the district provost marshal for the 1st District reported that his chief problem was convincing local Democrats that the drafting was done without partisan bias. But elsewhere in the state resistance to the draft grew violent. In Iowa's 5th District F. R. Van Eaton was killed trying to track down local guerrillas who had attracted deserters. Seventy-five deserters were arrested in the 3rd District; one deserter was shot and killed. The 4th District saw extensive antidraft activity, including reported secret societies, resulting in at least three deaths.[44]

Immediately to the east, Illinois and Indiana harbored pro-Confederate pockets, especially in those counties bordering the Ohio River. The 9th District in Illinois witnessed repeated efforts at organized draft resistance, including one occasion when two officers were shot delivering draft notices, and another episode when a provost marshal was killed attempting to arrest a draft resister.[45] In the southern tip of Illinois the provost marshals of the 12th District faced a wealth of challenges, particularly with citizens "who freely owned that their sympathies were with the rebels," and who thus took every opportunity to resist conscription or desert when called. In July 1863 a large body of detached cavalry arrested "about four hundred deserters" in Williamson County, and they faced another 130 men—"deserters and rebels"—who had "thrown up light fortifications" and seemed prepared to fight until they saw the size of the federal force. The following month draft resisters shot and killed Special Agent John P. Law in Union County just to the southwest. That December two more enrolling officers were killed in the county.[46]

Marshals in the southern counties of Indiana faced similar areas of organized resistance. In the 2nd District, just across the Ohio River from Louisville, Kentucky, some prominent citizens openly sympathized with the rebels and "were opposed to all conscription or enforced military service." In September 1864 an estimated five hundred deserters made camp in the southern part of the district, assisted by these local Confederate supporters. Much like in southern Illinois, the deserters dispersed when the Union military arrived, although the provost marshal reported that they arrested forty-one leaders.[47] Slightly to the east, the marshal in Indiana's 4th District wrote that disloyal civilians had killed two draft enrollers.[48] In July 1864 federal troops clashed with draft resisters calling themselves the "Butternuts of Sullivan County," resulting in the death of one Indiana protestor.

In the eastern states mobs responded to the draft in various cities, most notably in New York City, but also in Portsmouth, New Hampshire; several counties in Pennsylvania; and—in a more limited way—Boston. District provost marshals in these eastern states told a mixed story, with some districts holding enrollments and drafts with little or no problems, and other areas witnessing pretty serious conflicts, especially where marshals clashed with immigrant workers. Occasionally these episodes led to casualties. In Maine's 5th District Special Agent David Edwards was shot in the head and killed in October 1864, as he and a partner attempted to arrest two brothers who had resisted the draft.[49] Pennsylvania's notorious 11th District saw the deaths of several men assisting provost marshals, as well as the shooting of at least one draft resister by a district marshal. In Banks Township the district marshal reported an episode where an unnamed man was "murdered by some Irishmen living in the place."[50] Pennsylvania's Clearfield County saw some of the state's most organized draft resistance, and the most destructive violence, including the killing of a Colonel Butler who was attempting to arrest deserters.[51] Sometimes violence came in the form of planned vengeance, rather than spontaneous explosions. In Baltimore there were at least two cases where angry citizens set the property of enrolling officers on fire.[52]

The postwar district provost marshal reports provide a valuable, if impressionistic, window into the breadth of resistance to the enrollment and the four federal drafts as understood by the men charged with administering the drafts. Each rock thrown at an enroller, or conscript who ran off to join a camp of deserters, or woman who accosted a provost marshal on a city street, was a form of political dissent. Some—like the draft resisters in the border states or the southern portions of Indiana and Illinois—were openly rebels who found themselves on the wrong side of a dividing line between nations. Other northerners, including the editors and politicians who called on working-class draftees to resist, were politically opposed to some portion of the administration's policies. Perhaps they only resisted conscription, either in concept or in execution, or perhaps they had a broader objection to emancipation, the challenges to civil liberties, or the general execution of the war. Certainly most of these protestors were Democrats, either by affiliation or inclination, but we cannot always know what portion were antiwar in a broader sense as opposed to objecting to particular policies, such as conscription. For the rank and file who crowded streets attacking enrollers, or who joined impromptu camps of deserters and draft resisters, the stories are no doubt diverse, but one theme emerges from the district reports: the provost marshals consistently concluded that working-class protestors, and especially immigrants who were new to the country, were susceptible to control by Democratic leaders.

Some wartime dissent, particularly in response to the four federal drafts, emerged spontaneously in response to aggressive draft enrollers and unfavorable draft days, and in other occasions popular dissent followed angry public political discourse, in the form of speeches, editorials, and agitated talk on street corners or local taverns. Some stories involved individuals or small groups thrown together by the demands of war. In many communities dozens or even hundreds of deserters and draft evaders found common cause and shared sanctuary, often clashing with local militia or federal troops, or disappearing into the night when armed forces came hunting for them. It is fair to assume that most of these dissenters were ideologically aligned with the Democratic Party, although we cannot tell if they voted or attended rallies and the like.

Race and Riots

The 1866 reports demonstrate that desertion and violent resistance occurred throughout the North. In some communities fairly large groups of deserters gathered, challenging the federal forces to come and get them. In districts closest to the border states, citizens were not merely opposed to conscription but openly in support of the Confederacy. Even where the district provost marshals reported general successes they still contended with active resistance to both enrollment and conscription. Deserters and bounty jumpers faced arrest, organized resistance provoked violent responses, and across the home front blood was shed with some regularity.

In this four-year narrative of divisive "politics in the streets," the New York City draft riots stand out for the massive loss of life and property damage that rocked Gotham in the second week of July 1863. Draft day arrived in New York on July 11, and almost immediately the city erupted in violence. Within three days the city had experienced some of the worst and most destructive urban rioting in American history. But the story begins long before the 11th.[53]

Several contexts are worth noting. First, when the war began, New York's firemen enlisted in numbers and served valiantly in the ranks of the Union Army. They were a politically powerful group and not always satisfied by how the Union Army treated them. More importantly, the new Conscription Act removed the draft exemption previously offered to volunteer firemen. They were not pleased. Furthermore, by 1860 roughly 200,000 Irish men and women lived in New York, or roughly a quarter of the city's total population.[54] By 1863 many had served in uniform (including large numbers in various fire company regiments). As a group Irish immigrants—generally aligned with the city's Democratic machine—opposed emancipation, partly because of working-class hostility to labor competition from free Blacks and partly because of a broader antipathy to emancipation as public policy. In addition, New York's influential Irish Catholic Bishop John Hughes spoke in favor of conscription, but he had long opposed including emancipation as a war aim. Moreover, in June roughly three thousand dock workers—largely Irish men—went on strike, only to see African Americans hired to replace them. These events left Irish laborers grumbling about the economic threats posed by Black workers and the further potential threat implied by emancipation. And finally, as New York prepared for a citywide draft, Robert E. Lee and the Army of Northern Virginia invaded the North. The Battle of Gettysburg concluded on July 3, but the invasion left New York stripped of much of its available military manpower.[55]

Prior to draft day, several hundred enrollers had been assigned to the city, and in the weeks leading up to the draft they reported considerable resistance and multiple arrests. One newspaper story claimed that enrollment officers making their rounds were attacked by a woman wielding "an immense slingshot."[56] Meanwhile, as in many other parts of the country, Democratic politicians and journalists questioned the legality of the draft and the fairness of its implementation. In a July 4 oration immediately following the Battle of Gettysburg, Democratic governor Horatio Seymour offered the ominous warning that "the bloody and treasonable and revolutionary doctrine of public necessity can be proclaimed by a mob as well as by Government."[57] On draft day Benjamin Wood used the pages of his New York *Daily News* to remind readers that "the fact that the Conscription virtually exempts the rich and fastens its iron hand upon the poor alone, is sufficient demonstration of its injustice."[58] In their 1866 reports, the provost marshal for the Southern Division of New York and several district provost marshals noted the particular challenges they faced when political leaders and journalists contributed to a popular perception that the city's draft quotas were unfair.[59]

The actual drafting began in New York on Saturday, July 11. As chance would have it, the name of the captain of the Black Joke Fire Company was among the first to be drawn, prompting angry suspicions that festered throughout Sunday, when the draft was suspended but drinking continued. On the 13th a mob attacked the 9th District draft office, apparently assisted by a cart hauled by men of the Black Joke Fire Company. Over the next several days the riot swelled and the mob's agenda evolved. Homes of prominent politicians and buildings associated with the government became obvious targets. Police and military officers in the streets faced bloody beatings; some died. But while uniformed White men remained victims of violence, before long the rioters took to indiscriminate attacks on African American citizens and institutions, including the Colored Orphan's Asylum on 5th Avenue. Many African Americans fled the city, but an unknown number were beaten to death or hung from trees or lampposts. By the third day hundreds of special policemen had been sworn in and had started regaining control of the streets. The following day regiments from Gettysburg began to arrive and the worst of the violence was over. By this point well over hundred citizens, mostly Irish rioters, were dead; property owners would claim $2.5 million in lost property, and the nation looked on in horror.[60]

What explains this enormous carnage? Although there were many other violent episodes connected to northern conscription, no other riot in the northern states comes close to what New York experienced in July 1863. As with most large events like this, several variables conspired to produce the riot while sparing other divided cities similar catastrophes. One explanation is simply a matter of timing. It is much easier to limit urban disorder before it gets up a head of steam, rather than attempt to impose order on mobs who are already out of control. In this case the city's officials were stymied by the absence of those armed men who had been sent off to Gettysburg. But it also seems that the city was poorly prepared for the disturbances that broke out. After July 14 other community leaders across the nation had ample warning in New York's experience. That meant deploying manpower in the streets in advance of draft day, but it also meant taking vigorous steps to meet quotas and avoid major drafts. New York's riots became the most powerful incentive for other communities (and New York in future drafts) to raise bounty funds and focus on aggressive recruiting.[61]

But if circumstances conspired to produce the horrors of the draft riot, it seems fair to also point a finger at New York's divided political climate. In the aftermath, Republicans and supporters of the war effort were quick to blame city and state Democratic leaders and journalists for stirring up popular hostility to the war and the draft. And Governor Seymour's remarks on July 4 provided them with ample ammunition. On the 14th the governor stood on the steps of City Hall to address a crowd in the streets. Seymour promised to seek a suspension of the draft pending a decision on its constitutionality, and in the process the governor referred to his audience as "my friends." In context, those words were pretty innocuous, and he was not actually addressing rioters but peaceable citizens who had gathered, but the two words themselves gave Republican critics an easy target. In the aftermath of the riot they made every effort to blame the entire affair on malevolent secret plans by Seymour and New York City Copperheads.[62]

The city's Peace Democrats—agreeing with the gist of the governor's July 4 comments—countered with the argument that conscription itself, with its unconstitutional violation of civil liberties, invited violent responses, and that the city's announced quotas were unfair and tilted toward Democratic districts.[63] Certainly the city's provost marshals found local concerns about quotas to be a source of ongoing annoyance, promoting greater resistance. And, as the marshal for New York's Southern Division (which included the city) put it, "politicians and press joined in the popular claims," contributing to the ongoing problems.[64]

Both the large Irish immigrant presence among the ranks of the rioters, and their emphasis on Black victims and institutions, speak to the racial, ethnic, and economic climate in the city, but those characteristics also reflected broader national patterns. Immigrants, and particularly Irish immigrants, commonly objected to both conscription and emancipation and seemed most receptive to racial attacks. Even those Democratic politicians who steered clear of the most virulently racist rhetoric routinely stressed the threat to northern society if the free states were flooded by newly emancipated slaves. Meanwhile, Democratic journalists grew adept at presenting Blacks as a dangerous threat to White civilians. In New York City the virulently racist *Weekly Day Book* unleashed a steady stream of editorials aimed at Irish readers, proclaiming the dangers of Black men and women in their midst while warning that the Republicans were anti-Catholic. Newspapers across the North printed (and reprinted) violent stories of attacks on Whites by "savage Africans." A few months before the riots, the Albany *Atlas and Argus* asked if the New York *Tribune*'s abolitionist editor Horace Greeley was prepared to "listen at midnight for the fancied shrieks of violated women—the wailings of mangled children—the groans of tortured and powerless men?" The following year the *Daily News* ran a story claiming that Blacks in the West Indies had been feasting on the bodies of dead children, adding that such stories suggested the "possible fruits of Abolition."[65] Between their own racism and the unending stories about the economic and physical dangers posed by Black people migrating to the city, it is perhaps not surprising—but no less shocking—that some of the New Yorkers who joined the July mobs took the opportunity to beat Black civilians to death, hang others from lampposts, and burn African American institutions to the ground.

The New York City riots provided Union soldiers with further evidence that treasonous Copperheads were endangering the home front even while the troops risked their lives to protect the Union on the battlefield, provoking more letters from volunteers in the field.[66] The riots prompted diverse responses from the nation's Irish Catholic communities. In and around New York, some defended the rioters, or at least the circumstances that had led them to act. Even if the nation needed a draft, they insisted that the conscription laws really were unfair both on paper and in execution. Maria Lydig Daly, the wife of one of the city's prominent Irish leaders, blamed the riots on the "exceedingly unjust" three-hundred-dollar commutation fees, "obliging all who could not beg, borrow or steal this sum to go to war." Later, Daly pointed a finger at the city's African Americans. Although she was "very sorry and much outraged at the cruelties inflicted," she could not resist adding that "I hope it will give the Negroes a lesson, for since the war commenced, they have been so insolent as to be unbearable." Other Irish editors and leaders across the country—faced with a national backlash—defended Irish patriotism and rejected the acts of the New York rioters. Still, the damage to the Irish community was done, and Irish Americans became subject to increasing hostility.[67]

Even without the added tinder provided by conscription, northern towns and cities had already experienced a distressing amount of racial violence, usually triggered by angry White workers upset about real or imagined labor competition. In 1862 striking Irish and German stevedores battled Black workers hired to take their places, prompting a week of rioting and destruction. A few weeks later, a similar story unfolded in Toledo when white rioters attacked "a number of negro shanties," housing workers hired by "grain and produce carriers" to undercut white wages. Cities in Indiana, Ohio, and Michigan saw similar clashes, all provoked by Whites angry about Black labor competition.[68] Rising talk of emancipation, and the unending drumbeat of bigoted editorials in newspapers, contributed to a society thick with racial tension.

New York's three days of rioting shifted political discourse at home and shaped how other cities and towns would recruit prior to their draft days and prepare for the contentious drawings if they came. No other draft riot rose in scale or significance to the carnage in Gotham, but although we do not have the space for detailed descriptions, each episode illustrates some of the larger themes. The previous March some citizens in Detroit, Michigan, had recoiled against the combined news of the Emancipation Proclamation and the new Enrollment Acts, creating a tinder box awaiting a spark. Events obliged when local authorities charged a biracial man with the rape of two White girls. The local Provost Guard managed to maintain a semblance of calm, but when federal authorities removed these armed men the angry crowd turned into a mob, threatening to disrupt the city. A year later in Charleston, Illinois, antiwar Democrats swarmed the modest unarmed military force on duty as a new draft day neared, lead by the antiwar sheriff. The resulting riot left ten dead. Shortly after New York's draft riots, a mob of Irish men and women in Boston's North End assaulted two provost marshals and a policeman who came to their aid, before armed forces subdued the disturbance. Draft day disturbances disrupted other northern cities, including Fairfield, Connecticut; Wooster, Ohio; and Troy, New York.[69]

The histories of the North's draft riots and disturbances illustrate an array of wartime themes. There are certainly common threads. Ordinary citizens—particularly those of the working classes—objected to conscription both as an imposition on their individual liberties and as a means to support a war they disliked. Although northern men faced the threat of conscription, each episode saw angry women taking to the streets, standing up for their loved ones but also protesting unfair treatment at the hands of government contractors and other wartime employers who had taken the opportunity to exploit working-class women desperate for incomes. Moreover, as in New York, this hostility commonly intermingled with racism, objections to emancipation, and the belief that the draft was a means to free southern slaves. And, as in Port Washington and Cincinnati and Detroit, local economic and social dynamics shaped the narratives. Finally, these stories commonly had two principal components: First, the widespread sense of injustice in these communities bubbled up with the aid of a Copperhead press and outspoken local politicians. And second, communities exploded into violence—either large or small—when the instruments of public order failed to meet the occasion, illustrating that it is always easier to stop a riot before it is underway.

Secret Societies and Chimeras

During the Civil War many rumors floated about mysterious "secret societies" of pro-Confederates gathering in the northern states and threatening the safety of the nation. These secret societies, whether real or largely imagined, have proved an irresistible subject for historians. The scholarly analysis has generally divided into two broad camps. One perspective concludes that there were indeed important secret societies composed of treasonous Copperheads who posed a significant challenge to the United States in the midst of the war. They were, so the analysis goes, numerous, well-organized, and a serious threat to the Union. The alternative camp argues that these secret societies were largely chimerical, representing shadowy fears that permeated the northern mind. Although some groups might have gathered on occasion, and perhaps even invented secret forms of communication, they were in the grand scheme of things of little importance. A related version of that same analysis suggests that the federal government latched onto fears of secret societies as an excuse to suppress civil liberties.[70]

The most notorious Civil War–era secret society—in popular imagination but also in some form of reality—was the Knights of the Golden Circle. Founded—or really reestablished—in the 1850s by the notorious George W. L. Bickley, the Knights had their origins in various antebellum filibustering schemes in Mexico and Central America, none of which got very far.[71] During the secession crisis Bickley made limited efforts to support the Confederacy, but they did not amount to much. In the first year of the war rumors of chapters of the secret society emerged in the East, attracting the concern of the federal government. In January 1861 the House of Representatives appointed a committee to look into these stories. The representatives could find no evidence of such societies, but the committee's existence speaks to the level of popular concerns during the secession crisis.[72] In the months to come, talk of this secret society persisted in northern communities, often spurred on by overzealous journalists. The editors of the *Boston Herald* reported in April 1861, "It is undoubtedly true that a secret order exists in Boston, for the purpose of aiding rebels at the South." That same month the *Newark Daily Advertiser* claimed that there were "well-founded Rumors" circulating in the city about the Knights. The following month the *Philadelphia Inquirer* shared serious tales about a plot to burn down the city, urging locals to be particularly vigilant.[73]

In 1861 and 1862 published accounts about the Knights, including popular pamphlets, claimed that huge numbers of members were scattered across the North. In the popular memory, these shadowy secret societies—and the rumors about them—are commonly associated with the Midwestern states, perhaps thanks to the groundbreaking work by historian Frank Klement. But stories about the Knights of the Golden Circle cropped up all over the North in the war's first two years, including accounts of their activities in the Northeast. One scholar has uncovered 379 references to the Knights in the *Chicago Tribune* and a combined 233 references in the *New York Tribune* and *New York Times*.[74] Whatever else might have been true, false, or exaggerated, there is no doubt that talk of secret societies sold newspapers.

The district provost marshals picked up the narrative about secret societies with the federal drafts. Writing their reports in 1866, these agents had the benefit of hindsight, and presumably little incentive to promote false stories. Quite a few of these reports indicated that secret societies of one form or another were at work in the final two years of the war. The most extensive report on the secret societies came from Captain Robert Robinson, provost marshal of California's Middle District. Writing to the state's acting assistant provost marshal in late 1864, Robinson spun a detailed account of the activities of the local Knights of the Columbian Star as well as the larger Knights of the Golden Circle. Robinson relied on detailed information uncovered by a Hiram Potter, who had infiltrated the Knights of the Golden Circle deeply enough to learn details of complex cyphers, passwords, and countersigns, as well as a multitiered organization spread throughout the region. An official notice of "Obligation," also acquired by the provost marshal, revealed that the Knights' members swore "to support the constitution and the cause of Democracy and . . . not submit to the draft or conscription." According to Potter, the two organizations numbered as many as fifty thousand men in late 1864. Robinson's account, which was included in James Fry's 1866 report as part of the state's Middle District report, also found its way into the official record as an apparent insider's view of the Knights.[75]

Quite a few other reports mentioned the Knights or other secret societies, generally presented with complete confidence in their existence although without the details of the California report. The marshal for Indiana's 3rd District concluded, with some conviction, that "in this county several Lodges of the K.G.C. existed" during the war.[76] The marshal in Iowa's 4th claimed that both the Knights of the Golden Circle and another organization known at the "Order of American Knights" operated in the district.[77] In Boone, Iowa, a group of "modern Democrats" reputedly operated under the name "Society of the Golden Circle."[78] To the east, the marshals in the 11th District in Pennsylvania identified the actions of the Knights of the Golden Circle and also a group called the Sons of Liberty.[79] The Sons of Liberty likewise turned up in reports from Illinois, Indiana, and Ohio.[80] In addition to the many reports that identified secret societies by name, district provost marshals commonly noted the activities of unidentified "secret societies" in their territory without naming particular organizations. This sort of general language appeared in district reports from Illinois, Indiana, Ohio, and Pennsylvania, in addition to those reports identifying specific groups. At least thirteen district reports mentioned the actions of local secret societies. It may be that some of those marshals were simply repeating rumors of shadowy activity in their midst, but in most cases the reports seemed to indicate fairly precise knowledge.[81]

Ohio's 1st District, which included Cincinnati, developed a reputation as "among the most evasive draft districts in the country." In 1866, when the district marshal submitted his report, he noted the wartime presence of "formidable secret organizations to oppose the enforcement of the draft in almost every ward and township—composed of a population largely of foreign birth—clannish and of strong prejudices." But in this case the marshal claimed to have eased local tensions by mingling with the population, attending public meetings, and correcting falsehoods about conscription.[82]

Some of the best scholarship on wartime secret societies has come from historian Robert Sandow, who explored the opposition to the war in Pennsylvania.[83] Calling for a community-based analysis of wartime dissent and secret societies, Sandow digs deeply into events in two Pennsylvania counties in 1864: Columbia County in north-central Pennsylvania and Clearfield County in Appalachia. In November 1864 Richard Dodge—the provost marshal for the western part of the state—submitted a lengthy report to Provost Marshal General Fry, singling out both counties as sites of antiwar activity and draft evasion. There was, he reported, organized resistance in Columbia County amounting to roughly 500 men, while he estimated that between 1,200 and 1,800 deserters and kindred spirits had gathered in and around Clearfield County.[84] In some senses Dodge's description looked much like reports from elsewhere in the Union. Men who opposed the war or had resisted conscription had come together in armed groups, prepared to resist the imposition of federal authorities. But the scale of the resistance in these highly Democratic Pennsylvania counties was distinctive.

Sandow explains that the situation by the end of 1864 had evolved from the emergence of spirited Democratic Clubs in the spring of 1862. These groups, not unlike their Union League opposition, had a partisan political agenda, at least at the outset. But two years later they were better described as "mutual protection societies," willing to undertake armed resistance when circumstances called for it. And, rather like resistance groups elsewhere in the nation, they had their own rules, loyalty oaths, and organizational structures. And, as is often the case, the organizational leaders—who led the rhetorical charge against the tyrannical administration—rarely faced the legal penalties that fell on the rank and file who were swept up by federal forces.

In response to repeated reports, government officials—again following patterns that appeared elsewhere in the United States—turned to overwhelming force by sending military expeditions to root out the troublemakers. These expeditions yielded limited success. They captured some draft evaders and deserters but failed to confront a large armed resistance. Those results prompted the not unreasonable conclusion that these Copperheads had dispersed into the countryside, choosing to escape rather than fight. In February 1865 the editor of the Democratic *Clearfield Republican* argued that the military expeditions constituted a "fraud upon the government." He acknowledged that no doubt some individuals had "been indiscreet, and allowed themselves to commit acts, or use expressions, that are in violation of recent laws." But he insisted that there was no evidence of a broader criminal intent in their actions.[85] The following year, in his report on Pennsylvania's 19th District, the provost marshal reported that only half of Clearfield County's draftees had reported, and that the rest had been discouraged "by the most influential citizens of that county combined for the purpose of resistance, formed secret societies for mutual protection, encouraged the migration into their county of deserters from the army belonging to adjoining counties and when consolidated openly defied the government to arrest them."[86] In short, although the scale of local resistance was noteworthy, the report adopted language that shared much in common with comparable reports from other districts in other states. The real culprits were the "influential citizens" who led the rank and file astray.

Less than a month before Richard Dodge reported to Fry about the resistance in Pennsylvania, Judge Advocate General Joseph Holt issued an extensive, oft-cited report on a national network of secret societies, and especially the Knights of the Golden Circle, which threatened the Union war effort. In Holt's telling, Pennsylvania played a crucial role in this national secret world.[87] Holt's account, presented prior to the election of 1864 and with a war still to be won, was probably more fiction than fact, or at least he produced a narrative that served the government's purposes. That is, in what might be understood as the inherent binary of warfare, the architects of the U.S. war effort had every reason to stress the need for vigilance in stopping an organized threat to that war effort. And a highly organized network of secret societies calling themselves "Knights" surely fit that rhetorical bill.

Even if Holt had every reason to accentuate the danger of these secret societies for political reasons, there really were guns—in boxes if not smoking—that supported the narrative. On August 17, 1864, and again on the 20th, boxes of "revolvers of the best quality" arrived at the offices of Harrison H. Dodd & Company in Indianapolis. Over the previous several years Dodd had developed a reputation as an active, outspoken, antiwar Democrat in local politics and a leading figure in the Democrats' contentious conflicts with Indiana governor Oliver Morton. By the spring of 1863 Dodd was busily engaged in organizing Indiana Copperheads into a branch of the Sons of Liberty, writing letters, staging meetings, and throwing himself into the endeavor.[88] But these shipments of arms seemed to raise the stakes considerably. Governor Morton had been tipped off to their arrival; authorities confiscated twenty-six boxes in all and arrested three men, including a Mr. Harrison, the "Grand Secretary of the Sons of Liberty." The raid—which unfolded only weeks before the Democrats met in Chicago at their nominating convention—reportedly turned up a complete list of the local Sons of Liberty in Dodd's safe, including the names of several prominent local men. The press identified Dodd himself as the state's "Grand Commander of the Order of the Sons of Liberty."[89]

Days later the Democratic *Indianapolis Daily Sentinel* ran a lengthy story rebutting the core claims about this arrest, seemingly mirroring some of the defenses the secret societies offered in Pennsylvania. Yes, boxes of revolvers had arrived at Dodd's establishment, but the paper insisted that there was nothing remotely circumspect about the shipments, and that the residents of Indiana had every right to purchase and bear arms for their own needs. After all, various Union organizations had busied themselves with similar martial activities. Legal authorities, the *Sentinel* insisted, had yet to demonstrate "that the arms were brought here for unlawful purposes."[90]

Those claims did not last long. Soon the details of a complex scheme unfolded. Apparently Dodd and his cohorts had planned an elaborate revolution, with the order staging coordinated attacks on Columbus and Cincinnati, Ohio, and Chicago, Illinois. But wiser heads had prevailed, convincing Grand Commander Dodd to send a secret message to the various lodges calling off the plan.[91] The entire episode is evidence that at least in Indiana some men of substance engaged in serious revolutionary planning, including the acquisition of arms. But the scheme's abortive nature might support another analysis, minimizing the real danger. Perhaps these were little more than fanciful notions by powerless enthusiasts with powerful imaginations. But they did manage to get guns shipped to them. Several members of the scheme were freed after they signed loyalty oaths. A military commission convicted Dodd—who had escaped to Canada—of treason and sentenced him to death in his absence. Later, President Andrew Johnson commuted the sentence to life in prison. Months later still the Supreme Court reconsidered the case and concluded that the military commission had had no jurisdiction since civilian courts continued to function in Indiana, and Dodd and his co-conspirators were ordered freed, at which point Dodd returned from Canada and moved on to the next stage in his curious life.[92]

Given the tangle of scholarly accounts and the mass of contemporary evidence, much of which remains sketchy and incomplete, what should we conclude about these secret societies? It might be useful to reconsider the main lines of the historiographic debate. In the simplest terms, the discussion focuses on whether there was indeed a national network of secret societies that threatened the Union cause. Phrased in those terms, the conversation focuses on the Union war effort and the possibility of a truly dangerous treasonous organization within the United States.

Let us shift the paradigm just a bit, considering diverse secret organizations as a manifestation of grassroots political activism and dissent, rather than as a nationwide effort to undermine the entire war. The evidence suggests a few conclusions. First, the wartime secret societies were not entirely the product of Republican imagination or postwar fantasy. Groups of deserters, draft evaders, and their allies really did gather in clandestine groups. Many adopted the name the Knights of the Golden Circle, the Sons of Liberty, or some similar title. They had secret meetings, they developed formal rules and constitutions, some had secret means of communication. The most ambitious organizations planned paramilitary operations to free Confederate prisoners or otherwise destabilize the Union war effort. Or at least they talked about such things. The district provost marshals were aware of these groups, and on occasion they led military excursions to roust the dissenters. But second, the dissent aimed at conscription and the Union war effort emerged locally, from local conditions and following the specific demands of a distinct community and environment. Like the April 1861 mobs and the urban draft rioting, the community resistance to conscription—and the support for desertion and deserters—emerged out of hostility to national policies, but they reflected local populations and conditions, often driven by a powerful sense that things were unfair. No doubt information passed from group to group, and their core concerns were related, but there is little reason to see these local organizations as actively intent on creating nationwide movements or undermining the entire war effort. And it is probably fair to place these "secret societies" in a broader cultural context. A diversity of secret, or at least secretive, fraternal groups existed throughout the mid-nineteenth century. Other private bodies, less secret, organized to protect the Union, and some armed themselves. Armed militia groups also dotted the landscape. These particular secret societies really merited governmental attention because they disagreed with the war, or at least some policies, and spoke of armed resistance, not because they gathered secretly and constructed complex secret codes.

A final set of questions concern how we should understand this whole array of draft evaders, deserters, and secret societies. The framework that understands the Knights and their affiliates as an organized national institution quickly takes the next step, concluding that they were engaged in a treasonous effort to undermine the nation. That invites a complicated set of questions about what in fact constituted treason. Recent scholarship has considered the notion of "treason," both as a legal concept and as a term used in public discourse. In contested areas, journalists and military officials sometimes used the phrase "latent treason" to describe those in occupied territory whose "sullenness or silence could be construed as treasonous." General Henry Halleck used the term "military treason" to describe "noncombatants who displayed armed resistance against the occupation force." In general these notions of treason, which went well beyond constitutional law or familiar legal practice, targeted elites who directed such behaviors, and not the rank and file—such as members of secret societies—who might have put rhetoric into practice.[93]

In the simplest terms, those men and women who became affiliated with the Knights of the Golden Circle or some other group were committed to illegal activity. Ideologically they may have hated emancipation and distrusted the administration, but in practice their crimes were resisting the draft and perhaps conspiring to help others avoid conscription. Many seemed willing to fire on draft enrollers or provost marshals who came looking for them. Given the laws of the land, they were surely criminals. But what explains their individual and collective behavior? No doubt many simply did not wish to go to war, or to have their loved ones conscripted into uniform. To make matters worse, when the war became a conflict over emancipation, many of these recruits to local secret societies had a new incentive to resist the central government. And for many, the hostility to conscription became wrapped up in convictions that the entire process—from quotas to enrollment to selection to medical examination—was fundamentally crooked, as explained to them by partisan journalists and political elites within their communities. Those who gathered in small bands or aligned with local secret societies were convinced that conscription and emancipation were unconstitutional measures imposed on them by a federal government that did not have their interests in mind. Or, as Sandow explains, these individuals in the grassroots acted out of a "community desire for local autonomy" in the midst of a war that seemed to impose federal rules on local communities.[94] They disliked the war, or at least how it was being fought, but they did not see themselves as engaged in treason.

The accounts of wartime violence and dissent tell us quite a bit while leaving much in shadows. A large share of rioters were probably men and women of the working classes; a disproportionate number were likely first- or second-generation immigrants. Many were probably Democrats, or at least ideologically aligned with the party. Or at least this is the portrait presented by the district provost marshals and other federal officials. Although describing the actions of workers and immigrants, those marshals blamed Democratic leaders—politicians and editors—for riling up an angry citizenry.

The story of these Democrats and politics in the streets has a few simple conclusions: First, ordinary citizens—both women and men—who objected to wartime events or legislation sometimes resisted with the tools at their disposal, even when their actions turned from civil disobedience to violence. Second, the Democratic elites, including those officeholders and journalists who also pursued partisan political ends through elections and other traditional measures, found ample opportunity to influence the opinions of those who had grown disillusioned with the war. Sometimes some portion of those stirred-up citizens and consumers of political rhetoric took to the streets with their political opinions and their racial hatreds. And third, the actions of rioters, draft evaders, and secret societies became valuable fodder for the Democrats' political adversaries, who took pains to tar the entire party with the brush of treason. They became the face of the Democratic opposition as constructed by northern Unionists.

III

An Opposition Party

6

An Organized War, a Disorganized Party?

We return to the world of partisan politics in mid-1863, as Democrats struggled with definitions and roles. What did it mean to be the opposition party in the midst of civil war? Who was a "conservative" and what did that mean? New voices emerged and partisan conflicts grew more heated as the parties strove to define themselves and their opposition.

"Why I Am a Democrat"

Our story is about two years into the Civil War. It is a good moment to summarize national politics. Mid-nineteenth-century Americans cared deeply about presidential elections. Campaigns were energetic public affairs. Voter turnouts were high. But presidential election politics differed from the almost endless campaign cycle we see in contemporary politics. In April 1863 Abraham Lincoln was firmly in place as the president of the United States, and it would be another year before ordinary Americans turned to serious conversations about a new presidential election. Meanwhile, local and state partisan politics continued, with elections following their own calendars rather than any nationwide rhythm.[1] These too attracted considerable interest, at least among those citizens most committed to political debate. The midterm elections in 1862 had proved vital in shifting the makeup of congressional delegations, as energized Democrats regained seats from the party in power. And those results led Republicans to rethink their approach to future contests.

Certainly electoral politics mattered immensely, especially insofar as the Lincoln administration—pursuing a broad Republican agenda and a massive war effort—pushed at the outer limits of federal power. And congressional Democrats periodically pushed back. But in a broader sense, the life of northern men and women was rife with political debates and disputes, manifesting themselves in a host of ways remote from the ballot box. Men who resisted draft enrollers, and the women who supported them, acted out political dissent in their own communities, as did those rioters who openly resisted on draft day. These were political disputes, shaped by politicians and journalists as well as individuals' instincts for self-preservation. Meanwhile, border-state Democrats—whether they supported the war or not—discussed the implications of Republican inroads into the institution of slavery. Some Democratic journalists and other outspoken politicians, ministers, and dissenters strained at the boundaries of political speech, provoking occasional government backlash and new clashes over civil liberties.

In private homes and family gatherings, or in saloons or factory floors, or on street corners or before newspaper offices, citizens debated public policies. Some concerned themselves with the subtleties of constitutional law, while others spoke boldly—and without subtlety—about treason and tyranny. All of this was politics, even when party labels blurred. And meantime, the nation watched a war that continued on into the spring of 1863. Talk of lost battles, incompetent generals, administrative malpractice, and the ongoing trauma of war all filled newspaper editorials and excited conversations, as did continued debates about the implications of the Emancipation Proclamation and the ongoing tensions surrounding conscription. Soldiers in uniform eyed these events from military camps or on the march and assessed things from their own perspectives. Some, like William Standard, found little to support in the administration's actions and much to grumble about. Others welcomed emancipation as a valuable war measure even if they had no interest in racial equality. Many volunteers expressed outrage at cowards at home who resisted military service or spoke up against the war. A few soldiers sent angry letters to their local newspapers, accusing the worst of treason.[2] If politics was about the accumulation and application of power, all of this amounted to political debate. And the stakes were high.

In addition to governmental and military efforts to subdue treasonous dissent, the larger world of political debate leaked into hundreds or even thousands of local disputes. We have seen that in contested places like Kentucky and Tennessee, long-term community conflicts found their way into sometimes violent clashes. Meanwhile, Republicans across the North took advantage of local federal authorities—often the provost marshals—to point fingers at subversive activities in their midst. That is, they turned in Democrats who upset them. Sometimes the charges were for modest behaviors, or just for shadowy rumors. Proud patriots reported suspected Copperheads for careless public speech, sometimes aided by strong drink. Some Republicans infiltrated Democratic meetings to collect damning evidence. Only rarely did these cases turn up true treasonous activity, as hard as that was to define, although occasionally a loose-tongued Democrat called for resisting the draft or even mumbled about political assassinations. Anywhere between 18,000 and 38,000 northern civilians faced charges for potential subversive activities. Some were no doubt guilty of treason; many others had upset their neighbors.[3] In a historic moment fraught with ideological conflicts and local political squabbles, the Civil War exacerbated gaps that had already existed between Democrats and Republicans, and Democrats and Whigs not long before. They had differences over fundamental republican ideals, and with war they clashed much more rigorously about the role of the national government.[4] With the fate of the Union on the line, local Republicans across the North enjoyed a useful advantage in their intramural battles with local Democrats.

Into this cacophony of political discourse, the true nature of the Democratic Party can be challenging to identify and define. By mid-1863 the Republican Party had worked assiduously to establish itself as the party of Union and patriotism. A civil war was no time for partisan dissent, they argued. Since late November proud patriots in Philadelphia had been meeting to discuss how best to confront what they saw as treasonous antiwar Copperheads in their midst. By the end of the year what had been known as the "Union Club" rechristened itself as the new "Union League," including 253 self-professed leaders among the city's elite. These men insisted that the League was nonpartisan, although it was explicitly prowar. In fact, in its first incarnation Philadelphia's Union League included 135 Democrats and 75 Republicans (among those with known party affiliation). Elites in New York and Boston soon followed suit with their own autonomous Union Leagues, while a much broader Union League structure emerged nationwide, often marching under the banner of "No Party Now."[5]

The Republican Party, with the Union Leagues and their publication societies as valuable adjuncts, set its sights on defining its political adversaries as the nation's enemies. When elections rolled around, that proved to be an effective stick with which to pound away at the opposition party. And in many loyal Democrats, that argument found a receptive audience. Democrats like Joseph Holt or James Fry worked in the Lincoln administration without abandoning their political party.[6] Others saw themselves as part of a loyal opposition, committing to the war effort while dissenting on major points of policy, from emancipation to conscription. Some Democratic leaders and opinion-makers had either opposed the war from its outset or had come to conclude that the nation should abandon the conflict. Others found some middle ground where they claimed to be in favor of the war, and the men in uniform, while objecting to the tools selected to pursue victory. Thus, they rejected conscription and emancipation and political arrests while insisting that the war could be pursued with more conservative means.

Ordinary citizens did not necessarily view the war, or these political debates, through a strictly partisan lens, and certainly not through the same lens. Language blurred and labels evolved. For Democrats who objected to events or policies, the party in power often became simply "the abolitionists" or "the radicals." Those in opposition routinely characterized their side as noble "conservatives" standing up against a tyrannical administration. And those discussions varied from place to place, as did the issues shaping public opinion. In the second half of 1863, before nationwide political conversations turned to the presidential election, Democrats focused on a variety of local and state elections, including a series of crucial gubernatorial contests. In the process, politicians dueled over what it meant to be a Democrat, and what the party should stand for in the midst of civil war. If they could not define themselves, surely the Republicans would provide unsavory definitions for them. The answers the Democrats discussed were hardly obvious or shared across the nation.

Historians who look at this political moment tend to speak—quite reasonably—in terms of broad categories. Thus, a large portion of northern Democrats fall into a "War Democrat" camp. The label is fairly imprecise. Presumably a War Democrat had some loyalty to—or at least history with—the national Democratic Party, but when push came to shove they supported continuing the military conflict to a successful victory. Some of these would actively align with the current administration in the name of Union. Others remained in the party of opposition while insisting that their support for the war remained unbending. There was also, to some, a conditional aspect to that support for the war. That is, some Democrats came to suspect that Lincoln hoped to postpone peace until he had achieved emancipation. That was a line they would not cross.

Those Democrats who dissented from the administration's core policies were often labeled "Peace Democrats," in that they wanted the war to end sooner rather than later. Some contemporary observers, and later historians, called these Democrats "Copperheads." Some in the opposition embraced that label, but more often "Copperhead" became—especially by 1863—a term of derision tossed around by their adversaries, describing people who critics claimed were disloyal or even treasonous. One Illinois paper that summer made the Republican point clear: "Copperhead Democracy to-day means traitorism. . . . Those that are not for the Government *must* be against it."[7] Chicago's mayor Francis Sherman insisted that he was a patriotic member of the opposition, but his adversaries called him a Copperhead, calling into question who should get to affix the label on the historic actor.

That sort of binary language is certainly useful to understand the Democratic Party: some people supported the war, and others opposed it. But the labels mask complexities. People—both citizens and politicians—fell along a spectrum, and their positions on that spectrum were not fixed. Some northerners were unambiguously pro-southern and pro-secession from the early months of 1861. But other northern Democrats objected to *how* the war was being fought, and for some those objections left them openly hostile to the Lincoln administration and the war effort. Other civilians thought little about specific policy debates, but they objected to the war's destruction and the dangers it posed to themselves and their loved ones. Others still (and these categories overlapped considerably) were perfectly happy to see the Confederacy defeated, but not if that required destroying the institution of slavery or provoking a mass movement of freed people into the northern states. All of these people might be called "Peace Democrats," and their political adversaries could call them "Copperheads" or worse. But that is not to say they shared much in common, or that they were all universally or continuously at odds with more mainstream War Democrats.[8]

Party identities could easily blur where labels became tools of rhetorical combat more than portraits of ideological positions. Savvy politicians who sought to woo local voters had to navigate the demographics and core issues of their communities, as much as the national political issues that defined the war years. Chicago's Sherman could insist that he was a moderate Democrat, true to his party's long-term core principles and reaching out to partisan opponents, but his opponents did everything they could to link him to the *Chicago Times* and tar him with the brush of treasonous Copperheadism. These were challenging times for Democrats who found themselves seeking support in a particular place while also in the midst of a national debate about loyalty and patriotism. Although the labels were imprecise, and Democrats had a tough time defining who they were, there was no surfeit of political thinkers or opinion makers willing to take a stab at declaring what it meant to be a true Democrat in 1863.

As we saw in the introduction, by the middle of the war people calling themselves Democrats differed wildly about how the nation should proceed, and how the party should define itself. Arch-conservative Chauncey Burr used the pages of *The Old Guard* to defend his view of party purity. He believed in a very strict reading of the Constitution, where the administration's war and most of its constituent parts violated that Constitution, and any northerner who saw things otherwise did not deserve to call himself a Democrat. Meanwhile,

Indiana Democrat Robert Dale Owen had insisted that the only true path to a lasting peace would be to embrace emancipation, and not merely as a war measure.[9] When looked at closely, the opinions of Burr and Owen appear as very distinct points on a broad political and ideological spectrum. By early 1863 many such voices were weighing in, as the party gradually moved to a more clearly defined division over the Civil War and its opposition role.

In early February 1863 Kentucky congressman William Wadsworth (who would so disappoint Henry and Sarah Waller) wrote to Samuel Barlow offering his thoughts from a Washington perspective: "Our country is absolutely without hope for two years," the Democrat wrote. "Lincoln is as radical as Lloyd Garrison, & weak as infancy. Should we be unable to get possession of the leading state governments, & find some way to combine the strength of the country in some overwhelming way, against the Govt in its present hands, we will go to the Devil, before the people can change the senate & turn the sorry, stale, vulgar joke out of the Presidential chair. My hope is that the country will not be wholly broken down in a financial & military respect before the conservatives will be at the helm." Once conservative men of high principles are back in power, Wadsworth predicted, it would be possible for "the men in both quarters . . . to meet each other & settle the contest by compromise."[10] In Wadsworth's framework, the answer to the nation's ills was to inject more sensible conservatives into Washington's political debates. He had Democrats in mind. But more broadly Wadsworth saw a political world populated by radicals and sound conservatives.

James Wall, a one-time senator from New Jersey and a vigorous opponent of the war who had spent time in Fort Lafayette for his antiwar views, had—like Burr—lost patience with the War Democrats in his party. He had long since concluded that it was pointless for Democrats to define themselves as echoing the administration's positions. "It seems to me," he wrote, "to be . . . nonsense that the democratic party can cry out for a vigorous prosecution of the war, and yet expect to beat the party that is vigorously prosecuting it and controlling the sinews at the same time." Instead, Wall—an unabashed supporter of the Confederacy—offered a radical option: the Democrats should endorse a peaceful separation from the southern states. "I am for putting an end to this bloody scene, before it becomes more ensanguined," he announced. Here was an unapologetic Peace Democrat, and one who might reasonably be called a Copperhead. Few in his party would be willing to go so far.[11]

Journalist T. J. Barnett had spent years sparring with his friend and fellow Democrat Samuel Barlow. The two often disagreed about how the party should proceed. By the spring of 1863 Barnett felt confident that the rebellion would soon be defeated, and he argued that the other key policy decisions—including how to handle Reconstruction—should wait until victory was won. As a Washington-based correspondent, Barnett enjoyed substantial contacts with the administration and periodically had Abraham Lincoln's ear. Barnett liked the president and reported to Barlow that "he has been most absurdly managed by the New York Conservatives and by G—they have deserved his contempt, as a party." In Barnett's eyes Lincoln was a fairly conservative man, often at odds with radicals in his own party, but also frustrated with the opposition's unrelenting resistance to his administration. Barnett assured Barlow that "the stinking aroma of party politics has tainted the whole concern, quite as deeply as it has the Radicals; and the lines were drawn prematurely, and the issues were made without a proper consideration to cooperation." Barnett went on to report that "Mr. Lincoln, if he believes the men to be true to the Country, is quite as glad to listen to Conservatives as to anybody."[12]

While Barnett saw an ideological spectrum with the president somewhere near the center, facing radicals in his own party and seeking the support of any fair-minded conservatives in the other, the journalist wrote that administration insiders dismissed the peace men within the Democratic Party as little more than a pointless side show. "As to the Peace Party," he wrote in June, "they laugh at it here, and think that the most it amounts to is a proof that the Opposition have . . . cleared the way, for the present at all events, for the Republicans as a party—and, in this regard, they seem to like it." A month later, focusing on the opposition in the Empire State, Barnett told Barlow that "I am convinced now that the President apprehends nothing from the Peace Party. He looks upon it as an amalgam of the elements of discontent in New York." Men like Fernando Wood did not give Lincoln pause.[13]

Barnett perceived a national conversation among Democrats as the opposition party, with their focus occasionally shaded toward leading figures in New York. But before long this discussion would fragment into lively local debates. As events and elections progressed in the spring and fall of 1863, one key narrative concerned how the Democratic Party would continue to define itself while the Republican Party claimed to be the party of Union and of loyalty. Democrats individually and collectively had to construct an identity as the party of loyal opposition. But what might that mean in practice?[14] They would have to settle on a national message, at least by the presidential election the following year.

Taken in isolation, one might reasonably categorize Manton Marble and his *New York World* as a virulently Copperhead publication. At the least by mid-war the newspaper's editorial pages were full of strongly worded attacks on Abraham Lincoln and his administration. But set alongside Burr's *The Old Guard,* Marble's position seems more moderate. After all, the *World* began life with a very different editorial perspective, and Marble's own roots were in the Whig Party. But in late 1862 and certainly by 1863 the New York newspaper had become one of the North's most important opposition publications. Marble, who was friends with Barlow and the city's crucial Democratic figures, took the position seriously. In February 1863 he offered a lengthy discussion of the *World*'s role in the national political debate, and his sense of how the Democratic Party should function as the opposition: "It is the mission of the Opposition party not to break down or enfeeble the federal government, but to get possession of it and administer it on constitutional principles. . . . When the presidential canvass open in 1864 it will be proper for the opposition to define the principles on which they propose to administer the government if they carry the elections. But for the present it is wise to confine our efforts to simple opposition." In sum, Marble saw the Democratic Party's job as the opposition party, to oppose. And he saw the *World* as an important defender of the freedom of the press. "The function of the opposition party is negative," he concluded. "It is to expose administrative corruption, resist bad measures, and stand up against infractions of the Constitution." In those core critiques, Marble and Burr spoke with one voice on most issues. But the *World* would be a voice of opposition within an ongoing political debate, while *The Old Guard* had largely washed its hands of the whole thing.[15]

Democrats who thought broadly embraced divergent views on how the party should behave in national elections and public dialogue. Some took the notion of an opposition party quite literally and expansively. Others supported the administration in its overall war effort while dissenting on various particulars. Others still seemed content to keep their partisan powder dry until the shooting war had ended, while claiming some form of constitutional high ground in their dissent. In the meantime, across the North Democrats differed over issues large and small, and individual politicians and contests illuminated those core fissures in the Democracy.

Philadelphia Democrats, the *Philadelphia Age,* and Clement Vallandigham

Although hardly a microcosm of national politics, Philadelphia Democrats arrayed across a broad ideological range and were (mostly) not reticent in sharing their opinions, some of which put them afoul of legal authorities. In January

1863 a small but enthusiastic group gathered at the Girard House to mark the visit of James Wall, just released from Fort Lafayette. A week later the provost marshal ordered his men to Third Street to shut down the city's only daily Democratic paper, the *Evening Journal.* The officers arrested the proprietor, Albert Boileau, at his home and transported him to Fort McHenry. The *North American* reported that Philadelphians on the street sympathized with Boileau but agreed that the paper had been publishing secessionist screeds written by others. Specifically, the provost marshal took exception to an editorial comparing Jefferson Davis favorably to Abraham Lincoln. Diarist Sidney George Fisher found the action excessive and noted that he would not "be surprised if trouble grew out of this act." A local Republican agreed, noting that "we are bordering on anarchy." Writing from Washington, Charles Biddle did not share the popular sympathy for the editor, adding, "He is a miserable creature." In the end Boileau wrote a letter of apology, explaining that his paper had printed an editorial (perhaps by William Reed) that he had neither written nor approved.[16]

The following month the city's conservative Democrats met at the newly founded Democratic Club, where they celebrated George Washington's birthday and heard Charles Ingersoll rile up the audience. Diarist Anna Mercer LaRoche attended with her Democrat father and was pleased to report that Ingersoll "was splendidly received."[17] In March Philadelphia's antiwar Democrats celebrated the launching of the *Philadelphia Age,* a new daily newspaper. The editors promised "a national Democratic journal, conducted on national Democratic principles . . . devoted to the Constitution of the United States." They would stand for Union but asked, "What were Union without Liberty?" To that end they evoked Daniel Webster, "that immortal Statesman," as their guiding light. With this editorial the *Philadelphia Age* joined the fight, claiming Webster—the great Unionist Whig—as their inspiration.[18] It would be a fight for the Union but also for the identity of the Democratic Party.

The *Philadelphia Age* almost immediately took on the popular Republican rhetoric with an extended editorial asking, "Who is in favor of the Union?" The Republicans, it noted, had taken to calling themselves "loyal Union men," painting the opposition party as both disloyal and fundamentally opposed to Union itself. Following Chauncey Burr's analysis, the editorial argued that it was the Democrats who had fervently adhered to the Constitution and thus the core principles of Union, while the administration party had pursed abolition and other measures that challenged constitutional principles while claiming to listen to a "higher law." "Are these men now to sit in judgment of the National Democracy?" the paper asked. Turning to the debates surrounding the

Compromise of 1850, the *Philadelphia Age* pointed out that it was men such as Webster, Henry Clay, and Stephen Douglas who had found a path to compromise and the preservation of the Union, against the resistance of "the puritanical disunionists of New England," who went on to lead the Republican Party. Once again Democrats claimed great Whig Unionists—Webster and Clay—to their cause while also calling on the name of Stephen Douglas.

A few days later in a companion editorial, the *Philadelphia Age* asked, "What are we fighting for?" In this piece the editors laid out a core argument about peace. In the midst of warfare and bellicose rhetoric, prideful men would resist negotiation and peace. But the nation's southern adversaries were honorable men who "*could* accept" peaceful terms "if they were offered." Speaking for the Democratic Party, the *Philadelphia Age* concluded that despite current perceptions that peace would be impossible without military victory, men of honor could still find an honorable settlement with the Confederacy. "The Radicals," they noted, called such talk "treasonous," while they insist on unconditional surrender and the end of slavery. Sticking with the label "radicals," as opposed to Republicans, the *Philadelphia Age* spun an argument where reasonable and moderate men could craft an end to hostilities with the South, but one in which emancipation was not a condition of peace.[19] It was an argument that tracked internally and ran entirely counter to the logic in Democrat Robert Dale Owen's pamphlet. In this early statement the *Philadelphia Age* rebutted the core Republican claims that calls for an honorable peace were somehow disloyal.

Whereas the *Philadelphia Age* sought to portray itself as a loyal and Unionist response to the radical Lincoln administration, many in Philadelphia were not buying their characterization. On May 2 things grew tense when a Union soldier tore down a seemingly pro-Confederate account of the defeat of General Joseph Hooker at the Battle of Chancellorsville, posted on the *Philadelphia Age*'s bulletin board. The episode drew a small crowd to the Chestnut Street building and attracted modest attention in the press. A week later a larger scene unfolded in front of the newspaper office, once again triggered by an upsetting article on the bulletin board. This time a crowd of several hundred gathered, murmuring about Copperheads and "that Vallandigham." Before things got out of hand, the ubiquitous Mayor Alexander Henry showed up to calm the crowd. As the crowd dispersed, a few punches were thrown and one fellow took to swinging a cane. At this point members of the Philadelphia police—among the nation's most organized police departments—arrived on the scene and carted a few people off to Central lockup, where they were soon released.[20]

Although the *Philadelphia Age* claimed a public position as the loyal opposition, insisting that the paper represented proper Union sentiments, the crusty

Fisher was not impressed, dubbing it "a secession journal" and noting that "after defeat their opinions were especially offensive and irritating." The whole affair annoyed the diarist, who declared that "these Democrats can see in this great war only a party contest," celebrating every military failure and providing comfort to the enemy.[21]

The timing of the riot at the *Philadelphia Age* offices is worth noting. On the one hand, the catalyst for the tensions seemed quite local. A new Democratic daily, with decidedly antiwar views, had begun publication; it was just a matter of time before it attracted angry attention. But the immediate trigger came when the newspaper posted a story about the Union's latest military failure, making a local dispute national. Moreover, as some in the crowd noted with their jeers, local tensions about Copperheads had become intermingled with national politics. On May 9 Philadelphia Democrats once again welcomed ex–New Jersey senator James Wall to speak at the party headquarters on Walnut Street. A considerable crowd of angry Republicans gathered outside the hall, where they cheered Lincoln and the Union, to counter-cheering from the Democrats inside. Once again Police Chief Samuel G. Ruggles and his officers arrived on the scene to calm the waters and arrest the most boisterous. But a worried Anna LaRoche recorded that "everyone threatens us with Revolution."[22]

The reporting on the Walnut Street episode—like the stories on the hubbub at the *Philadelphia Age*—illustrate that these clashes were part of an expanding national political story. As we have seen, similar conflicts emerged in Ohio following the news from Chancellorsville, and in early May ex-congressman Clement Vallandigham attracted public ire and federal attention when he spoke in Mount Vernon, leading to his arrest. Members of the crowds on Walnut Street and Chestnut Street (only blocks apart) yelled about "Vallandigham" and his dangerous influence. Vallandigham's arrest had been part of a conflict between federal officials and local dissenters in Ambrose Burnside's Department of the Ohio, but the military arrest became a national rallying cry for antiwar Democrats and a major rhetorical point for Republicans seeking to paint the opposition party as fundamentally disloyal. Thus, spontaneous gatherings on Walnut and Chestnut Streets in Philadelphia became occasions for the loud expression of public anger about military events in Virginia and a political arrest in Ohio. The *Philadelphia Age* defended Vallandigham, insisting that "if he has transgressed the law, let the law punish him," but that was a task for the civil courts rather than overreaching military courts.[23]

Things came to a head on June 1 when riled up Philadelphia Democrats staged a rally in Independence Square, protesting Vallandigham's treatment and his banishment from the Union. The day before, Fisher wrote that "a disturbance is feared" as he had heard talk of an attack on the meeting. But on the day, a large crowd showed their enthusiasm for the cause, and a heavy police presence helped ensure that all remained calm. Rather than hearing from the city's more famed rabble-rousing Copperheads, the Independence Square assembly featured speeches from the likes of Democratic congressman Charles Biddle and one-time mayor Peter McCall. Fisher seemed pleasantly surprised with the proceedings, noting that the published accounts of "resolutions and speeches . . . are of a superior order to others of the same party." In Fisher's eyes, it seemed, some local Democrats were truly beyond the pale whereas others constituted a coherent loyal opposition. Within days, more news from Burnside's Department of the Ohio again stirred up Philadelphians, as word reached the East that federal forces had shut down the *Chicago Times*.[24]

The following week Democrats assembled at the Democratic Club in Manayunk, in northwestern Philadelphia, where they heard from the iconoclastic conservative Charles Ingersoll. Ingersoll sang a familiar tune. He was disgusted with the Republican Party's threats to the nation's fundamental values. "The Republicans, as led by the Abolitionists," he declared, "have not about them an iota of conservatism; they are essentially a revolutionary party, and the Democrats are the conservatives of the United States." "Their course towards the Democratic party is perilous," he warned, painting a picture of angry Republican mobs attacking conservative Democrats. The answer, echoing Congressman Wadsworth's conclusions, would be "to vote them out" before it was too late. The *Philadelphia Age* found it a "sound and patriotic address." As Ingersoll had explained in a similar speech to the city's 15th Ward Democrats a few weeks earlier, "What the Democratic party wants is, their Union and Constitution back again; the Union and that Constitution which the leaders of these misled Republicans have, for years, been denouncing."[25] The sharp-tongued Ingersoll presented himself as a loyal, conservative patriot, dissenting against a government that had run amuck.

In this ongoing conversation about the identity of the Democratic Party, Clement Vallandigham had become a national lightning rod. For Democrats like Biddle and McCall, Vallandigham's arrest smacked of the violation of civil liberties and proper judicial practice. For the North's more rabid antiwar Democrats, Vallandigham's image and words made an appealing rallying cry. And to Republicans of all stripes, the Ohioan came to symbolize the worst excesses of northern Copperheadism and treason.

The aftermath of Burnside's arrest of Clement Vallandigham fills an important chapter in Lincoln lore. By trying the politician in a military court, Burnside had invited Democratic objections about process as well as result. Even though the ex-congressman had been a persistent thorn in his side, Lincoln recognized that Vallandigham would be even more troublesome as a martyr, particularly with a strong legal case. For a time the administration contemplated suspending the privilege of the writ of habeas corpus specifically for Vallandigham. But wiser heads concluded that such an unorthodox measure would probably not survive the Ohio courts, and so Lincoln abandoned the idea.[26] Instead the president took a politically savvy step. He ordered Burnside to free Vallandigham from military prison and instead banish him to the Confederacy where Lincoln hoped he would be out of harm's way. But meanwhile, Vallandigham's arrest had sent shockwaves among Democrats in the region, and across the nation.

Philadelphia's Independence Square gathering was hardly unique, as angry Democrats coalesced around their new martyr. New Yorkers met at the city's Democratic Headquarters to hear Congressman James Brooks—another prominent Peace Democrat—assail the Lincoln administration and Vallandigham's arrest.[27] On May 16 Democrats gathered in Albany to share their indignation about the arrest, but irate Union soldiers burst in to disrupt the meeting.[28]

The Albany gathering rose to particular significance when the attendees prepared a letter to the president calling the arrest unconstitutional and accusing the administration of approaching military despotism. Rather than accepting the merits of this critique, Lincoln prepared one of his famed public letters, addressed to Erastus Corning, the first signatory on the letter. Lincoln's "Corning Letter" became his most extensive defense of his administration's approach to civil liberties. In times of civil war, he argued, suspension of the privilege of the writ of habeas corpus was appropriate and necessary, and circumstance sometimes called for the use of federal military courts rather than local civil courts. In the letter's most famous lines Lincoln asked the question: "Must I shoot a simple-minded soldier boy who deserts, while I must not touch a hair of a wiley agitator who induces him to desert?" In this fashion Lincoln recast Vallandigham as an enemy of the nation at odds with the innocent boys who sacrificed their lives for the Union.[29]

Just a day before that Albany meeting, an anonymous Democrat who went by "Jackson" published a long letter in the *Philadelphia Age* explaining to the world "Why I am a Democrat." It was a long manifesto, presented in eleven numbered paragraphs. Jackson began by announcing his fealty to the Constitution and the nation, which had prospered for generations until "abolitionism, with its fanatic teachings" had taken over the government. With that statement in place, he worked through many of the familiar issues that concerned Democrats: habeas corpus, free speech, fraudulent government contracts, an overly powerful centralized government, attacks on freedom of the press, and the protection of states' rights. Jackson—who presumably took his name from the great Democratic president—went on to critique the Emancipation Proclamation, which threatened to provoke insurrection while uniting the South and dividing the North. This litany of issues led him to conclude "that the salvation of our Government can be obtained only by the elevation of the Democratic Party to the control of the Government." It was a comprehensive list of where the Democrats differed with the Lincoln administration on public policy, organized around the broad theme that the Democracy was best suited to protect the nation's constitution and laws. What was absent was any discussion of the war itself. He shared no thoughts about military matters, or even conscription. Moreover, this Democratic manifesto offered no opinion about how or when the Civil War should come to an end. Jackson's allegiance to the Democratic Party seemingly left him outside of either of the party's two identified camps.[30]

State Electoral Politics

Soon after Vallandigham's arrest, the *New York Herald* recognized that Burnside had handed the outspoken Ohioan a gift, noting that prior to this spurt of publicity, "his chance of being elected Governor of Ohio was small." Democrats in the East and Midwest made it clear that even if they disagreed with what Vallandigham had to say—and many did—they defended his right to say it.[31] On June 11 Ohio Democrats nominated Vallandigham for governor while the candidate languished in Canada. Many Ohioans rallied to his cause more as a symbol of free expression than as a harsh critic of the administration. Sunset Cox, a moderate Democrat in some senses, took to the stump supporting the banished candidate. Congressman Cox privately told the *World*'s Marble that he did "not approve of anything Vallandigham says, only his right to say it." The Ohio platform that year was long but did not include any actual peace plank. Although the candidate's surrogates sought to focus on civil liberties and other constitutional concerns, Vallandigham himself had made so many outrageous pronouncements that the Republicans had ample fuel for campaigning against him.[32] Union soldiers writing home grew increasingly incensed about the seemingly treasonous talk they heard from the home front. One member of the 101st

Ohio reported that "Coperheadism has brought the soldiers here together more than anything else."[33] As if to underscore that point, and to remind politicians that the troops were watching, some Union soldiers took to mailing Ohio Copperheads nooses, suggesting the price of their treasonous positions.[34]

Ohio's Republicans, organized as the Union Party in the state, nominated War Democrat John Brough to battle Vallandigham, with Charles Anderson as the candidate for lieutenant governor. The state's Republicans and War Democrats embraced the ticket, emphasizing the dangers Vallandigham represented. The always colorful William Tecumseh Sherman wrote to Anderson, sharing his distaste for Vallandigham and his ilk. "Thank God the Southern men sunk as they are in crime are yet too proud to admit Vallandigham as an associate," Sherman added. "They are willing to have him as a Stink Pot, but not as an associate."[35] But Anderson's own family illustrated the complexities of state politics and Democratic identity. On the eve of the election, Union Captain Thomas McArthur Anderson wrote to Anderson, his uncle, with regrets that his father—the candidate's brother—had been on the stump speaking for Vallandigham. This appalled his son, both for familial and ideological reasons.[36]

For the Democratic Evans clan of southern Ohio, a possible Vallandigham nomination held no appeal. Although a lifelong Democrat, Andrew Evans felt disgust for "stay at home Democrats" or those who opposed conscription, and he declared that he would "not vote for anyone unless he is of unquestionable Loyalty to his Government." Andrew's soldier son, Samuel, writing from camp in Tennessee agreed: "My politics is the men who can and do most to put down this 'Rebellion.' As you, I do not make political preferences toward the army." He added later that the great Democrat Andrew Jackson would have dismissed Vallandigham's candidacy.[37] When he heard the news that Ohio's Democrats had nominated Vallandigham, Andrew could barely contain himself, telling his son that "I am fearful that I cannot fill this page without swearing." It was "a disgrace to the State and a slander to the name, Democrat." Sharing his son's affection for Jackson, Andrew embraced the nomination of Brough as "an Old Hickory Democrat."[38]

While some Ohio Democrats supported Vallandigham despite his most offensive rhetoric, others saw him as a fine spokesman, both because of his views on the war and his frequent comments on race and emancipation. One Ohio newspaper ran the slogan "WHITE MEN SHALL RULE AMERICA" on its masthead, with a longer comment just below: "THE CONSTITUTION AS IT IS, THE UNION AS IT WAS, THE NEGRO WHERE HE IS." It was a popular sentiment.[39] A Dayton, Ohio, newspaper backed Vallandigham and the Democratic ticket, with a masthead declaring simply, "THE CONSTITUTION AS IT IS, THE UNION AS IT WAS."[40] But a Gallipolis, Ohio, newspaper that supported Brough for election noted, wryly, that the Copperhead *Ohio Statesman* had pointed out the whole idea of restoring the Union "as it was" had become "impossible." And it seemed that none of the Vallandigham supporters had contemplated that simple fact.[41]

Certainly a case can be made that although many observers saw Vallandigham as the most important national voice for the amorphous northern Peace Party, and Republicans were pleased to tar the entire Democratic Party with that brush, his Ohio gubernatorial candidacy was not quite so easily defined. His arrest and banishment symbolized to them the excesses of the Republican administration, which—as the *Herald* had noted—proved politically invaluable. Yet, to oppose the administration and call for the defense of the Constitution was not quite the same as demanding immediate peace or wishing for the failure of the Union Army in the field. As directed by Ohio Democrats, this was not a treasonous candidacy, and the party was on firm ground in concluding that the ex-congressman had been poorly treated by the military commission. But in the battle for public opinion, the national Union Party succeeded in defining both the candidate and his candidacy.

Although it looms large in Civil War memory, Vallandigham's unsuccessful bid for the Ohio statehouse was not the first statewide campaign launched by a Peace Democrat. In February Connecticut Democrats had met in Hartford and nominated Thomas Hart Seymour as their candidate for governor. Whereas Vallandigham's judicial martyrdom would muddy his state's waters several months later, the Connecticut decision seemed clear. Seymour, a popular ex-governor and military hero, had been a consistent voice for an "honorable peace" from early in the war. When the party renominated him for governor, it actually went further than Ohio would, passing a platform including a resolution that "the democracy of Connecticut, sympathizing with their conservative brethren in the Middle and Western State, pledge themselves to unite with them in the adoption of all honorable measure having in view the secession of hostilities." Or, as one delegate declared at the convention, "We are against the War."

In the campaign, Connecticut Republicans worked to define their adversaries as treasonous Copperheads, while the Democrats fought back, calling their opponents radical abolitionists. The Hartford press launched into partisan battling and cartoonish portrayals of their enemies. On April 6 Connecticut voters selected Republican William A. Buckingham, but by a mere 2,634 votes. Democrats claimed political dirty tricks, arguing that the administration had manipulated military furloughs so that more Republican men could come home and vote. Connecticut Democrats had opted for a fairly unambiguous statement calling for an end of the war. Although they came close, the message in their failure seemed clear to the party nationwide. (Of course more moderate Democratic candidates had not fared better in statewide elections in New Hampshire and Rhode Island that spring.)[42]

Kentucky's mid-1863 state elections followed familiar patterns, shaped by geography and the persistent significance of the peculiar institution. On June 23 Thomas Elliott Bramlette announced his plans to run for governor. Bramlette, a Whig judge who had long been an annoyance to Governor Beriah Magoffin, declared that he was comfortable with Lincoln's Emancipation Proclamation, so long as federal measures did not interfere with slavery in Kentucky. Candidate Bramlette aligned with the state's Union Party and made it clear that he was no supporter of the administration's constitutional excesses, or its use of Black soldiers in the Union Army. Although campaigning on vastly different terrain, Bramlette's core arguments resonated with Horatio Seymour's campaign in New York. Both conservative politicians questioned the administration and defended a Constitution under siege. But each candidate was a staunch Union man, despite reservations about Lincoln. Bramlette faced Charles A. Wickliffe, a true Peace Democrat whose political beliefs aligned more clearly with Midwestern Copperheads. Both Bramlette and Wickliffe assured Kentuckians that they opposed arming Black men and would resist emancipation's incursion into the Bluegrass State. In the end voters in the crucial border state sided overwhelmingly with the Unionist Bramlette, who won 68,306 votes against the Copperhead Wickliffe's 17,386. The state's overall voter turnout declined by 40 percent, although assisted by considerable votes of Union soldiers, but Bramlette still won by a healthy margin.[43]

A month after Ohio Democrats nominated Vallandigham, the political world seemed to shift as the Union's military fortunes improved. In the first week of July Robert E. Lee's Army of Northern Virginia invaded Pennsylvania, only to be stopped in the bloody three-day battle at Gettysburg. The following day, on July 4, Confederate forces surrendered Vicksburg on the Mississippi River. Victory was not quite within sight, but it seemed imaginable. Those events complicated the arguments of the Peace Democrats. Those who were simply tired of the bloodshed or unable to see an end to the conflict had reason to rethink their stance.

Three days after Pickett's Charge in Gettysburg, T. J. Barnett sent Samuel Barlow another long letter, offering his sense of politics in flux. "The invasion must have killed the Peace party in Penna and New York," Barnett wrote. "The hatchet must be buried with Mr Lincoln, on the War question—the Conservatives ought to seek every occasion to show exactly what their position is (such men as Seymour and yourself &c).” Failing that, the distinctions between their conservative beliefs and “the other war men will be utterly lost sight of, & the Conservatives will find themselves without an efficient party,” he warned. Barnett, always savvy about political developments, insisted that “the victories must be Conservative victories; the energy of the war must be Conservative energy; the paeans of praise to the conquerors must be Conservative paeans; Democracy must stand . . . under the flag and of the side of its contributed authorities.” Conservative men like Barlow, who had supported the war while opposing the administration, must claim these victories for their cause rather than letting them be seen as a defeat for Democrats.

Barnett found this strategy obvious, and the Democrats' failings frustrating. He wondered when the Democracy would stop playing into the hands of their Republican adversaries, letting the party's most radical voices claim the spotlight: “When will they command the heart of the nation, instead of swaying with its whims and its fears? When will they discard such oracles as Fernando Wood, James Brooks, & Ingersoll, and Wall, and Vallandigham, and Voorhees, & not sporadically, but by a general voice.” The problem, he insisted, was that the party's conservative center had failed to wrest control of the party—and the Democracy's identity in national eyes—from those angry antiwar voices.[44]

George McClellan Writes a Letter

Pennsylvania's 1863 gubernatorial election proved crucial to defining the Democrats' political position moving forward. And indirectly, that campaign helped shape the party's presidential campaign the following year. To understand that narrative we must pick up the career of General George McClellan.

After Lincoln removed him from command not long after the Battle of Antietam, George and Ellen McClellan relocated to New Jersey; soon they moved to the 5th Avenue Hotel in New York City. For months the general rubbed shoulders with New York society, preferring the company of the city's leading Democratic politicians, journalists, and wirepullers. His admirers soon presented the McClellans with a home on West 31st Street. The general was careful to make no public statements hinting at a political career, and McClellan biographer Stephen Sears argues that well into 1863 there is no indication the trained military man had designs on political office. We know that as late as December 6, 1863, he told his mother that "I feel very indifferent about the White House," and that he was perfectly happy to leave the whole matter up to "Providence." Instead, he focused much of his energies on drafting a detailed account of his time as commander of the Army of the Potomac.[45]

But if McClellan had no political ambitions, that did not stop Democrats and Republicans from discussing his future. Often interested observers reported speculation that McClellan would return to uniform, saving the Union Army from the next disaster. Emma Biddle told Charles that she had heard rumors McClellan had "been sent for" only a week before the disastrous Battle of Fredericksburg. Nine days later Emma reported that "Burnside's stock seems low," perhaps paving the way to another change in command.[46] In January the general visited his father in Philadelphia, and loyal Democrat John L. Smith dropped by their house for an evening soiree, where the younger McClellan was the toast of the gathering.[47] Late the following June, as Robert E. Lee's army headed into Pennsylvania, the *Philadelphia Age* argued that the Army of the Potomac should be under McClellan's command. A few weeks after the battle, the *Philadelphia Age* published a humorous story describing how many Union soldiers who fought at Gettysburg actually believed that General McClellan had been in command.[48]

Meanwhile, McClellan's name was never far from Democratic talk of the political future. Maria Daly, who knew both McClellans and thought well of them, worried that "McClellan has injured himself by too much tampering with the ultra-Democrats" in New York.[49] On May 15, two weeks after Hooker's failure at Chancellorsville, as talk of recalling McClellan again rose, T. J. Barnett told Samuel Barlow that the administration's policies were "mad," and "for his own sake, McClellan should not be recalled." Barnett had great hopes for McClellan's political future, but he worried that a return to the military would only do the general harm. Barnett concluded that the general was too free in socializing with highly conservative Democrats whose devotion to the war effort might have been suspect. Ohio's ex-governor William Dennison agreed, warning that McClellan's political contacts risked undermining his public future.[50] As if to underscore that point, two weeks later notorious antiwar Philadelphia Democrat William Bradford Reed told Barlow that "I think the very good chance, of making Genl McClellan the Democratic Governor of Pennsylvania." If McClellan had national political aspirations, he would probably have been wise to steer clear of Reed and his crowd.[51]

Repeatedly friends and associates urged the general to make some public statement about his political beliefs and expectations. In May he gave an interview with the *Baltimore American,* which might have solidified his prowar credentials, but then he refused to let the editor publish it. Ohio War Democrats tried to convince him to run for governor, which would have demonstrated that he was no Copperhead, but he declined. In June he passed on an invitation from Thurlow Weed to speak to a New York audience, but he did agree to submit a public letter underscoring his belief that the war should be fought to an honorable conclusion while also supporting the rights of loyal citizens to own slaves. Generally, McClellan would not speak on national politics.[52]

In June 1863, not long after Ohio Democrats nominated Vallandigham, Pennsylvania Democrats selected Judge George Woodward to challenge Republican Andrew Curtin for governor. At the time Woodward appeared to be an excellent choice, and Governor Curtin—who was handicapped by charges of corruption as well as poor health—seemed like an appealing target. A well-known conservative, Woodward had a long resume in Pennsylvania courts, including an extended stretch on the state supreme court. The *Philadelphia Age* praised the decision: "He is a Democrat without a blemish upon his political record," the paper gushed, "and has never wavered in his devotion to the great doctrine of State rights and strict Constitutional construction."[53] Woodward was not a professional politician or a particularly savvy campaigner, but he enjoyed widespread respect as a solid conservative.

Shortly after his nomination Woodward took an important step by selecting Charles Biddle to serve as the chairman of the state Democratic Party's State Central Committee, where he would be in charge of Woodward's political future.[54] Biddle had valuable personal and familial connections and immense political acumen, as well as a politically useful background in the U.S. Army. A few weeks later, when Lee invaded Pennsylvania, Biddle took leave from his position to return to uniform, further solidifying himself as a Democrat who was also a proud patriot. Not long after Gettysburg, Biddle agreed to return to his post steering the party's gubernatorial election.[55] The battle between Curtin and Woodward was going to be close; Democrats statewide seemed optimistic that their man would unseat Curtin. In late August James Buchanan, who continued to watch politics from Wheatland, wrote, "I concur with you in believing that no better nomination could have been made than Judge Woodward, & from all my information I think he will be elected."[56]

As election day approached, Biddle calculated that the campaign needed a boost. On September 2 he drafted a letter to McClellan. Although not a Pennsylvanian, McClellan had strong ties in the state and enjoyed an enthusiastic following among voters. On the other hand, he had resisted overtures to make partisan statements, especially those that might be understood as criticizing the Lincoln administration, particularly since he remained in the military and perhaps still entertained hopes of returning to command. The general was already a national figure, and his objections to the Lincoln administration, and specifically to the president's approach to emancipation, were well known. He had every political incentive to keep his head down and sit out the 1863 state elections.

The crafty Biddle's letter adopted just the right strategy. "I beg leave to bring to your notice the fact that in the present political canvass in Pennsylvania your name is used in a manner inconsistent with truth and with the best interests of our country," he wrote. Specifically, local publications had claimed that McClellan was supporting Governor Curtin's reelection. With this in mind, Biddle wrote, "I solicit you to make or authorize a statement of the fact that you agree with those who believe that the election of Judge Woodward the Democratic candidate for governor of Pennsylvania would be the political event most favorable to the [ ] of civil liberty and the restoration of the Union."[57] Biddle calculated that McClellan's support would be an invaluable aid to the judge's campaign, particularly because Woodward had alienated Union soldiers by suggesting they should not be allowed to cast absentee ballots. Reporting that McClellan's name had been linked to Curtin seemed a wise strategy for luring the general to the Woodward camp.[58]

For McClellan and his New York advisors, the Pennsylvania election raised important discussions. On the 25th he wrote to Barlow, assuring the political insider that he was well aware of the "Penna proposition" and "shall give it full & fair consideration." Barlow advised that McClellan could save the election in Pennsylvania if he were to openly endorse Woodward, while his silence could undermine his future aspirations.[59] At the end of the month McClellan traveled to Philadelphia, much to the interest of political observers. David H. Williams—a longtime comrade of McClellan—wrote to Barlow from Pittsburgh, reporting that "I have heard to day, that at the urgent request of some distinguished Democrats, that Genl McClellan would soon, in a public speech in Philadelphia, define his position politically and declare his preference for Judge Woodward in the present contest." Williams felt that such an endorsement would be good for an additional ten thousand Woodward votes, although he worried that it could hurt the general's national political prospects.[60]

McClellan visited Philadelphia but did not deliver a speech. He did, however, have one extraordinary political conversation. Sometime around midnight on September 29, a messenger came to Biddle's Philadelphia home, summoning him to General McClellan's hotel. The next day Biddle shared a detailed account of his "interview with the General" with his boss, Judge Woodward. "There had evidently been some misconception of his views and immediate intentions, in his visit to this city," Biddle reported. "What I now write to say is that Gen. McClellan so expressed himself to me about yourself and the cause that a similar expression from him, with such publicity as he would think fit and agreeable, would do great good at the present time." Biddle offered Woodward his assessment of the general's political abilities: "He is not so conversant as you may suppose with our state politics, or the opinions of individuals. A frank and friendly exposition of matters from yourself will no doubt give him much information on those subjects." In sum, Woodward's political manager had met with McClellan in the dead of night and suggested he endorse Judge Woodward, fully aware that the general was not particularly aware of local politics.[61]

A few days later Biddle, whose capacity for political manipulation was matchless, sent a letter to General Andrew Porter. Porter had been the provost marshal for the Army of the Potomac and had married a member of the massive Philadelphia Biddle clan, but most importantly, in September 1863 he was in Philadelphia and in regular contact with McClellan. Biddle addressed General Porter as Andrew, and he made it clear that this note was a backchannel route to communicate with the general. Biddle was unambiguous. Porter could share his letter with McClellan, and if it was "not found agreeable," the general could refuse it and "it need not be considered as any formal way delivered to the General, and the matter need not go further." In this fashion, Biddle wrote to McClellan, through Porter, in a form that could be easily denied.

Biddle went on to suggest text that McClellan might use in a public statement. His proposed text included, "Were I now a resident and voter in Pennsylvania my vote should be cast for the candidates of the Democratic party, because the principles set out in the platform and entertained by the great mass of that party, and also as I am well-assured by Judge Woodward, its candidate for governor, are principles that accord more closely with my own than those avowed by any other party now in the political field." Biddle was using an indirect route, through a relation by marriage, to ghostwrite a public statement by McClellan supporting his candidate. Biddle explained to Porter, "This is, in substance, what I understood the General to intimate that he would desire to say, if he should determine to say anything for publication by his authority."[62]

Less than two weeks later McClellan sent Biddle a letter for public consumption. Versions of this public letter appeared all over the local and national press, and in broadsides aimed at workers and soldiers. McClellan's letter began by noting that the Philadelphia *Press* had published dishonest stories, claiming that he had endorsed Governor Curtin for reelection. "I cannot longer maintain silence under such misrepresentation," he declared. Instead, he wanted Biddle to explain that the *Press* had printed untruths and that

> having some few days ago had a full conversation with Judge Woodward, find that our views agree, and I regard his election as Governor of Pennsylvania, called for by the interest of the Nation. I understand Judge Woodward to be in favor of the Prosecution of the War with all the means at the command of the Loyal States, until the Military power of the Rebellion is destroyed. I understand him to be of the opinion that while the War is waged with all possible decision and energy, the policy directing it should be in consonance with the principle of humanity and civilization.

McClellan's letter concluded, "Believing that our opinions entirely agree upon these points I would, were it in my power, give to Judge Woodward my voice and vote."[63]

So, what had happened here? The simple answer is that at the eleventh hour, General George McClellan endorsed Democratic Judge George Woodward in the Pennsylvania governor's race in 1863. The judge went on to lose a close race against Curtin.[64] The results certainly mattered tremendously for the history of the state and the nation during the Civil War. But when we consider McClellan's role and his political future, there are two intertwined questions of some interest.

First, why did McClellan endorse Woodward? Sears notes that McClellan's support of Woodward illustrates his political naïveté, particularly when faced with rumors that he had supported Curtin. Sears argues that the decision to endorse Woodward reflected careful discussions with his New York advisors, especially Samuel Barlow and Manton Marble. It was, they felt, a gamble, but one that made the best sense in the grand scheme of things.[65]

Another version of the same narrative accepts that McClellan was indeed naïve, or at least a political neophyte who was too arrogant to recognize his inexperience. In this version, Congressman Biddle, a man who understood people and politics, played McClellan like a cheap violin. First, he established to McClellan that the rumors the general had endorsed Curtin were widespread and disturbing. Then, when faced with the unbelievable opportunity after McClellan invited Biddle to his Philadelphia hotel after midnight, Biddle sold him on the general concept that he should meet with Woodward and he should be open to a public statement endorsing the Democratic candidate. Finally, as a *coup de grâce,* once McClellan had chatted with the candidate, Biddle sent Porter a

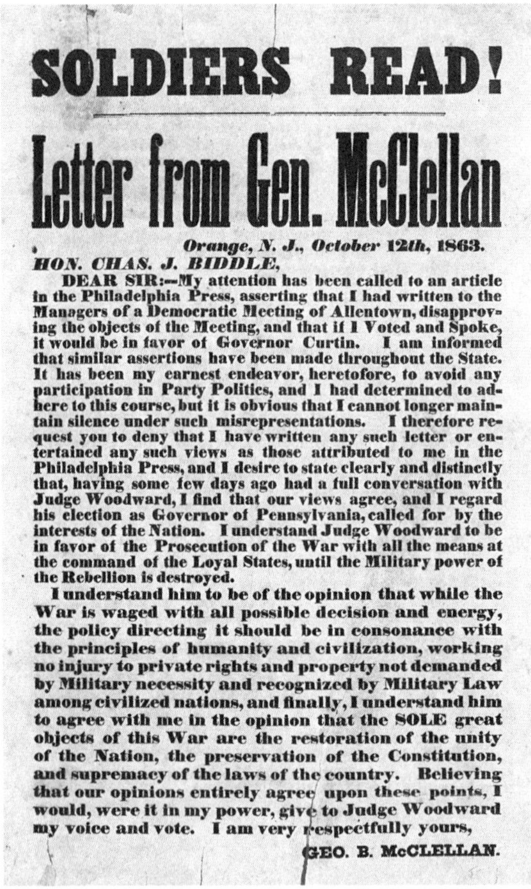

SOLDIERS READ!

Letter from Gen. McClellan

Orange, N. J., October 12th, 1863.

HON. CHAS. J. BIDDLE,

DEAR SIR:—My attention has been called to an article in the Philadelphia Press, asserting that I had written to the Managers of a Democratic Meeting of Allentown, disapproving the objects of the Meeting, and that if I Voted and Spoke, it would be in favor of Governor Curtin. I am informed that similar assertions have been made throughout the State. It has been my earnest endeavor, heretofore, to avoid any participation in Party Politics, and I had determined to adhere to this course, but it is obvious that I cannot longer maintain silence under such misrepresentations. I therefore request you to deny that I have written any such letter or entertained any such views as those attributed to me in the Philadelphia Press, and I desire to state clearly and distinctly that, having some few days ago had a full conversation with Judge Woodward, I find that our views agree, and I regard his election as Governor of Pennsylvania, called for by the interests of the Nation. I understand Judge Woodward to be in favor of the Prosecution of the War with all the means at the command of the Loyal States, until the Military power of the Rebellion is destroyed.

I understand him to be of the opinion that while the War is waged with all possible decision and energy, the policy directing it should be in consonance with the principles of humanity and civilization, working no injury to private rights and property not demanded by Military necessity and recognized by Military Law among civilized nations, and finally, I understand him to agree with me in the opinion that the SOLE great objects of this War are the restoration of the unity of the Nation, the preservation of the Constitution, and supremacy of the laws of the country. Believing that our opinions entirely agree upon these points, I would, were it in my power, give to Judge Woodward my voice and vote. I am very respectfully yours,

GEO. B. McCLELLAN.

Broadside: Letter from General McClellan. In 1863 General George B. McClellan broke his long political silence when he wrote his public letter to Charles Biddle endorsing George Woodward, the Democratic candidate for governor in Pennsylvania. The letter was immediately reprinted in newspapers across the North and also in single-sheet broadsides. (Library of Congress)

draft of a public statement that McClellan *might* issue. Before very long, McClellan had sent Biddle a public letter that looked an awful lot like Biddle's draft. Barlow and Marble might have been right that on balance it made sense for McClellan to endorse Woodward, but it is hard to read the evidence without crediting Biddle with making it happen.

This leads us to a second big question: was it a mistake for McClellan to endorse Woodward? In terms of Pennsylvania politics, it is hard to see that his endorsement—coming on the eve of the election—mattered much. It obviously did not push Woodward over Curtin. McClellan's New York advisors may have been correct that the public letter established McClellan as a loyal Democrat. It certainly established him as politically engaged, rather than just an observer watching from the sidelines. And that probably cost him any slim chance of returning to a military post.

But from the perspective of McClellan's political present and future, the crucial issue was whether it was a mistake to attach his name to that of Judge Woodward. This was—and still is—a thorny question. The national Democratic Party was divided in the spring and fall of 1863, and they would be even more so the following November. Democrats in Connecticut and Ohio had both nominated men who opposed the war, and the New England candidate had already run unsuccessfully on an antiwar platform. McClellan's political challenge was to establish himself as a loyal patriot while also marking out territory as an ideological critic of Lincoln and his administration. The astute political path was as a member of the loyal opposition, but not as a treasonous Copperhead. Where did Judge Woodward fit into this emerging Democratic spectrum?

Woodward's admirers—both in 1863 and since then—have portrayed him as a dedicated jurist with strong conservative sensibilities. On occasion his legal opinions or personal inclinations ran counter to the administration's perspective on major constitutional issues. During the secession crisis, Woodward had indicated that it was constitutional for states to leave the Union, and he worried that the Republican victory placed the institution of slavery in immediate jeopardy.[66] No supporter of federal activism, he had questioned the Legal Tender Act and seemed inclined to rule against conscription as well. In the eyes of many Democrats, Woodward was a man of strong conservative convictions but hardly a treasonous Copperhead who opposed the war itself. His defenders were quick to point out that Woodward had two sons in the Union Army, one of whom had been wounded at Gettysburg.

Rather like the Ohio Democrats' platform, the resolutions passed by Pennsylvania Democrats in Harrisburg on June 17 made it quite clear that they objected to the current administration, and particularly the Emancipation Proclamation and multiple transgressions of constitutional law, but they stopped well short of questioning the war itself, and the resolutions did not call for immediate peace. They did, however, declare that Democrats would "hail with pleasure and delight any manifestation of a desire on the part of the seceded States to return to their allegiance to the government of the Union." Pennsylvania's Democrats would be perfectly happy to welcome back the Confederate states in a mutually agreeable peace, and with no suggestion that slavery would be affected.[67]

Because he maintained his position as a sitting judge while running for governor, Woodward had a good excuse for saying almost nothing about the policy issues of the day. Even as northerners debated the constitutionality of federal conscription, Woodward declined to offer an opinion since the issue would soon appear before him in court. But the relative absence of a public record left the field open for creative Republican operatives to define Woodward to voters. In addition to charging him with bias against soldiers, Republicans managed to repeat a wealth of rumors that cast the judge in the most unfavorable terms. One story claimed that he had not only endorsed the constitutionality of secession but had suggested that perhaps Pennsylvania should join the seceding states. Another claimed that Woodward—who was known as having no personal objections to slavery—had questioned the constitutionality of abolition. A particularly creative rumor reported that after Woodward's son was wounded at Gettysburg, the judge told his child that he wished the boy had been killed.[68] Between Woodward's known and presumed opinions, and a wide assortment of published rumors, the judge's adversaries managed to paint him as a traitorous Copperhead. And on the eve of the election, McClellan, who—as Biddle noted—knew little of Pennsylvania politics, issued his public endorsement.

Chauncey Burr's *The Old Guard* embraced Woodward. The Copperhead journal praised the judge's previous stances on secession and states' rights, and his occasional comments that seemed to endorse the right to own slaves. But while Burr liked Woodward's conservative constitutionalism, he stopped short of claiming the Pennsylvanian as a kindred spirit when it came to peace, noting Woodward's two sons in the army and arguing that as governor he would support constitutional means to subdue the rebellion.[69]

Biddle, the veteran of two wars himself, did his best to defend his candidate with Woodward's own words. In mid-September the Democratic State Central Committee published a pamphlet combining Woodward's December 1860 address on the secession crisis and the party platform passed in June. Biddle authored a short introduction to the pamphlet, explaining that the publication's goal was to counter the waves of misinformation about the candidate. The judge, he insisted, had been "the subject of constant misrepresentation and misquotation by partisan speakers and writers," as the actual texts would demonstrate. But at that point the battle for public perception may have been lost.[70]

While the *Philadelphia Age* praised Woodward's candidacy and underscored that he was not a crazed antiwar candidate, John Forney's Philadelphia *Press* adopted a very different approach. On September 17 the paper declared that electing Woodward would make Pennsylvania "an enemy of the Union," comparing the judge to Kentucky's Governor Beriah Magoffin.[71] On the day McClellan endorsed Woodward, the *Press* insisted that "Woodward may not be a traitor, but every traitor is for Woodward."[72] Forney's paper reprinted

McClellan's letter to Biddle in full. The *Press* discussed the implications of McClellan's latest claim that he and Woodward saw eye to eye on major issues. This, the editorial suggested, would seem to indicate that McClellan—like Woodward—was an enthusiastic supporter of slavery, and one who would happily "place Pennsylvania at the feet of the rebel Confederacy." The *Press* concluded that if it turned out McClellan really wrote this letter, "he has ended his career," because loyal soldiers and citizens would never accept him.[73] The *Philadelphia Age,* in stark contrast, praised both the general and his letter, but it did predict that McClellan's endorsement of Woodward would invite attacks from Woodward's many enemies.[74]

Elsewhere in the state, newspapers responded to the endorsement according to their partisan leanings. Clearfield's *Raftsman's Journal* took McClellan to task for turning his back on Curtin, who had always been a great supporter, and suggested that the general had been the dupe of unscrupulous New York Democrats who had taken "the quality of manhood" from McClellan.[75] The *Sunbury American* took its lead from the *Press,* arguing that McClellan's letter had been "extorted from him" by Woodward's people, and agreed with the Philadelphia paper that if it turns out the general really wrote the letter, it could only hurt him in the long run.[76]

The public letter also received substantial attention nationwide. On October 13 the Republican *Chicago Tribune* noted that Iowa, Ohio, and Pennsylvania all faced crucial elections, where "the victory of the Copperheads" would have dire consequences. The *Tribune* saw McClellan's letter to Biddle as a feeble attempt to appeal to soldiers. But, the paper concluded, the letter would not help Woodward, but it would surely hurt McClellan: "The letter proves the General to be a puppet in the hands of politicians."[77] In some cases editors merely reprinted McClellan's letter, or a short summary, with little or no comment.[78] More took the occasion to fire salvoes at either Curtin or Woodward, and some had a few choice words for McClellan as well.

The *Cleveland Morning Leader*—another important Republican paper—ran an extended editorial on McClellan's endorsement of Woodward. The paper pointed out that it was a good thing McClellan had made this announcement, which essentially put his cards on the table. By endorsing Woodward, the editorial claimed, McClellan had revealed himself to be a Copperhead: "It places him at once and forever among the enemies of his country."[79] Warren County, Ohio's *Western Reserve Chronicle* joked at how McClellan's endorsement of Woodward simply meant that both men would go down together.[80] The *Chicago Tribune,* quoting an unnamed Pennsylvanian, noted the election results, and concluded that McClellan's letter was "powder wasted" and evidence that he was not "a clever politician."[81]

Many of the contemporary accounts, like the *Chicago Tribune,* perceived a clear connection between the Pennsylvania election and others—most particularly Ohio's—that involved antiwar Democrats. To these journalists, the Woodward campaign was understood as part of a national Copperhead scourge, and McClellan's letter to Biddle had made him complicit. The Wilmington *Delaware State Journal and Statesman* pulled no punches. Dubbing McClellan a "Moral Traitor," the paper declared that the general had "long been accused of being in the secrets of the Copperhead disunionists of the Vallandigham-Seymour school," invoking the names of the Democratic gubernatorial candidates in Ohio and Connecticut. For the longest time, the journal insisted, McClellan's true sympathies had been suspected, and even his battlefield performances questioned, but with his endorsement of Woodward the general's true colors had been revealed.[82] The *Baltimore American* published very similar sentiments, which were reprinted in a Wheeling, West Virginia, paper. "Next to Vallandigham," the editorial declared, "there is no man in the country whose loyalty has been more strongly impeached than Judge Woodward." By ending his silence and endorsing Woodward, McClellan had made his true sentiments known.[83]

If we accept Biddle's general narrative of events, it seems that the general and the judge did sit down for a friendly chat about politics, where McClellan concluded that Woodward shared his general vision about the war and the future of the nation. That was a conservative vision, and one that had no enthusiasm for emancipation as a war aim, but it was also a prowar perspective that did not deserve the label "Copperhead." And, as Biddle suggested, McClellan probably knew almost nothing of the negative talk about Judge Woodward when he signed the public letter to Biddle.

Although Woodward might have defined himself as a political conservative and constitutional purist, and McClellan might have seen him in those terms as a kindred spirit, northern newspaper readers, and especially Republicans, received ample contradictory evidence. Many accounts linked the Pennsylvania elections with the gubernatorial contests in Ohio, Connecticut, and New York. McClellan's critics presented him as in league with the Copperheads, if not as a traitor to his country. Moving forward, some northern voters would have McClellan firmly yoked to Judge Woodward and his losing campaign, and for many that placed the general on the antiwar wing of the Democratic Party a full year before the election of 1864. It was a charge he would have to combat in the year to come.[84]

If Democrats in 1863 lacked unanimity in their stance on the war, or how best to define themselves and proceed as the party of opposition, their partisan adversaries had effectively moved into the unoccupied ideological terrain, painting Democratic candidates and their supporters as Copperheads and disloyal advocates of treason. And they had made major headway in tarring the party's likely presidential standard-bearer with the same brush. Observers like T. J. Barnett were left to tear at their hair in exasperation.

Pulpits and Politics

On October 3, 1863, shortly before McClellan wrote to Biddle endorsing George Woodward, Abraham Lincoln issued a Thanksgiving Proclamation calling for a national day of thanksgiving on the last Thursday in November. Coming roughly a year after his Preliminary Emancipation Proclamation, this new proclamation focused on peace and victory, but also healing without retribution. He did not touch on the crucial, but potentially divisive, themes related to emancipation and freedom. Lincoln hoped that the day of thanksgiving would bring the nation together. He also ended up laying the groundwork for an annual holiday. New England wags noted that the president had proposed a national day celebrating Union, grafted onto an existing day of thanksgiving already celebrated in many states.

Following the president's suggestion, Protestant ministers across the North delivered sermons of thanksgiving on the announced day. The addresses were generally patriotic, celebrating Union rather than explicit military affairs, although the recent victory of Union forces at the Battle of Chattanooga certainly made the day that much sweeter. Some abolitionist ministers took the opportunity to commemorate emancipation and freedom while anticipating reunion.[85] Across the North, local newspapers reported on the Thanksgiving Day sermons delivered throughout the community. They continued a pattern that had begun in the first months of the war. Northern religious leaders had grown accustomed to using their pulpits to blend religious teaching with talk of Union, loyalty, and duty. Congregations periodically distributed the most powerful to broader audiences in privately printed pamphlets.[86]

This national coming together in a day of spirituality and patriotism had symbolic weight, yoking houses of worship with the national cause and underscoring the overall power of Union.[87] But like other wartime moments when words and symbolic actions reflected a surge in patriotism, there was—for some—another side of that coin. The expectation that ministers would use their positions to endorse the national cause posed challenges for some men of the cloth. No doubt some northern ministers privately—or not so privately—opposed the administration and perhaps even supported the Confederacy. Or, like Bishop John Henry Hopkins, they retained dreams of rejoining with their co-religionists in the Confederate states.

Some evangelical Democrats and their ministers disagreed with abolitionists and Republicans on spiritual grounds. Some placed the Bible and the Constitution on the same plane, concluding that their political adversaries could not run roughshod over the Constitution while still being on the right side of the Bible. Others, even those who did not embrace the teachings of a Bishop Hopkins, concluded that abolitionism ran counter to the nation's spiritual well-being. The Democratic press ran articles with titles such as "Why Christ Did Not Proclaim Emancipation."[88]

But for others the call to use the pulpit to celebrate the Union, and lecture young men on their patriotic duty, posed more complex dilemmas. From after Fort Sumter, some Protestant ministers, and many Catholic priests, had refused to use their spiritual voices for what they saw as political—or at least secular—ends. With the passage of time, this became a more difficult conviction to observe. Here, once again, the weight of broadly shared patriotic fervor produced forces—in the hands of civilians, government officials, and military authorities—that sought to silence or punish dissent.[89] The examples are many. In Allegheny City, Pennsylvania, Reverend William Plumer, a Presbyterian minister, had established a successful church and a growing flock. But when the war came he declined to pray for military victories, and he refused to respond when Lincoln called for national days of prayer. And while other ministers dutifully read official decrees from their pulpits, Plumer insisted on steering clear of all hints of politics, even when pressured by prominent church members. Eventually, members of his flock and the larger community came to question Plumer's loyalty. Plumer—who did have personal ties with the South—refused to budge on a position that he insisted was based on his sense of the proper role of a minister. On September 17, 1862, the day Union and Confederate blood flowed along Antietam Creek, Plumer—facing a divided flock, a hostile local press, and an unsupportive presbytery—abandoned his ministry.[90]

In the border states, where local and federal authorities worried most about disloyalty in their midst, recalcitrant ministers became repeated targets, as notions of the separation of church and state seemed to dissolve in the face of military conflict. In early 1863 the provost marshal in Baltimore ordered that churches fly the American flag. When Methodist minister John Dashiell repeatedly declined to display the stars and stripes, supported in his stance by his flock, Provost Marshal William S. Fish ordered him thrown in jail.

To the west, clergymen dedicated to neutrality, or opposed to using their position for political speech, faced pressures from civilians and authorities. For some, this rejection of "politics" became a route to dodging the moral issues surrounding slavery, often when speaking to congregations full of slave owners. In contested portions of Kentucky and Missouri, clergymen found themselves pressured to sign loyalty oaths, despite their hopes of remaining "neutral" on political matters. Jesse Bird, a southern Methodist minister in Missouri, refused to preach after congregants displayed Union flags over the doors of the churches where he worked. Locals turned him in to the military authorities, and when Bird declined to sign a loyalty oath they banished him from the state. On multiple occasions, border-state ministers ran afoul of the authorities when they failed to follow federal suggestions about fast days and prayers of thanksgiving.[91] In other episodes in Missouri outspoken Democratic clergy faced a greater threat from angry crowds threatening violence.[92]

In the most celebrated border-state case, Samuel B. McPheeters, a North Carolina native who was the minister at the Pine Street Presbyterian Church in St. Louis, agreed to swear loyalty oaths to both Missouri and the Constitution. But beyond that he insisted on being entirely neutral, declaring that he was not "a friend or advocate of any party or section, but an ambassador of One whose kingdom is not of this world." McPheeters insisted that he expressed loyalty by declining to pray for the Confederacy or support it in any way. Union forces demanded a more positive affirmation of where he stood. Like Plumer's congregation, McPheeters's flock divided, with a large portion insisting on further evidence of loyalty while others approved of his claims of neutrality.

Things came to a head in June 1862 when a congregant brought his son to be baptized with the name "Sterling Price," as an homage to a notorious Confederate general. McPheeters did as he was asked, infuriating many Unionists. The provost marshal banished McPheeters from the state. McPheeters did not go gently. He traveled to Washington and found a receptive audience in Attorney General Edward Bates and then with President Lincoln. Lincoln ordered the minister reinstated, and on January 2, 1863, the chief executive issued a statement noting that McPheeters had sworn a loyalty oath and had not seemed to violate it. Moreover, although he left ample room for federal impositions on church autonomy, the president wished that federal forces should not "undertake to run the churches." The provost marshal allowed McPheeters to return to St. Louis, but despite Lincoln's decree the marshal refused to let McPheeters preach at the Pine

Street Church. It would not be until a year later that the ban was lifted, which merely reignited controversy. Finally, in 1864 the presbytery heard the case and voted to support the Unionists at Pine Street who wanted McPheeters gone.[93]

The stories of Plumer and McPheeters and a host of other wartime ministers underscore some key points about free speech and loyalty during the Civil War. When Lincoln called for a day of thanksgiving, most Protestant ministers—even those in the border states—happily accepted the premise and joined in affirming their commitment to the Union. Some who declined—either out of political beliefs or because they objected to engaging in politics at all—faced pressure from civil or military authorities who wanted displays of loyalty.

In the McPheeters case, the popular story seems to be that in the end Abraham Lincoln stood up for freedom of religion (at least if you signed a loyalty oath). But despite the president's statement, the St. Louis officials did not allow McPheeters to preach for another year. More importantly, both McPheeters and Plumer faced the greatest pressure from Unionists in their own flocks, as well as from members of the larger community. And they received no support from larger religious authorities. One historian notes that collectively these cases "reveal the limits of enforced loyalty in the North."[94] That point is well taken. Civilians remained divided in the border states. But the broader story is that whereas military authorities could do little to control the actions of the clergy, time and again ministers who either privately opposed the war or who held strong convictions about politics in the pulpit confronted strong-minded Unionists in their congregations and communities who rejected such stances.[95]

In some border-state congregations, political opinions split and dissenting congregants found tools to critique Unionist ministers. Some angry members refused to attend prescribed Thanksgiving Day events and even withheld expected tithes. And the other side of this coin was that in border-state congregations full of Democrats, ministers faced different sorts of support and pressure. In some cases these congregants pooled resources to pay commutation fees to help members avoid service. Where congregations split over politics, Democrats banded together to start new churches.[96] In the end it was individual parishioners, not government forces, that probably had the most powerful hand in controlling ministerial speech in the wartime North.

The president's Thanksgiving Day proclamation, and the other national days of prayer, called on northerners to come together to pray for the Union. These became public events, with local newspapers running entire pages of stories on how churches marked the day of thanksgiving. Such national spiritual occasions, rather like the rebranding of the Republican Party as the Union Party, and the partisan efforts to define opposition Democrats as treasonous, helped craft a national Republican discourse where true loyal citizens were cut from the same cloth. In this fashion, it was public opinion—more so than governmental action—that suppressed the freedom to dissent.[97]

Adversaries fought this political battle over religious behavior on multiple fronts. Openly disloyal ministers risked arrest, especially in the border states. The Republican press commonly insisted on patriotism from the North's ministers, and some took to charging those who declined to address politics from the pulpit as inherently hypocritical, using their reticence to mask disloyalty. Northern ministers, puffed up with their righteous patriotism, fired salvoes at their brethren who disagreed with the administration or the war. One minister in the Methodist Episcopal Church made it clear: a "Copperhead cannot be a Christian; and he who is not a Christian is not a proper person to preach the Gospel."[98] He was hardly alone. Large numbers of ministers at annual conferences in Illinois, Indiana, and Ohio faced disciplinary trials during the war, largely for charges of disloyalty, and often on the flimsiest of evidence.[99] The Democratic press fought back, although badly outnumbered. One Pennsylvania columnist bemoaned "that the distraction of our country has been produced by introducing politics in the pulpit" to the detriment of true spiritual discourse.[100] *The Old Guard* noted the war and politics creeping into religious sermons and asked, "Could the madness of the hour leave us no spot, not even the altars of religion, free from the embattled elements of the world?"[101]

The accused ministers sometimes spoke eloquently in their own defense, On October 18, 1864, a year following Lincoln's Thanksgiving Proclamation, Henry J. Van Dyke, a Democrat and Presbyterian minister from New York, delivered an angry sermon on "The Spirituality and Independence of the Church" to the Presbyterian synod. Responding to the synod's resolution endorsing emancipation and the Republican Party, Van Dyke unleashed a vigorous dissent. Citing the recent McPheeters case, where the assembly "did apparently sanction the interference of the secular power with the spiritual affairs of our churches," Van Dyke offered a series of resolutions calling on the church to return to its core principles, to "preach the gospel" without allowing the "interference of civil magistrates or military commanders," and without endorsing any political party.[102] Van Dyke wanted his church to keep out of politics, and he especially disliked the arrogance of the spiritual claims made by northern abolitionists. He had his say in the synod and suffered no official sanctions. But he did face threatened violence from an angry abolitionist mob. Thus was the danger of speaking against the national Union consensus.[103]

Miscegenation

Near the end of 1863 two journalists for the Democratic *New York World* took a creative, and thoroughly dishonest, stab at defining the differences between Democrats and Republicans, adding a new wrinkle to the ongoing battles over the meanings of Union, duty, loyalty, and patriotism. David G. Croly and George Wakeman concocted a scheme to write and publish a long and curious pamphlet called *Miscegenation: The Theory of the Blending of the Races, Applied to the American White Man and Negro.* The seventy-one-page pamphlet appeared in print at the very start of 1864. The authors, publishing anonymously, coined the term "miscegenation" to describe the mixing of the races. Their underlying "theory," presented in faux scientific language, argued that the long-term solution to the nation's racial problems was to encourage greater racial mixing, producing a congenial society of multiracial Americans.

It was a complex scheme. The idea was to convince voters that the nation's Republicans supported this notion of "miscegenation," with the assumption that most voters would recoil at the idea. Of course that presented an additional challenge: how could they convince northern voters that Republicans backed this race-based social engineering? The authors primed the pump by publishing their document with an "Appendix" of statements from leading abolitionist writers and newspapers, including Wendell Phillips, Harriet Beecher Stowe, Theodore Tilton, New York's *Independent* and *Tribune,* and other publications. But while those passages imagined a world of racial justice, they predated Croly and Wakeman's manifesto and did not really endorse its sentiments. The challenge was to lure abolitionists into supporting the actual text, so that they could portray the opposition as the radical party of racial mixing. On February 17 Sunset Cox—unaware that the pamphlet was a fraud—took a major step toward that argument when he rose in Congress to deliver a speech assailing the pamphlet, with copious quotations from the text, and reading from the letters of abolitionists who supposedly had endorsed its arguments.[104]

The reporters from the *World* had undertaken an ambitious version of what a century later would be termed "dirty tricks." They had fabricated an entire Republican argument for why the races should mix, socially, sexually, and genetically, hoping to appall Democrats. The idea was to affect future elections by turning voters against Lincoln and the Republicans. Time would tell whether the fake pamphlet would serve its purpose. While other Democrats across the country were attempting to define what the Democratic Party really stood for,

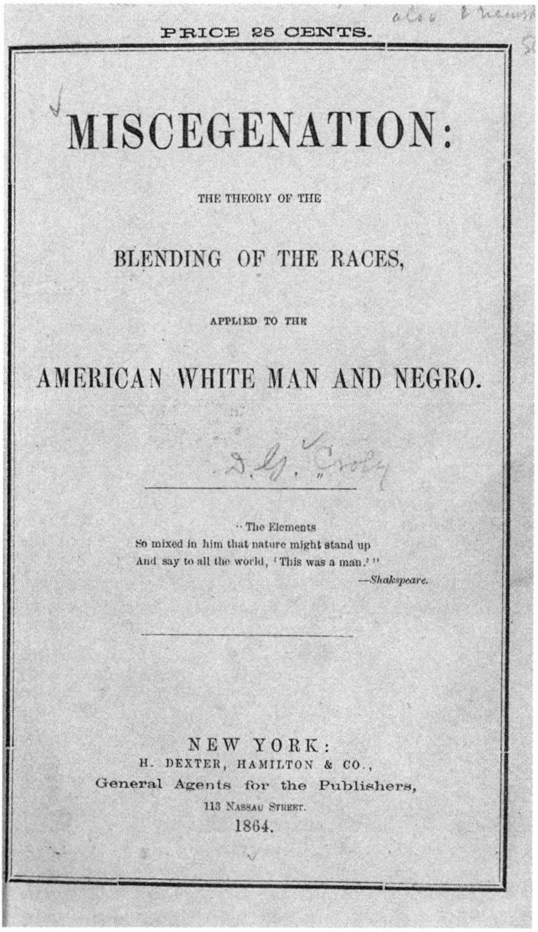
PRICE 25 CENTS.

MISCEGENATION:

THE THEORY OF THE

BLENDING OF THE RACES,

APPLIED TO THE

AMERICAN WHITE MAN AND NEGRO.

"The Elements
So mixed in him that nature might stand up
And say to all the world, 'This was a man.'"
—*Shakspeare.*

NEW YORK:
H. DEXTER, HAMILTON & CO.,
General Agents for the Publishers,
113 Nassau Street.
1864.

Pamphlet: *Miscegenation; The Theory of the Blending of the Races, Applied to the American White Man and Negro,* 1864. This lengthy pamphlet by David G. Croly and George Wakeman was the product of an elaborate hoax. Published in New York in 1864, the pamphlet purported to present a highly scientific argument in favor of "the blending of the races." In truth, it was an early case of "fake news," where the author sought to turn White northerners against abolitionist Republicans. (Library of Congress)

and what it meant to be of an opposition party in wartime, Croly and Wakeman, not unlike the Republicans who perfected the art of calling those opposition leaders disloyal Copperheads, had taken an important step in constructing a competing version of their partisan opponents. If Democrats were traitors to their nation, then let the Republicans be defined as traitors to their race. And so a crucial election year began.

7

Bracing for an Electoral Clash

The year 1864 would prove crucial to the Civil War and the nation's political history. The presidential election at the close of the year promised to settle key questions about the future of the military conflict, slavery, and the relationship between the United States and the Confederacy. It would surely be vital to the future of the Democratic Party.

The State of Political Discussion

By the first weeks of 1864 national political leaders in both parties had shifted their attention to the presidential election that would close the year. Although Abraham Lincoln was the nation's commander in chief in the midst of a bloody civil war, many in his party were not quite settled on renominating the president, preferring instead to consider several more radical alternatives. Meanwhile, the opposition Democrats were badly divided about how to proceed. And the Republicans commonly campaigned under the banner of the National Union Party, inviting patriotic Democrats to abandon party for nation, an appeal that attracted some portion of northern Democrats. Political professionals had much to discuss.

The North's rank-and-file citizenry looked at things with concern and skepticism. The crucial policy debates that had driven the state elections in 1862 and 1863 persisted as the nation approached the end of the war's third year. Although the July 1863 draft under the federal Enrollment Act had been numerically the largest federal draft, and the source of the greatest civil unrest, the federal government would declare three further drafts in 1864, each provoking active enlistment drives and substantial resentment.[1] As the year began, it was anybody's guess how many more men the United States might need to defeat the Confederacy or how many new drafts might be announced.

By January 1864 the Emancipation Proclamation had been in effect for a full year, but that did not mean emancipation and its potential impact on the northern states was somehow a settled political—or social—issue. The controversial pamphlet *Miscegenation*—or at least the themes it raised—had struck a nerve among some northern readers, seeming to promise—or threaten—a future blending of the races as freed people made their way into the free states. As the United States armed Black men in the nation's service, the most racist and antiwar Democratic publications banged the miscegenation drum, stressing the dangers these Black men in blue uniforms posed to northern society. When the 20th Regiment of the United States Colored Troops marched out of New York City in March, many locals gathered to give them a patriotic sendoff, and much of the local press marked the occasion with modest approval. But for others, like Manton Marble's *New York World,* the parade became the occasion for wry commentary about lovely White maidens waving their handkerchiefs as uniformed Black men marched by. *The Old Guard* printed the names of 152 "shameless women" who had signed a banner celebrating the Black men and offering their "love and honor," inviting readers to draw their own conclusions. A few months later a similar procession in Chicago prompted the *Chicago Times* to claim that "white women were in attendance to bid farewell to black husbands." Democratic newspapers in Philadelphia and New York took these miscegenation themes to their logical conclusions, publishing stories about White women marrying Black men, commonly blaming such "depraved" behavior on Republicans.[2]

While this interconnected network of radical Democratic newspapers stressed the social dangers of racial interactions and the elevation of Black troops, their editors eagerly grasped onto any stories—true, imagined, or exaggerated—that portrayed Black soldiers as violent or as sexual predators. The Columbus, Ohio, *Crisis* ran a detailed account of eighteen members of the United States Colored Troops accosting and killing an elderly Tennessee man, and then drowning the man's son and four grandchildren. In early 1864 the *Crisis* published a story alleging that several Black members of the 55th Massachusetts Regiment had raped a White woman. The *Chicago Times* ran a lurid story about Black troops in Vicksburg who had "committed the greatest possible outrages on the women." New York's *World* and *Daily News* regularly printed similar stories underscoring to their readers the fundamental dangers of Black men, and particularly armed Black men in uniform.[3] Fear of conscription and concerns about a post-emancipation racial world knew no party, or at least civilians across the political landscape worried about both issues. Still, the radical voices in the national Democratic press stressed these twin themes most urgently.

As winter turned to spring, Americans in both the United States and the Confederacy shifted their attention to the battlefield. In March Abraham Lincoln called General Ulysses S. Grant, who had enjoyed considerable success in the western theater, east to take over command of the entire military operation. Grant chose to command from the saddle, and that spring he embarked on a long and bloody offensive against Robert E. Lee and the Army of Northern Virginia. Their armies sparred in a succession of destructive battles, from The Wilderness to Spotsylvania Court House to North Anna and beyond. The casualties on both sides seemed to overwhelm comprehension, but the Army of the Potomac gradually made progress toward Petersburg, Virginia. Shocking body counts, and endless columns of newspaper print listing the fallen, came to dominate conversation in private homes and public spaces. Some who had supported the war for years had had enough, others insisted that Grant was making progress and the North must see the war to a positive conclusion. In a very real sense, events on the battlefield—for good or ill—promised to dictate the results of the presidential election to come.[4]

By early June partisan clashes in the capital had grown testy. In one notorious episode, Michigan's burly senator Zacharia Chandler, dining with Republican colleagues at the National Hotel, was overheard sharing some thoughts about northern Copperheads. Indiana's Democratic congressman Daniel Voorhees—known as "The Tall Sycamore of the Wabash"—took exception and confronted Chandler. The senator slapped Voorhees in the face, and soon the two large men were wrestling on the floor of the hotel dining room. With Chandler nearing victory, another Hoosier grabbed a pitcher of milk and bashed it over the Michigander's head, then pummeled him with a chair for good measure. Eventually other diners separated the two politicians, but not before all had a fine tale to share with folks back home. It would seem that the parties were preparing for a rigorous electoral season.[5]

But we are getting ahead of ourselves.

August Belmont Hosts a Meeting

On the evening of January 12, 1864, a distinguished group of Democrats braved the snow to gather in Manhattan at the Fifth Avenue mansion of wealthy financier August Belmont. They came from all over the country, and all branches of the party, although storms in the West kept some key Midwestern Democrats from attending. Belmont chaired the Democratic National Committee, and this was their first meeting since mid-1860. Belmont was an immensely powerful fellow, with a fascinating history. An Austrian-born Jew, Belmont had emigrated to the United States in 1837, where he became a highly successful banker and a celebrated figure in social and political circles. Belmont had thrown his considerable might behind Stephen Douglas in 1860. Since the start of the Civil War, Belmont had cast himself as among Lincoln's loyal opposition, supporting the war even when he opposed the administration's policies. Looking to the upcoming election, Belmont saw George McClellan as the man to replace Abraham Lincoln.

That January gathering had pretty limited responsibilities. They agreed that the party's convention should meet on July 4 (it did not), and they decided that the convention should be held in Chicago—to honor Stephen Douglas—rather than Cincinnati. Some hoped to accomplish more. Rather than merely setting the stage for the convention, they hoped to lay down markers establishing some core party positions. But in the end the gathered Democrats agreed to leave such matters to the party's national convention.[6]

Still, the gathering at Belmont's estate marked the start of the party's 1864 campaign. For political wirepullers there were many questions to answer, but two were most obvious. First, who should the party standard-bearer be in 1864? And, even more challenging, what should the party's stance be toward the war that continued to rage? Some Democrats would be happy to pursue an immediate peace, while others—including Belmont—insisted that they must stand for military victory. The most cynical kept one finger in the air, assessing how the wind was blowing from distant battlefields. In January that wind was pretty cold and calls for immediate peace found receptive audiences. Hanging over debates about the proper path to peace, both Republicans and Democrats would have to face the thorny policy challenges posed by a postwar world.

The Democratic leadership that met on that January evening focused on the politics of the presidential election to come. But that complex campaign—or series of campaigns—would be fought against the backdrop of events on the battlefield, and intertwined concerns about race and reconstruction. And while powerful insiders met in the occasional smoke-filled room, or discussed plans in private correspondence, their political operatives navigated the evolving world of partisan discourse that would shape how they communicated with a divided citizenry. Certainly the war itself had a huge impact on how political debates unfolded, but the national political culture was also evolving in a wealth of ways, ultimately affecting how voters thought about politics.

The Civil War arrived at a moment when all sorts of economic and cultural matters were in flux. Such things are always in flux, although a good case can be made that the mid-nineteenth century was a moment of unusually rapid change. And here is an inescapable, although rather uncomfortable, irony. The American Civil War wreaked tremendous damage on American society, both North and South. Lives were lost; families were destroyed; previously apolitical women and men became obsessed with developments on the battlefield. But although all that was certainly true, after the first months of the war the northern economy did quite well. Unemployment was low, productivity was high, many people were making money, attending the theater, and enjoying life while keeping one eye on the newspapers. Other civilians, however, suffered from the lost wages of soldiers and the material challenges that accompanied the war's devastation.[7] On November 21, 1863, only days before ministers across the land delivered prayers of thanksgiving, *Harper's Weekly* ran a cover illustration by artist Winslow Homer portraying a scene from New York's "Great Russian Ball at the Academy of Music," commemorating the visit of Russian diplomats. It was an orgy of celebration and excess, played out in a city where just months earlier angry rioters had burned buildings and murdered soldiers and African Americans. Some observers noted the contrast between extreme wealth and pageantry and the distressed daily lives of ordinary people on the streets, but most appeared to just enjoy reading about a spectacular party.[8]

Life on the Civil War home front became increasingly intertwined with a changing popular culture, fueled by evolving communication and public debate. Two episodes, both in New York, illustrate how partisan politics took on new forms in this fluid political culture.

The Politics of Celebrity: Emma Webb Goes to Brooklyn

The Civil War emerged at a moment when popular fascination with fame, celebrity, and what we today call "the media" was shifting in important ways. Thanks to the telegraph, and reductions in printing and distribution costs, newspaper production had expanded, and news that might have been of only local interest a decade earlier had become part of national discourse. These changes had an enormous impact on what voters could read during the upcoming campaign. Meanwhile, developments in the technology of photography meant that fans could purchase inexpensive *cartes de visite* of their favorite celebrities.[9] These celebrities might have been generals or politicians, or they might have been actors and actresses, orators, or anyone who attracted the admiration of consumers. Fame had exploded in the midst of the Civil War.[10]

Carte de visite: Emma Webb, actress and orator. Before the Civil War Emma Webb and her younger sister, Ada, had been a moderately successful singing and acting duo. In early 1864 Webb turned to politics, launching a short tour speaking for Democratic candidate George B. McClellan. Webb's career, and the occasional photographs featuring her (alone and with Ada), illustrate the commingling of celebrity and politics during the war years. (Library of Congress)

In 1863 the worlds of celebrity and politics (and gender) intersected when Republican politicians at the state level concluded that the orator Anna Elizabeth Dickinson might help their cause. Dickinson, a young Philadelphia Quaker, had earned attention as a public speaker, championing the rights of both women and African Americans. By 1863 Republican operatives had begun offering Dickinson substantial sums to lecture for their candidates. The sole support of her mother and sister, becoming the paid spokesperson for Republicans brought Dickinson's financial needs and ideological convictions into line. Although Dickinson would be legally barred from federal elections for nearly sixty years, and she personally never exercised her franchise, she became an important voice for women in politics, and a national celebrity during and after the Civil War.[11]

Stung by Dickinson's effectiveness, some Democrats cast around for a female speaker to balance those scales. They settled on actress and singer Emma Webb, a member of a celebrated touring sister act with her younger sister, Ada. Teenagers when the Civil War began, the Webb sisters had toured for several years prior to secession. They began their singing careers in New Orleans but soon took to the stage in San Francisco. Before long they had appeared across the South and in theatrical venues in Milwaukee and New York City (and many stops in between).[12] In early 1860 the sisters attempted a brief stint as theater managers, rechristening New York's Broadway Boudoir as the Webb Sisters Theater. That venture only lasted a few weeks, at which point they once again hit the road.[13] In the first years of the war the sisters' fame grew. Notices of their performances appeared regularly in the *Cleveland Morning Leader* and the *Chicago Tribune,* as well as in other newspapers in and around Ohio. The pair also turned up on stages in New York City, offering more evidence of their national reputation. Dedicated fans purchased *cartes de visite* of the pair together or alone.[14]

On March 4, 1864, Emma took a hiatus from the stage and began her career as a political lecturer, with her first stop at Brooklyn's Atheneum. By the time she took to the platform, her managers had done a superb job of advertising the event. The *New York Herald* ran a short notice announcing the "Contest of Female Wits." "Miss Webb," the paper noted, "is said to be a capital speaker, pungent and satirical."[15] The *Cleveland Morning Herald* took note of Webb's new career, noting that she was "a very fair actress" who might well have something to say about "the poor white slaves of the country."[16] The *Daily Ohio Statesman,* a Democratic paper, echoed the language from the *Herald,* noting that Webb—who had spent some time in the West Indies and therefore knew of what she spoke—promised to speak for the "vindication of the rights of the poor white slaves of this country."[17] The Democrats behind Webb's lecture had done a good job of producing a healthy buzz.

Webb devoted much of her Atheneum address to a direct refutation of Dickinson and her abolitionist rhetoric. The war, she explained, had forced her to think hard about political issues and other "unwomanly matters." Webb claimed to have an equal number of friends on both sides of the nation's conflict, providing her with a particular perspective on the war. While Dickinson tended to paint a romantic vision of the war, she focused on the universal "horrors" of war and the damage done to its "innocent victims," the common soldiers on both sides. Shifting from her unambiguous critique of war, Webb tackled emancipation. She spoke of her own experiences with "the fertile West India Islands" as evidence to support the argument that "slavery is the normal condition of the negro," whereas emancipation would harm African Americans while doing unimaginable damage to poor Whites. Turning to politics, Webb reminded her audience that Dickinson had frequently mocked George McClellan, while she insisted that "his is a name that faction and fanaticism dread and fear."[18] When Webb finished her lecture, the crowd called Ohio congressman Sunset Cox from the audience onto the stage. Cox, who claimed that he just happened to be present, said a few words praising Webb followed by some highly partisan words attacking the Republican Party.

Webb's inaugural lecture seemed to have met the organizers' expectations. The *New York Tribune,* not fans of Webb's message, acknowledged that she had "a fair audience" and that the actress did a good job of delivering her lines.[19] The *Daily National Republican* quoted an array of Democratic newspapers approving of Webb's performance.[20] Webb shared much in common with Dickinson, both in her performance and in the public responses. Both were powerful speakers, prone to sarcasm and sharp commentary. Both played with gender conventions, declining to adopt a traditionally feminine approach to their topics while still attracting particular attention because they were women. They were also similarly radical, although diametrically opposed in their positions.

The published commentary on Webb's Brooklyn lecture mapped out the intersection of gender and politics. Much as Democrats sought to belittle Dickinson, Republican and moderate newspapers were quick to diminish Webb's intellectual role in her performance. The editors of the *Rutland Weekly Herald* described Webb as an agent of the Copperheads who ably delivered a speech "prepared for her by the leaders of the Peace Democracy."[21] Other newspapers explicitly credited Cox with writing her speech. All seemed to agree that the talk was distinctly "copperheady," appealing to the peace wing of the party.[22] Within a week of the Atheneum lecture, the *Chicago Tribune* was already reporting that the wind had fallen from Webb's sails with the revelation that "she doesn't write her own lectures."[23]

The rumor that Webb was a mere mouthpiece for the words of men outraged the actress. On April 1 she penned a public letter to Horace Greeley at the *New York Tribune.* Webb insisted that she presented her own opinions in her own words, based partially on her childhood experiences. And, as a final bid for greater relevance, Webb offered to debate Anna Dickinson or—failing that—Greeley himself.[24] This gambit apparently yielded no response. A month after her first appearance in Brooklyn, Webb's career as a political lecturer was on the decline. In late April she spoke to an audience of 140 in Troy, New York, prompting another round of commentary about women speaking in public.[25] By that fall the Webbs were back on the stage in Ohio, leading the *Cleveland Morning Leader* to conclude that Emma was a better actress than she was a speaker.[26]

Although Webb's political star shone bright for only a short time, her brief political tour says much about wartime politics and Democratic messaging. Certainly there is an important gender story here. Although a transparent response to Dickinson's great success, the mere fact that the conservative Democrats put this young woman on the stage to support their cause speaks volumes about the shifting roles of American women in public political life. But then there is the matter of Webb's actual message. Perhaps most startling, Webb stood on the stage with an explicitly antiwar message. She pointed out that warfare does horrible things to young men. Although the point was obvious, few in either party made it.[27] Webb also wove a somewhat distinctive argument about emancipation. She endorsed the familiar Democratic point that emancipation posed a threat to White northerners, and particularly the working classes. But she added an argument—purportedly based on her personal experience—that slavery was in fact the best status for African Americans. Webb was explicitly racist, really more so than many Democrats, and—despite Republican claims—she seemed to know her own mind. Webb's lectures are worth noting also since she always endorsed McClellan for president, even though the Democrats had yet to nominate the general and he would certainly not have embraced her core messages.

George McClellan (Almost) Wins a Sword

As the Democrats were sending out Emma Webb to do partisan battle, the North's patriotic civilians launched an ambitious series of fundraising fairs to help fill the coffers of the United States Sanitary Commission. In the final years of the war many northern cities and towns ran fundraising fairs to assist men in the field. The largest were staged in New York, Philadelphia, and Chicago. These gala events raised money for branches of the Sanitary Commission or for local organizations. They also offered an opportunity for patriotic women and men at home to support the war. Noncombatants could be *involved* in the conflict by attending meetings, preparing exhibits, volunteering at tables, and so on. The cynic could note—and many did—that these events allowed for highly public displays of patriotism, including the publication of the names of key volunteers and donors. The Sanitary Fairs were nominally nonpartisan. They supported the war while declining to take political positions. Democrats were welcome to buy tickets and make contributions; even antiwar Democrats who merely wished to enjoy the festivities could drop by. But these fairs, like the Union Leagues, were bulwarks of nationalism and the Union war effort.[28]

The fair organizers developed a range of strategies to turn prowar fervor into donations, yoking patriotism and commerce. They sold admission tickets to the fairs themselves, and in advance of the larger fairs committees solicited donations from all sectors of the economy. When the visitors arrived they were greeted with rows of tables, where other volunteers—often comely young women—sold all manner of things. One of the more clever fundraising techniques was for the organizers to offer a fancy gift to be given to a favored public figure. Visitors could then donate a small fee to vote for who should receive that token of their admiration.

The most successful of these schemes were the "sword votes," which brilliantly turned celebrity into cash donations.[29] New York's Metropolitan Fair perfected the art. Visitors to the fair's Arms and Trophies Department would see a beautiful sword on display, donated by Tiffany & Company, and valued at $2,000. Each guest could—for the price of one dollar—vote for which Union general should receive the sword.[30] During the three-week fair, and in the newspaper articles summarizing the event, the sword competition attracted a disproportionate share of interest, both in New York and across the country. The *New York Post* called the competition "the most exciting feature of the fair."[31]

Certainly part of the excitement was owing to the beauty of the sword and the pageantry of the contest. Pundits noted that the savvy businessmen at Tiffany & Company had won far more than $2,000 worth of free advertising with their gift. But much of the interest in the sword contest centered on its two main competitors, Generals Ulysses S. Grant and George B. McClellan. The two men were quite a contrast in style and situation. Grant, the low-key Midwesterner, had moved east to take over as commander in chief of the Union armies barely a month before the fair began. A few weeks after the event closed its doors, Grant would be leading his men on their spring offensive into Virginia. McClellan, who had been living with his wife, Ellen, in New York City, had not commanded an army in the field since the Battle of Antietam more than a year and a half earlier. Meanwhile, although Grant seemed generally apolitical, he had become the face of the Union war effort, while McClellan had been the darling of the Democratic Party for years and seemed to be the party's likely presidential nominee.

As the fair neared its close, McClellan appeared to have a commanding lead in the sword vote, and interest remained high. In a particularly snarky, and widely reprinted, essay, the *New York Herald* noted that Ulysses S. Grant's wife, Julia Grant, had visited the fair without fanfare, casting her vote in the sword contest. Meanwhile, the paper noted, Ellen McClellan was a highly visible visitor to the fair, staffing a table just a few feet from the sword vote and doing her best to be seen. As an interesting coda, Mrs. Grant actually cast her vote for McClellan, leaving readers to wonder if that was an act of sportsmanship or sarcasm.[32]

On the Friday night before the close of the fair, the man they called "Little Mac" had 1,600 more votes and seemed to be well on his way to winning a lovely sword and some additional fame barely a half-year before the election. But the following day saw an explosion of voting tilted heavily toward General Grant. By one reckoning McClellan received 6,000 votes on Saturday while Grant garnered 22,000. This surge in voting was aided by shifts in the rules, which allowed soldiers and civilians to vote from afar, or even in large anonymous groups. It certainly appeared that the organizers of the Metropolitan Fair had no intention of letting the Democrat McClellan walk away with the fair's biggest trophy. The *Boston Transcript* poked fun at McClellan's last-minute loss, noting that "as usual, he did not bring up his reserves" in time to seal the victory. The Democratic *World* took the fair's organizers to task for turning a regular vote into a "pecuniary contest," where Grant's supporters were able to buy the election.[33]

New York diarist and frequent visitor to the fair George Templeton Strong did not buy the corruption argument, suggesting instead that the city's Democrats got snookered. Strong concluded that the "the Union League Club and other subscriptions in Grant's favor had been held off, judiciously, to the last minute." Thus, when leading Democrats August Belmont and Samuel Barlow dropped by the fair on Saturday they concluded that McClellan had the contest sewn up, and they only spent a few thousand additional dollars, "to give him a handsome majority." When the Democrats learned their man had lost, they were "full of wrath and confusion." Strong insisted that he was glad of Grant's victory, not from any "partisan feeling" but because it was more important for Grant to be elevated in the eyes of his men.[34] But although Strong claimed to be nonpartisan, other observers saw the affair as a partisan exercise, and not one which reflected well on the Union League's nonpolitical ideals. One local paper described the sword vote as little more than a political canvas in advance of the upcoming election.[35]

When the crowd gathered to hear the final totals, the votes were overwhelmingly in Grant's favor. He had received 30,291 votes to McClellan's 14,509, with just a smattering of votes to other officers. In preparation for announcing this surprising result, the organizers arranged for twenty-five policemen to be on hand. The *New York Herald* claimed that the cheers for Grant went on for five to six minutes, although the paper also acknowledged that the policemen came in handy maintaining order among the angry McClellan supporters.[36]

In the end the Metropolitan Fair's sword vote was a grand success. It raised over $45,000 for the Sanitary Commission. But it was also a highly publicized, much watched, partisan battle in the midst of an event that was supposedly a celebration of nonpartisan patriotism. We are left to wonder precisely why some voters selected McClellan over Grant. For some he was simply the local favorite. But for others McClellan represented a Democratic option to the Lincoln administration, and perhaps to Grant's military leadership. As an interesting wrinkle in wartime politics, the New York press published selected lists of the individuals and groups who voted for Grant or McClellan. Some of those named voters suggested something of the political fights to come. For instance, Mrs. James Gordon Bennett, the wife of the editor of the *New York Herald* and a longtime McClellan supporter, gave two hundred votes for McClellan. Wilbur Storey, the publisher of the *Chicago Times*—the Midwestern paper that had been shut down for its treasonous opinions—added 245 more votes for McClellan. And finally, the local press noted that Ada and Emma Webb had each cast a ballot for McClellan, thus indicating their political preferences and also their enduring celebrity in New York society. McClellan, who was not yet a candidate for president, was being openly endorsed by leading antiwar Democrats.[37]

The sword vote was a classic "popularity contest" between two widely known Union generals. But it was also an early skirmish in a political battle, staged before the official candidates were even on the field. While fair visitors had a bit of fun in the name of fundraising, leading Democrats were weighing in on the bigger issues that continued to divide the nation.

Reverdy Johnson Weighs in on Emancipation

The North's wartime public conversation on race unfolded at various levels, aimed at different constituencies, with partisan politics never far from the surface. Most, although not all, White northerners believed in fundamental racial inequalities. In the border states, slavery existed before the war and a large portion of the slaves in those states remained enslaved a year after the Emancipation Proclamation; many border-state Democrats walked that fine line where they supported the war while defending their peculiar institution. In much of the northern states, White citizens had little personal experience with African Americans, but judging from the columns of radical Democratic newspapers, many worried about an imagined world where Black men and women might invade their communities. For these people, emancipation somehow represented a threat to their way of life. This was the sort of home-front fear that Democrats like Emma Webb appealed to when she insisted that emancipation was bad for Blacks and threatened Whites. In a short story published early in the war, satirist David Locke, writing in the voice of his Copperhead character Petroleum Nasby, mocked how residents of his imaginary Ohio town of Wingert's Corner quickly abandoned their abolitionist sensibilities when it seemed that a handful of Black men and women had migrated to their White community.[38] One measure of the politics of race and racism was White northern fears of Blacks in their midst.

Then there were the complex political, moral, and constitutional debates about slavery and emancipation. Many in the North recognized slavery as morally wrong, while others embraced a religious or economic understanding that approved of—or even celebrated—the institution. With his Emancipation Proclamation, Abraham Lincoln had yoked the emancipation of slaves held in the Confederacy with the Union's military war effort. That framework allowed him to assert the proclamation as the prerogative of the commander in chief, and it provided for a public policy that maintained slavery in the border states as well as in those areas of the Confederacy already captured by Union troops. Framed in those terms, as a necessary war measure, War Democrats could accept military emancipation without backing universal emancipation. Looking to the future, political observers recognized that broader action, either through legislation or constitutional amendment, would be necessary to rid the nation of slavery.

In this national discussion about race and politics, Maryland's Democratic senator Reverdy Johnson emerges as an important figure. Johnson, like many of his conservative colleagues in the border states, had been a Whig politician before that party crumbled, serving in the U.S. Senate in the 1840s and as attorney general under President Zachary Taylor. With the collapse of the Whigs, Johnson turned to the Democratic Party, and in 1860 he supported Stephen Douglas's candidacy. With time Johnson had grown disillusioned with slavery and freed his own slaves, while maintaining a conservative approach to the constitutional issues surrounding states' rights and the peculiar institution. A friend of Abraham Lincoln, the senator had opposed the secession movement in Maryland.[39]

Johnson had been an early supporter of the Emancipation Proclamation, joining fellow War Democrats in accepting the proclamation as a war measure. A year later in February 1864, Johnson surprised some political observers by publicly endorsing a proposed constitutional amendment ending slavery. The historian Michael Vorenberg notes that as the third year of war ended, the Democratic political establishment seemed prepared to set aside emancipation as a useful partisan political issue, even while party members remained ambivalent about more sweeping constitutional measures. The general election committee for New York's Tammany Hall met in March and issued a statement declaring "slavery, as a subject of political agitation, has passed from the politics of this country." Other Democrats lined up to support this position, prompting Republican concerns that the opposition party was trying to steal emancipation as a political campaign point. But although the worm was slowly turning, emancipation still appeared to be a Republican issue.[40]

On April 5, 1864, Johnson rose in the Senate Chamber to deliver an important address "in support of the resolution to amend the constitution of the United States." It was a long and complex speech, befitting the senator's reputation as an ardent and erudite defender of the Constitution. The speech came in the midst of a heated, and generally partisan, Senate debate on the proposed amendment to abolish slavery. Johnson set up his contribution with extended thoughts on the history of slavery in the United States. Although the peculiar institution had long and deep roots in the nation's past, the senator insisted that hostility to slavery had almost as long a lineage, and many had been confident that slavery would die out on its own accord. Johnson reminded his listeners that in the midst of the secession crisis he had called for compromise, and he blamed radicals on both sides for the outbreak of war. But once the war was underway, he had supported the president and the United States. Now three years later, he had grown convinced that in order for the "terrible war" to come to a close, slavery must be ended, and that in fact the institution was "already fatally wounded." Moreover, the constitutional scholar had become convinced that the correct path to ending slavery was through the Constitution, rather than legislation or presidential fiat. In short, the proposed constitutional amendment was just and necessary.[41]

It was a crucial moment in the debates over emancipation. Some War Democrats had supported the Emancipation Proclamation as a measure to win a war that must be won, but the party's crucial legal thinkers balked at broader efforts to end the institution. They worried about violating the constitutional rights of slave owners and the individual states. Johnson had now declared that slavery must go, and that goal could only be legally achieved through a constitutional amendment. Such a move was morally correct and structurally necessary. In the interest of Union, the claims of states' rights should not surpass the demands of united federal power. Johnson's careful argument effectively omitted partisan rhetoric in the midst of a debate that had seen little else.

One historian called Johnson's April address "the crowning speech of his career." Vorenberg notes that the heated senatorial debates about the amendment had largely eluded the national press and the broader public consciousness until Johnson stepped into the discussion. Coming from his side of the aisle and speaking as a great legal authority and a leading border-state senator, political pundits suddenly took notice, some noting the strange times that led a "stiff" conservative like Johnson to become a "radical" at such a moment. The *New York Herald* reported that the speech had "created much sensation." The *Chicago Tribune* compared the damage to the Confederate cause with the fall of Vicksburg the previous year. Kentucky Unionist Robert J. Breckinridge, who had two sons in the Confederate Army and one fighting for the Union, embraced Johnson's message. The following day Maryland voted to hold a new convention to draft an antislavery constitution.[42]

The April speech was certainly important to the emancipation narrative that eventually led to the 13th Amendment. Vorenberg seems on solid ground in arguing that Johnson's words sent a political tremor through the North's most concerned political observers, while also marking a key moment in an ongoing evolution of national political thought. For Democrats who paid attention to Washington politics, and who read the major political editorials produced by the national press, it was a crucial episode. For rank-and-file northern Democrats, it is not clear how much they worried about the constitutional details. Emancipation—some still feared—promised unwanted threats to Whites in northern society. And some worried that the administration's insistence on emancipation could be a stumbling block in negotiations for peace. Confederate representative might balk at laying down their arms if that meant handing over their slaves.

Manton Marble and "Freedom of the Press"

By the spring of 1864 Democrats had grown more open in critiquing the war and questioning the administration. Casualty lists and constitutional debates provoked critics to risk charges of disloyalty to fire rhetorical shots at Lincoln and his people. On the battlefield progress had been slow and frustrating. In the first weeks of May northerners desperate for good news from Grant's spring offensive read of startling carnage at places like The Wilderness and Spotsylvania Court House. Voters across the political spectrum looked to the election of 1864. Democrats saw an opening with a nation tired of war and popular objections to a legislative agenda that included conscription, emancipation, and the suppression of civil rights. Reporters and editors printed their objections with growing audacity, and the frustrated administration periodically fought back.

Amid these developments Manton Marble became one of the most interesting characters in the burgeoning conflict over journalism and treason. Marble, at twenty-seven years old, owned and edited the powerful and controversial *New York World.* Marble's own career as a journalist began in Boston, before he took a position at New York's *Evening Post,* eventually moving on to the *World.* The *World* had supported the administration at the outset of the war. In the spring of 1862, with the paper struggling financially, young Marble managed to borrow enough money to buy the newspaper. As those debts came due, Marble looked around for backers. Finally, late in the year, Marble cast his lot with a group of local Democrats who opposed the Lincoln administration. That group included Fernando Wood, who had been the city's Democratic mayor when the war began; August Belmont, the chairman of the Democratic National Committee; and Samuel L. M. Barlow, leading banker and political insider. In the gubernatorial election that year the reconfigured *World* made its politics known by endorsing Horatio Seymour—a strong Lincoln critic—for governor. With this powerful new platform Marble almost immediately became one of the city's loudest voices against the Lincoln administration, attacking the Emancipation Proclamation, the arrest of Clement Vallandigham, and other affronts to the Constitution as it was.[43]

Life for Marble and the *World* took a disturbing turn on the early morning of May 18, 1864, the day before the editor's scheduled wedding. At dawn the paper published a presidential proclamation requesting a national day of "fasting, humiliation and prayer" while calling for 400,000 recruits, a huge number. It was an ominous sounding announcement, particularly arriving in the early stages of General Ulysses S. Grant's bloody Overland Campaign. As the papers were publishing long casualty lists almost daily, the president's call for 400,000 more men seemed to promise casualties without end. It hardly appeared to be a presidential proclamation designed to encourage patriotic enthusiasm. And, in fact, it was not.

By the end of the day, the Lincoln administration had confirmed what many suspected: the proclamation was a forgery. Copies had been sent by courier to newspaper offices all over the city. In some cases the offices were not open; other newspapers smelled a rat and declined to print the fake proclamation after checking with Washington. The *Herald* initially fell for the ruse, running off twenty thousand copies before discovering the truth. Only two New York newspapers published and distributed the fake proclamation: the *World* and the Democratic *Journal of Commerce.* These were the city's two most notoriously anti-administration dailies. Things surely looked bad for the Democratic opposition. William Prime, the editor of the *Journal of Commerce,* and Marble both insisted that they had been fooled by a skillful forgery. Marble offered a five-hundred-dollar reward for the apprehension of the culprits. Several other local editors confirmed that anyone could have made the same error. But the fact remained that the city's two openly opposition newspapers had been the ones to distribute the false proclamation.

Lincoln—acting on the urging of Secretary of State William Seward and the approval of Secretary of War Edwin M. Stanton—signed an order calling for both papers to be shut down and their editors arrested. General John Adams Dix, the military commander in New York, ordered the arrests. Many in the local and national press objected to the administration's actions, insisting that the newspapers had made an honest mistake.[44]

The crisis for the two New York papers did not last long. Soon after ordering the arrests, General Dix countermanded his order. Dix ascertained that the counterfeiter was an associate editor of the *Brooklyn Eagle,* who hatched his plot in hopes of manipulating gold prices. Privately even Lincoln's closest associates and admirers thought that he had mis-stepped. Secretary of the Navy Gideon Welles wrote that "the seizure of the office of the *World* and the *Journal of Commerce* for publishing this forgery was hasty, rash, inconsiderate, and wrong, and cannot be defended." Although the editors were no doubt enemies of the administration, the secretary saw no virtue in their incarceration, which he largely blamed on Seward. While the administration's actions damaged their standing, the accused did not suffer much. The arrested did not get as far as Fort Lafayette, and on the 21st both newspapers resumed publication.[45]

The entire episode took only a few days. In the midst of ongoing partisan rancor, it would be possible to imagine a moment when both sides reflected and realized that perhaps they had erred. True, the *World* was (apparently) duped by a fake, but nearly every newspaper in the city managed to avoid contributing to the fraud. And, yes, the fake proclamation did real damage, if only for a very short time, but perhaps Welles was right that Seward, Stanton, and Lincoln applied too heavy a hammer to the case. Even if neither side would acknowledge fault, maybe they could turn the page and move on to the next skirmish.

That might have been the case for other newspapermen. But Marble was not one to leave a useful card unplayed. As soon as the *World* was back up and running, he published a long indictment of Lincoln and the whole affair in his newspaper. Marble began his column—which he wrote as a letter to President Lincoln—by noting that whereas in a monarchy "the King can do no wrong," the same protections are not available to the president. Marble summarized the facts surrounding his arrest, and almost immediate release, in terms that observers familiar with the facts would have accepted. From this point he framed the episode as part of a larger federal attack on the press. "To characterize these proceedings as unprecedented," he wrote, "would be to forget the past history of your administration." Marble insisted, not unreasonably, that had the *Herald* or the *Times* been fooled instead of the two Democratic dailies, Lincoln would have behaved differently. Moreover, by recalling his order to imprison the two editors, the president really did nothing to "confess and repair your mistake." While other wartime Democratic editors might have been suppressed for undermining the war effort, encouraging desertion, disrupting conscription, or various other treasonous activities against the federal war effort, in this case Manton Marble presented himself as the innocent victim, mistreated by a tyrannical administration.

Marble's letter in the *World* attracted considerable attention in the press. Wheeling, West Virginia's *Daily Intelligencer* acknowledged that both New York newspapers had "a case against the administration and they know it," but it concluded that Marble's public letter was "not in good taste" and "too venomous."[46] The *Cleveland Morning Leader* summarized Marble's letter while adding that the administration's behavior was more reasonable than the editor had claimed.[47] The *Chicago Tribune* called it "silly twaddle" produced by a "humbug."[48] *Der Westbote,* a German-language Democratic newspaper published in Columbus, Ohio, published the entire letter, as did southern Pennsylvania's harshly anti-Lincoln *Bedford Gazette.*[49] These, and many other, northern newspapers devoted space to Marble's critique of the administration, generally using the occasion to replay established partisan battles with other publications. Republican editors who had sided with the *World* when it came to unfair treatment at the hands of the administration changed their tune upon reading Marble's melodramatic letter.[50]

With his lengthy public letter, the shrewd editor managed to help turn a seventy-two-hour event into a national debate that lasted for weeks. And before the controversy had fully died down, Marble arranged for his letter to be reprinted by the Society for the Diffusion of Political Knowledge as a pamphlet entitled *Freedom of the Press Wantonly Violated: Letter of Mr. Marble to President Lincoln, Reappearance of the Journal of Commerce, Opinions of the Press on This Outrage.* The president, by acting a bit too quickly and harshly, had provided useful fodder for the loyal, and not so loyal, opposition.[51]

Debates over Reconstruction

It is commonplace in America's wars that debates about peace are joined well before the competing armies leave the field. That was the case during the American Civil War. Before military victory felt comfortably in hand, northerners discussed the terms under which the Confederate states should be allowed to return to the Union. Multiple concerns shaped those discussions, complicated by the concern that harsh terms of surrender might delay the peace. Opinions fell across a fairly wide spectrum, as some legislators saw victory—when it came—as the opportunity to reshape the Old South while also to punish the rebels for the carnage they had wrought.

This national political debate raged long before 1864. In September 1863 Massachusetts senator Charles Sumner, one of the most radical Republican voices in Congress, delivered a speech on "Our Domestic Relations; or, How to Treat the Rebel States." Sumner—speaking for the radicals in his party—laid out an argument that by dissolving the Union, the Confederate states had essentially become territories under congressional jurisdiction. Or at least they would be as soon as they were defeated. Pushing back against efforts the president had already made to ease defeated portions of the Confederacy—most notably in Tennessee and Louisiana—back into the United States with minimal fuss, Sumner saw the defeat of the Confederacy as a fine opportunity to impose social revolution on the slaveocracy. And he felt sure that the Constitution's balance of powers was on the side of Congress.

The following month Postmaster General Montgomery Blair, a conservative with little in common with Sumner and his ilk, delivered a rebuttal in Rockville, Maryland. Blair had much more faith in the fundamental loyalty of the southern people, blaming the current state of things on the South's slave-owning aristocracy. He also had more confidence in Lincoln's approach to bringing the Confederate states back into the fold, as opposed to Sumner's claims of jurisdiction and his preference for punishment. The two important speeches effectively set out the terms of debate within the Republican Party. Blair's version matched the president's perspective and generally met with approval from moderate Republicans and Unionist Democrats.[52]

In his third annual message on December 8, 1863, Abraham Lincoln laid out his plan for the future in his "Proclamation of Amnesty and Reconstruction." The proposal, following the language set by Blair, promised rebels considerable leniency. Any ex-Confederate who swore an oath of allegiance would receive a full pardon and the return of all his property, except his slaves. Once the list of men in any state signing oaths numbered 10 percent of the total votes cast in 1860, those newly loyal citizens could become the basis for writing a new state constitution and returning to the Union. Those new constitutions would have to approve emancipation and make certain basic provisions for the civil rights of freed people. Like Blair, Lincoln seemed confident that large portions of rank-and-file White southerners remained inclined toward the Union but were controlled by radical elites in their midst. But while Lincoln's proclamation seemed much more moderate than what Sumner and his colleagues had in mind, it was still too radical for many Democrats. After all, men seeking amnesty would be required to abandon their slaves, and the entire 10-percent proposal seemed inherently antidemocratic and probably unconstitutional. At bottom, they saw Lincoln's proclamation as turning emancipation into a condition of peace, which threatened to prolong the fighting.[53]

Lincoln's proclamation seemed designed to promote an easy transition from war to reunion, and in the first several months following the proclamation new Unionist governments formed in portions of Louisiana and Arkansas, suggesting the first fruits of this generally generous policy. But Republicans in Congress found Lincoln's plans unsatisfactory, and they welcomed an opportunity to reassert congressional control over the nation's future. Various congressmen floated plans to counter the proclamation. Finally, on July 2, 1864, Congress passed a bill sponsored by Republican congressman Henry Winter Davis of Maryland and Republican senator Benjamin Wade of Ohio. The Wade-Davis Bill raised the stakes of reentry considerably. Under the proposed law, fully 50 percent of voters in each state (based on the 1860 returns) would have to sign oaths of allegiance, and as a preliminary step to returning to the Union these Confederate states would have to elect delegates to new state constitutional conventions. Only men who were willing and able to sign an "iron clad oath," declaring that they had never supported the rebellion, would be allowed to participate in that vote.

The Wade-Davis Bill represented a radical departure from Lincoln's Proclamation of Amnesty and Reconstruction. Following Sumner's earlier logic, it claimed for the legislative branch crucial control over how Reconstruction would unfold, and it raised the expectations on White southerners seeking to return to the Union. Of course, placed in the context of what was to come, rather than compared with the president's proclamation, even the Wade-Davis Bill only imposed modest reconstruction on the rebel states. They would have to abandon slavery, but even the wartime Republicans in Congress were not prepared to call for universal Black manhood suffrage or major civil rights protections.

From a partisan political perspective, this reconstruction debate, culminating in the July 2 legislation, was essentially a Republican affair. Congressional Republicans shared the conviction that they should shape how the Union would be reunited, but only the more radical portion of both houses would have signed on to Black manhood suffrage or more radical reforms. The resulting legislation reflected a political compromise between the two wings of the Republican Party. But even that compromise went much too far for the president, who feared the loss of progress that had been made in Louisiana and Arkansas and generally looked at the debate through the lens of a war still underway. Better to reach out to southern unionists rather than signal a tough reconstruction policy. Rather than signing the bill, which enjoyed overwhelming Republican support, Lincoln chose to pocket veto it by letting the session expire without signing it into law. On August 5 Wade and Davis responded to Lincoln with an angry "Manifesto," which took umbrage at Lincoln for failing to sign a bill that reflected the will of congressional Republicans and for instead opting for an essentially conservative path. As historian Elizabeth R. Varon notes, there was an "irony lost on no one," as radical Republicans and conservative Democrats had come to agree that the president's "policies were motivated by his lust for power."[54]

But despite this interesting confluence of anger, in most essential ways this was an intramural conflict between Republicans in two independent branches. The radicals in Congress had forged a compromise with some of their more moderate colleagues, but the president's position was more moderate still. This conflict, which focused largely on the demands that should be placed on rebel leaders, coexisted with a more subtle constitutional disagreement that remained a concern for conservative War Democrats. The Wade-Davis Bill not only insisted on the iron-clad oath before ex-Confederates could participate in their states' political life; it also required those new states to accept emancipation. But as Reverdy Johnson had articulated a few months earlier, it was not at all apparent that the Constitution allowed the federal legislature to mandate emancipation in individual states. Far better to amend the Constitution.

Looking to the upcoming election, it was not clear how these legislative debates over reconstruction might affect the contest. After all, Abraham Lincoln had claimed fairly conservative ground on the topic, alienating radicals in his own party, some of whom would clamor for a new candidate, but offering little of use to the Democratic opposition. For Democratic voters hoping for an honorable peace, one concern might be which presidential candidate was best suited to negotiate peace with the rebels. Few had the stomach for imposing social revolution on the Confederacy, and they would surely resist the sort of radical transformative measures imagined—or not yet imagined—by the radical Republicans in Congress. They had to decide which Democratic option would be more effective in negotiating with the rebels.

Democrats in Search of a Candidate

Back in July 1863 some observers might have understood that the Civil War was nearing its end, or at least the tide had turned in favor of the United States. After all, the first week of July witnessed two almost simultaneous Union successes with the Battle of Gettysburg (July 1–3) ending Robert E. Lee's invasion of Pennsylvania, and the fall of Vicksburg (July 4) leaving the Union Army in the West—under the command of General Ulysses S. Grant—with control over the crucial Mississippi River. But a year later the war raged on, leaving the future of the Civil War, and the Lincoln administration, in doubt. The best long-term strategy for the Confederacy had always been to convince northern voters that they no longer wished to support the war. And the best way for them to articulate that conclusion would be at the polls. It may have been unclear how some other president would proceed, but by mid-1864 it was surely a good bet that the Lincoln administration would pursue the war to victory, which would include emancipation and likely more conscription.

On August 23, 1864, the president walked into a cabinet meeting with a small sheet of paper, folded over and sealed so it could not be read. That memorandum, forever called the "Blind Memo," read as follows: "This morning, as for some days past, it seems exceedingly probable that this Administration will not be re-elected. Then it will be my duty to so co-operate with the President elect, as to save the Union between the election and the inauguration; as he will have secured his election on such ground that he can not possibly save it afterwards." His assembled cabinet members all signed the piece of paper without reading it.[55] This was a fascinating moment in American political history for a host of reasons, many of which have little to do with our concerns here.[56] Some things are relevant to our discussion of wartime Democrats. First, Lincoln did not come by this conclusion casually. The president had an extensive network of political advisors, both in the capital and scattered across the nation. In the weeks before he drafted the memo Lincoln had received substantial political advice, both in writing and in private visits. There seems to be every reason to conclude that he believed the words he had written. It was still possible, but by mid-August unlikely, that radical members of his own party might successfully replace him as the Republican candidate. It was more likely that he would lose to the Democratic nominee. And although the Democrats had yet to meet and nominate their candidate, Lincoln was presumably guessing that man would be George McClellan.

In short, although Abraham Lincoln would go on to win the election of 1864 by a healthy margin, that fall this was hardly a foregone conclusion. Events on the battlefield would be crucial, but so would decisions made by politicians. Serious political minds had much to discuss.

The conversations about the election occupied observers for many months before the parties met in their nomination conventions. In 1860 the Democratic Party, struggling mightily to balance its northern and southern wings, had failed to maintain a cohesive identity. Once the southern proslavery wing broke away and nominated its own candidates, that which had seemed unthinkable—the victory of a regional Republican Party—became quite possible. In 1864 the men of the Democracy had not forgotten the lessons of the previous election. Could this new party, absent those southerners of the slaveocracy, manage to establish common ground as the party of opposition?

For years New Yorker Samuel Barlow had been the friend and advisor of George McClellan, while occupying a central place in the party's inner circle. Democrats peppered Barlow with letters about the state of politics and the future of the party. In January New York's Democratic congressman Henry Stebbins wrote a long letter, offering a grim assessment of the party from the congressional perspective. Stebbins concluded that the party, when assessed "through the language and actions of the Reps in this Congress, was in a state of hopeless disintegration." Not at all pleased with what he was seeing, Stebbins challenged Barlow: "I am amazed that men like yourself," he wrote, "so full of reputation and sagacity, do not seize the facts, and use them for the preservation of the party." Stebbins explained that there were two distinct camps within the party's congressional delegation. "One class," he explained, "is for a rigorous prosecution of the war." They believed that voters would never support a party opposed to the government's war measures. "The other class of Democrats," he continued, "is for peace at any costs." While they might claim to support the continuation of national unity, Stebbins suggested that "their acts fail to correspond with their words." The congressman was not fond of his antiwar colleagues. Looking to the future, Stebbins noted that "abolition of slavery" would be central to the next campaign, and that the recent success of African American troops would pose a continuing political challenge.[57] Although a few months later it seemed the Democrats were prepared to concede key points around emancipation, the

New York congressman correctly gleaned that the party's fundamental split on the war itself would be a huge problem, and that issues of race and emancipation would continue to challenge the Democrats to take a coherent position before voters went to the polls.

As is so often the case, political insiders assessed the Democratic Party's future as a fascinating horserace. Six months earlier informed pundits might have put their money on New York's popular and powerful anti-administration governor Horatio Seymour. But while Seymour remained a long-shot candidate in early 1864, his actions surrounding New York's draft riots had tarred him—not entirely fairly—with the charge of treason, leaving Democrats casting around for better options. One man's name appeared at the top of most speculative lists. In late December Ohio congressman Samuel Cox dined with John Hay, one of Lincoln's private secretaries and a young man with his ear to the ground in Washington circles. That evening Hay recorded in his diary that he asked the congressman "whom his party would nominate." Cox responded, "General McClellan. We will run McClellan. He is our best ticket. He lost some prestige by his Woodward letter. But it was necessary. He never could have gotten the nomination without it." The congressman dismissed popular talk that the Democrats would turn to Ulysses S. Grant. "Grant belongs to the Republicans," he asserted. And, besides, he doubted that the general would trade his current role for the presidency.[58]

On March 10 Republican General David Hunter wrote to his old Democratic comrade Irish-born humorist Charles Graham Halpine, noting that "it appears to me the Presidential contest is narrowing down to Uncle Abe & McClellan." Hunter added that "the old man looks very anxious."[59] On the same day Congressman Cox wrote to Samuel Barlow from Ohio, reporting that in the West McClellan was more popular than General Grant, offering his early handicapping of the race to come.[60] A week later New Yorkers gathered at the famed Cooper Union for a rally endorsing McClellan for president.[61] Long before the Democrats would meet for their convention, it was clear that General McClellan would be a formidable candidate for nomination, and to challenge the president.

Cox's comments to Hay the previous December underscored a key issue for the Democrats: McClellan was enormously popular and one of the most widely known men in America. Both traits were particularly important if, as Cox assumed, Grant was not an option for the party or for the White House. But Cox's remark that the general had "lost some prestige by his Woodward letter" struck at the marrow of the problem, especially for deeply interested Democrats. McClellan was popular and charismatic, but he also had been fired from his position as commander of the Army of the Potomac, and many observers questioned his performance on the battlefield. And worse, in his first and only previous political action, McClellan had publicly endorsed Pennsylvania gubernatorial candidate George Woodward, a man many had termed a treasonous Copperhead. Cox was willing to see McClellan's Woodward letter as an act of political pragmatism, but party insiders and rank-and-file voters still needed to know more about Little Mac before he could win the party's enthusiastic endorsement.

McClellan may have been a political neophyte, but he was no fool. The lengthy report he had begun in early 1863 amounted to a detailed document, full of explanations for decisions and actions, and inactions. The *Report on the Organization of the Army of the Potomac, and of Its Campaigns in Virginia and Maryland* took months to draft, but in early August—just under two months before McClellan would endorse George Woodward—McClellan submitted a 756-page manuscript defending his sixteen months in uniform. The Government Printing Office agreed to publish the full report but without the extensive accompanying texts from McClellan's subordinates. The published version, which ran to 242 printed pages, appeared in February 1864. Although on its surface McClellan's *Report* read like an extensive defense of his military career, the document immediately became almost the equivalent of a campaign biography, introducing the general and his ideas—including the crucial letter he gave to Lincoln at Harrison's Landing—to the voting public.[62] Party insiders, anxious to assess the presumptive nominee, now had three documents to contemplate: his public letter on Woodward, his letter written at Harrison's Landing, and this long account of his military career.

A few weeks in advance of the publication date, Stebbins reported to Barlow that he had received fifty letters in the previous week, and all but five requested copies of the general's *Report*.[63] In April another Democratic correspondent wrote from St. Louis, claiming that local Republicans were trying to block the distribution of McClellan's statement.[64] But the *Report* sold well, assisted by a cheaper edition produced by a New York editor.

Still, true insiders and engaged voters also had to come to terms with that Woodward letter. Congressman Cox read the document as an act of political compromise, an argument that appealed to the professionals. In April a Pennsylvania soldier sent a friend a long letter about McClellan and national politics, noting that "last fall he wrote a letter in favor of Judge Woodward for Governor of Pennsylvania, now this was a hurt to him, for Woodward is considered of copperhead principles." The soldier—who denied being a Democrat—insisted that the charge was unfair, for McClellan was "much of a Union man."[65] Postmaster General Montgomery Blair remarked in May that "I am distressed too at the attitude on which McClellan has placed himself. If he could have left himself out of politics I am sure he could have been at the head of his army." Blair went on to argue that "the Woodward letter places him. Many look upon it as a bid for the nomination to the Presidency by the Woodward party in opposition to Lincoln." The postmaster general would have been much happier if the general had just kept his nose out of politics.[66] Months later, as election day neared, one-time Democratic congressman Joseph McKibben sent Barlow a letter from Pennsylvania, describing a chat with Republican governor Andrew Curtin, who had no enthusiasm for Lincoln's reelection. "The whole tenor of the conversation," McKibben wrote, "was that nothing but the letter of Gen McClellan in favor of Woodward, prevents his coming out on our side."[67]

And even as many insiders had come to terms with the general's endorsement of the judge, the national press—particularly Lincoln loyalists—regularly reminded its readers how McClellan had supported Woodward. In August, as Democrats prepared to nominate its candidate, the Philadelphia *Press* mocked the *New York Herald* for seemingly distancing itself from McClellan. The paper reminded readers that the previous fall the general had endorsed Woodward, "the candidate of the peace faction," although in McClellan's recent speeches he seemed to have shifted his message.[68] Newspapers all over the country took shots at McClellan for his supposed hypocrisy.

This ongoing discussion of McClellan gets us a bit ahead of our story. Back in January when the Democratic National Committee met at August Belmont's house, the assembled insiders had agreed to open their convention in Chicago on July 4. But as that date approached, key Democrats were inclined to postpone their convention. The core question was not who their standard-bearer should be. Although George McClellan was hardly a shoo-in to be the nominee, his handlers had no particular reason to postpone that decision. The problem was that it remained unclear what the Democratic Party should stand for. Or, more precisely, what should the party platform say? The party was split, and disinterested party members might have reasonably concluded the party's approach to the war as a military conflict should be dependent on the state of events on the battlefield. Perhaps best to wait a few months and see how the war was going before writing a platform.

For quite awhile the party's preferences remained unclear. In mid-June St. Louis Democrat James Steel wrote to his brother in Pennsylvania, sharing plans to meet in Chicago the following month. "I presume there will be little difference of opinion among the delegates as to the propriety of nominating Genl McClellan," he wrote. "*There should be none. He must be nominated.*"[69] But a few days later New York congressman and ex-mayor Fernando Wood dropped Barlow a note, acknowledging the movement to postpone the convention, which he interpreted as an anti-McClellan effort. Wood insisted that "I am *uncommitted*—my friends are uncommitted I want success—but with a man who will close the war without more fighting and without disunion." He went on to insist that "if satisfied that McClellan is this man I am for him—especially as I believe he can pull more votes than any other Democrat living."[70] Belmont telegrammed that Horatio Seymour and other leading East Coast Democrats were on board with a postponement to the convention, but only weeks before it was slated to begin the chair of the Democratic National Committee remained uncertain.[71]

In simplest terms, Democratic leaders were still divided over the message they should present to voters. One option would be to declare the Civil War essentially a failure. In this view, the United States should pursue a negotiated peace that would end the bloodshed as soon as possible. But the other option would be to embrace a patriotic perspective, calling for pursuing the fight to a military victory while rejecting emancipation and other administration policies as unconstitutional. Wise, and unapologetically cynical, Democrats recognized that the body counts from Grant's spring offensive in Virginia had disillusioned many northerners. Why not postpone the convention for a few months to see whether popular enthusiasm for the war continued to wane, or whether Grant achieved successes that might affect that partisan message? To put the same issue more broadly, some of the men who did their work in smoke-filled rooms thought it best to convene in Chicago when the military future seemed more apparent and the party could be more clear about its overall goals, and thus its likely candidate.[72]

Barlow, who was effectively McClellan's campaign manager, received unending advice on these issues. Two weeks before the scheduled convention, New York congressman John V. L. Pruyn wrote that McClellan "has been gaining greatly since Grant's campaign commenced." Better, he thought, to let the casualties mount before putting McClellan forward.[73] Journalist A. Banning Norton checked in from Ohio, warning Barlow that "men who have heretofore been warm friends of McClellan are expressing the desire that he will in some manner define his position more satisfactorily for this peace element." In a perfect illustration of the challenges McClellan faced, Norton wrote that he found the general's address at West Point—which McClellan had delivered the previous week—"magnificent," whereas the antiwar Democrats in Norton's universe "are very violent in denunciation of its war tone." With only weeks before the party was slated to declare a nominee, Democrats recognized that McClellan was a leading candidate while dividing on what they felt he should—or did—stand for.[74]

While some savvy Democrats wished to postpone the convention, Democrat David H. Williams—who had commanded Pennsylvania's 82nd Infantry Regiment—was not pleased. Williams, a strong defender of the war, wrote to Barlow from Pittsburgh on June 23. "It will be better to place our candidate in the field upon a bold and vigorous platform at once, than to await the chances of the future," he insisted. As Williams saw it, the advocates for delay were hedging their bets. "The argument is generally illustrated by saying that if General Grant should capture Richmond between now and the time for holding the election," he wrote, "he could be elected by the Democrats beyond a doubt and if it is not captured we can elect almost any person that we should select." But rather than putting their faith in hopes of Union military failure, Williams argued that the party should make its best case against the actual "errors and crimes of the administration," campaigning for McClellan on the substantial written record "as announced in the Harrison Landing, Judge Woodward, and other letters." A few days later, having learned that the party had decided to postpone the convention for eight weeks, a disappointed Williams wrote again: "Reason appears to have almost entirely lost its sway and men are almost exclusively guided by their passions, which holds good as well in our party as in the opposition." But Williams remained optimistic: "There is a vast difference in the instincts and impulses of the two parties and upon this difference, favorable to the Democratic Party, I alone have hope for the future."[75]

While these machinations unfolded, George McClellan sat in New York and stewed. On June 15 he had delivered a well-attended patriotic address at West Point at the dedication of a monument honoring the Civil War dead from the regular army. Careful to avoid sounding too political on the occasion, McClellan took pains to make it clear that the war was a just cause, so long as its prosecution did not drift into other matters, like emancipation. The speech was well-received by his supporters and would be the basis for his campaign to come.[76] But now he faced talk of a postponed convention, engineered by Democrats who did not share his core views on the war. His friends Barlow and Belmont were uncertain about the postponement. Sunset Cox opined that the whole idea was intended to provide fodder for the antiwar wing of the party. Better, he argued, that the Democrats get on with things and lay the groundwork for a vigorous campaign. The *World*'s Manton Marble agreed that postponement was a poor idea. When news of the decision reached the general he threw up his hands, telling Marble that "I feel now perfectly free from any obligation to allow myself to be used as a candidate. It is very doubtful whether anything could now induce me to consent to have my name used."[77] The candidate would eventually calm down, but the postponement opened up two more months of back-room negotiations about the party's future.

In the eight weeks between early July and late August, Democratic insiders and the deeply engaged continued to try to fit McClellan into their own worldview. Barlow's aged aunt Anne G. Wright—no supporter of the war—pored over McClellan's writings and rejected her nephew's candidate. "They so plainly show he has not the first idea of true Democracy or Republican form of government," she declared. "Great God! A man claiming to be a Democrat & a Christian gentleman, advocating a continuance of this [ ] & bloody course, initiated by that disgrace to humanity & decency Abe Lincoln!"[78]

Democrats scattered across their end of the political spectrum did their best to take the nation's partisan temperature, musing over whether they could pick off a few conservative Republicans who had grown frustrated with the president, while monitoring Grant's progress on the battlefield. The pressure on McClellan grew more intense. On July 21 Judge Francis Blair summoned McClellan to meet with him at New York's Astor Place. Blair, the patriarch of one of the century's great political families, had an unparalleled confidence in his own political power and acumen, and he had thoughts to share with the general. Blair was a long-term Democrat turned Republican who supported the war, and he had a proposal for the general. Given McClellan's commitment to the conflict, Blair felt that the logical conclusion would be for him to refuse the Democratic nomination and instead make himself available to accept a commission in the army from Lincoln. That is, rather than challenging the president at the ballot box, the general should implicitly endorse the administration by accepting a new military command. Although Frank Blair's son Montgomery was a conservative in Lincoln's cabinet, it seems likely that the elder Blair was not acting as an official emissary of the administration. Still, the idea was not absolutely insane on paper. Lincoln and Grant did discuss reinstating McClellan, and Montgomery had also expressed his frustration to Barlow about McClellan's political aspirations.

McClellan dismissed Blair's suggestions. He rejected the premise of the meeting in a letter to Blair, nearly three decades his senior. McClellan denied that he was involved in any active pursuit of the presidency or even the nomination. If the Democrats chose to nominate him, that was their concern. And if the Democrats were to select McClellan, he was certainly not going to step aside for Abraham Lincoln. As he explained, although he was committed to pursuing the war to military victory, McClellan wanted no part of a path that would involve leaving the way open for Lincoln's reelection. He supported the war but disagreed vigorously with how the Republican Party had been violating the Constitution in the name of military victory. McClellan's biographer concluded that the general opted to not send his reply to Blair. And, in fact, Lincoln and Grant discussed putting McClellan back in uniform, a conversation that would not have occurred had they seen his letter.[79]

The leaders of both parties recognized that the election might well turn on events on the battlefield. By August all eyes turned to Atlanta. On August 2 Colonel Durbin Ward of the 17th Ohio Volunteers sent a long letter to Ohio Congressman Cox from "before Atlanta." In this rather extraordinary eight-page missive, Ward—a prowar Democrat—offered Cox his extended thoughts on the state of the party and of politics. Ward wrote confidentially, worried that his political opinions might cost him his commission, but he insisted that "in the true American sense I am a Democrat. I believe in the liberties of the people being guaranteed by written Constitution," including in the proper balance between federal and state powers, and "in the perpetuity of the Union." But despite his core convictions, the colonel warned that "I may not *vote* with the Democratic Party. I believe War is at present necessary to preserve the Union—; not War against the Institutions, or for the *Subjugation or extermination* of the people of the South, but War for the overthrow of the Rebel government. I shall vote for no party that does not seek these things." For these reasons, he added, "I am very anxious as to the Presidential election. Lincoln is not at all my choice and it is difficult for me to conceive a contingency in which I shall vote for him. But still even a worse may be elected."

With these words Ward was defining himself quite explicitly as a prowar Democrat. He was committed to defeating the Confederacy, yet he had no confidence in the Lincoln administration, and he did not wish a war that would destroy slavery, particularly because he could not see the South surrendering under such terms. So, looking to the Chicago convention, Ward had strong words for his congressman. The party simply must nominate a candidate capable of winning the war, and that candidate must run under a strong prowar platform. Given those constraints, he recommended, "If you nominate on such a platform and he accepts—Genl Grant—his election is certain. Next to him in popularity and far abler in my judgment is McClellan; and I think it very likely that he would be elected." Ward promised that if the party were to nominate McClellan and prepare a strong war platform, the general would have his enthusiastic support. Like many of his peers, Colonel Ward had done his homework on McClellan, precisely as the general had anticipated. "I have McClellan's Report and have read it carefully," he reported. "It is an unanswerable vindication. I read also with great interest his West Point speech. It is both eloquent and beautiful. I have always admired McClellan but was not prepared to find him an orator and an elegant scholar as well as a military hero."

But the prescient colonel worried over how the Democrats would handle Chicago. The delegates would, he assumed, fail to nominate Grant. And although they would turn to McClellan, they would "not make a winning platform" for him. Rather, "you will nominate your candidate but then put a load on his back."[80]

Only a few days later Charles D. Robinson, the Wisconsin editor of the Green Bay *Advocate,* sent a concerned letter to Abraham Lincoln. Whereas Ward supported the war but remained loyal to the Democratic Party, Robinson—also a veteran of the Union Army—wrote to express his concern over the administration's position about slavery and peace. "I am a War Democrat, and the editor of a Democratic paper," he explained.

> I have sustained your Administration . . . because it is the legally constituted government. I have sustained its war policy, not because I endorsed it entirely, but because it presented the only available method of putting down the rebellion. . . . It was alleged that because I and my friends sustained the Emancipation measure, we had become abolitionized. We replied that we regarded the freeing of the negroes as sound war policy, in that the depriving the South of its laborers weakened the . . . Rebellion. That was a good argument. . . . It was solid ground on which we could stand, and still maintain our position as Democrats.

Robinson reminded Lincoln of a public letter the president had written to Horace Greeley and the *Tribune* two years earlier: "We were greatly comforted . . . by your assurance that if your could save the Union without freeing any slave, you would do it; if you could save it by freeing the slaves, you would do it; and if you could do it by freeing some, and leaving others alone, you would also do that." But now, with the presidential election looming, Robinson expressed his concern about recent discussions of peace and Lincoln's declaration, "as we understand it, that no steps can be taken towards peace . . . unless accompanied with an abandonment of slavery. This puts the whole war question on a new basis, and takes us War Democrats clear off our feet, leaving us no ground to stand upon. If we sustain the war and war policy, does it not demand the changing of our party politics?"[81]

Robinson's letter holds a place in Lincoln lore because the president drafted two responses that seemed to leave the door open a crack for the possibility of a negotiated peace without emancipation as a condition. But Lincoln apparently never sent his reply, presumably leaving Robinson—and many other pro-administration Democrats—in a continued quandary. It was one thing to support the administration, emancipation and all, if the ending of slavery was a war measure, as articulated by the Emancipation Proclamation. But what if the ending of slavery was a war aim in itself? And further, what if the Democrats would—as Ward hoped—nominate a candidate who would commit to military victory without emancipation? The Democrats faced a complex political challenge. Ardent Peace Democrats wanted to see the conflict come to an abrupt end. War Democrats held commitments to both the party and the Union, and individuals might break either way when it came to voting. And meanwhile, party insiders continued to believe that there were conservative Republicans who were sufficiently unhappy with the administration that they might be lured by the right Democratic candidate.

August 1864: Chicago

At the end of August Democrats poured into Chicago—the site of Abraham Lincoln's Republican nomination four years earlier—to select their candidate and settle on a party platform. Barlow remained in New York, receiving a flood of letters and telegrams on events as they unfolded. Some of his allies felt that Barlow should be on hand in Chicago to steer McClellan's nomination, but the New Yorker worried about having too many political managers on the ground.[82] The general's chances seemed excellent, or at least that is what Barlow heard from his fleet of advisors and informants. Ohioan Thomas Marshall Key, a one-time member of McClellan's staff, sent a detailed analysis of the political terrain as the convention opened. The strongest antiwar "opposition from Ohio will cluster about Pendleton and Vallandigham," he reported, without seeming to be too concerned. Meanwhile, Key noted some possibility that the New Yorkers would rally around Horatio Seymour, posing a bit of a challenge.[83] August Belmont was feeling less sanguine when the convention opened on the 29th, recalling the disasters of four years earlier. "It will not be as easy as expected," he wrote. "The people are all right but the leaders have learned *nothing* since Charleston."[84]

Key's letter nicely mapped out the fissures in the Democratic Party in 1864. The party agreed fundamentally on the broad legal and constitutional issues. Whatever rhetoric they selected, there was a consensus that the Lincoln administration had wildly exceeded its constitutional authority by pursuing emancipation, enforcing conscription, violating civil liberties, and other misdeeds. They disagreed over whether the United States should pursue the Civil War to victory, presumably without emancipation. Or should the new president abandon the effort as a failed venture and seek immediate peace? Beneath this split there were important geographic differences, most of which had been in place since before the war began. Midwestern Peace Democrats, led by Clement Vallandigham, had an important center of power in Ohio. Meanwhile, although McClellan spent much of his time in New York, and relied on a cluster of powerful New York Democrats in his inner circle, the state's Peace Democrats enjoyed substantial influence. Politicians who knew how to count delegates recognized the power of both geography and personality. Meanwhile, the delegates from the border states—with their own concerns about slavery and civil liberties—commanded attention. The Maryland delegation held long-term grudges against McClellan for his role in the arrest of state legislators in September 1861. Kentucky's delegates expected to have a strong voice in the proceedings, and perhaps a candidate on the party's slate.

Historians can read these divisions differently. Most important newspapers of the day were profoundly partisan, and the private correspondence that survives commonly pulled no punches about adversaries. But the brilliant political historian Joel Silbey reminds us that despite internal conflicts over real policy, "the will to remain united was obviously there" in 1864. "As bad as internal factional differences might be," he added, "there was much more distance between Democrats and all Republicans than between blocs of Democrats (or Republicans)."[85] It remained an open question if this commitment to unanimity would survive a convention.

At the very least, the so-called Chicago Wigwam promised to provide a few days of fine political theater. When each delegate arrived, he was presented with a carefully printed pamphlet that combined McClellan's Harrison's Landing Letter and his West Point address. Together these two documents affirmed the general's patriotism and commitment to the war while underscoring his core conservative values.[86] It would reassure the convention's War Democrats while also—in the future—appeal to conservative Republicans who had not forgotten about that Woodward letter. But it did not reach out to the party's Vallandigham wing.

Journalist Noah Brooks, an occasional confidant of the president, attended both political conventions in 1864. Before Brooks departed for each, Lincoln asked Brooks to send him any interesting gossip from his trip. Shortly before setting out for Chicago, Brooks chatted with the president about the Democrats. Lincoln, always the astute political observer, told Brooks that "they must nominate a Peace Democrat on a war platform, or a War Democrat on a peace platform; and I personally can't say that I care much which they do." Those predictions came just a few weeks after Durbin Ward declared that both options would be disastrous.[87]

Three decades later Brooks wrote his memoirs and published a short and entertaining account of the two conventions in the *Century*, reporting on the key characters and events and capturing the overall feel of Chicago in 1864. Brooks recalled a lively train ride to Chicago, in cars packed with leading Democrats and Union soldiers heading home. The high point was when a traveling colonel managed to convince a carload of Indiana troops that he was in fact George McClellan heading west. When Brooks arrived at the party's "wigwam" on Chicago's lakeshore, he found what he called a "Peace Democratic Convention," where Ohio's Vallandigham and Alexander Long and Maryland's controversial Benjamin Gwinn Harris were the acknowledged "stars" of the affair. When Ohio's Sunset Cox rose to speak, the assembled crowd shouted him down, calling him a "War Democrat." It was, in Brooks's recollection, a raucous affair.

Once the formal proceedings began, New York's Governor Seymour presided over the convention. Brooks came away impressed with the governor's leadership, even while rowdy participants shouted for Vallandigham and his more radical colleagues. One of the major developments in that first day was the placement of Vallandigham on the platform committee, a huge victory for the assembled advocates of peace. On the second day the committee presented its work to the convention, including the crucial clause that reflected Vallandigham's input: "After four years failure to restore the Union by the experiment of war, during which, under the pretense of military necessity, or war power higher than the Constitution, the Constitution itself has been disregarded in every part, . . . the public welfare demands that immediate efforts be made for cessation of hostilities with a view to an ultimate convention of the States, or other peaceable means to the end that at the earliest practicable moment peace may be restored on the basis of the Federal union of the states." It was a powerful broadside against Lincoln and the Union war effort, fired by one of the administration's most strident critics. And now, despite the vigorous efforts of McClellan's allies on the committee, it was in the middle of the Democrats' proposed platform.

Brooks, with his flair for the dramatic portrait, recalled that "S.S. Cox clasped his hands on his lap and dropped his head, a picture of despair," and "August Belmont . . . looked profoundly sad." Meanwhile, "Vallandigham and Alexander Long," antiwar Ohioans, "rubbed their hands with unrestrained glee" as the convention voted to adopt Vallandigham's resolution.[88] One might argue that just over four years earlier, when the southern delegates walked out of the Democratic Convention in Charleston, their inability to find common ground with their northern brethren sealed the fate of the Democratic Party. Now in Chicago, it seemed that perhaps the same had happened again. The party had done precisely what Colonel Ward had feared, and Abraham Lincoln had predicted. Or at least they had done half of it: they had written a strong antiwar resolution into their platform. Or, to put it more simply, the Chicago Democrats had thrilled Vallandigham. A beaten Belmont wrote to McClellan, explaining that "we had to fight against the western peace men, who are very ultra."[89]

Historian Silbey quoted Brooks's recollections, but he read the events a bit differently. In Silbey's view, Barlow and his faction—who Silbey called the "Legitimists"—were intent on keeping the party together while finding some common ground with the "Purists" who opposed the war. Although Vallandigham's role in the platform committee and the language of his second resolution in the platform ran counter to what McClellan believed, Silbey argued that the Legitimists saw it as a victory for the party that nobody walked out of the proceedings.[90]

With the platform passed, the delegates turned their attention to nominating a candidate. But first they devoted the rest of the second day to listening to angry delegates sharing their objections to McClellan. Harris and his delegation from Maryland reminding the assembled delegates that McClellan, when he was still in uniform, had been complicit in arresting Maryland legislators accused of disloyalty early in the war. McClellan's defenders pointed out that when he was an active general, McClellan was part of a military chain of command and not personally engaged in arbitrary arrests for his own amusement. Then Ohio's Long took his turn, calling McClellan "the worst and weakest man." Far better to nominate Vallandigham or Seymour, rather than McClellan. The day ended without a candidate, or even a vote. It was really an afternoon for angry politicians to vent their spleen before turning to the business at hand.

Day three was the day for voting. Although McClellan's nomination was all but assured, his managers quickly found that some clusters of Peace Democrats were not willing to go down without a fight, or at least some bargaining. Vallandigham and the Ohioans, who had already outmaneuvered McClellan's managers to control the platform committee, officially opposed the general's candidacy, as did the Peace Democrats from New York and much of the Maryland delegation. Although prior to the convention Barlow had indicated his managers would be in Chicago with no authority to make deals or compromises, Brooks reported that in the end there was considerable horse trading, and a few broken promises. In the first ballot McClellan earned 150 votes; Connecticut's Thomas Seymour, 43; and New York's Horatio Seymour got 7 votes. After that first vote, the delegates from Missouri, who had backed Thomas Seymour, split their votes on the second ballot between the two leaders. Finally, after much manipulation, McClellan won the nomination over Thomas Seymour. At this point Vallandigham, silent for most of the day, mounted the rostrum and moved to make the vote unanimous. Brooks recalled that "the pent up feelings of the crowd broke forth in the most rapturous manner," with much praise aimed at Vallandigham for his actions. But although that was how Brooks recalled the vote thirty years later, a few days after the vote he noted that some of McClellan's strongest critics refused to cast their lot with the general.

With McClellan's name finally selected, the convention turned to a vice-presidential candidate. Some of the established War Democrats, including party chairman Belmont, hoped that the party would select Kentuckian James Guthrie, but the assembled delegates floated a long list of candidates. Border-state representatives from Kentucky and Indiana believed they had been promised the vice presidency in exchange for their support of McClellan. While the party contemplated many options, they settled on Ohio's George Pendleton, thus giving a final win to the Ohio Peace Democrats.[91]

Barlow received a steady stream of telegrams reporting on events and congratulating him on his man's nomination. Theodore Romeyn celebrated the nomination but added the ominous note that "there is some disappointment at the platform."[92] Daniel Devlin weighed in from New York, sharing his enthusiasm for the candidate and noting that "although I submit to every line & word of the Chicago Resolutions I'm sorry to say as a whole they do not give entire satisfaction to a large number of our friends, and disappoint thousands of wavering Republicans who were ready and anxious to come over to us." If the overall plan had been to woo some conservative Republicans into the Democratic camp, Vallandigham's resolution hardly seemed likely to seal the deal.[93]

In some senses modern readers would recognize the main lines of the Chicago convention. Delegates were excited and boisterous, and some drank a lot. Democrats jockeyed for opportunities to deliver orations, even when they held minority views. And important events transpired behind the scenes. Of course if we were to compare 1864 to modern conventions, we would have to select one of the rare recent meetings where important decisions were actually made at the gathering. That was surely the case in the Chicago Wigwam. Although nominally committed to unanimity, delegates divided on important issues, and some of the loudest voices had no trouble pointing out their disgust with the presumptive nominee. And whatever broad similarities might have linked the past with the present, important variables set the nineteenth-century process apart.

Perhaps most central to our story, the nominee—or even the presumptive nominee—had no control over the content of the party platform or the name of the nominee for vice president. In Chicago the Democrats weighed political and geographic interests. Perhaps McClellan's West Point oration and lengthy *Report* reassured some voters that he was a prowar patriot, but those same reassurances caused problems for the party's peace faction and its powerful Midwestern contingent. Thus, the party leadership agreed to let Vallandigham write that strong antiwar plank into the platform. And the delegates agreed to name Pendleton, an outspoken advocate for peace, to the ticket. It was a complex balancing act, where the party wanted to keep all Democrats in the fold while they also hoped to lure conservative Republicans—unhappy with the administration and the progress of the war—into the party. And the eventual nominee had almost nothing to do with how events transpired.

There was another crucial distinction between then and now. In modern elections it has long been typical for presumptive presidential nominees to stay out of the convention until they have been selected, at which point they can swoop onto the rostrum to deliver a rousing acceptance speech, followed by a carefully constructed tableau with presidential and vice-presidential candidates holding their hands raised in anticipation of victories to come, surrounded by adoring family members (and falling balloons). In 1864 George McClellan—following current custom—was nowhere near Chicago. Still, in the age of the telegraph, news traveled fast. Barlow in New York and McClellan in New Jersey received word of the key votes within hours of their completion. Once nominated, all the general had to do was fire off a short telegram accepting the honor and promising to run a fine campaign. A reasonably organized candidate might have had that letter of acceptance drafted and ready to go before the serious drinking had begun in Chicago.

But the situation was hardly typical. McClellan was bitter over the antiwar plank in the platform and the decision to nominate Pendleton. Correspondents shared his disappointment, but some insisted that he was not really bound by the convention's core decisions. It was clear that Vallandigham's plank did not match McClellan's many public statements. Some supporters hoped that McClellan would issue a response that reconciled his actual beliefs with the platform his party had passed. That would be a complex tightrope to walk. At the very least, McClellan would have to officially accept his party's nomination.

Shortly after the convention, James Buchanan wrote to fellow Pennsylvanian Lewis S. Coryell about the convention. "The nomination of McClellan was the inspiration of popular feeling," the ex-president concluded. "The Chicago Convention was a mass meeting to ratify the decision of the people. I trust he may be elected because he is greatly better in every respect than the present incumbent." But Buchanan acknowledged that "the platform is rather muddy. Peace would be a great blessing; but it would cost too dear at the expense of the Union."[94]

For days McClellan remained publicly silent while privately he labored over multiple drafts of a letter accepting the nomination.[95] Correspondents from across the country flooded Barlow with letters, underscoring the importance of the general's acceptance letter. One September 2 letter was typical: "Many thousands of votes depends on Gen'l McCellan's letter of acceptance. The Platform does not suit the Conservative Rep. not that I think there is any doubt of the General's election, but if he can so shape his answer so as to appease the 'People' that he means to bring the war to a close by an honorable piece, or if necessary by the force of arms it would have a great effect."[96] Democratic journalist William Cassidy wrote from Albany, predicting that a careful treatment of the platform would help attract conservative Republican voters, and insisting that previous candidates had rejected portions of their party's platforms without great problems.[97] But while many correspondents urged McClellan to accept the nomination as a War Democrat, others hoped he would embrace the platform as drafted. Philadelphia's William Reed, the controversial antiwar Democrat, wrote to Barlow urging the candidate to stand with the platform, and when Barlow suggested a different path, Reed replied, "Depend on it—this will be a fatal mistake. I speak with entire confidence as to the feeling here—and throughout—this commonwealth. You cannot carry Pennsylvania on a war policy."[98]

There is no good reason to conclude that McClellan seriously considered declining his party's nomination, although history could forgive him if he had done just that. After all, he had agreed to let the party nominate him, and they had saddled him with a hostile vice-presidential candidate and a platform that he would have to run from rather than embrace.

In the week after the convention McClellan drafted six different letters accepting his nomination. The challenge was partially ideological. How could McClellan accept the nomination while explaining to potential voters what he really believed? But in a broader sense McClellan's letter was a political document. He needed to select a path that would maximize political support from among voters who embraced at least part of that platform, and from those who agreed with the general's earlier writings but worried about Vallandigham's antiwar plank. In the end McClellan accepted the nomination but did his best to separate himself from the platform's more troublesome words. His letter affirmed his enduring commitment to the Union, promising that peace would only follow a reunion of the states, whose core constitutional rights would be respected. He gambled that the disappointed peace advocates would stick with the party in the campaign to come.[99]

3

1864

ELECTING A PRESIDENT

Once both candidates had been selected, the national campaign began in earnest. It was a hugely important election for the future of the American Civil War, and a valuable campaign for explaining midcentury partisan politics.

Democrats Campaign for the Presidency

To recap just a bit: on August 23, 1864, Abraham Lincoln presented his cabinet with his "Blind Memo," declaring that he might lose the upcoming election. It was only a few days later that the president chatted with Noah Brooks, predicting that the Democrats would likely nominate a presidential candidate whose ideals were at odds with the party's platform. On the 31st the Chicago convention closed after the party had done just that. On September 3 General William Tecumseh Sherman sent a telegram to the president informing him that "Atlanta is ours, and fairly won."[1] That success had a huge impact on the popular mood in the North. By the time McClellan formally accepted his party's nomination on September 8, it is a good bet that the president would have revised his gloomy prediction. And by the time the Democrats met in Chicago, the great Union cavalry commander Phillip Sheridan had launched his Shenandoah Valley campaign against the equally famed Confederate general Jubal Early. Finally, on October 19—just in time for the election—Sheridan's men routed Early's forces at Cedar Creek.[2] No doubt military matters would have a huge impact on vote totals.

But despite these successes in the East, violence in the slave-owning border states had grown progressively worse, both at the hands of roaming bands of guerrillas and in the increasingly brutal responses by federal forces. The impact on partisan politics was complex, as some moderate Unionists evolved

Political cartoon: "Little Mack & His Party 'Going Up' Salt River on a Gunboat." This 1864 political broadside mocks an assortment of antiwar northern Democrats as they prepare to do electoral battle against Abraham Lincoln, who stands to the left. Long a staple in political humor, "going up salt river" referred to political campaigns that were bound to fail. (Library of Congress)

into hardliners calling on federal forces to do their worst, but other long-term War Democrats watched violence in their midst and the rising role of African American soldiers and abandoned the national cause. One Kentucky Unionist watched her community become occupied by Black troops and finally turned on "the low tyrant Lincoln" and the "tyranny, oppression and injustice" that had become "a matter of course."[3] In September the Confederacy sought to tip the political scales in Missouri by launching an invasion of Sterling Price's Army of Missouri, with twelve thousand cavalry. For over a month Price and his men—aided by local guerrilla groups—terrorized Missourians, taking particular aim at African American and German civilians. Finally, Union troops under William Rosencrans crushed the invaders, but not before Price and his men had provided Missouri dissenters with much-needed assistance.[4] Even though the war in the East seemed to be nearing a conclusion, voters in the western border states continued to face disruption and despair.

While the Democrats were delaying their convention before selecting McClellan as their candidate, the Republicans had been navigating their own complexities. For months various groups of radical Republicans had discussed challenges to the president. At the end of May the latest such effort resulted in a convention in Cleveland that nominated John C. Frémont, but by then the chances of a successful challenge from the president's radical flank had fizzled. Meanwhile, the party—following earlier state moves—had officially renamed itself the National Union Party, hoping to attract loyal War Democrats such as Wisconsin's Charles Robinson. That newly branded party met in Baltimore in the first week of June and renominated Abraham Lincoln. On the 9th he penned his acceptance letter, two months before McClellan formally accepted his party's nomination.

When the two parties had settled on their nominees, it was two months until election day. Civil War historians love to speak of crucial "turning points." Those conversations commonly focus on key military events but invariably the election of 1864 makes the list.[5] Scholars and general readers recognize the huge significance of the election. It was unusual enough for a nation to hold a full election in the midst of a civil war. And in this case the issues on the table were momentous, even if a bit murky. But in those discussions, most of the interest focuses on events leading up to September, and then on the election results themselves.[6] The two months of campaigning after McClellan accepted the nomination are not generally the focus of attention, perhaps because events on the battlefield and in the military camps would be more determinative. But those months are a useful window into who the Democrats were, what they thought about themselves, and how the leaders communicated ideas with the rank and file. They capture not only the issues of the day but the evolving state of party politics in the nineteenth century.

George McClellan's most substantial contribution to his own campaign was probably his letter accepting his nomination. That public document presented his own ideas but also provided some interested Democrats with a version of their party that they could embrace, even if they could not stomach portions of the platform. In fact, the spokesman for the Union veterans of New York's McClellan Legion wrote that their political club had "repudiated the Chicago platform, as an insult to the soldier," but they had embraced "the frank and honest Letter of Acceptance" that the candidate penned. They would cast their ballots for the Democrats, even while rejecting the platform.[7] Maria Lydig Daly happily noted that "the Democratic candidates and their principle supporters have overthrown" the Chicago Platform.[8]

Following tradition, McClellan declined to campaign for his own candidacy. When Pennsylvania Democrats wrote urging him to make a public appearance, the general refused, explaining that as a rule "it would be better for me not to participate in person in the canvass." The following day he resisted Barlow's

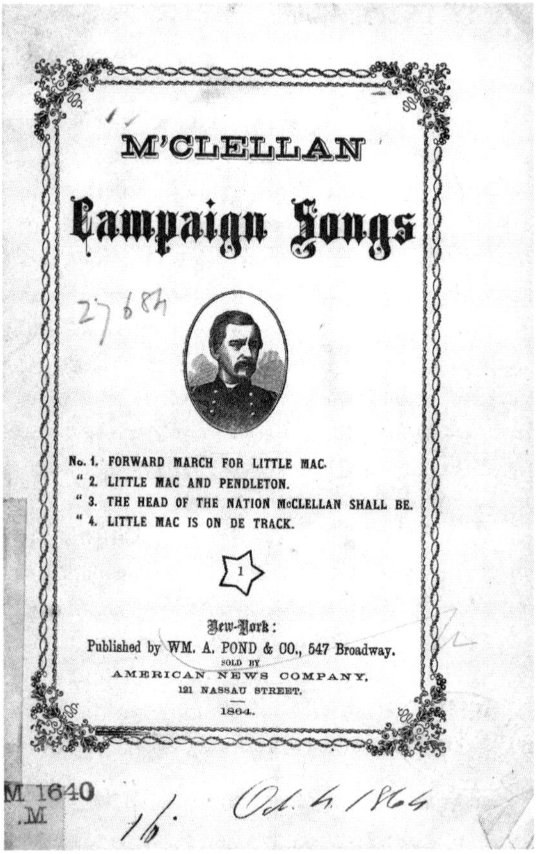

Booklet: *M'Clellan Campaign Songs.* With the election of 1864 looming, partisans on both sides produced both song sheets and small booklets of campaign songs. This small booklet, produced in New York, featured four pro-McClellan songs. (Library of Congress)

invitation to New York and added that if he did come it would only be as a secret visit.[9] He made one partisan trip to Newark and visited New York City to review troops from the balcony of his 5th Avenue Hotel room. But for the duration of the campaign McClellan spent most of his time in the McClellans' New Jersey home in Orange Mountain, assisted by a single secretary.[10]

For those two months the candidate kept up a substantial correspondence. He occasionally exchanged notes with Barlow and a few other party luminaries, but although those letters involved the nuts and bolts of the election, it is striking that the correspondence between the candidate and his chief political advisors offered few hints of a national campaign strategy. The general wrote to some of his old military comrades, reassuring them of his broad aims and seeking their political assistance and support. In this way McClellan—following the advice of those advisors—sought to shore up military support.[11] Meanwhile, the general still had to navigate around the continuing effects of his Woodward letter of the previous year, particularly reassuring Andrew Curtin's Pennsylvania supporters that he had meant no disrespect to the governor.[12]

McClellan also quietly battled to reassure Democrats about the platform and his own positions. He wrote to one skeptical War Democrat, insisting that his letter of acceptance "effectively knocked on the head any ideas of bringing in the Peace Party," even though "many of my conservative friends regret that I wrote that letter."[13] Of course some of those conservative Democrats, who felt that Vallandigham's plank spoke for them, had to be courted as well. William Reed, the outspoken peace man, warned Barlow from Philadelphia that McClellan should stand by the party's platform. When McClellan accepted the nomination but distanced himself from the peace plank, New York congressman Fernando Wood called for a new Democratic convention "either to remodel the platform to suit the nominee, or nominate a candidate to suit the platform."[14] For McClellan and his political advisors, the first major battle was to win over both wings of their own party.

In New York Barlow received reports from all over the nation, monitoring McClellan's chances and keeping the banker-politician abreast of various concerns. Some of the most intense behind-the-scenes conversations concerned McClellan's vice-presidential nominee, the Ohio Peace Democrat George H. Pendleton. The candidate's explicit rejection of the peace plank had won some converts, but it risked losing others. Former New Jersey senator John Wall wrote to McClellan immediately after the nomination, pledging his support for the campaign and assuring him that Pendleton "is an elevated high toned gentleman of rare ability."[15] But this was before McClellan had penned his letter of acceptance. In the days after that letter became public, Barlow and his colleagues worked assiduously to keep leading Peace Democrats in the fold. By September 12 Barlow had made substantial progress with many of these conservatives, but he was still unsure about the vice-presidential candidate himself, "to whom all our friends are telegraphing." The following day McClellan reported that he had heard promising support from leading Pennsylvania Peace Democrats, including William Reed and Samuel Randall.[16] Reed told Barlow that we "are laboring in good faith to put an end to disorganization and aid General McClellan," but it was still tough going.[17] As late as the 23rd McClellan had still not heard from Pendleton, and political insiders recognized that a public statement of support from the vice-presidential candidate would hurt in some places even as it helped in others.[18] It was not until a week later that the crisis seemed to be averted. Henry Myer Phillips reported from Philadelphia that "I have this morning a very excellent letter from Pendleton: he will say or do nothing calculated to harm—there had evidently been a western pressure to persuade him he had been slighted," but the waters had finally smoothed.[19]

In the weeks between the Chicago convention and the election, although McClellan did not appear on the stump and the party lacked a centrally controlled national political message, leading War Democrats rallied to the cause, making the case that McClellan presented the best option for a successful resolution to the conflict and a lasting peace with the Confederate states. Democratic governors played crucial roles in this national contest with distinctly regional implications. New York's Horatio Seymour, still understood as one of the party's most influential voices, maintained his prominent position among the loyal opposition, backing the administration's war measures while calling for a change in national leadership. In Kentucky Governor Thomas Bramlette—another loyal War Democrat with a conflicted relationship with the administration—remained, in the words of one historian, "an ideal surrogate for McClellan in Kentucky." Both fundamentally moderate Democratic governors reminded their constituents that McClellan was best situated to navigate the nation to victory and a lasting peace without imposing unconstitutional social revolution on the southern states.[20] Meanwhile, the party's key wirepullers orchestrated a multitiered campaign, constructing and delivering the Democratic message to a diverse electorate.

Robert C. Winthrop: New England Whig

The challenge for McClellan and his supporters was to bring a successful message—or perhaps messages—to voters. Their efforts reflected the diversity of Democrats, and potential Democratic voters, as well as the evolving nature of partisan politics. While party insiders exchanged correspondence with each other, and occasionally with their candidate, it would be a mistake to imagine presidential campaigns being controlled with some firm central hand on the tiller. The Democratic National Committee had limited resources, and it is hard to see the work of McClellan or his core lieutenants on many of the statements distributed in the name of the candidate and the party. It is perhaps better to imagine a national political contest fought out at multiple levels, engineered by different architects and aimed at very different voters.

One of the first major party gatherings after the convention occurred at New York City's Union Square on September 17.[21] On the anniversary of the ratification of the U.S. Constitution, and the second anniversary of the Battle of Antietam, Robert C. Winthrop delivered an address endorsing McClellan. It was an interesting speech from a somewhat unlikely voice. Winthrop, a one-time Speaker of the House and Whig senator from Massachusetts, was a strong conservative from one of New England's most distinguished families. During the antebellum decades Winthrop had been known as a "cotton Whig," representing that portion of the party most willing to work with slaveholding southerners. With the demise of the second party system and the rise of the Republican Party, many New England Whigs found common cause with their Free-Soil brethren in joining the new party, but not Winthrop. In 1860, no longer in politics, he had supported Constitutional Union candidate John Bell, declining to cast his lot with the representatives from either major party. During the war Winthrop occasionally corresponded with McClellan, who shared many of his conservative sensibilities, but he remained politically independent.[22]

On this occasion Winthrop anchored his words in his own past. He was an old-time New England Whig, and a disciple of Daniel Webster, the great defender of the Union. He pointed out that he was speaking to them in New York's Union Square about the man who fought to defend the Union. He was before them not to advocate for a political party but "with the single and simple view of restoring Union and Peace to our distracted land." With these core themes firmly pounded into place, Winthrop turned to some of the more contentious issues of the day, establishing his essentially conservative perspective. While the war should be purely about the "restoration" of the Union, some had become distracted by grandiose "projects and theories of *reconstruction*" that threatened to destroy entire states. Winthrop reminded his audience that once the war had begun, the Union came together to pursue victory even though it was the policies of the Republican Party that had provoked the conflict. He happily acknowledged Lincoln as a patriot, but now—Winthrop declared—"he desires to be enrolled as the great Liberator of the African race." Such ideals, however worthy, were inhibiting the larger goal of peace and a restored Union. Turning to the candidate, Winthrop reminded his audience of McClellan's Harrison's Landing Letter and his West Point address, as well as the general's extensive report on his military career. Winthrop also pointed out that McClellan had effectively dismissed portions of his party platform. Instead, "Gen. McClellan has made his own platform" with his previous words and in his superb letter accepting the nomination.[23]

Winthrop's friend William Endicott, another ex-Whig, privately praised the speech and recognized its potential importance, declaring, "Among these members of the old whig party, who like yourself have acted with no political organization for many years, there has been but one response—all are gratified by your course, and more than gratified by what you said. It is indeed no time for neutrality, and indifference is impossible." Endicott underscored the crux of the matter as he saw it: "The forcible abolition of slavery, in violation of the Constitution, means war, grand and petty, for years, and then a civil turmoil and confusion hardly preferable to war, and leading to results, too fearful to contemplate. And I know of no principle of sound politics or pure religion that can sanction such a course."[24] The war must be pursued to a military victory, but the unconstitutional pursuit of emancipation and social revolution through military means promised disaster.

Winthrop's New York speech stands as a valuable articulation of McClellan's support from an independent New England conservative. Very much in keeping with the Democratic slogan, Winthrop wished for the restoration of "the Union as it was, and the Constitution as it is." He had no interest in calling Lincoln a tyrant or raising the specter of hordes of freed slaves heading north to threaten White culture, but he was convinced that now was the time for McClellan to step in and return the nation to the Union as loved by Daniel Webster, undisturbed by talk of universal emancipation or a revolutionary Reconstruction. This was a statement that War Democrats and disgruntled conservative Republicans could embrace, and it offered little solace to the peace wing of the Democratic Party. Winthrop's address thrilled McClellan, who called it "far above . . . the political speeches of the present day & so like those of the better days of the Republic."[25]

The September 17 meeting at Union Square and Winthrop's address attracted substantial notice. Marble's *New York World* ran an exhaustive account of the day's celebrations, including the text of Winthrop's speech. Washington's *National Intelligencer* published nearly six columns from the *World*'s report and added an editorial urging "members of the old Whig party" to heed the gentleman's words.[26] The *Chicago Times* ran a short account of Democratic events on the East Coast, quoting liberally from local newspapers. It noted that even New York's *Sunday Mercury*—a Republican paper—reported that the event drew a huge crowd and that Winthrop "made a great speech." The same account appeared in a Democratic paper in Wisconsin. The following Saturday morning the Democratic *Ohio Statesman* reprinted the report from the *Times,* in an issue thick with local Democratic news from across the country.[27] In this fashion newspaper readers across the nation saw reports of the event within days of Winthrop's address.

Most of these published accounts followed a partisan script. Nearly all daily and weekly newspapers were affiliated with one of the political parties, and most were strongly partisan, even if they varied in how they made their case.[28] The Democratic *Daily Register,* in Wheeling, West Virginia, underscored that Reverdy Johnson, Millard Fillmore, and Robert Winthrop, "long recognized as leaders of the Old Whig Party, support McClellan and Pendleton." In so doing, the paper linked the Democratic candidate with a long conservative tradition in the Whig Party while also taking pains to keep Pendleton in the conversation.[29] Pennsylvania's *Columbia Democrat and Bloomsburg General Advertiser* adopted a similar analysis, noting that Winthrop, the senatorial successor of Daniel Webster and a "life-long Whig, and one of the ablest men in Massachusetts," had spoken in New York. The paper urged "every man not wedded to abolition and miscegenation" to watch men such as Winthrop and Johnson, who were backing "McClellan, Union and Peace."[30] Democratic papers stressed Winthrop's conservative credentials while claiming an affiliation with the old Whig Party, rather than stressing the current partisan conflict.

Opponents sought to tar Winthrop with the brush of hypocrisy. A Republican paper from Portland, Maine, noted the oddity in seeing Robert Winthrop on the same dais as New York's outspoken Copperhead Fernando Wood.[31] The *Cleveland Morning Leader* mocked Winthrop's speech, and particularly his comments about the platform, commenting that "the politicians of New York City have kicked over the Chicago platform and snubbed the Pendleton wing."[32] James Gordon Bennett's highly independent but Democrat-leaning *New York Herald* devoted a long column to mocking the Democrats and the rather challenging position they had constructed in Chicago. The *Herald* noted the awkward difficulties posed by the presidential candidate, vice-presidential candidate, and platform, concluding that New York had witnessed an awkward balancing act when Winthrop and Fernando Wood stood on the same stage.[33]

In sum, the address that pleased McClellan so much called on voters to embrace a conservative approach to the future, where the famed general would lead the Union to victory in war while resisting the revolutionary transformations that the Republicans would impose on the South and the nation. And the fact that Winthrop's ideological roots were with the Whigs, rather than either of the two competing parties, was all the better. Meanwhile, advocates of the National Union Party did their best to yoke both McClellan and Winthrop to the New York Peace Democrats, reminding them of the platform's peace plank, Pendleton's position on the ticket, and the continuing presence of Democrats like Wood.

In October Winthrop delivered another well-attended lecture at New London, Connecticut, once again drawing a distinction between McClellan's conservative approach to victory without revolution to the dangers that a continued Lincoln administration threatened. This time Winthrop floated the notion that President McClellan would be better at navigating postwar Reconstruction. A McClellan administration would be less alienating to defeated southerners contemplating a return to the Union, thus easing the transition to peace. The *New York World* described it as "the most brilliant and effective speech of the campaign."[34] (Unionist wags noted that Winthrop was arguing that voters should embrace McClellan because the enemy would like him more.) When McClellan read the speech he unleashed another round of hyperbole, assuring Winthrop that "I know of no political speech of the present or the past that will bear comparison with yours."[35]

The historian Michael E. McGerr has argued that American politics in the decades after the Civil War saw a gradual decline in the popular politics of torchlight parades and celebratory events, toward at least some new focus on what he termed "educational politics," where party leaders actively sought to teach voters with pamphlets and other more substantial written materials.[36] When Winthrop spoke in New York City, it was more than nineteen months since Democrats had gathered at Delmonico's and founded the Society for the Diffusion of Political Knowledge (SDPK). In their first year of operations the SDPK, under the direction of Samuel Morse, had published and distributed a steady stream of pamphlets, presenting the party's core beliefs and key speeches to a national audience.[37] It was this body that republished and distributed Bishop John Henry Hopkins's *Bible View of Slavery.*

Once the party settled on a candidate and the platform, the SDPK and the Democratic Party, under the auspices of the Democratic Central Executive Campaign Committee (DECC), launched a new numbered series it called "Campaign Documents." The pamphlets differed quite a bit, but collectively they made the party's case. The first number reprinted McClellan's letter of acceptance, bundled with the party's platform and his West Point oration. In Document No. 3, the SDPK published McClellan's full *Report* in 144 pages of double-columned text. The fourth pamphlet reproduced a lengthy McClellan campaign biography. Throughout the campaign the DECC published several dozen pamphlets of varying lengths, all seemingly aimed at a fairly attentive literate public. The Campaign Documents, which numbered twenty-six items, included both Winthrop's New York and Connecticut speeches, distributed as separate numbers.

The Democratic publication societies sought broad audiences, although many of their publications seemed aimed at elite—or at least persistent—readers. They published 200,000 copies of the New London lecture and made it available through Democratic newspapers and other venues throughout the country.[38] The DECC's published versions of Winthrop's speeches, like many of their other pamphlets, inserted items to fill in the space left at the end of the publication. These decisions are instructive. At the end of the published version of Winthrop's New York speech the pamphlet included an excerpt from Henry Clay's 1839 oration to the Senate on abolitionist petitions. By turning to this quarter-century-old speech, from another Whig hero, they underscored the power of Union and the dangers of emancipation. Clay had been worried about abolitionism undermining the Union and warned of the threat of freed slaves disrupting White northern communities. By highlighting Clay's words the Democrats again reminded readers that Winthrop's endorsement was not a matter of partisanship.

The DECC also had a supply of pithy McClellan quotes from his various speeches and writings, which it inserted under the heading "Watchwords for Patriots." Winthrop's Connecticut speech was reprinted in ten double-columned pages. They added McClellan's letter of acceptance, his Harrison's Landing Letter, a longer text of Clay's 1839 speech, and a full page of quotations. Interested readers, willing to work through long speeches and short squibs from the candidate, would come away with a pretty clear and consistent version of what McClellan and his supporters wished voters to know. He was a soldier and a Union man who could be counted on to bring the war to a successful conclusion while protecting the Constitution along the way. And, perhaps not coincidentally, Winthrop's speech and pamphlet invoked Whig icon Daniel Webster, and the pamphlets from McClellan added long references to Democratic hero Henry Clay. Patriots recalled Webster and Clay as great nationalists and grand defenders of the Constitution. Both leaders died in 1852. The conservative Democrats wished to remind readers—and voters—that they defended the nation's great history.[39]

The Miscegenation Ball and the Politics of Racism

If newspaper editorials and political pamphlets made extended arguments, battling it out for the minds of northern voters, other political efforts aimed at different targets. One of the oddest products of the 1864 election was a large

Political cartoon: "Miscegenation Ball." This anti-Republican cartoon was produced by G. W. Bromley & Company in 1864. The large lithograph mocks an event staged at the Lincoln Central Campaign Club at Broadway and 23rd Street in New York on September 22, 1864. The highly racist image portrays well-dressed White men and African American women dancing together, with the portrait of Abraham Lincoln overlooking the scene. (Library of Congress)

colorful lithograph called "The Miscegenation Ball." The image, purporting to capture the goings on at a Republican meeting in New York on September 22, shows a crowd of well-dressed dancers enjoying a formal ball, with a large portrait of Abraham Lincoln on the back wall overseeing the festivities. The striking feature of the lithograph is that the crowd is interracial, and all the White men are dancing with Black women. The suggestion was clear: Lincoln's reelection would open up a world of unfettered miscegenation, with Whites and Blacks cavorting together unchecked by law or culture.

The key message behind "The Miscegenation Ball" was hardly new. As we have seen, nearly a year earlier two journalists with the *New York World* published a fake seventy-two-page booklet claiming to be a scientific treatise on the virtues of the "blending of the white and black races." Like most political cartoons and lithographs, "The Miscegenation Ball" was not the product of party officials but rather privately produced by entrepreneurs. In this case the image was one of a series created by the firm Bromley & Company, working with the anti-Lincoln Democrats of the *World*. The event in New York was real, and there apparently actually were guests of different races present, but from there the Democratic press and the artist took immense license, regaling readers with talk of interracial debauchery. The *World* ran a long story on "Miscegenation in Earnest" illustrated by the ball, suggesting that the "colored belles" produced quite a stir, attracting the "love sick glances of the Republicans." The city's *Weekly Day Book* reprinted the *World*'s entire story. Albany's *Atlas and Argus* had its own prejudiced fun, commenting on the "negro ball" where leading Republicans danced with "ebony damsels."[40]

Much like the reports of Winthrop's New York speech, the stories about this Republican gathering spread quickly in the nation's Democratic press. A paper in Columbus, Ohio, ran the entire article from the *World* on its front page only days after the event.[41] The Democratic newspaper in Wheeling, West Virginia, acknowledged the original stories in an editorial titled "Miscegenation." It had initially questioned the *World*'s credibility, but when the *Journal of Commerce* confirmed the stories the Wheeling *Daily Register* reprinted their account and added its own outraged commentary. The whole thing illustrated "the future that is in store for the American people" should Lincoln win reelection.[42] Delaware's *Wilmington Gazette* published the story from the *Journal of Commerce* under the heading "Shame."[43]

The image itself was probably more important to modern historians seeking visual depictions of campaign racism than it was in shaping the opinions of 1864 voters, but the lithograph and the newspaper coverage does illustrate several themes. At the core of broader political debates was a continuing cultural hysteria about an interracial society, stirred up by the feared arrival of huge numbers of freed slaves. Throughout 1864 a portion of Democratic editors scoured newspapers for accounts of the dangers of race mixing. In April 1864 the Philadelphia *Press* ran a letter professing to describe two wealthy White women who had taken Black men as their spouses and were flaunting their relationships on the streets of New York. The *World* immediately picked up the story and blamed the whole thing on Republicans. That November the *Philadelphia Age* claimed that a local White woman had abandoned her husband to run off with a Black man. Meanwhile, the network of radical Democratic papers reveled at any accounts of violence involving Black men and White victims.[44] This latest story and lithograph of Republican men frolicking with Black women provided further grist for this racist mill. The printers at Bromley & Company, assisted by the men at the *World,* knew their audience.

We should be precise about the buttons being pushed here. "The Miscegenation Ball" and affiliated stories, much like broader concerns about "amalgamation," focused on fears of an interracial society. African Americans made up only a tiny percentage of the U.S. population in 1864, clustered largely in the slaveholding border states. The previous year angry New Yorkers, triggered by federal conscription, had unleashed brutal attacks on free Blacks. These rioters had followed some combination of impulses, including raw racism, a hostility to fighting a war with emancipation as a crucial goal, and the conviction that Black laborers were threatening their jobs. This particular brand of printed discourse in 1864 appealed to White fears about the implications of emancipation, followed by Black migration into northern communities.

The logic behind this public conversation was quite different from constitutional arguments against federal emancipation, or the public rhetoric of a Robert Winthrop—and many other leading Democrats—who wished to divorce the social goals of emancipation from the military goals of Union victory. In fact, the Democratic platform made no reference to slavery or emancipation at all, and it only nodded in passing at the ideal of states' rights, which could be used to support why border states—as well as conquered Confederate states—should not be forced to abandon their slaves. The Democrats in Chicago recognized that emancipation was not a winning issue at the national level.[45] The party leadership objected to abolitionism as the source of war, and emancipation as an illegal and dangerous policy at odds with Union, but they did not actively warn voters about what might happen in their own communities if slavery ended. That message was left to others, and only aimed at some voters.

But although historians can reasonably dismiss, or at least discount, the power of "miscegenation" talk or "White supremacy" rhetoric as central to the Democratic political ideology as articulated by the party leadership, that does not eliminate the appeal of such imagery to a portion of Democratic voters and shapers of public opinion. Many Democratic newspapers published racist humor and caricature, and quite a few took every opportunity to warn readers of the threats of Blacks in their midst, linking such dangers with Republican emancipation. Two themes often intertwined: emancipation (and Black migration) threatened White society, and the Republican commitment to emancipation would unnecessarily prolong the war. The Democratic *Hartford Times* reminded readers that on election day they would declare "which they prefer—UNION AND PEACE AND THE SALVATION OF THE COUNTRY, or, PERPETUAL WAR IN A VAIN EFFORT TO EMANCIPATE SOUTHERN NEGROES."[46] Precisely the same paragraph had been published a week earlier by a small newspaper in Wyoming Valley, Pennsylvania, and it would be reprinted several weeks later by another Pennsylvania paper. And no doubt there were many others. The loose network of Democratic editors across the North shared squibs and stories and editorials, often appealing to their readers' concerns about emancipation, and frequently speaking directly to the racism of those voters.[47] That is not to say that the Democratic press had a monopoly on racially charged rhetoric, or that the party officials embraced the most offensive messages. But fears of miscegenation became intertwined with calls for the pursuit of peace without emancipation.

Sandwiched between Winthrop's two campaign speeches the DECC printed an eight-page Campaign Document no. 12 called *Campaign Songs.* Published songbooks had long been a staple in northern life, and quite a few popular pamphlets or small books appeared during the war, often focusing on patriotic themes but also producing political messages put to song. Campaign Document no. 12 was a small pamphlet, much like the others in the series, and included the lyrics to a dozen songs of differing lengths, some presented to be sung to some popular tune. Well over half the songs were explicitly about the life and career of George McClellan, including "McClellan, the Pride of the Nation"; "McClellan the Brave"; and "Rally Round McClellan." Quite a few of the others were in the voice of a soldier, prisoner, or veteran, celebrating patriotism and the military. The offering that adopted the most angry, partisan tone was "Traitors Clear the Track." This song cast McClellan and his supporters against the nation's enemies, portrayed in one verse as architects of the "'free-soil' fraud," and in a later verse as "Abolition knaves."

Overall, these songs articulated McClellan's message, building on his own career and character, and his connection to the Union fighting man. The songs ignored slavery or emancipation, and only rarely took shots at northern abolitionists. Following the campaign songs, the pamphlet included a short—unsigned—essay on "Freehold without the Negro or Leasehold with the Negro—Which Shall You Have?" This piece, aimed at northern landowners, argued that the unexamined price of emancipation would prove overwhelming for ordinary property owners.[48]

Document no. 12, presented as a more or less official publication of the Democratic campaign, marks a stark contrast to another wartime book of song sheets called *Copperhead Minstrel.* This was a longer book, running to about sixty pages and just over forty songs. That songbook appeared originally in 1863, and its editors released a revised version the following year for the election. The editors took many of the songs and poems from the Democratic press, including quite a few from the journal *The Old Guard.* The 1863 version differed from *Campaign Songs* for the obvious reason that there was no Democratic candidate to endorse. These were verses from the not-always-loyal opposition. Many attacked Lincoln and his administration, and others criticized emancipation and conscription or other government policies. A few were unapologetically antiwar, decrying the destruction the nation had endured. Unlike *Campaign Songs,* quite a few of these songs presented a raw racial prejudice, attacking a war fought to free slaves, as well as the abolitionists at its core. Some of these were written in a mocking Black vernacular, and many were free with the word "n—r" in titles and lyrics. None, however, were built on themes of miscegenation or "amalgamation." The lyrics were often thick with racial stereotypes, and many hated a war fought to free slaves, but they did not contemplate a postwar interracial society, for either good or ill.

Historian Mark E. Neely, who consulted both editions of *Copperhead Minstrel,* concludes that of the thirty-nine songs in the 1864 edition, "six dealt mostly with race, but one third (thirteen) did not mention race at all," and "only five were written in the telltale dialect of minstrelsy."[49] That is, like the original edition, the election issue of the *Copperhead Minstrel* criticized politicians and policies while also embracing a broader racism. It was not a book in the minstrel tradition, but—in songs and poems culled from the Democratic press—it included a substantial group of songs appealing to racism, themes almost completely absent in the party's quasi-official book *Campaign Songs.*[50]

The comparison of the two 1864 volumes is a useful mapping of where official partisan politics and grassroots political beliefs diverged as the election approached. Men like Barlow and Belmont and McClellan were not calling on their followers to embrace the powerful cultural racism of the moment, and those messages were often absent in the official documents supporting their candidate. And their closest followers seem to have absorbed that message. A survey of over three hundred letters written directly to candidate McClellan from interested voters revealed that fewer than 10 percent of these correspondents wrote about "race and slavery," and even fewer betrayed any semblance of raw racism.[51] But potential Democratic voters on the streets of northern communities still had ample cartoons and songs to feed those racial sensibilities, leaving no doubt that they saw their opposition as the party of racial amalgamation.

"A Traitor's Peace": The Battle for the Working Man's Vote

In the two months between the Chicago convention and the election, potential voters faced a barrage of political statements coming at them from different directions and pitched at various levels. Certainly many of the longer and most complex pamphlets, and the oratory from leading politicians, spoke to an important slice of voters and opinion makers who absorbed their messages and discussed them in their homes or at social or political gatherings. Producers of other pamphlets and publications directed their materials to different audiences, where perhaps they became the subject of talk at firehouses or neighborhood saloons, or on street corners. Meanwhile, the partisan newspapers inundated readers with editorials, reprinted news stories, and short squibs making key political points. During election season it was not unusual for a small-town newspaper to devote an entire page or more to reprinting partisan political news from all over the nation, reflecting its own editorial position on the candidates. Stories of street disorders that seemingly supported a newspaper's stance about African Americans or Copperheads or rabid patriots would find their way into columns of print hundreds of miles from the event. Although some historians have argued that we exaggerate the public interest in partisan politics at mid-century, no doubt in the months before the election of 1864 the air was thick with political talk in print.[52]

As these piles of pamphlets and newspapers produced a multilevel public political discussion, there remained a broader political conversation on city streets and in community squares. Some portion of this political life came in the form of torchlight parades and political rallies, continuing a long antebellum practice of political exuberance. Ever since Lincoln's first election the Union had seen hundreds of such gatherings, some organized and others emerging spontaneously. In February 1861, with Lincoln soon to be inaugurated and the nation debating the virtues of compromise and conciliation, representatives from skilled labor organizations from across the North had converged in Philadelphia for a national meeting and a grand parade, urging the nation to pursue compromise. Only months later, with the firing on Fort Sumter, crowds took to the streets to express patriotic fervor and outrage with suspected secessionists. In the subsequent three years northern citizenry had lived through an exhausting array of public assemblies in response to elections, calls for conscription, news from the front, and visits from the politically famous and infamous. Some provoked loud cheers and celebrations, others were occasions for violent resistance. Bulletin boards outside of newspaper offices became gathering spots for citizens interested in the latest news, updated casualty lists, or names of draftees. Sometimes such public congregations devolved into fistfights or worse. All had a political aspect in that the air filled with talk of public events. And for citizens in border states, or in some eastern communities, this sort of public politics became overlaid with guerrilla raids,

Confederate invasions, and frightening rumors. The realities of occupation and armed conflict created their own politics.

By the Civil War this messy world of public politics featured large broadsides posted on public buildings, headlines on bulletin boards outside newspaper offices, and humorous lithographs designed for public display. Both the technology of printing and the fervor of politics elevated the significance of such ephemeral publications during the Civil War, perhaps coming to a head in 1864.

One of the most complex themes embedded in these conversations in the public square, particularly in larger cities, concerned the political behavior of the White working man.[53] Certainly matters of class, geography, and ethnicity shaped the political thinking of White northern laborers, who were far from a monolithic group. Many workers had strong ties with the Democratic Party, especially in cities, like New York, dominated by party machines. Strong resistance to conscription, particularly among urban ethnic families, turned many against the administration, but they were hardly the only ones. By 1864 more and more White northerners objected to what they saw as a "rich man's war" fought by poor men, particularly with emancipation as an end that threatened to delay peace and extend the conflict. Explicitly race-based appeals found increasingly appreciative audiences in some quarters, including those who felt their economic livelihood most threatened by Black laborers and possible Black migration.

After nearly four years of war, both parties contemplated how workingmen would vote and what appeals would reach them. The key point here is that northern workers, or even urban laborers, did not simply align with one party or the other, nor were they exclusively prowar or opposed to the war. Nativity no doubt influenced opinions and the information they received, but working-class immigrants were hardly of one mind. After all, roughly a quarter of Union soldiers were immigrants (generally from Germany or Ireland), and nearly another one in five had at least one foreign-born parent. Some of these men joined regiments with their countrymen, but others found themselves serving with native-born soldiers. There is no guarantee that all these uniformed immigrants still embraced the war in 1864, and some portion were draftees or substitutes whose loyalty to the cause might have been more conditional.[54] Certainly foreign-born Americans celebrated loyalty and Union as much as their peers with deeper family roots in American soil, but when it came time to vote, matters of class—perhaps as much as ethnicity—tugged at them in various directions. One political historian who made a close reading of Massachusetts voting returns concluded that in communities across the state foreign-born nativity constituted the best variable predicting McClellan votes. Irish- and German-born voters generally lined up behind McClellan, although they were not numerous enough to turn the results in his favor.[55]

In 1864 working-class votes were up for grabs. On the one hand, northern workers—and perhaps especially immigrants—had particular objections to conscription and to the primacy of emancipation in administration thinking, and they felt the rising sting of war-related pricing and taxation. On the other hand, as the great labor historian David Montgomery insisted, northern workers tended toward patriotic nationalism, and despite appeals aimed at their votes, "few urban workers . . . 'went Coppery.'"[56] Montgomery might have protested a bit too much, but certainly neither Democrats nor Republicans could take the working-class vote for granted. Arguments had to be made and disseminated.

A survey of broadsides, pamphlets, and editorials printed and distributed in those crucial campaign weeks suggests something of the political strategy and practice from both parties as they appealed to working-class voters. The specific appeals varied, although patterns emerge.

In February 1864 a large group of workingmen—probably unionized artisans—gathered at a mass meeting at New York's Stuyvesant Hall, where they charged the president of the Workingmen's United Political Association with naming a committee "to draft an address to the Workingmen of the United States." On August 4, 1864—a month before the Democrats had a platform and a candidate—that committee, chaired by McDonough Bucklin, produced a lengthy address that appeared in the press and soon emerged as an eight-page, double-columned pamphlet. The first half of the address, called "The Origin of Our Troubles," offered a narrative of how the nation had reached this point, from a moment four years earlier when "labor generally received its due reward." The short version was that a revolutionary party of abolitionists, and people blindly pursuing racial equality, had made a mess of things, leading the nation into this terrible war. The committee's second section traced events under the "abolition Republican Party." The result was a litany of battlefield carnage, divisive conscription, violated civil liberties, and all sorts of horrors. But turning to slavery as a political problem, the authors dismissed the argument that southern slaveholders represented a southern aristocracy, at odds with republican forms of government. After all, the great founders like Washington and Jefferson had been slaveholders. In fact, the writers concluded (echoing Emma Webb), slavery was the natural place for the Black man and in the best interests of the White working man. As they saw it, the danger was if the war persisted and slavery eventually ended, tossing White workingmen into their own economic slavery. The address concluded by focusing on how the war had economically wounded the working man, and on the broader argument that the war could never be won. For Bucklin and his committee, neither the Civil War nor emancipation promised anything good for workers. With Democrats preparing to meet in Chicago, they called for a peace platform that would serve the interests of White workers.[57]

This was hardly an unpopular stance among workers. The war had produced years of destruction and economic dislocation for many, and the Republican focus on emancipation and race seemed an affront to the future of the White working man. Such arguments appeared less persuasive once the Democrats had nominated their candidate and adopted their platform, which largely endorsed the war effort. Now messages from the National Union Party directed at workers focused on the dangers of a premature peace, arguing that the working man was wisest to align with the administration because it would ensure true and lasting victory. Republicans, they argued, were best prepared to win the peace.

Shortly after the Chicago convention, an unknown printer produced a small single-sheet broadside directed "To Workingmen" and signed "DEMOCRAT." Building on the military successes enjoyed by Grant and Sherman, the author—supporting the National Union Party—insisted that "the rebels wish you to elect a man who will stop the war, and give them a chance to prepare for it again." DEMOCRAT argued that the Democrats' platform promised they would pursue peace, and that such a peace would only be a prelude to another destructive war. Turning to a celebrated bare-knuckle prize fight from April 1860, the broadside asked readers to "remember the prize fight between Heenan and Sayers, when Sayers was nearly used up, his friends outside the ring interposed a 'Cessation of Hostilities.'" The reference was telling. John Heenan was an America pugilist who journeyed to Hampshire, England, to take on English fighter Tom Sayers in a brutal battle over more than forty rounds. In the end, Sayers, whose loss had seemed almost assured, recovered enough to achieve a draw with his American opponent in this highly celebrated (and entirely illegal) event. In this metaphorical telling, the reinvigorated southern slaveholders—having achieved peace—would reintroduce the slave trade, threatening "free labor" in the United States. "Do you want any more Negroes in this country?" DEMOCRAT asked.

Finally, the author shifted to an explicit class analysis, where the South was the nation of wealth and privilege. "Gen'l McClellan is a tool used in the hands of these men," he insisted. "They manage him to suit themselves. They will betray you! True Democrats and true men are for Freedom, and against

Aristocracy." "Workingmen, stand by your order," DEMOCRAT concluded. "Lincoln and Johnson were poor men and worked for their living. They rose to high places, as you, their comrades, may rise, unless you by your votes give the country to the aristocrats! The order of liberty is your order! You must not be deceived, but stand by your colors and vote for Free America, united and strong, and THEN LET ENGLAND INTERFERE IF SHE DARE." In this clever appeal to northern workers, and presumably particularly to immigrant hostilities to the English, the broadside cast McClellan as the candidate of the elites and claimed that a Democratic victory would result in more African Americans in northern society.[58]

This message to patriotic Democratic workingmen recurred in various forms. One Philadelphia broadside addressed to "Democrats Who Love the Union!" began with an extended quotation from the *Charleston Mercury:* "If we hold our own and prevent further military successes on the part of our foes, there is every prospect that McClellan will be elected, and his election upon the Chicago platform must lead to peace and our independence," the South Carolina paper had effused. This prompted the simple question for northern workers: "Do you desire to strike hands with Rebels, and help them to break up the Union? If you do, then vote the Democratic ticket!"[59] A similar broadside addressed to "Democratic Workingmen" in New York City the previous fall adopted a comparable strategy. The nation faced the ultimate danger of "A traitor's peace!" undermining three years of war, it declared. And, as evidence, the broadside quoted extensively from a *Richmond Enquirer* editorial, enumerating the terms under which the Confederacy would seek peace with Union negotiators. Here again the crucial argument was that the Democrats were the party of acquiescence. McClellan was the friend of the White southerner.[60] It would be up to the McClellan Democrats to convince voters that they would not abandon the war until victory had been achieved.

In this sort of appeal, the National Union Party sought to convince working-class Democrats that they should reject the Democratic Party specifically because a McClellan victory would eventually jeopardize the long-term fruits of military victory. Voters who wished for a lasting peace should stick with the Lincoln administration.

An editorial in the four-page leaflet *The Workingman,* published in New York City on October 22, 1864, addressed "Workingmen Who Are Not Politicians" and perhaps had given little thought to the niceties surrounding the upcoming election. For those voters "who care little for the success of any or either party" but who are worried about the preservation of the Union, the answer was clear.

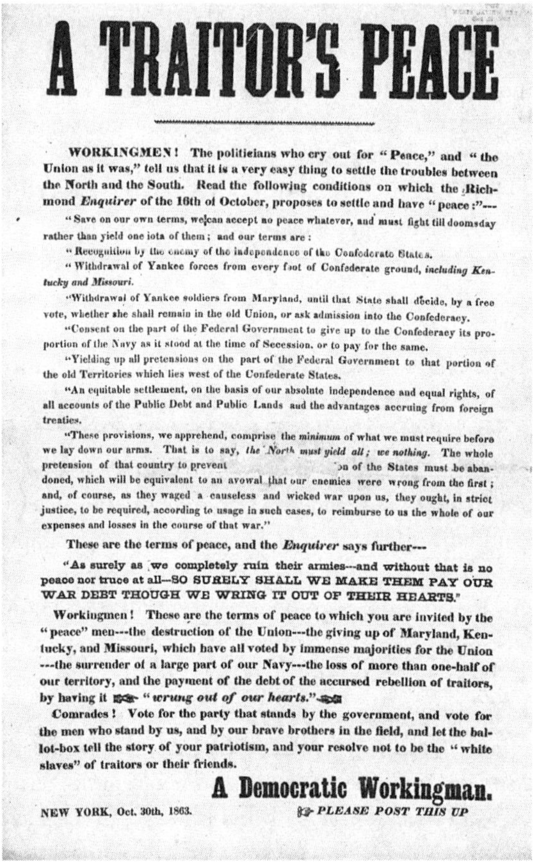

A TRAITOR'S PEACE

WORKINGMEN! The politicians who cry out for "Peace," and "the Union as it was," tell us that it is a very easy thing to settle the troubles between the North and the South. Read the following conditions on which the Richmond *Enquirer* of the 16th of October, proposes to settle and have "peace:"---

"Save on our own terms, we can accept no peace whatever, and must fight till doomsday rather than yield one iota of them; and our terms are:

"Recognition by the enemy of the independence of the Confederate States.

"Withdrawal of Yankee forces from every foot of Confederate ground, *including Kentucky and Missouri.*

"Withdrawal of Yankee soldiers from Maryland, until that State shall decide, by a free vote, whether she shall remain in the old Union, or ask admission into the Confederacy.

"Consent on the part of the Federal Government to give up to the Confederacy its proportion of the Navy as it stood at the time of Secession, or to pay for the same.

"Yielding up all pretensions on the part of the Federal Government to that portion of the old Territories which lies west of the Confederate States.

"An equitable settlement, on the basis of our absolute independence and equal rights, of all accounts of the Public Debt and Public Lands and the advantages accruing from foreign treaties.

"These provisions, we apprehend, comprise the *minimum* of what we must require before we lay down our arms. That is to say, *the North must yield all; we nothing.* The whole pretension of that country to prevent [illegible] on of the States must be abandoned, which will be equivalent to an avowal that our enemies were wrong from the first; and, of course, as they waged a causeless and wicked war upon us, they ought, in strict justice, to be required, according to usage in such cases, to reimburse to us the whole of our expenses and losses in the course of that war."

These are the terms of peace, and the *Enquirer* says further---

"As surely as we completely ruin their armies---and without that is no peace nor truce at all---SO SURELY SHALL WE MAKE THEM PAY OUR WAR DEBT THOUGH WE WRING IT OUT OF THEIR HEARTS."

Workingmen! These are the terms of peace to which you are invited by the "peace" men---the destruction of the Union---the giving up of Maryland, Kentucky, and Missouri, which have all voted by immense majorities for the Union---the surrender of a large part of our Navy---the loss of more than one-half of our territory, and the payment of the debt of the accursed rebellion of traitors, by having it "*wrung out of our hearts.*"

Comrades! Vote for the party that stands by the government, and vote for the men who stand by us, and by our brave brothers in the field, and let the ballot-box tell the story of your patriotism, and your resolve not to be the "white slaves" of traitors or their friends.

A Democratic Workingman.

NEW YORK, Oct. 30th, 1863. *PLEASE POST THIS UP*

Broadside: *A Traitor's Peace.* By late 1863 partisan Democrats and Republicans were becoming increasingly adept at publishing political appeals aimed directly at the North's working men. This broadside, published in New York, calls on workers to reject the peace proposals of northern antiwar Democrats. (Library of Congress)

The blame for the current war was with the slaveholders, and they "must be rebuked" to protect the nation's institutions. Any party that proposed "to yield even in the slightest degree to the insurgents" constituted a threat to the nation's future. To underscore the point, *The Workingman* followed the lead editorial with the lively lyrics to "A New Yankee Doodle," which declared that "Lincoln is the man we need, Johnson too is handy," while including verses celebrating the military exploits of William T. Sherman, Jubal Early, and Admiral David Farragut, and adding a swipe at McClellan's military leadership. *The Workingman* added a lengthy address from new California senator John Conness. The Irish-born Conness had been a cabinetmaker in New York before heading west to seek his fortune, giving him the credentials of a skilled laborer and no mere politician. "I know what it is to give my daily toil for years in the acquisition of a mechanic's trade," he reminded his audience. And the honest laboring man should stand with the government. Conness, *The Workingman* explained, was "a true friend of the Union, and of equal rights for workingmen"[61]

On the eve of the election a Republican newspaper in Union County, Pennsylvania, addressed an editorial of "Plain Words to Workingmen." Those words were quite clear. Yes, the war had been very costly and workers had born a huge price, but the Confederacy represented the interests of southern "aristocrats . . . who look down upon the workingman with contempt." And, echoing the arguments by core Republicans, the article pointed out that anything short of a full military victory would constitute capitulation to Jefferson Davis: "Our only hope of better days is in putting down the Rebellion, and so gaining a Union peace."[62] On November 3 Vermont's *Rutland Weekly Herald* left no doubt about its intended audience, printing a short announcement that Irish workers from Dublin had sent a notice to their kinsmen in the United States, urging them to vote for Abraham Lincoln. The notice, the paper reported, had been written by Reverend Thaddeus O'Malley of the Catholic Church.[63]

The Republican appeal to northern workers had diverse strands but several key points: An enduring Union victory would be best for the nation and for the working class, and that meant sticking with the Lincoln administration. And when viewed from a class perspective, Lincoln and Johnson were men of the people, while the southern slaveocracy represented all the evils of aristocracy.

Democrats countered these appeals with their own publications. One large, multicolored broadside simply read "Victory, Union, Peace" in large blue letters running vertically down a flag of red, white, and blue. The message was clear. It was really the Democratic Party that promised military victory, followed by the restoration of the Union and lasting peace.[64] A short newspaper squib titled "Workingmen Beware" circulated in the North, warning innocent workers that an organization calling itself the "Democratic Workingman's Association" was in reality a group of abolitionist scoundrels intent on "flooding the country with lying handbills endeavoring to deceive the workingmen into the support of the present corrupt and imbecile administration."[65]

As September neared to a close, Ohio's Democratic *Ashland Union* surveyed recent events and concluded that "there seems less and less prospect of relief for the poor laborer, the workingman." The poor man, the paper declared, absorbed the nation's financial debts and its military carnage, while "the rich can escape" the war's greatest horrors. Building to its logical conclusion, the newspaper called on "Voters! Workingmen! [to] remember who has wrought all this."

The current administration had brought arbitrary arrests, unfair conscription, and mass casualties on the nation's least powerful, and it was up to workers to "remember all this in November."[66] About ten days later the Copperhead *Dayton Daily Empire* reprinted a passionate letter from a local working man, presenting a detailed critique of capitalism's inequities, as exacerbated by war. Four years earlier the nation had been prospering and peaceful, until the current administration provoked the disastrous Civil War. "I appeal to you, as a humble workingman," he concluded, "lay aside your party prejudices . . . by voting the entire Democratic ticket."[67] A short notice in various Midwestern newspapers made the Democrats' case succinctly: "Workingmen who want more war, no Union, heavy taxes, quarterly conscription, and high prices for all they use in their families, will vote for Mr. Lincoln? Workingmen who want peace, the old Union, and a return to the good old Democratic days of gold and silver will vote for McClellan!"[68] A newspaper article on "Plain Facts for Taxpayers" made the party's case in economic terms, enumerating the war's many costs that had been passed on to the laboring man, no doubt leading to new tariffs and other impositions: "Chose ye, then, between these two: McClellan with the old Union, the old Constitution, the old laws, peace prosperity and low taxes; or Lincoln and war, disunion, negro equality, and hopeless bankruptcy."[69]

These class-based messages to northern workingmen, particularly in cities, often intersected with newspapers aimed at Catholic Irish and German immigrants. As we have seen, editorials in many of the nation's ethnic newspapers encouraged immigrants to question administrative policies ranging from conscription to emancipation. As the election approached, Catholic editors differed on various axes. Nearly all endorsed the Democratic Party, but they divided on whether to support the war or endorse the peace movement. Moreover, in the past many Catholic leaders had steered clear of politics, but for this crucial election an increasing number of Catholic newspapers entered the partisan fray. Whether or not they believed in the war effort, most endorsed McClellan's challenge to Lincoln. The *Boston Pilot,* the newspaper of the city's archdiocese and long a critic of abolition although not a supporter of draft disturbances, made its message to Irish readers clear in 1864. "The Democratic party," it wrote "has been . . . the only home and refuge to which the oppressed of Ireland could flee." In contrast, the Republican Party "has distinguished itself by . . . its narrow bigotry . . . and its open hatred for the rights of the poor and laboring classes." It was an argument that yoked ethnic loyalties and class hostilities into a call for Democratic votes. In New York, the key Catholic journals the *New York Tablet* and the *Metropolitan Record* joined the *Pilot* in endorsing McClellan and pointing its Irish readers toward the Democratic challenger.[70]

The appeal to workers from both parties shared the same promise: we are the party that will ensure a lasting peace. Democrats reminded working-class voters of the trauma and injustice they had endured at the hands of Republican legislation. And Irish editors pointed to the nativist roots in the Republican Party. By election day northern voters, even working-class citizens outraged by conscription, emancipation, and inflation, recognized that circumstances had shifted. Good news from multiple military fronts promised victory sooner rather than later. It remained an open question whether the Lincoln administration's commitment to emancipation might prolong the war, but the Union Party made every effort to warn workers that a McClellan administration might negotiate away the fruits of victory. Even laborers who had hit the streets to object to administration policies in earlier years might have been receptive to the argument that the sacrifices of war required an enduring conclusion. Montgomery argues that when all the votes had been counted, years of political grievances "brought no stampede of workingmen to the Democratic ticket," at least in the major urban centers. For leading labor leader and publisher Jonathan Fincher, the electoral calculus was clear in 1864: "One thing to which all else must assume a subordinate position is, the 'United States' must forever be a fact, we can tolerate no division." No doubt many working-class voters disagreed, but on balance the case for a military victory and a successful Reconstruction remained strong and compelling.[71]

Voters and Voting

Despite Abraham Lincoln's serious concerns several months earlier, on November 8 he won reelection for a second term. It was not really all that close. Lincoln received 400,000 more votes than McClellan and won 212 of the 233 electoral votes. He carried all but three states: New Jersey, Kentucky, and Delaware. The latter two were border states that still held slaves. As with most major elections, the results allow for multiple interpretations and finely tuned analysis about class, ethnicity, and region.

If we paint with a very broad brush, the results can be explained by a very few things, all of which were part of the conversations the president had with his advisors before he wrote that Blind Memo. First, and no doubt most important, things had gone well on the battlefield. By November Atlanta had fallen to Sherman's men, and Phillip Sheridan's army had enjoyed celebrated successes against Jubal Early in the Shenandoah Valley. Second, despite McClellan's efforts to distance himself from his party platform (and vice-presidential candidate) with multiple documents, the Democrats still presented an ambiguous message, ripe for attacks from a party that had renamed itself the National Union Party. Lincoln's supporters could easily link the general with a variety of familiar Copperhead names, suggesting that Democratic success would sacrifice the fruits of military victory. Arguments that McClellan would work more easily with the vanquished Confederacy did not always strike a hopeful chord among those intent on revenge or on transforming the South. And, finally, although their votes were not determinative, the available evidence suggests that Union soldiers voted overwhelmingly for Lincoln, as opposed to for the popular Union general.[72]

But we should not go too far down this path, attempting to explain why Lincoln won so handily in 1864. After all, 1.8 million voters cast their ballots for the opposition candidate in the midst of a bloody civil war. In fact, the total Democratic votes in northern states had increased since 1860, even as their total percentage slipped a bit. Despite demographic shifts during the war, the evidence suggests little change in voter turnout between 1860 and 1864. Democracy, and a vibrant two-party system, persisted in the midst of war, particularly if one focuses on the core states in the Electoral College.[73] In fact, given four years of almost absurd turmoil and despair, perhaps the more important story is that the two northern political parties did not completely transform themselves. There were, however, some shifts in party fortunes. After mid-war Democratic victories in crucial elections, the Republicans made significant gains in 1864. They won a 42–10 majority in the Senate, and a commanding 149–42 majority in the House. In Ohio, the home of powerful Peace Democrats Clement Vallandigham and George Pendleton, the Democrats' congressional delegation shrunk from fourteen to two. Moreover, Democrats lost control of all the state legislatures they had won two years earlier, and the party only won the New Jersey governorship. The Union Party won comfortable gubernatorial elections in the crucial states of Ohio and New York, and Pennsylvania's Governor Andrew Curtin managed to squeak by in a close contest. But despite gains by the administration's Union Party the general shape of the partisan divide remained in place. Consider the crucial state of Indiana. In 1862 the Democratic Party won 52.5 percent of the vote; two years later that number had dropped to a still respectable 47 percent. In the earlier election they had won seven seats in the statehouse, enough to give Republican governor Oliver Morton fits. Two years later, despite a marginal shift in overall votes, Indiana Democrats only won three seats in the state legislature. In sum, Democrats continued to contest crucial elections even as their overall success dwindled. The historian Joel Silbey put the thing succinctly: "They remained very close to their opponents and always posed a threat." And in still more fine-grained electoral analysis, Silbey concluded that "there was very little movement at the county level in each state."[74] This was true despite the awkward fact that they were the opposition party in the middle of a civil war.

The story of the soldiers' vote, both in the 1864 election and in previous state elections, is a complex one that has been nicely unraveled by Jonathan White. In many regiments state legislation enabled Union soldiers to cast absentee ballots in the field, and in some cases the military furloughed regiments so that they could go home to vote. Neither process was without partisan bickering and potential biases. Democrats complained that federal authorities tipped the scales in favor of Republican regiments when it came to furloughs and access to the vote.

The available data—which is quite substantial—indicate that 78 percent of soldiers voting in the field cast their ballots for Lincoln. This figure has been used to support the argument that Union soldiers rejected the one-time Union general in favor of emancipation and the Republican Party. White argues that at least 20 percent of Democratic soldiers declined to vote, either because they feared retaliation or out of frustration with their own party. Much of that frustration came from the party's ambiguous platform, or from an association—not entirely fair—of the national Democratic Party with the treasonous Copperheads. But Union troops also connected the Democrats with legal objections to soldiers voting in the field, as articulated by constitutional conservatives like Pennsylvania's George Woodward. Thus, although McClellan had commanded troops in the field, Republicans claimed the mantle as the pro-soldier party. White argues that historians have looked at those voting returns and mistakenly concluded that by 1864 the Union was overwhelmingly Republican and that ordinary soldiers had experienced a profound "ideological conversion to the Republican war measure of emancipation." A more accurate assessment would be that perhaps one in five opted out of voting for personal or strategic reasons, and that many other citizen-soldiers remained loyal Democrats whose chief priority remained military victory and loyalty to the Union.[75]

There is a broad macro story about vote returns, and there is a true "in the weeds" analysis about how individual states and counties behaved. This is all the stuff of excellent political analysis, but there is another way to tell this story, focusing on the comments of individual northern Democrats in 1864. Given the flood of political speech—in person and in print—aimed at northern voters, what did individuals actually do? What did they think about what they did? And what might we glean about how they came to their personal conclusions? We turn now to the written thoughts of a handful of Democrats we have already met. The conclusion seems to be that northern Democrats thought diverse things about the 1864 election and commented about that contest in diverse ways. That should come as no surprise. They were a pretty varied lot. Here are just a few examples.

Philadelphia printer John Smith had accumulated considerable skills but not much capital when the Civil War began. A dedicated Democrat and committed observer of public events, Smith lived alone and had yet to begin a family. He worked hard, generally filling independent printing contracts, and was often in Philadelphia's streets and public squares when politics became public. Although not a man of wealth or stature, Smith was a fellow who knew people, and as a Democrat living in the heart of Philadelphia, he periodically bumped into celebrated Democrats on the streets of the City of Brotherly Love, recording chats in his diary.[76]

Smith recorded entries in small pocket diaries, rarely writing much but often commenting on political events. In 1860 he had been a Breckinridge Democrat with a strong distaste for abolitionists and no confidence in Abraham Lincoln. When the press reported an attack on a Democratic home, newspaper, or institution, Smith would write an outraged entry. He was an engaged rank-and-file Democrat.

Smith grew increasingly angry about racial politics throughout the war, and over time his entries became peppered with the word "n—r" and other racial invectives. He was outraged at the idea of recruiting Black soldiers, hiring Black men to dig ditches around Vicksburg, and numerous accounts of Black rioting in distant cities.[77] In July 1864 he inserted a clipping announcing a meeting of Black citizens to discuss the city's segregated streetcars, adding a scrawled racial caricature in his own hand.

Although a young man with a modest profession, Smith occasionally socialized with prominent local Democrats. In early 1863 he attended a reception at a "Dr. McClellan's" where he met General McClellan and other luminaries. The following month he was in the crowd at the Concert Hall when the Democratic Club celebrated Washington's birthday. When Clement Vallandigham came through town, Smith was there cheering him on. In early 1864 Smith began attending the "Saturday Evening Club," an invitation-only gathering of elite Democrats. The club—which seemed to involve a meal and good cheer—met in different members' homes, and Smith happily received invitations to individual gatherings while hoping to earn a permanent membership. His discussions of these events were short, but over time he mentioned meeting a long list of

Philadelphia Democrats, including George Woodward, Peter McCall, Charles and Edward Ingersoll, George Wharton, Charles Biddle, and Dr. McClellan.[78]

When the Democrats gathered in Chicago, Smith noted the nominations, but with no commentary about the platform or the party's decisions. Over the next several weeks Smith described a series of processions and public events and added frequent criticisms of the "abolitionists." On election day he noted that he had voted for McClellan and Pendleton with no further comment. The following day he reported that his party was "apparently swindled out of the election again."[79] With the new year Smith's racial anger seemed to grow. On January 31, 1865, he wrote that "the n—r party has passed a bill abolishing slavery." When Richmond fell, his chief observation was that "n—rs" had been the first into the city. When Abraham Lincoln fell to an assassin's bullet, the printer recorded quite a few entries about the news of his death and burial and related events, but he indicated neither joy nor sorrow about the assassination.[80]

As is often the case with diarists, John Smith's small journal provides a fascinating and incomplete glimpse into this young man's thinking. As a political actor he was engaged in the events of the day. In many senses Smith's politics seemed tied to partisan loyalty as much as broader ideology. If he read political pamphlets or detailed editorials, he did not reveal that in his diary. His comments and the language he used suggest that his feelings were particularly animated by racial hostility. He generally spoke of the opposition party as the "abolitionists," rather than employing some other partisan label. Meanwhile, Smith—like many of his Democratic peers—spoke of his own as the "constitutional party" (or some variation) rather than by party name, but he did not devote any energy to articulating particular constitutional opinions. Perhaps most interestingly, many 1864 Democrats would have characterized the party as deeply divided between those who favored a vigorous war effort to a negotiated peace and those who hoped for an immediate end to war. But nothing in Smith's journal indicates that these debates consumed him, and his socializing and attendance at public events seemed to include affection for Democrats on both sides of that divide.

Philadelphia diarist Katherine Wharton was the young wife of Democratic lawyer Henry Wharton when the war began. Not personally very engaged in partisan politics, in January 1861 Wharton wrote that "H gave me a long political lect. this Eve. saying that most Amer. women knew very little of the politics of their country." The diarist did not take umbrage at his remarks, and in her particular case they were probably not far off the mark. But like many of her peers of both genders, the nation's trauma attracted more of her attention, even as she lived her routine life. Throughout the secession crisis she recorded regular short comments about the national excitement, admitting after the firing on Fort Sumter that "I had no idea I wd care so much." Before long the impact of the war came closer to home, as her brother Godfrey left town with the local Washington Grays. Wharton noted that with the arrival of letters from Godfrey, "it is amusing to see how entirely father has changed his views, which some time ago inclined very much to the Southern side." In September 1862, as the Army of Northern Virginia moved north, Henry and Katherine had long talks about how he might have to go and fight with the Home Guards, a prospect that terrified her but which she resolved to accept without objection.[81]

In all of these entries Wharton wrote about her support for the war, without any talk of internal political conflicts. But when the president relieved McClellan from command she penned a long entry supporting the deposed general and adding, "I am at last getting discouraged." A few months later, when a visitor asked Henry if he was "a Union man," Katherine wrote that in fact he was personally very conservative and opposed the administration, but did so quietly. When a dinner companion a few months later argued that the war would likely end without victory, she recorded that "H cd not stand his saying that," and things got heated. In mid-1863 Wharton noted that with all the carnage of war, "I have personally suffered nothing," but in August the family learned that Godfrey had died in a South Carolina hospital.[82]

Throughout 1864 Katherine and Henry remained unambiguously prowar. A regular in various voluntary organizations, Katherine did her part to support the city's Great Sanitary Fair. Henry, who felt unable—or unwilling—to go to war, diligently made "all the arrangements for getting a substitute, as he might be drafted." Her entries never betrayed any objections to conscription, and she seemed to give emancipation and racial politics little heed at all. When the Democrats met in Chicago, Katherine wrote that she was pleased with McClellan's nomination but added no further discussion. A month later, she recorded an extended entry on northern politics. "God knows I dont want a dishonorable peace," she declared, "if for no other reason than for the sake of my brother who gave up his life for the cause. . . . But I think that the administration has mismanaged everything." As the election grew near, Wharton reiterated that she was strongly opposed to the Lincoln administration, but she worried that most Democrats would decline to vote for the Chicago platform, presumably because of its peace plank. On election day Katherine reported that "Henry says he has never felt so uneasy as he does now." Although he disliked Lincoln, he refused to vote for McClellan. Katherine privately hoped that McClellan would win, although it is unclear if she shared those thoughts with her husband.[83]

John Smith and Katherine Wharton lived at different social tiers in the same Philadelphia Democratic world. The Whartons had more wealth and a second home they occasionally visited. Smith had an apartment that was no more than a few blocks from Henry's law office. They knew many of the same people, and perhaps even knew each other. And when all the dust settled both supported the election of McClellan. But how did they come to their political convictions? Both diarists paid attention to the news of the day, although Wharton seemed more absorbed with the progress of the war as opposed to politics. Both observed the vibrant public discourse on Philadelphia's streets and in its halls. Of the two, Smith was more likely to attend a public rally, and his sympathies ran toward the likes of Vallandigham. The Whartons took a more low-key approach to politics and seemed to be more firmly prowar Democrats. Despite all of the Democracy's efforts to craft their candidate's personal narrative and shape his case for the presidency, the two Philadelphia diarists seemed driven most by their distaste for the current administration.

Across the North, individual Democrats viewed the 1864 election through the prism of their own circumstances and experiences. In Kentucky, slave-owning diarist Ellen Wallace supported the war while having no patience for Lincoln and the continuing threat of abolitionism. In late 1864, with her town of Hopkinsville occupied by Union troops—including dreaded Black soldiers—Wallace wrote that she hoped for a McClellan victory but feared that Lincoln would triumph. On election day Wallace vented her spleen in her journal: "The election for president was held today. There was a marked difference between the men who voted for McClellan and those who supported Lincoln. Just the same difference that there is between the men, comment is unnecessary. We are afraid to indulge in any hope, but the darkness will be tenfold greater when that hope is removed by the election of Lincoln." A few days later, with the returns in, she ended a similarly gloomy entry with "Farewell Liberty."[84] For Wallace and many of her fellow Kentucky Democrats, support for the war persistently clashed with her commitment to the state's peculiar institution.

Across the Ohio River in Ohio, Andrew Evans and his family remained loyal to the Democratic Party while evolving on some of the key issues of the day. Although living in a county thick with Copperheads, Andrew and his soldier son, Samuel, rejected the appeals of Vallandigham and his supporters in favor of John Brough, the War Democrat nominated by the state's Union Party. In August 1863 Andrew agreed to run for the state legislature, and although he appeared indifferent about his own victory, both father and son found the successes of prowar candidates in Ohio and Kentucky to be "glorious."[85]

When the parties began their presidential nomination processes, Andrew and Samuel viewed events as essentially nonpartisan, prowar patriots. Shortly before the Democrats convened in Chicago, Sam told his father that "we will soon know who the Copperheads intend to run for President. I have not been studying Politics. I now think I never Shall. Abe and Johnson Will do me for President and Vice President." After the nomination Andrew replied, "Well the Peace men had to take a War Democrat at last, if McLellan sticks to his doctrine." Neither father nor son seemed to see the upcoming election in partisan terms. They did not speak of Lincoln, their chosen candidate, as a Republican but as the best option to win the war. And despite the pains McClellan had taken to make his case to the voters, the Evans men wasted little time discussing the general's virtues, beyond noting the party's platform and his Copperhead ties. "Mac has got into bad Co.," Samuel concluded.[86]

Not all the Evans family embraced the Union Party banner. In 1863, with the state elections approaching, Mary Evans had written to her brother that "all the girls around here are Valls [supporters of Vallandigham]" and that their cousin "Little Jane is a strong one" who had plans of attending a "Val meeting" soon. A year later, shortly after McClellan's nomination, cousin Jane—who was about twenty—fired off a long and angry letter to her cousin in the field. By this point Sam had become an officer in the United States Colored Troops, against his father's wishes. Jane did not share his impulse toward racial justice, declaring that "I would not mind freeing the negros if they could be sent off and not come back here again." Moreover, Jane could see no virtue in supporting the Lincoln administration. "You may call me a Rebel secesh or a butternut or copperhead or anything you please, I am for peace. I am getting [tired] of this war," she insisted. And in a powerful dissent against her uncle and her cousin, Jane continued, "There is no true hearted Democrat that will vote for him."

This was a harsh letter, illustrating complex family dynamics filtered through age and gender difference. Samuel did not take his younger cousin's words well. He sent his father a long letter, quoting Jane's harshest lines and noting that he had no idea "she was so much Reble." That was a telling remark, since Jane had really only objected to the war; she had not praised the Confederacy.[87] Finally, Sam responded to Jane. Writing from Memphis, Sam chastised her "unlady like" letter, and he objected to her liberal use of "treasonous language." Engaging the partisan point, Sam dissented from Jane's critique, pointing out that "we are Democrats and love the Union. Not such as you, Jeff Davis, Vall and Co." And in a particularly telling passage about language and race, Sam took Jane to task for using the word "negur," adding the parenthetical "you mean Negros."[88]

In the end Andrew and Samuel Evans did not embrace the Republican Party, but they gladly cast their lot with Lincoln and the war. Nothing in her letters suggested that Jane Evans supported McClellan, but she opposed the war and the administration that pursued it. None of these Ohio Democrats seemed disturbed by the nuances in party platforms or constitutional details. All things came down to how they felt about the war.

In Fulton County, Illinois, Jane Standard continued to run the family farm in her soldier husband's absence. At the end of March 1864 Jane sent William a long letter describing a brutal political argument her father, a Republican, had with a family friend who was a local Democratic leader. Cannah, the Democrat, insisted that the war would never end as long as the Republicans ruled, and Jane's father countered that he was content to sacrifice "every man, woman, and child" to subdue the South. As Jane reported, "[They] did not strike one another but I thought sometimes they would." Despite her father's inclinations, Jane remained loyal to the Democratic Party. In early October, in a telling window into gender and politics, Jane had planned to attend a local Democratic meeting, but the woman who had agreed to care for her children did not show up. She had gone to the meeting instead.[89]

By the fall of 1864 William Standard was a colonel with the Union Army in Georgia. He remained unhappy with military life, and with the Lincoln administration, but he seemed resigned to staying in uniform. He wrote to Jane frequently, commenting occasionally about politics. On August 21, only weeks before the Democrats met in Chicago, William declared that "I am for any man for the next President that will use his influence to put a stop to this unholy war, and give us peace and prosperity again." "Old Abe" seemed intent "on refusing any terms of peace that did not include the abolition if slavery," a stance William could not accept. The following month, after having taken part in the capture of Atlanta, he wrote, "I see from a paper from Chicago that McClellan has been nominated by the Democrats for President. That is what I desired they should do. I think that he will give us some peace if selected."[90]

Both Jane and William lived in politically divided communities, one at home and the other in the military. William seemed to feel that many of his comrades had grown sick of the war, but in one telling comment he noted, "I am a very good abolitionist while I am in the army."[91] Judging from his letters, William received his news from whatever newspapers passed his way. Jane attended occasional political meetings and took part in some lively partisan talk. Neither gave any indication that they were reading political pamphlets, studying speeches, or poring over editorials. Both, like so many other Democrats, seemed to look at the election of 1864 as a referendum on Lincoln and his policies, rather than an assessment of McClellan, although William did seem to feel that the Democratic candidate promised an easier path to peace.

St. Louis's William Steel offers a different window into Democratic thinking. A highly active prowar Democrat, Steel occasionally wrote political editorials, some of which he sent to his brother James, a newspaper editor in Pennsylvania. In June 1864 William wrote to James about the upcoming convention in Chicago, which they both planned to attend. Steel remained a dedicated Democrat and declared that "Genl McClellan . . . *must be nominated.*"[92] A few weeks later he visited Julia Grant at her father's home. His conversation with Frederick Dent, Ulysses S. Grant's father-in-law, proved particularly interesting. "Old Mr. Dent has no faith in the ability of the Government to subjugate the Southern states," he wrote. He "told me distinctly 'they never could completely break down that Southern people.' He remarked that Vallandigham was a pure patriot—quite as loyal as A. Lincoln." But although it was possible to glean the political opinions of the general's relatives, no one had "been able to get from *him* an expression of *his own* views on forcible abolition of slavery and other violations of the Constitution, now attempted by the party in power." If Grant were in fact on the correct side of these issues, Steel felt sure the Democrats would nominate him "by acclimation." Steel still preferred McClellan, except that he thought Grant would be unbeatable.[93] Echoing Colonel Durbin Ward's letter from Georgia that August, Steel was happy to have McClellan on the ticket but eyed General Grant longingly as the ideal solution.

Back in Philadelphia, young Anna LaRoche was once again not quite in the thick of things, but not far from them. On October 31 she spent the afternoon at the offices of the *Philadelphia Age* at Fifth and Chestnut, "looking at the Democratic transperancies[,] torches[,] flags[,] &c which passed in one continuous stream," broken occasionally by fistfights or other violence. "What hateful times we live in," she declared. The following evening she was at home playing cards when another Democratic torchlight parade passed in front of their home on Locust Street, accompanied by more violence and "7 or 8 pistol shots." Anna's father wanted to go out and see what was up, but his family convinced him to remain inside. "Our house was one selected to be mobbed," Anna wrote, "but a Republican spoke in our favour" and they were spared.[94] As in April 1861, Philadelphians played out the drama of politics in the city streets, although perhaps the intervention by this one Republican signaled some reason for optimism, at least for the city's upper-crust Democrats.

New Yorkers Charles and Maria Daly were hardly typical Democrats, but for four years of war they had been consistent in their support for the war and in their distaste for the president. Maria had commented on local and state elections, and the goings on in the Democratic Party, but for most of the conflict her interests had been elsewhere. As the presidential election loomed, the diarist grew increasingly partisan, concluding a week before the election that "Lincoln is cheating as hard as he can." On the day before the election Maria worried at how "unscrupulous" the Republicans had become, vowing to shutter the doors and keep out visitors to protect Charles, who had been announced as a McClellan elector. Daly had come to see the election as a contest between good and evil.[95]

The Democratic Party's rank and file came to their conclusions for various reasons, but for many the ultimate decision in 1864 seemed most dependent on how they felt about the current president and administration or the war itself, as opposed to the character of the man challenging Lincoln. For the party insiders perhaps the die had been cast with the Chicago platform, or really with the capture of Atlanta. In those last weeks before the election, letters flowed into Samuel Barlow's office from all over the country, offering prognostications about national politics and local results, sometimes peppered with the insights of hindsight.

Kentucky congressman William Henry Wadsworth had been tracking local politics with care. In early October, a month before election day, Wadsworth told Barlow that he had been canvassing widely from Indiana and Ohio to Connecticut, Pennsylvania, and New York. He felt confident about his home district, and about Kentucky voters as a whole, but he worried that military and political interference would hurt Democratic chances, and "I am very sorry, I wanted the Union again, & the restoration of peace & liberty. Lincoln will lose us all these. In 6 mos. after his reelection, new & widespread insurrections will finish the face of republican govt. The people whom I know cannot possibly support four years more of his wicked & bloody reign," he feared.[96]

Samuel Butterworth wrote from San Francisco, suggesting that the party's resources would be better spent in other states.[97] John Thomas Doyle also checked in from San Francisco, concluding that the cause was lost: "I think we would have done better had the general run distinctively as a war democrat, pitching the peace men overboard from the start."[98] Delaware's James Asheton Bayard assured Barlow that "we are peace men here, but we will give the vote of the state to McClellan."[99] Writing from St. Louis, James Harrison worried about the intervention of the military in the election.[100]

On voting day Lincoln earned 55 percent of the popular vote. Wadsworth and Bayard had been correct in calling their home states of Kentucky and Delaware for McClellan, but the only other state he carried was his home state of New Jersey. Most Democratic insiders were probably not surprised by the results, but there is always room for angry recriminations. Henry Douglas Bacon wrote to Barlow a few weeks after the election, offering his two cents: "Your predictions & hopes in regard to McClellan are disappointed," he wrote. "I am sorry for you & the Genl, but regret for his feelings is much mitigated from his accepting the nomination on a Platform, that up to that moment I deemed totally at variance with his views & unworthy of him either as a patriot or statesman." Whatever McClellan's efforts after the fact, Bacon was not going to forget Chicago.[101]

There are various ways to interpret the final numbers. Perhaps Lincoln's National Union Party had successfully convinced a portion of northern voters that the Democrats were the party of traitors, populated by antiwar Copperheads and legions of secret-society conspirators.[102] Certainly for some the Republicans were the party of emancipation and racial justice, as well as the best choice to ensure a military victory. Conversely, some Democrats saw McClellan as the best option for military success and negotiated peace, unencumbered by debates about emancipation. Others saw in Lincoln a political activist who ran counter to core conservative principles. No doubt many northern Democrats voted for the Democratic candidate out of long-term loyalties to the party and its principles. The military definitely mattered. Multiple successes on the battlefields in the East meant that by November the end of the war appeared to be merely a matter of time. These developments softened some antiwar sentiments.

It was a huge victory, and a loud endorsement of the administration's policies. But it is not as if four years of warfare had completely destroyed the nation's partisan political structure. Some portion of Democrats who had opposed Abraham Lincoln in 1860 opted to support his reelection in 1864, presumably because of their continuing support of the war. Those War Democrats embraced the rhetorical point offered by the National Union Party: this was an election about supporting a war and not the time for partisan disagreements.

Varying Shades and Hues

An analysis of the election results in 1864 comes down to a host of variables, although the simple, and not entirely off-base, argument would be that it was a referendum on the Civil War, staged only months before the war would end. But what if we shift our focus to ask what that momentous election tells us about Democrats and the Democratic Party? Both historians and historic actors like to fit people into particular pigeonholes. Thus, histories of the Civil War, and of the election of 1864, often divide Democrats into two groups: War Democrats and Peace Democrats. Or, depending on who is doing the dividing, War Democrats and Copperheads.

In a world where simple binary divisions are often the best way to describe and understand human behavior, these divisions have some virtue. But as is so often the case, the actual human actors divided along a fairly broad spectrum, even though in the end the voters had two choices. What if we shift our focus from northern voters to Democratic voters, regardless of who they voted for in 1864? What can we glean about how Democrats thought and behaved, from the combined evidence of documents aimed at them, comments by party insiders, thoughts expressed by ordinary voters and their spouses, and the numbers themselves? Several patterns emerge, even though much still remains in shadows.

Let us begin with what voters might have gleaned from the two party platforms. The Republican platform, approved in Baltimore in the first week of June, had 11 resolutions, running to just under 4,500 words. Democrats approved their controversial platform at the end of August in Chicago. It had 6 resolutions and over 2,500 words.[103] Voters who opted to read both short party statements—and many no doubt did—would have found various platitudes, several key differences of opinion, and no surprises. Both parties declared great fealty to the Constitution, although they read the document differently. The Republicans had a long resolution praising Abraham Lincoln. The Democratic platform did not quite call the president a crazed tyrant, but it came close. Both Democrats and Republicans praised the nation's soldiers and sailors; the Democrats took pains to note the nation's prisoners of war, while the Republicans spoke of ensuring fair pay to soldiers, including African Americans. The Republican platform supported emancipation across the entire United States. The Democratic Party notably made no mention of slavery or emancipation. The Republicans had resolutions showing their support for immigration, a transatlantic railroad, and paying off the public debt. They were opposed to foreign governments interfering with the United States. Each of those last resolutions would be important in the future, but it seems unlikely that any swayed many voters in 1864.

The resolutions that attracted the greatest attention concerned the Civil War itself. The Republican's second resolution announced "that we approve the determination of the government of the United States not to compromise with rebels, or to offer them any terms of peace, except such as may be based upon an unconditional surrender." Over two months later the Democrats declared "that after four years of failure to restore the Union by the experiment of war, . . . justice, humanity, liberty, and the public welfare demand that immediate efforts be made for a cessation of hostilities." The difference between the two platforms was stark. The Republicans wanted unconditional surrender; the Democrats called for a negotiated peace. Embedded in the Democratic resolution was the charge that under the guise of military necessity, "the Constitution itself has been disregarded in every part, and public liberty and private right alike trodden down, and the material prosperity of the country essentially impaired." They objected to how the war had been fought, and they declared the whole venture a failure. Of course various mitigating factors closed the gap between the two parties. First, McClellan made it clear that he did not endorse that resolution. Second, by November 1864 there was reason to conclude that the military war was no longer a "failure," even if a voter agreed that the Lincoln administration had run roughshod over the Constitution.

When we stack up the diverse evidence, what can we conclude about Democrats in 1864? As one great historian—writing of a few years earlier—put it, "No one generalization covers all the Democrats of the period; they were of varying shades and hues."[104] Here are a few thoughts about those "shades and hues" as they looked in November 1864.

First, some large portion of northern Democrats remained deeply loyal to their party, and to its fundamental conservative vision, especially when it came to the Constitution. As the 1864 platform and many of their public and private writings demonstrate, these voters felt differing degrees of outrage about how President Lincoln went about administering the Civil War. Many of these dedicated conservatives simply voted with their party, as they had for decades.[105] Others could not vote against their nation in time of war, or—like Henry Wharton—they just could not stomach George McClellan.

Second, for a substantial portion of voters who saw themselves as Democrats, the 1864 election seems to have been more a referendum on Lincoln and the war than it was a consideration of McClellan. Although their candidate did his best to present a strong version of his beliefs and accomplishments, and Democrats took pains to present an alternative to the current administration, in their private writings ordinary party members seemed most interested in discussing the president and the war. William Standard was perfectly happy with the McClellan nomination, but he clearly voted *against* Lincoln. Andrew and Samuel

Evans were dedicated Ohio Democrats, but in 1864 their thoughts focused on winning the war, and that meant backing Lincoln.

Third, many northern Democrats certainly viewed events through the lens of race, and they began to do that more so over time. John Smith peppered his diary with angry comments about African American soldiers and the progress of emancipation. He became increasingly free with the word "n—r" in his entries. In Kentucky, where Unionist Democrats saw their slaves joining the U.S. Army, while armed members of the United States Colored Troops marched through their communities, race hatred and fears for the future shaped their political opinions and in some cases shifted their loyalties. Political rhetoric, particularly aimed at the working classes, continually raised the specter of freed Blacks moving into White towns, producing unsettling interracial societies. And yet, in political terms we should take care not to overemphasize the political power of racism. Most northerners of both parties harbored fundamentally prejudiced beliefs and assumptions about inherent White superiority. As a matter of political strategy, the Democratic Party did not campaign against emancipation in 1864, and while John Smith might have grown almost obsessed with race hostility, the wirepullers writing to Samuel Barlow were not. Throughout the war, Democrats—in their public speech and private writings—had objected to radical abolitionists, who they felt had destabilized the nation and threatened the Constitution. But it is not clear how these beliefs translated into voting behavior in 1864, when most in the party had largely accepted that emancipation was a foregone conclusion. Some overviews of the war seem to see the Democratic Party as the racist, proslavery party in 1864. That misses the many hues at play.

The Democratic platform in 1864, and the private and public writings of many of the party leaders, made a pretty consistent argument that the Lincoln administration had violated the Constitution in a host of ways. Some of the Democrats who had grown tired of the administration still lined up in favor of the Union and the war, voting for Lincoln. Others who also styled themselves War Democrats cast their ballots for McClellan, presumably concluding that the general would successfully lead the nation to a just peace rather than an abject capitulation.

On election day Abraham Lincoln won by a comfortable margin, no doubt supported by the fact that the soldiers in blue had enjoyed successes on the battlefield. But 45 percent of voters voted against the president, even though it looked as if the Confederacy would soon be defeated. No doubt some sliver of those voters were no longer loyal to the Union. Most remained loyal to the United States and the Constitution, but they concluded that McClellan was the better option at the helm. Meanwhile, some portion of Democrats, perhaps still simmering with anger at administration policies, remained dedicated War Democrats, supporting the war over party. They became part of the 55 percent voting for Lincoln, even while they saw themselves as loyal Democrats. But despite all this talk about voters changing parties, the simplest explanation for 1864 may be that it was a high voter turnout election, and there were just more Republicans in the northern states.[106]

Less than a month after the election, Ohio Democrat Washington McLean wrote to Samuel Barlow, taking an early stab at the search for a silver lining. He believed that in the long run the election would be "to the benefit of the Democracy, although I did not so think previous to the Election." Democrats who played the very long game had reason to conclude that the party was best off not defeating Abraham Lincoln as the war was winding down.[107]

9

Peace and an Uncertain Future

The election of 1864 had been a loss for the Democrats, but at least the war seemed about to end. Big questions remained, including the future of slavery and the eventual return of the Confederate states to the Union. Soon events would destabilize how Democrats would see their present and imagine the party's future.

A Fallen Party

As the voting returns came in that November, conservative northern Democrats—those with long roots in the party's history and ideology—who thought back over the previous five years might have had good reason to kick themselves. Or others in their party. After all, in the spring of 1860 the party's radical southern members had walked out of the Charleston convention, severing the final national political party and paving the way for the upstart Republicans to win the White House. They walked out because they were worried about their slaves. When Lincoln won they worried more, and despite the president's claims that his party had no designs on southern slavery, the leaders of the Slave Power divided the nation. They had killed their party and their country in order to protect their claimed right to own slaves. Moderate and conservative northern Democrats had every reason to be displeased with them.

With secession underway and war threatening, the North's moderate voices—including many of those same Democrats—tried to move Heaven and Earth to find some path that would conciliate the South. But Lincoln and his party pointed out that in politics score is kept by counting votes. Southerners were welcome to accept the core Republican assurance that the nation would not seek to emancipate southern slaves, but insofar as they also wanted promises that they could move their alleged human property to federal territories, they were out of luck. Pennsylvanian James Buchanan knew how to read history and politics. He ruefully concluded that civil war exploded thanks to the actions of radicals on both sides. He was essentially correct, although the moral ground on which those radicals stood was hardly similar.[1]

Skipping ahead just over three years, our conservative northern Democrat might have had some hopes that the party could regain the executive branch in 1864. But once again history, and fellow Democrats, took the plans off the rails. The party had little chance unless they could agree on a candidate and a core platform, with those two fitting together. They failed in that pursuit. Meanwhile, Robert E. Lee and the Confederate strategists had long understood that the best path to success was not victory on the battlefield but political success shaping the minds of the northern citizenry. If enough northern voters preferred a negotiated peace to more bloodshed, the Confederacy might just survive as an independent nation. Lee saw in the North's antiwar movement some glimmers of hope that success might come at the ballot box. And Peace Democrats, who read talk of negotiations running aground if Lincoln demanded emancipation as a price of peace, had something of a rallying cry. But all that peace talk, especially from northern Democrats who saw themselves as loyal to the Union, depended on military stalemates and more long lists of casualties. When the U.S. military made sufficient progress on multiple fronts the election returns became close to inevitable. This time perhaps it did not matter that the Democrats had failed to find unanimity. The Civil War would soon be over.

Ending Slavery and Preparing for Peace

The issues surrounding the end of slavery in the United States are a bit opaque. We recall Abraham Lincoln as "The Great Emancipator" with some good reason, but the road to universal emancipation did not really go through the White House. To recap: Lincoln's Emancipation Proclamation, which took effect on January 1, 1863, only announced that enslaved people held in states and portions of states still in rebellion were forever free. Lincoln was both an astute scholar of the Constitution and a wise reader of politics. The expressed logic of the proclamation was that the measure would further the nation's military aims by undermining the Confederate war effort, and thus it was constitutional for the president as commander in chief—not as a protector of morality and justice—to issue such an order.

By the close of 1864 a large portion of northern Democrats had accepted the core logic of the Emancipation Proclamation as a military measure. Many border-state Democrats continued to cling to the hope that their own slaves would be untouched, while others had manumitted slaves or attempted to divest themselves of the institution. The party's leading constitutional thinkers, such as Maryland's Reverdy Johnson, agreed that full emancipation depended on a constitutional amendment rather than a presidential proclamation. Democratic advocates for a negotiated peace objected to federal negotiators making emancipation a condition of reunion. It is not clear that they really cared about slavery at all, but they objected to conditions that might delay an end to the war, and—as a matter of constitutional theory—it seemed a violation of states' rights to force emancipation on the vanquished. (That argument presumed that the individual Confederate states still had any rights that the United States was bound to respect.) By the election of 1864 the Democratic Party had no interest in digging in its heels about emancipation, or really talking about it at all. But raw racism remained a useful rhetorical tool in some quarters.

Republicans in Congress had been discussing a constitutional amendment ending slavery for nearly a year, and many leading Democrats were already on board or at least had come to accept the handwriting on the wall. In April 1864 the Senate approved the amendment thirty-eight to six, taking advantage of the Republicans' huge majority. But that June the measure failed to receive the requisite two-thirds vote in Congress, thanks to the resistance of congressional Democrats. Although the measure, which would go on to be the nation's 13th Amendment, was certainly historic, the whole matter attracted little attention during the 1864 presidential campaign. The Republicans supported the amendment in their platform, the Democrats ignored the issue. Nobody really campaigned on the matter.[2]

Despite the fact that the election did not seem to turn on the emancipation amendment, Lincoln and the Republican Party won handily in 1864 and the 39th Congress, set to take their seats in March, would be packed with Republicans. Lincoln hoped that the members of the House in the outgoing 38th Congress, which had already turned down the amendment, would take up the matter again before their terms expired. Once both houses had passed the amendment it would go to states for ratification, essentially moving the matter out of Washington. That would also mean that the talk of emancipation as an obstacle to peace would seemingly be off the table. The matter would be in the hands of individual states. Here the constitutional and reconstruction numbers got tricky. A constitutional amendment required the approval of three-fourths of the states, but in order to reach that figure the amendment would need the approval of two formerly Confederate states. And this would be most easily accomplished if Congress backed Lincoln's 10-percent plan, thus easing the rebel states back into the Union.

These events opened up a great congressional debate, where Democrats—especially those representing border states—mounted familiar arguments against emancipation, either as a general idea or as implemented in this form. The debate produced grand theater, where Lincoln and his people proved adept at the rough game of congressional politics. The historian Elizabeth Varon reads the entire drama as one where "images of Southern deliverance were central to the case for the amendment." Republicans argued that they sought to "liberate the South" from the evils of slavery. Democrats, in the end not at a loss for unintended irony, took that deliverance theme in a different direction and—in Varon's words—argued "that the death of slavery would mark the death of abolitionism." Many recalcitrant Democrats just saw that they were fighting yet another losing battle, although they despaired that the amendment was a new measure strengthening the central government and weakening state autonomy. The Civil War had effectively killed slavery, and now was the time to recognize its demise. Even if the 38th Congress balked, the next group would have the numbers. On January 31, 1865, ten Democratic congressmen flipped their earlier votes, eight were "conveniently absent," and the 13th Amendment squeaked by in the House of Representatives. It was a day for celebration, although hardly a moment marking a sea-change in northern thoughts about slavery and emancipation. In the lengthy ratification process, Maryland, Delaware, and Kentucky would each vote down the amendment.[3]

Slavery was effectively dead in the United States. Or at least it would be when the Confederate states returned to the Union under the condition that they must endorse the amendment. Still, there was a war to be won, and a peace to negotiate.

On March 4 Abraham Lincoln delivered his Second Inaugural Address. In one of the great speeches in the English language, the president offered a message of reconciliation and hope, fueled by an uncharacteristic spiritual contemplation. Examining the harsh hand of providence, Lincoln presented slavery as the essential cause of "this terrible war," and he argued that both sides had properly suffered "the scourge of war" created by the institution's evils. With the war nearly at an end, Lincoln rejected any impulse to triumphalism. He did not speak to the radicals in his own party. Instead he called for national reconciliation, "with malice towards none, with charity for all." It was a speech that promised some level of generosity for vanquished rebels while stressing to all that four years of bloodshed constituted God's proper punishment for centuries of slavery. In the address itself Lincoln recognized the fundamental evils of that institution while offering little specific hope for freed people in the future.[4]

Lincoln's Second Inaugural is fascinating for many reasons, including the simple fact that the president was addressing people who had abdicated their citizenship in the United States. The better inaugural addresses make some effort to speak to those voters who did not support the newly inaugurated president. Here the president was reaching out to those White men who had taken up arms against the country while also doing his best to soothe the urge to punish among radicals in his own party. He may have been less concerned about pleasing the members of the opposition party. No doubt several of his key points did not find a receptive audience among the North's Democrats. For many it was not slavery itself, but fanatical abolitionism, that explained the 1860 election and the coming of the Civil War. And even if political forces had moved the nation toward emancipation, Democrats rejected the notion that the hand of providence had somehow weighed in to cause the war and then end slavery. The last four years did not represent providential forces but rather the crazed actions of extremists in the North and South. And insofar as Lincoln envisioned a truly reconstructed South in the postwar years, his conservative political opponents resisted any talk of imposing revolutionary changes on the vanquished Confederacy.[5]

In Kentucky Ellen Wallace read of Lincoln's victory and his inaugural speech and was not impressed. "Another four years of darkness, tyranny and blood if they bear any resemblance to the past term," she wrote. "It is the opinion of the people that the Confederacy is in the last ditch. But General Lee is the greatest General of the age, and his principal officers are men of undaunted courage and great ability. This of itself is reason for hope even though the case other wise seems hopeless." Although a prowar northern Democrat, Wallace—like so many slaveholders in the border states—remained torn about her loyalties to individuals.[6]

On that day in March Lincoln might have been forgiven for seeing his political challenges coming from other directions. After all, thanks to his considerable coattails in the recent election, the 39th Congress featured a politically toothless Democratic Party. In the Senate 37 Republicans outnumbered the 9 Democrats, with 2 senators representing "Unionist" campaigns. The new lower house had 132 Republicans, 14 Unionists, and only 40 Democratic congressmen.[7] As he looked ahead to the next four years, Lincoln recognized that he had a huge, often independent-minded Republican delegation in Congress, which would push hard to control the terms of Reconstruction. Meanwhile, he faced an immensely complicated Confederacy he would have to steer back into the Union. Assuming that some form of his 10-percent plan determined the return of the rebel states, the next questions concerned what sort of southern unionists the defeated Confederacy would send to Washington to claim the many open seats in Congress.

But first there was the matter of winning the war.

Richmond, Appomattox, and Ford's Theater

Events moved swiftly in the six weeks after that wondrous Second Inaugural Address. On April 3 Richmond fell to Union forces. The following day Abraham Lincoln walked the streets of the one-time capital of the Confederacy. Headlines across the North celebrated the victory, and politicians prepared for the end. With Richmond again in the hands of the United States, Robert E. Lee guided the remains of his Army of Northern Virginia through the Virginia countryside, with Ulysses S. Grant and his men in unbending pursuit. On the 8th the two commanders met at Appomattox Courthouse, where they both signed a carefully prepared agreement, setting out the terms of surrender and effectively laying the groundwork for peace.[8] Kentuckian Ellen Wallace read of Lee's surrender and was ready to see the war over. And the sooner the better. But she worried what the future might bring.[9]

On April 14, 1865, everything changed. That evening Abraham Lincoln attended a performance of "Our American Cousin" at Ford's Theater, and John Wilkes Booth—a southern actor—shot Lincoln in the back of the head. Witnesses carried the fallen president across the street to a boardinghouse, where they placed him on a humble bed too short to accommodate the lanky president. That night one of Booth's co-conspirators attempted to assassinate Secretary of State William Seward in his home. Seward survived his wounds, but the following day the nation learned that Lincoln had died.[10]

Historians point out that Lincoln's assassination brought the entire nation—or at least the northern states—together in a moment of mourning, occasionally leavened by angry talk of vengeance. Civilians decorated their homes with black crepe; newspapers—regardless of their political affiliation—ran special issues with the columns framed in black ink. In pulpits across the North, clergymen spoke of the national tragedy. Coming barely a week after General

Lee's surrender to General Grant, the shock of the tragedy seemed almost too much to bear. For that moment in April 1865 Black and White northerners came together in a national moment of mourning.

For northern Democrats, events following April 15 presented particular challenges. Although in the emotions of the moment they may have missed the comparisons, the politics of public display certainly had much in common with events in the North four years earlier. In April 1861, after months of talk about compromise and conciliation, word of the firing on Fort Sumter had brought (most) northerners together to declare their solidarity with the Union and their fury with the secessionists. And for those whose opinions were conflicted, or who had simply not mastered the art of symbolic displays, angry crowds—especially in cities—roamed the streets demanding affirmation of patriotism from ordinary citizens. Those northerners who had personal ties with the new Confederacy, or who blamed events on crazed abolitionists, or who simply still imagined a world where the nation would not be divided by war, had tough choices to make. In April 1861 angry mobs had little interest in nuance; they wanted to see flags waving. Most northerners in most communities rallied to that flag, and dissenters generally kept quiet.

Four years later news of Lincoln's assassination prompted most Democrats to polite silence, regardless of how they felt about the murdered president. Certainly not all northerners had been Lincoln supporters. Although the president's 1864 electoral victory had been substantial it was hardly overwhelming. Not everyone was thrilled with the president or his administration, even among those who voted for his reelection. On the other hand, news of the brutal murder horrified many northerners who had not been Lincoln supporters, and the fact that the assassination was at the hands of a southerner, and the suspicion that Booth and his co-conspirators were part of a larger Confederate plot, made the killing more outrageous. Even observers who disliked Abraham Lincoln on April 8 openly and honestly mourned his passing a week later. Most probably agreed with Democrat James Asheton Bayard, who wrote on the 19th, "This shocking murder of Presdt Lincoln will prove most disastrous to the country, and I can see nothing but evil to flow from it and trust that everyone connected with it may meet speedy and unrelenting justice."[11] Even Chauncey Burr, the crusty editor of *The Old Guard,* declared that "the death of Mr. Lincoln is the greatest calamity to our country" just as he was preparing to "speedily end our civil strife, and give rest to our bleed land."[12]

But while we know that Lincoln's assassination had a massive impact on northern society, not everyone responded identically.[13] Some, in their private or public speech, provoked hostile reactions; others chose to be quiet. The Philadelphia *Public Ledger* declared that "past political differences [are] forgotten" in the face of the horrific news. But the *Ledger* added that any locals caught expressing joy at the president's murder risked attacks at the hands of angry citizens.[14] As one East Coast diarist noted, "It is almost as much as a man's life is worth to dare . . . to show any joy at our country's loss."[15] This, then, was—and perhaps still is—the rub. All sorts of private writings and public publications noted that the aftermath of the Lincoln assassination saw a grand moment of public unanimity and mourning, but then in the next breath the same observers pointed out that northerners dissented from that unanimity at their own peril.

Across the North upset Unionists reported that antiwar Democrats in their midst had opted for judicious silence. One Brooklyn observer wrote that there were "plenty of Traitors & copperheads hanging out mourning," which he felt smacked of hypocrisy. A sergeant with the 15th New Jersey Volunteers noted that none of his comrades "dared to cheer," although he was sure some were itching to celebrate the assassination.[16] Others, according to historian Martha Hodes, "refused to disguise their true sentiments." Northern diarists recorded stories of Copperheads who revealed those true feelings, provoking social derision or—in the case of some Irish laborers who were too free with their opinions—lost jobs. For some of the North's more virulent racists, even as the nation mourned the fallen president, Lincoln remained a hated symbol of abolitionism and racial equality, hostilities they shared more or less publicly.[17]

Talk of celebrating Copperheads enraged northerners who mourned their president and saw his death as an act of war. Many privately yearned to punish the enemies in their midst. Bostonian Caroline Dall passed men in the streets who wore no mourning and seethed that she "could have killed them." A Chicagoan reported seeing an "indignant crowd" attacking a woman seen tearing down mourning drapery. In upstate New York rumors circulated that a woman named Susan Hews had "clapped and cheered at the news" of the assassination, prompting locals to call for her exile while one citizen "called her a 'dirty low-minded ignorant disloyal contemptible *Thing*.'" Hews denied the claims, but apparently to no avail. In April 1861 private homes and businesses had risked attack if they failed to display the flag and other patriotic symbols, regardless of their political intent. In these heady days four years later reports flashed across the land of crowds attacking homes and businesses that failed to display mourning. Multiple stories circulated about accused pro-secessionists suffering rough treatment at the hands of the irate. Sometimes local police intervened.[18] In some cases individuals who openly expressed glee at Lincoln's assassination faced arrest and legal charges.[19] Throughout the war, northern pulpits had become places for political speech intermingled with religious sentiments. Following the assassination, some ministers turned their wrath on northern Copperheads and all who had criticized the president.[20]

This, then, is the story as we know it. Hodes, who has done a huge amount of research in contemporary materials, tells a tale of a nation nearly unanimous in mourning, broken only by small numbers of northern Copperheads who "spewed enough glee to make clear that they had not melted away." Thus, in the aftermath of the assassination, "mourners had to contend not only with the defiant Confederates but also with a faction of northern citizens who had turned the Union home front into a battleground."[21] But although there is no doubt truth to this narrative, it might invite further scrutiny.

As is so often the case, we face the equally thorny matter of sorting out private thought and public speech. Two things seem to be clear. First, most conservative northerners were honestly appalled at the assassination. And second, in most corners of the United States it was pretty clear that openly expressing glee at Lincoln's murder would have been a dangerous act. The accounts of open Copperhead speech are fairly limited, and generally come from their political adversaries. Thus, diarists commented on the "hypocrisy" of people who wore mourning who they felt really did not mean it. Or civilians such as Susan Hews, who no doubt had been free with her opinions before April 15, were accosted in the street even when she insisted that she had said nothing. And as a matter of symbolic speech, northern Democrats risked the ire of loyal patriots if they failed to display the proper mourning symbols on their homes or their persons (leading Caroline Dall to see red). Sometimes these people were probably making a symbolic statement with their symbolic silence, but the whole thing called to mind the Philadelphia business that accidentally raised a flag upside down in April 1861, to near disastrous results.

The decision to make any public utterance expressing satisfaction at the president's assassination required a person of particular beliefs and character. Certainly most northerners who had ideological objections to Lincoln and his administration were not the sorts to *say* such things, even if they thought them. But meanwhile, it is easy to imagine spontaneous groups attacking members of their community who had a history of attacking the administration, regardless of how they behaved on that sad day. No doubt there were people who really celebrated the assassination in public, or accidentally let their feelings be known. But it is worth wondering whether these were generally people who were ideologically Copperheads, as opposed to individuals who were full of anger unregulated by more complicated political thought. Conservatives like Chauncey Burr—who disliked everything about the war—were likely more typical in their circumspect responses.

For some of those northern conservatives, the horror at the assassination eventually gave way to discomfort with the public obsequies. In the week after his death, Lincoln's casket traveled across the North, where thousands of mourners turned out to pay their respects in each location. Edward Waln, a Democratic diarist, visited a friend on Walnut Street in Philadelphia to witness the spectacle. He was not impressed, declaring that "the procession was a failure." He added that "Poor old Abe—they have tried to make a great man out of him, but he was a failure . . . as a statesman he was a mere puppet."[22] Many others, like Katherine Brinley Wharton, admitted that "little did I suppose I should ever shed tears for him." Still, she had her limits. "Horror stricken as I was," she wrote, "I would say that I think things were carried to a ridiculous length," and she personally declined to wear mourning when she went out in public.[23] It is a fair assumption that neither Waln nor Wharton shared their ambivalent thoughts in public.

New York diarist Maria Lydig Daly's responses were typical of many elite northern Democrats. When she learned the news, Daly wrote, "Poor Lincoln!" followed by a long entry about the attacks, adding, "God save us all." A few days later Daly recorded a lengthy, introspective entry. After attending church on Easter Sunday, the diarist reported that the clergymen were asserting that "he was sacrificed on Good Friday." She demurred, arguing that she deferred to nobody in her patriotism but insisted that the Union's "success must be ascribed to God alone" and not the fallen president. In this entry, only days after Lincoln's death, Daly added a long discussion of Lincoln's many failures as a president and commander in chief, noting that "all this will be forgotten in this shameful, cowardly act of his assassination" on the eve of peace. And, in a surprising moment of historic reflection, the judge's wife pointed out that "it was the rejection of Douglas by the Charleston Convention four years ago that elected Abraham Lincoln and Jefferson Davis, and it was not any fault of Abraham Lincoln. Nor can we blame him that when elected by a legal majority, he accepted the Presidency. Every American feels competent for any place." Nearly a week later, when the funeral procession reached New York to lay in state at City Hall, Daly wrote that "I shall not go to see the show" but would allow the servants to attend. "I am sick of pageants." As an afterthought, Daly added that a house a few doors down had been tarred by a crowd for failing to display mourning. Still, "tomorrow the theaters reopen and then, I suppose, all will be over."

Daly certainly felt sorrow for the nation's loss and even added her concerns for "Poor Mrs. Lincoln!"[24] But even in her honest sympathy for the fallen president, she dismissed the talk that he was an iconic hero. In a moment of generosity, Daly admitted that it was not really Lincoln's fault he had been elected, nor could she blame him for believing—in true American tradition—that he was fit for the job. But in her view he had been a disaster as a president. Moreover, after a week of mourning, Maria Daly seemed thoroughly sick of the whole affair. Yet it is a very good bet that Judge Daly's home, unlike the one a few doors down, featured carefully arrayed mourning arrangements installed by loyal servants. The Dalys were War Democrats and not Copperheads, but Maria had been no supporter of Abraham Lincoln. If she and her husband made no public displays of their sentiments, that probably said less about their ideology than their sense of etiquette.

Edward Ingersoll Pulls a Pistol

While the Dalys were inclined toward polite circumspection, Philadelphian Edward Ingersoll and his brother Charles had fewer filters controlling their public speech. They both were free with their opinions on abolitionists and Republicans and the Lincoln administration. They disliked them. As it turned out, Edward was not only loose-tongued; he also had terrible timing. On Thursday April 13 Ingersoll delivered a dinner talk in New York to the local "Anti-Abolition State Rights Society." Surrounded by ideological kin—and perhaps spurred on by spirits—Ingersoll declared that "I yield to no man in sympathy to the people of the South," and he went on to declare that he "embrace[d] the doctrine of secession as an American doctrine."[25]

Under normal circumstances this would likely have been dismissed as familiar crazed Copperhead talk, if it were noticed at all. But the following evening—Good Friday—Abraham and Mary Lincoln attended Ford's Theater. The New York press picked up the story, and before long news had traveled far and wide. A few days later Philadelphia's *Evening Bulletin* ran a column on "The Ingersoll and Booth Doctrine." Other newspapers, not always attentive to the order of events, suggested that Edward deserved physical punishment. Ingersoll's brother-in-law Sidney George Fisher noted that in truth the published remarks were fairly typical of Edward's private conversation, but now—with Ingersoll's rhetoric appearing in print alongside lengthy accounts of the president's final moments—the understated Fisher noted that Ingersoll might "be in a very dangerous position."[26]

On the morning of the 27th Edward returned from New York by train, where a small crowd awaited. A Captain Withington of the 198th Pennsylvania Volunteers accosted the forty-eight-year-old Copperhead, cursing and demanding that he issue a public apology to his nation and to all his fellow soldiers. Undaunted, Ingersoll suggested that the soldier "go to hell." At this (because history is just more entertaining than fiction), the two irate Pennsylvanians squared off to do battle with their canes, as bystanders closed in. Ingersoll appeared to be holding his own until his cane shattered and things seemed dire. But as the captain and his associates sensed blood, Ingersoll reached into a pocket and pulled out a pistol. At this, the crowd drew back a step, but before they could learn precisely how tough Edward Ingersoll really was, two policemen appeared to break up the melee and arrest the agitated Democrat. They probably acted to protect Ingersoll from harm, but it was also illegal to carry a concealed weapon in the City of Brotherly Love.

Fisher, Peter McCall, and various other conservatives of sane mind thought it wisest if Edward—who was, after all, filthy rich—were to quietly leave town for one of his other properties. Edward's brother Charles—not always among the more sane local Democrats—openly worried about Edward skulking away for fear that his brother should "do nothing unworthy of a gentleman." In the police station angry witnesses stressed that Edward had illegally flashed a pistol, to which he crowed, "Yes, & when I drew it, you ran like sheep." Early that evening Charles went to the station to visit his brother, and the waiting mob—still stirred up and seeking Ingersoll blood—set on him. By the time they were finished and the police took Charles home by carriage, blood covered the beaten Copperhead, and several of his Democratic friends had been roughed up. Observers claimed that the policemen declined to step in until the mob had done considerable damage on the unrepentant Ingersoll. That evening Fisher wrote that Charles had not been badly hurt, although he looked terrible. His brother-in-law "was not the least cast down" by the experience. The following day Edward posted a considerable bail and the authorities released him from jail. He followed his friends' advice and took refuge out of the city.[27]

The separate Philadelphia episodes involving the two Ingersoll brothers illustrate crucial aspects of public life in the days immediately following the assassination of Abraham Lincoln. But Edward Ingersoll's sins had been more subtle. He had shared his thoughts on secession and the administration at a private dinner in New York. He could not have known what would happen in Washington the following evening. Once reports of his talk hit the newspapers, sometimes without noting that he spoke before Booth acted, Ingersoll could have issued some sort of public apology, but apparently some combination of personal convictions and elite arrogance kicked in. He refused to retract his words when challenged at the train station and mocked his attackers later at the police station. And Charles, equally arrogant and unrepentant, ended up bloodied and battered by an angry crowd, although it is not clear that he said anything to insult the fallen president.

Much like in 1861, the episodes in Philadelphia in April 1865 seemed to have attracted disproportionate attention in the national press, where newspapers reprinted stories and added their own commentary. Time after time, accounts presented both brothers as not merely dissenters but treasonous, and they described the beatings both brothers faced as completely warranted.[28] Not all agreed. About eighty miles to the northwest, the editors of the antiwar *Clearfield Republican* described Ingersoll as "a distinguished Democrat" who had been "assaulted by a mob" for his speech in New York. The *Republican* predicted that ten years from now, "nine out of every ten of this infatuated rabble will practically endorse every word said by Mr. Ingersoll."[29]

Historians should not be in the business of making moral judgments, but we might all agree that it was not a bad thing both Edward and Charles Ingersoll got smacked around a bit in April 1865. Still, the highly publicized stories about their separate encounters with angry crowds and only slightly protective police fit a different narrative. In the week after Lincoln's assassination the national press ran many entertaining stories about these elite Copperheads getting attacked by angry patriots. But although both Ingersoll brothers were certainly arrogant Copperheads by any measure, the contemporary accounts give no evidence that either expressed any glee at Lincoln's assassination. They were victims for things they had said and published before April 15, but they fit easily into a narrative about unrepentant Copperheads celebrating a national tragedy.

Restoration or Reconstruction

The fifteen years following Lee's surrender at Appomattox are some of the most important, and most complex, in American history. The scholarship on the period we call "Reconstruction" is vast. Many of the key issues concerning the period—including the proper timing of the end of the Civil War and of the end of Reconstruction—remain contested in interesting ways. If we restrict our attention to the postwar political experiences of the northern Democrats in the first seven years, the scholarship shrinks considerably but is still substantial. A few key issues are worth noting.[30]

Certainly many of the crucial political issues that the United States faced in those years concerned the nature of reunion and the future of the defeated Confederate states. From the end of 1863 and into 1864 (and beyond) Abraham Lincoln and the more radical members in his party had haggled over approaches to peace. After Appomattox, policymakers wrestled with the terms under which the defeated states would return to the nation and many related topics, including how postwar power to decide these questions would be divided among Congress, the president, and the individual southern states. More importantly, the postwar political world—again with its many constituent parts—debated how to welcome freed people into the body politic. When would African Americans get the franchise, and what laws and actions would protect that right? To what extent should the federal government and military exercise their powers to protect the civil rights and personal liberties of African Americans? And, again, which political entities would make these decisions?

Beyond the shifting morass of issues that defined postwar Reconstruction, politicians in these years debated a host of other evolving topics. A short list would include postwar debts and financial issues; expansion, both on the continent and beyond; ongoing conflicts with western Indians (certainly all wrapped up with expansionism); and responses to corruption at all levels of government. And each of these issues became intertwined with core concerns about the power of the federal government.

In the middle of 1865 the national Democratic Party had a terrible hand to play, and things were only going to get worse. First, they had opposed the administration in a civil war that the nation had just won. Even though the party's 1864 presidential candidate supported fighting the war to a successful conclusion, the Republican Party had done a superb job of painting the Democratic Party as the party of traitors. With time they would become adept at what became known as "waving the bloody shirt," reminding voters which party had been against the Union Army. Second, even the War Democrats had spent the war opposing Abraham Lincoln. At the time that had no doubt seemed like politics as usual, but now the president was the victim of an assassin's bullet, and the Democrats were remembered as adversaries of the century's great martyr. Third, after the 1864 election the Democrats were hugely outnumbered in Congress, with little power to sway proceedings except in concert with moderate Republicans.

Then there was the matter of Andrew Johnson. In 1864 Lincoln had selected the Tennessee Democrat as his running mate. Johnson had been a strong

Unionist, and his presence on the ballot nicely balanced the ticket. His future in the executive branch got off to a rocky start when he attended Lincoln's inauguration so drunk that observers noticed. Once he became president, Johnson—a Jacksonian Democrat—was not so much the leader of the Democratic Party as he was a political outsider and an angry, socially inept figure with few friends or supporters in Washington. Still, in those first few months Democratic newspapers supported the new president, much to the annoyance of his Republican adversaries. And some northern Democrats did their best to court Johnson and his enormous ego. In the long run for Democrats, the problem was that as a vocal adversary of the radical Republicans, the new president was a natural—but hardly comfortable—political ally.[31] And, assisted by a disastrous election of 1866 for the Democrats, Johnson's public behavior just made Congress more radical in its opposition. For the remainder of his term the accidental president faced hostile Republicans in Congress who battled him at every turn.

Fate and poor decisions left the national Democratic Party particularly hamstrung in the years immediately following the Civil War. Those who remained in Congress maintained their core conservative beliefs, which put them perpetually at odds with their radical colleagues. In the simplest terms, the postwar Democrats saw themselves as a largely ineffectual brake on radical changes. They wished to see the Confederate states returned to the Union with a minimum of fuss and dislocation, and they thought that such a thing could be accomplished. Left to their own devices they would have preferred a smooth return to a unified nation, with the southern states—and thus southern White men—controlling their own destinies. Looking more to the past than the future, they opposed the continuing rise of the central government, and they believed in the power of individual states' rights. As the 39th Congress neared a close, northern Democrats sided with Reconstruction proposals that would allow for a short-term military occupation of the South and fairly modest limitations on how the southern states should proceed in writing new constitutions. In all of these stances postwar Democrats—as they had been during the war—saw themselves as the defenders of the Constitution and "the Union as it was."

Of course this ideological purity, if it existed, became intertwined with practical political concerns, which in turn became all wrapped up in questions of racial justice. In principle, these northern Democrats did not support extensive federal efforts to defend African Americans and protect their right to vote, either through constitutional amendment or military intervention. But in practice, such stances aligned with the goals of southern White supremacists, who sought to disenfranchise Black voters. Those southern Democrats in the Old

Confederacy adopted the slogan "the Union as it was, the Constitution as it is" as their own, with clear racial implications. And, needless to say, those Black voters would support Republican candidates in both local and national elections. So constitutional purity became entangled with political pragmatism. One result was that northern Democrats, who after all had resisted emancipation during the war, became understood as central to the party of White supremacy.

In 1868 the Republicans nominated the heroic Ulysses S. Grant as their standard-bearer. In the end Clement Vallandigham, that boisterous Ohio Copperhead, called on Democrats to nominate New York's ex-governor Horatio Seymour. Seymour, despite some uncertainty, became the party's nominee, running for office on the argument that the Reconstruction Acts constituted an unconstitutional expansion of federal power. Grant won the election easily, with the crucial help of newly enfranchised southern African American men.[32]

A New Departure and a Shocking Departure

In the first several years of the Grant administration, reports of threats and violence against southern freed people roiled national politics even while those actual attacks wrecked havoc on southern society. Northern Democrats, still smarting from their association with their antiwar stances and their resistance to emancipation, recognized that tales of Ku Klux Klan violence in the South continued to damage them. Faced with these political dilemmas, one-time Ohio congressman Clement Vallandigham began to push his party toward his version of a "New Departure." Rather than appearing to resist Reconstruction and the key constitutional amendments that supported Black citizenship and voting rights, Vallandigham—who had lost in an 1867 bid for the Senate and an 1868 bid for the House—now argued that the party should accept the changes that had been made and work to reassure southern Black voters that they were not hoping to wind the clock back. Only by accepting some level of racial progress in the South could the Democrats hope to regain a more powerful national voice for their economic agenda. The enterprising Vallandigham had drafted a version of his New Departure for a county-wide political meeting, and the text had begun to earn some traction in Democratic circles.[33] Republicans saw this movement as little more than a cynical ploy in the face of political losses. One Republican journalist noted that "it is not made from conviction, but merely for the purpose of attaining power."[34]

In 1871 Vallandigham (despite his recent electoral failures) maintained his position as a significant national political figure, but he was also a distinguished trial lawyer. That brings us to his fellow Ohioan Thomas McGehean. McGehean was a bit of a shady character. He had been a shoemaker, but later in life he moved into some combination of politics and fishy finance. He had been linked to a celebrated fixed prizefight, and he had been charged with counterfeiting. Whatever else he was, McGehean knew his way around saloon culture. The third character in this little story was Thomas S. Myers, a one-time partner of McGehean who had become an enemy and bitter rival. On Christmas Eve 1870 Myers walked into the American Saloon in Hamilton, Ohio, and went upstairs to the saloon's "game room." McGehean arrived shortly thereafter, where he found Myers at the faro table. Here is where things got murky. Immediately after the fact it was known that someone threw a rock at Myers, and someone fired a shot, and Myers was dead. McGehean—not unreasonably—faced murder charges. He turned to Clement Vallandigham to defend him.

Vallandigham was an extremely accomplished politician and lawyer, but on June 16, 1871, he was a bit of a bonehead. On that day Vallandigham was in his law offices in Lebanon, Ohio, preparing a dramatic closing argument for the jury. The trial had been going on for ten days, and in his final statement Vallandigham hoped to convince the jury that Myers had walked into the saloon with a revolver in his pocket, "California style," and had actually shot himself by accident. Vallandigham and his colleagues had prepared two revolvers, one loaded for various ballistic tests and the second unloaded, for the courtroom demonstration. Somehow, in practicing for his closing argument, Vallandigham confused his props and picked up the loaded gun, shooting himself in the abdomen. The great Copperhead died the following morning.

On the day of Vallandigham's death, the Ohio Democratic press covered the congressman's final moments in painstaking detail. They also ran detailed excerpts from an interview Vallandigham had just given about the future of the Democratic Party. "There can be no more political campaigns fought on the issues of the last few years—they are dead," he declared, "and if the Democratic Party refuses to move to the front to accept the new order of things, it will simply pass away and some other party made up of the earnest progressive elements of both the old parties" will emerge and take over the government. Vallandigham praised President Grant as an individual, noted Grant's own talk of a "new departure," and explained that the president "would do right if the politicians would let him." Vallandigham went on to endorse talk of expansionism in San Domingo and Cuba, offering a broad understanding of Manifest Destiny. Turning to the past, Vallandigham resisted all claims that he had been a "disunionist" during the war, insisting that he had followed his principles. And, in a prescient look to the future, the Ohio Democrat announced that "if the Democratic Party fails to become the party of progress and advanced ideas, and I, from conscientious convictions, decide to act with any other political party, that other political party will not stop to inquire about my past political record has been." He would not survive to see the truly strange bedfellows the future would bring together.[35]

With Vallandigham gone, Ohio Democrat Durbin Ward—who we last heard from outside of Atlanta in 1864—took over McGehean's defense. After several trials, a jury finally found McGehean innocent, and indignant citizens urged him to leave Hamilton. McGehean's own story ended a few years later, after he returned to Hamilton and purchased his own saloon. In June 1875, almost precisely four years after Vallandigham's death, an assassin fired a shotgun through the saloon's window, killing the owner.[36]

The 1872 election saw the rise of the "Liberal Republicans," who broke with Grant over a host of issues and nominated Horace Greeley, the celebrated abolitionist and editor. The Liberal Republicans, who included many leading old abolitionists in their ranks, sought to move beyond the politics of Reconstruction. Greeley famously promised to "clasp hands across the bloody chasm," bringing peace to the nation seven years after Appomattox. The northern Democrats' notion of a new departure looked somewhat like the political goals floated by the Liberal Republicans, and they certainly shared their antipathy to Grant and his administration. Once again the Democratic Party found itself in an untenable situation going into a presidential election. To nominate their own version of an anti-administration candidate would (again) split the vote, guaranteeing a Grant victory. So instead, the Democrats met at their convention in Baltimore and nominated Greeley as their candidate, meeting Vallandigham's final predictions. More or less.

Grant beat Greeley by a substantial margin. In what must have been a bitter pill, the editor of the *New York Tribune* won only six states, all in the former slave South. Political observers noted that Democratic turnout in the national election dropped considerably below their participation in state elections. On November 29 Greeley died, only weeks after the election. The sixty-one-year old's wife had died a few days before the election, leaving the candidate heartbroken. Meanwhile, the Democratic Party was in disarray, and talk of a New Departure had fizzled.[37]

This story concludes with the quixotic failure of the Liberal Republicans—and their Democratic allies—in 1872. But perhaps we should end by looking back at Clement Vallandigham in Ohio the previous June. Six years before, Vallandigham was known as a virulent racist who had led the Copperhead movement and had been, in the eyes of many, a treasonous scoundrel. Now in 1871, with talk of the party's future heating up, and perhaps his own political future hanging in the balance, Vallandigham—not known for his sense of humor—floated two large ideas. The first was that he had personally not been a "disunionist" during the Civil War or in any way a disloyal traitor to his country. The second grand idea was that the Democratic Party must redefine itself as the "progressive party," reaching out to the South's African American citizens and voters. It remains to be seen how those positions meshed with the core wartime beliefs embraced by Vallandigham, his fellow Copperheads, and the northern Democratic Party.

CONCLUSION

Were Democrats Traitors and Racists?

This book began with an introduction that included six numbered observations about Civil War politics, sometimes straying beyond the bounds of pure partisan conflict. What follows focuses on two large questions about the northern Democrats as a national political party: loyalty and racism.

History has not treated the Civil War's northern Democrats very kindly. And with good reason. After all, during the war members of the party were on the wrong side of history on two huge fronts. First, some Democrats opposed the United States in a horrible war to defend the Union. Second, the party resisted emancipation, both as a military measure and then as national policy. So, looking backward, history sees a political party that sided against two important wartime goals, and the war's crucial legacies for the future.

This raises some additional considerations: Can we consider the wartime Democrats without the aid of hindsight? And, perhaps more complicated, is it possible to unravel what the diverse Democrats actually believed? To put the thing more bluntly: how far can we go in understanding people who believed things that we, as observers of the past, wish they had not? Let us focus on two clusters of questions.

On Copperheads, Traitors, and Labels

Political conflicts tend to encourage combatants to call each other names; political conflicts in wartime produce even nastier talk. During the Civil War, Republicans took to calling Democrats "Copperheads" and "traitors" and such. Democrats responded by calling their adversaries "abolitionists" and "radicals." (The Republicans won that rhetorical battle.) Historians have applied a wealth of labels to northern Democrats. Some were honorable "War Democrats," while others were "Peace Democrats," "Copperheads," "disloyal," and "traitors." The labels used, particularly in the broader historical surveys, tend to be imprecise if not entirely inaccurate.[1] Moreover, summaries of wartime politics are often vague about what portion of Democrats actually fit various labels, sometimes lumping the entire party together as a treasonous opposition.[2]

In the hands of political adversaries, the term "Copperhead" was usually an insult, often encompassing a host of vices. In more serious discussions, the defining characteristic of northern Copperheads was that they opposed the Civil War. The leading scholar of the Copperheads explains that they "generally came from one of three strands of American life." They were either "Southern or of Southern heritage"; "German or Irish immigrants, most likely Catholic"; or "firm believers in the Jeffersonian-Jacksonian approach to democracy."[3] Although northern Democrats who came to oppose the military conflict shared some core opinions, it is best to think of the Peace Democrats as a vocal interest group, rather than an organized party or political movement. They followed divergent paths to comparable conclusions. Moreover, Peace Democrats and War Democrats (insofar as those categories made sense at any given time) agreed on many things even while they disagreed on the ultimate implications of those beliefs.

There is also the matter of chronology. Many northerners, Democrats and Republicans alike, opposed the approaching military conflict in the first months of 1861, hoping for some sort of compromise that would keep the Union together. After all, a majority in both houses of Congress supported a constitutional amendment protecting the future of southern slavery. But once the fighting began, northerners of each party—both in public oratory and in street demonstrations—embraced the war as a just cause. Others preferred peace, even if they kept their opinions to themselves. This group included transplanted southerners, like Pierce Butler, as well as those with strong ties to the seceded states, including residents of the border states. Other northerners, largely conservative Democrats, believed that the southern states had a constitutional right to secede, and perhaps the rest of the United States would be best off letting them go. These Democrats followed different paths to their early war convictions. Some actively hoped for Confederate success and independence; others had a limited sense of the correct role of the federal government in national political life. Still others seemed to bridge those two groups. Thomas Hart Seymour, the powerful Connecticut Democrat, opposed the war for conservative Democratic reasons, but he also harbored a strong affection for aristocratic White southerners.[4]

With the passage of time, Democrats developed a broader critique of the Lincoln administration and its various legislative and judicial measures. Conservative Democrats assembled a list of actions that they found objectionable, including federal overreach on financial matters, the suppression of civil liberties, and early measures that elevated the civil rights of African Americans. Democrats had been skeptical about Lincoln and his party in 1860, and it did not take long for events to confirm their fears, provoking greater partisan hostility. And these clashes had a clear geographic dimension.

The national tensions had coalesced into broad constitutional critiques of the Republicans by September 1862, when Edward Ryan delivered his "Address to the People of the Democracy of Wisconsin." And the criticisms grew more pronounced with the Emancipation Proclamation and the emergence of federal conscription. The key point here is that Democrats across the North shared much of the constitutional outrage that Ryan expressed. The question remained whether that anger should translate into abandoning the war. Even Ryan argued that Lincoln was really much more moderate than the Republican radicals who he felt were steering the president in bad directions. Insofar as the Democratic Party split, it was over the primacy of the war itself—and the primacy of preserving the Union at all costs—as a national cause.

Two weeks after Ryan gave his address, the nation absorbed news of the bloodiest day in the history of North America, as Union and Confederate forces clashed along Antietam Creek. That reminds us of another thread that wove its way through northern discourse: the human cost of the war had become overwhelming, and it was only going to get worse. While matters of legislation and federal power certainly drove many conservative Democrats to distraction, other northerners tired of the long lists of dead and wounded soldiers, and the threat these casualties posed to each family. Walt Whitman famously predicted that "the real war will never get in the books," but northerners surely got glimpses of its horrors in letters home from men in the field.[5] When Emma Webb spoke in Brooklyn in March 1864, she delivered a classic Copperhead political speech in many senses, but it included these lines, which were met with rousing applause: "Whatever may be the crimes of the politicians on both sides there is no eye that does not weep for the private soldiers who are the innocent victims.—These soldiers who share none of the blame of the war must endure the hardships and lay down their lives on the altar of other men's ambition."[6] Those words struck a nerve with Webb's New York audience. In less than two months they would be reading of huge losses in places like The Wilderness, Spotsylvania, Cold Harbor, and Virginia battlefields in between.

This steady increase in war-weariness interacted with rising hostility to the federal draft. Groups of northerners—presumably Democrats—objected to conscription and all its component parts. They resisted draft enrollers, rioted on draft days, deserted when called up, and sometimes joined shadowy secret societies. Some of these draft resisters were clearly of that group described as "German or Irish immigrants." Northern immigrants were among these violent draft resisters, particularly those who rioted in New York streets in July 1863. But insofar as these draft resisters were Copperheads, they were certainly not all of foreign birth.

Events in the summer and fall of 1864 illustrate how some northern antiwar sentiments remained conditional.[7] It was that August when Lincoln wrote his "Blind Memo," indicating his serious expectation that he would not be reelected. Many variables led Lincoln and his key advisors to this conclusion, but much came down to developments on the battlefield. Lincoln worried that he might lose—presumably to George McClellan—because the war dragged on under his watch. Democratic insiders read the same tea leaves and adjusted accordingly. When the party leaders met at August Belmont's house in January they had planned a convention for early July. But they ended up postponing the Chicago meeting to late August. They changed plans largely because they were not sure what sort of message they should bring to the public.

Actual events, like the Democrats' Chicago convention, produced muddy results. When the delegates convened, William Tecumseh Sherman was still stalled outside of Atlanta, but not for long. The Democrats, intent on keeping all portions of the party under the tent, gave Peace Democrats an important hand in writing the platform, and they ended up with another Copperhead—George H. Pendleton—on the ballot. The overall strategy worked in that prominent Midwestern and East Coast Peace Democrats cast their lot with McClellan, giving the party some semblance of unanimity. On the other hand, McClellan was stuck with a platform he disliked and a running mate who did not share his views. None of which mattered in the long run. Timely news from Sherman in Atlanta and Phillip Sheridan in the Shenandoah Valley probably sealed the victory for Lincoln. Which brings us full circle: if we accept that the political professionals on both sides of the aisle knew their business, that would indicate that a substantial—quite crucial—portion of antiwar votes were conditional in 1864. A few more months of military disappointments and devastating body counts might have changed the election results.

The president won a substantial victory in the Electoral College, but George McClellan won more than 1.8 million votes. These Democratic votes no doubt included citizens (White men) who believed various things. Any voter who was a committed Copperhead had little choice but to support McClellan or sit out the election. On the other hand, the general promised to bring the war to an honorable conclusion, and he no doubt garnered votes from patriotic War Democrats, including some portion of loyal men in uniform. The labels blur even more. Since so often the term "Copperhead" was applied by political opponents, or later scholars, we are left to mull over the correct label for a voter who was sick of the war and hostile to the administration but who also yearned for an honorable negotiated peace.

In sum, if by "Copperhead" we mean northern voters who wished for a speedy end to the Civil War, it is important to recognize a few key points. First, they followed various routes to that conclusion. They were not a coherent party or even a coherent subset of the Democratic Party. Second, peace sentiments for most rank-and-file voters changed with the passage of time. Some northerners privately hoped for Confederate success, and some concluded early on that the entire enterprise was unconstitutional. Others who wore the Copperhead label honored the flag and supported the men in uniform but at some point lost faith in the war.

That brings us to the cluster of corollary labels that often accompanied the word "Copperhead." When were Copperheads literally traitors? No doubt political opponents sometimes tossed around such terms with abandon, but others were quite serious.[8] And in specific cases they had a good point. At the outset of the war Congress purged a handful of representatives whose loyalties were suspect. In divided communities some civilian women and men aided pro-Confederate guerrillas. In Kentucky Willie Waller—and others like him—enlisted in the Confederacy and then returned to his home state to enlist young men to the rebel cause. These efforts to join or aid the enemy were certainly "disloyal."[9]

In addition to internal warfare on the border, the North witnessed occasional organized actions against government institutions, or failed plots with similar intentions. When Harrison H. Dodd received a shipment of revolvers at his Indianapolis office, he might well have been engaged in the perfectly innocent arming of a local militia group for self-preservation, but when Dodd and his buddies in the Sons of Liberty exchanged letters about plans to free prisoners of war in various locations and otherwise destabilize the government, it is fair to say that they were up to no good. Even if we conclude that these were foolish fantasies constructed by silly men, they were still traitors.[10] The many civilian men and women who resisted the draft through various illegal and sometimes violent means were violating laws, but perhaps not committing treason.[11]

Much like the 1866 provost marshal reports, wartime officials in search of treason focused on leaders who shaped anti-administration public opinion. Copperhead publishers drove public officers and military commanders to distraction with editorials criticizing the administration, pessimistic reports on military developments, and extended commentary about the constitutional horrors perpetrated by Lincoln and his men. There is little indication that the government had a coherent policy to suppress disloyal newspapers, but there were many occasions when officers shut down newspapers for short periods of time, particularly in divided communities (or occupied territory) where active dissent might pose a serious danger.[12] The newspapermen who the government targeted were mostly Copperheads who openly opposed the war, or at least many of the key war measures. It is a greater stretch to call them disloyal or traitors, although editorials questioning conscription—either in theory or in practice—tottered on the edge.

Although freedom of the press did not die during the war, some government decisions also tottered on the edge.[13] Manton Marble used the pages of his *New York World* to batter the Lincoln administration with a steady stream of criticism, but he did not deserve to be tossed in jail in May 1864. In fact, it is not at all clear that Marble was even a Copperhead, much less a traitor. Wilbur Storey's *Chicago Times* was so annoying that the local provost marshal recalled the damage the paper did two years later, but it was a strategic and constitutional error to shut the paper down. Neither Storey nor Marble thought of himself as disloyal, but they both wrote strong editorials to the loyal opposition.

Military officials also worried about disloyal members of the clergy. Here again geography mattered. Clergymen in Kentucky, Missouri, and Maryland faced particular scrutiny. In communities where congregants might have been tempted to abandon the Union cause, it became particularly important for ministers to point their flocks toward the path of patriotism. Most Protestant ministers across the North seemed happy to comply. They delivered sermons supporting the war, encouraging listeners to embrace their civic duty, and commemorating official fast days. They were not coerced. It was a moment when religious belief and patriotic conviction coincided in pulpits across the North. Life became more complicated for ministers who opted for a different path. Some of these men privately, or not entirely privately, supported the Confederate cause. Others had congregations packed with slave owners, and they declined to celebrate emancipation. Another group of unclear size simply refused to let politics of any sort come to their pulpits. Military officials pushed them to sign loyalty oaths and make other proactive public announcements of their patriotism, to mixed success. Quite a few northern ministers ran afoul of military authorities, but it is unclear how many of these men—even if we should call them Copperheads—were guilty of treasonous, or even disloyal, thoughts or actions.

This Civil War record on civil liberties is mixed. Military officials and government authorities periodically used their power to sanction editors or ministers whose loyalty was suspect. Sometimes the actions stand the test of time, and other decisions were abrupt and poorly considered. But any narrative of Copperheads and freedom of speech must consider the power of public opinion and of collective harassment. Editors and ministers who were even suspected of disloyalty risked attacks by congregations. By one reckoning, as many as 111 northern newspapers faced mob violence.[14] When it came to civil liberties, ministers and publishers may have faced greater threats from angry civilians than military officials.[15]

The northern politicians and writers who became known as leading Peace Democrats also followed various paths and came to somewhat different conclusions. Most became actively critical of the Lincoln administration, but after that their profiles diverge. The man most popularly associated with the Copperheads, both during the war and in historic memory, was Clement Vallandigham. But although Vallandigham became the center of a legal battle when General Ambrose Burnside ordered him arrested, his public statements steered clear of treason. In his January 22, 1863, speech to Congress, for instance, Vallandigham offered a lengthy critique of the Lincoln administration's actions that combined to create "the iron domination of arbitrary power," shattering constitutional norms. He declared that the war as a military conflict could not be won, and that it was "a most bloody and costly failure" provoked by radical abolitionists. It was a powerful congressional swan song that attracted substantial attention, but his hostility to the administration did not mean he was disloyal to the nation.[16]

Chauncey Burr and the Men He Admired

We can identify Democrats who were wrongly accused of disloyalty, and others who were Peace Democrats for at least some portion of the war, and politicians at all levels who were clearly disloyal or at least did disloyal things. But it is more difficult to create a coherent portrait of the radical fringe of the Democratic Party. This is where Chauncey Burr comes in handy. The reader met Burr, the conservative editor of *The Old Guard,* in the first pages of this book. Burr was an unapologetic Peace Democrat who opposed Lincoln and abolitionists and the war. He lived and breathed the party slogan "the Union as it was, the Constitution as it is." In his vigorous defense of the Constitution, Burr rejected labels applied by his opponents. "Every true Democrat is a Union man," he insisted. Burr was not a big-tent Democrat. People who called themselves "War Democrats" baffled Burr because they had rejected the party's core positions.[17]

Given his passionate writings, Burr's opinions on his ideological kinfolk are illuminating. *The Old Guard* began regular monthly publication in January 1863. That first number opened with a steel engraving of New York's recently elected governor Horatio Seymour. Over the next two years *The Old Guard* followed a similar pattern, beginning nearly all issues with a portrait of a famous Democrat Burr liked, followed later by a short essay on why the individual had been selected. In 1863 and 1864 nineteen Democratic men won this honor.[18] May 1864 was a bit of an anomaly, with the illustration and essay featuring eighty-eight-year-old Roger Brook Taney. Burr admired Taney's *Dred Scott* decision, but the judge had not really weighed in on wartime politics in quite awhile. The other eighteen provide a glimpse into what Burr thought of his most favored colleagues.

All eighteen Democrats either held political office or had run for a major position: eight had been congressmen, two senators, five governors or candidates for the job. A New Yorker, Burr revealed some inclinations toward his home state, with five members from the Empire State. But those five New Yorkers also reflected the state's relative position in the peace movement. Burr also portrayed four men from New Jersey, five from Ohio, and one each from Pennsylvania, Delaware, Connecticut, and Indiana. Collectively, the eighteen represented a good cross-section of where important Peace Democrats could be found.

Burr sometimes selected men for their strong commitment to the Constitution, regardless of what they had said about peace. Others, particularly by 1864, were deep in the marrow Peace Democrats. Three had run into trouble with federal authorities or would do so. When he was a New Jersey senator early in the war, James Wall had annoyed his Republican colleagues by speaking forcefully against the war. Soon he found himself tossed into New York's Fort Lafayette. Ohio Democratic congressman Edson B. Olds had a similar history. In August 1862 he delivered an antiwar speech that led authorities to arrest him for discouraging enlistments. He also ended up spending four months in Fort Lafayette.[19] Burr devoted considerable space in his February 1863 issue to Clement Vallandigham, who had recently outraged Congress with his anti-administration parting shot to his colleagues. Burr praised the Ohio congressman's positions and added that "if his doctrines are treasonous, then the platform of every democratic convention has been treasonous."[20]

On several occasions Burr singled out politicians whose commitment to the Constitution pleased him, even while they were early in their public careers. New Jersey's Joel Parker was only thirty-five when he was elected as the state's Democratic governor. Burr was particularly happy with Parker's inaugural address and its strong words defending the Constitution and challenging the administration. Indiana congressman Daniel W. Voorhees, who began representing the 7th District when he was thirty-three, earned similar praise for both his youth and for demonstrating "the classic style of Burke."[21] Sometimes Burr's favorites disappointed him. In early 1864, after several governors delivered their annual addresses, *The Old Guard* ran an extended critique of Democratic governors Horatio Seymour of New York and Joel Parker of New Jersey. Both governors had demonstrated an appropriate fealty to the Constitution, and a proper hostility to Abraham Lincoln, but they had revealed themselves to be War Democrats. Burr found this astonishing and ideologically incoherent. He accused Parker of "self-stultification" for his contradictory beliefs.[22] The following month Burr, enamored with the word, wrote an essay on "Democratic Stultification." It followed old themes, where the core point was that true sovereignty rested with the individual states, and that there could not be "Union without Liberty." In a familiar attempt to reclaim key words from the Republican Party, Burr declared, "Let Democracy, and Liberty, and the Union live!" Just not on abolitionist terms. The problem for Burr was that too many leading Democrats failed to grasp the fundamental constitutional flaw in backing the war.[23]

Burr also praised right-thinking conservatives, even when they were not peace men. In a particularly long essay about Pennsylvanian George Woodward and his campaign for governor, Burr applauded the judge for his constitutional principles and his insistence on using only constitutional means to subdue the rebellion, but the editor stopped short of claiming Woodward as a Peace Democrat.[24] *The Old Guard* featured Ohio congressman Sunset Cox, who had an impressive history for firing rhetorical salvoes at the Lincoln administration, but Burr acknowledged that Cox called himself "a war Democrat," "most unaccountably to us."[25]

Others of the eighteen featured men earned explicit praise for being true peace men. New York's Fernando Wood, who found the whole conflict "madness and criminal," earned Burr's praise as an early proponent of peace.[26] A few months later *The Old Guard* profiled Wood's brother, New York editor and congressman Benjamin Wood, a long-term advocate of peace.[27] In the summer of 1864 Ohio congressman Alexander Long attracted Burr's attention for giving a widely discussed antiwar speech in Congress.[28] Connecticut ex-governor Thomas Seymour won Burr's most profuse praise. In February 1864, when Burr still had hopes for his party in the presidential election, *The Old Guard* featured Seymour as an "unflinching and unswerving Democrat" who had always opposed radical abolitionism. Burr suggested that a presidential pairing of Seymour and Vallandigham would be just the ticket.[29] Here were two giants in the Peace Democrat universe. They would protect the "Union as it was" as well as "the Constitution as it is." And that was a Union where the individual states, even the slave-holding ones, enjoyed constitutional autonomy. And it was a society grounded in "White supremacy."

Chauncey Burr's writings give us a window into the extreme conservative wing of the Democratic Party.[30] They all revered the Constitution, as they saw it, and they each pleased Burr by speaking ill of Abraham Lincoln. Quite a few solidified their identities as true peace men (Burr did not use the label "Copperhead"), but others with strong conservative credentials disappointed the angry editor. This group, like most in their party, abhorred radical abolitionism as a destructive political force that had produced the war and a host of other problems. Quite a few openly embraced a radical racism, and no doubt many of the others would have signed on for a party devoted explicitly to "white supremacy."[31] Yet most explicitly endorsed an 1864 candidate who rejected the party's peace plank, and a platform that said nothing about slavery or race.

On Race, Slavery, Emancipation, and Politics

When we talk about race and politics we tend to conflate words with distinct meanings, such as "bias," "stereotype," "prejudice," "racist," and "institutional racism." In the simplest terms, we can ask how people perceive racial differences, what they think about human capacities and race, what they believe about interracial interactions, and how might rules and laws respond to racial differences. This section does not attempt to explain what northern Democrats thought about racial differences, and it certainly does not pretend to defend them for their beliefs, which were in many cases quite disturbing. It is not really the goal here to offer moral assessments, or to demonstrate my capacity for moral outrage at historic actors. But I do hope to offer some thoughts on what these Democrats said about race and emancipation, particularly as a political issue.

We have seen that quite a few Democratic newspapers across the North loved to print horribly racist stories about African Americans committing all sorts of outrageous misdeeds.[32] A good story might be reprinted in a host of newspapers. Some Democratic songbooks included similarly anti-Black messages. The false pamphlet *Miscegenation* and the widely discussed lithograph "The Miscegenation Ball" probably hold a more important place in our historic memory than they did at the time of their production, but they do illustrate a crucial point. Both the pamphlet and the image played on the false charge that Republicans hoped for a real interracial society, with complete intermingling of the sexes. The claim was untrue, and it is unlikely that many northern White voters believed it to be literally the case, but the specter of free Blacks moving into White communities proved politically potent.

White voters in northern free states had little personal experience with African Americans, yet many had internalized massive prejudices about Blacks and overwrought fears about a post-emancipation world. Although most Whites beyond the slave-owning border states of the lower North rarely interacted with African Americans, they still embraced huge prejudices. They lived in a world where popular culture included a wealth of satirical images and stereotypes, demeaning Blacks individually and collectively. Long before the war, minstrel shows—with their stock Black characters—had become a mainstay in popular culture aimed at mass audiences.[33]

The intersection between racism and politics presents a conundrum when we consider the antebellum northern Democrats and the patterns they had established before the war destabilized their worlds. Certainly the party's political leaders understood the racist tropes that would appeal to some in the rank and file. They used language and imagery that called to mind those minstrel shows and familiar characters. Racial prejudice regularly found its way into antebellum political language.[34] In terms of laws and national public policy debates, much of the political heat followed debates over the future of slavery in the federal territories and in newly created western states. A large portion of White southern Democrats had been adamant about defending their claimed right to move enslaved people into newly occupied federal lands. Northern Democrats split on the issue, and some portion ended up gravitating to the newly formed Republican Party. For other Democrats, "popular sovereignty"—the policy that would allow newly formed states to solve the slavery riddle for themselves—constituted an appealing route out of a thorny political thicket, with Stephen Douglas as the great architect of the Kansas-Nebraska Act of 1854. But that was a political debate about unfree Black labor, sometimes opposed by voters who hated the institution of slavery while also wanting to block the migration of free Blacks. A decade earlier, in the early 1840s, Henry Clay—the Kentucky Whig who would become a subject of Democratic iconography two decades later—laid down important markers about race, as opposed to slavery, in the territories. Clay warned that radical abolitionists who had emerged in the North in the 1830s and 1840s threatened the tranquility of northern and western society by encouraging the wholesale movement of newly freed people into their White communities. Clay's argument was about the implications of emancipation, and it would prove useful to northern Democrats once war broke out.

One careful study of Democratic newspapers published between the Kansas-Nebraska Act and the 1860 election complicates the analysis. While these newspapers printed deeply prejudiced racial language, when it came to the crucial political issues of the day the analysis was rarely driven by race. In engaging with politics and policy, these antebellum Democrats rarely assessed issues through the lens of race, even when those issues involved the future of Kansas or the aftermath of John Brown's 1859 raid. Instead, these northern Democrats—in keeping with the party's long traditions—looked at those disruptive issues as threats to order and stability.[35]

During the war small numbers of runaway slaves and contrabands migrated to the almost all-White agricultural communities in the Upper Midwest. They arrived on their own or with the assistance of Union troops. Although this had been strong Lincoln territory in 1860, the local residents did not initially open their arms to the new arrivals. Instead they saw the Black newcomers as a threat to racial hegemony as well as jobs. Eventually, and aided by the realization that the communities needed new laborers, things settled into some sort of rapprochement. But such developments took time.[36]

For those White northerners who remained isolated from free Black human beings, the war culture continued with expanded images of African Americans. The two most popular national weeklies, *Harper's* and *Frank Leslie's,* peppered their audiences with commentary and images with racial content. Both periodicals were prowar and ostensibly nonpartisan, doing their best to reach large northern audiences. They celebrated the arming of Black recruits and praised the valor of the United States Colored Troops in the field, and Black contributions as noncombatants. Occasionally they remarked on the challenges faced by African American contrabands. In various senses these national weeklies endorsed the racial progress that accompanied the Civil War, but that did not stop them from publishing racist language and stereotypes and cartoons thick with bigoted imagery. Such talk permeated many levels of northern popular culture.[37] But even those images portrayed Blacks as a distant "other," swept up in the war's grand narrative. Novels and short stories published in the North about northern society rarely included African American characters, and even the wartime satirical cartoons included few images of northern Blacks. African Americans were, after all, largely a part of a distant world for most northern Whites.[38]

At the other end of the popular culture spectrum, northern readers found John H. Van Evrie. Van Evrie, a rabid racist, published the *New York Day-Book* and authored various publications printed at the *Day-Book* offices. After its first year of publication, Van Evrie's printing presses produced Chauncey Burr's *The Old Guard.* Van Evrie is credited with being one of the first public advocates of the term "White supremacy," and one historian has argued that "no individual contributed more to racism in United States history."[39] Van Evrie's publications are commonly linked to the Democratic Party, but although rank-and-file Democrats no doubt absorbed his racist contributions to northern popular culture, party regulars explicitly distanced themselves from the man and his message.[40]

In their personal writings, the northern Democrats examined here varied greatly in how they expressed racial prejudices, although it seems fair to assume that they all would have shared core assumptions about Black Americans. A few, including Philadelphia printer John L. Smith and Illinois soldier William Standard, sometimes dripped with racist venom in their writings. Others, like the Wallers of Kentucky and the Hales of Tennessee, wrote with almost saccharine paternalism about slave men and women while indicating little sense of what the Black people they wrote about believed or wished. Others still, particularly several diarists and correspondents in Kentucky, worried about the implications of racial changes in their midst, and of the presence of Black armed soldiers patrolling their communities. Diarist Maria Lydig Daly wrote little about race, yet she periodically acknowledged her deep distaste for Black northerners. In many of the diaries and letters examined here, the notion of slavery did not appear in discussions as a human experience or even a moral issue. Slavery appeared as a political issue when diarists attacked those "radical abolitionists"—as individuals or as a party—who had destabilized the Union and provoked civil war.

Democrats Talk about Slavery and Emancipation

Throughout this volume readers have encountered Democrats speaking and writing about political contests or broad political issues. Their public words tell us something about what they thought, and also about the issues and arguments they wished to bring to Democratic voters or to their colleagues. The topics they chose and the arguments they made are a valuable window into what they thought about race and politics. Here we shall return to some of our key public characters.

Stephen Douglas hovered over much of this book's first chapters. Long before the election of 1860, the senator from Chicago had established his reputation as an advocate of "popular sovereignty." The Illinoian cared deeply about the Union and national expansion and partisan politics. He embraced his own brand of racism, making it clear in his writings that he felt Blacks were inherently inferior to Whites. If he cared about the morality of slavery, that was not a major driving force. For Douglas the future of slavery in the territories was as much as anything a political obstacle to navigate.[41] At his passing, northern Democrats recalled Douglas as a great defender of the Union, rather than as a man who either supported or decried slavery.

When Douglas died six weeks after the firing on Fort Sumter, much of the nation mourned, and John W. Forney eulogized the fallen Democrat as "preeminently and always a national man." Only four days earlier Joseph Holt—another nationalist—wrote his public letter laying out the case for remaining unambiguously in the Union. Holt attempted to convince Kentucky slave owners that it was their best bet to support the federal government. Despite northern abolitionist rhetoric, the reality was that the national laws and judiciary promised the best protection of the peculiar institution. Holt's letter spoke to White citizens about practical matters of politics and power. A slaveholder who would personally wrestle with the institution and finally become a strong abolitionist, on this day Holt had nothing to say about the moral issues behind the conflict.[42]

In early March the following year, one-term congressman Charles J. Biddle rose to speak to his colleagues on "The Alliance with the Negro." A military veteran, Biddle supported the war, but he was worried about what he saw as revolutionary measures that had enhanced the civil liberties of northern free Blacks and promised to arm African Americans. Biddle insisted that he had "never been blind to the disadvantages and evils of slavery," but he worried about the radical changes he witnessed that he felt circumvented constitutional law. Despite his comments about the immorality of slavery, Biddle made a political argument to his politician audience. Congress should not tamper with constitutional issues, and neither the federal government nor the U.S. Army should be tasked with freeing slaves without appropriate process. In the end Biddle said little about slavery and race and much about a conservative reading of political rules.[43]

As Biddle was articulating the strongly conservative ideas of an elected War Democrat, Philadelphian Charles Ingersoll was penning and publishing his

Letter to a Friend in a Slave State. Undeterred by formal partisan concerns, Ingersoll presented his unapologetic Copperhead "letter" in fifty-six meandering pages. He blamed the war on abolitionist agitators and declared that he saw no military end in sight. "Emancipation is a word which sounds to virtue," he wrote, "for who can doubt that slavery is a blight to any region in which it is tolerated?" Still, Ingersoll pointed out that the northern states would resist any idea of emancipated freed people pouring onto their soil. The only solution would be a peaceful settlement leaving southern institutions undisturbed.[44]

A few months after Biddle spoke before Congress, radical Ohio congressman Sunset Cox spoke on "Emancipation and Its Results—Is Ohio to Be Africanized." Like Biddle, Cox objected to the legislative progress congressional Republicans had been making on Black rights, and he worried about the direction things were taking. Grounding his argument in geographic concerns, Cox painted a picture of members "of the black race by millions" heading for Ohio (whose African American population numbered 1.6% in 1860).[45]

When Edward G. Ryan delivered his "Address to the People of the Democracy of Wisconsin" in September 1862 he spoke for Wisconsin Democrats, but the address laid out a strong set of national party principles on the eve of Lincoln's proclamation. On slavery, Ryan declared, "We regard it as a great social evil. But we regard it as a misfortune, and not a crime." Or, more precisely, the blame for slavery rested with previous generations who introduced the "social evil" to the colonies. And thus Ryan argued that slavery as an institution was in effect settled law, and only constitutional measures could change that. In the meantime, radical abolitionists were responsible for creating the national crisis by insisting on seeing slavery as an "abstraction," rather than a constitutional issue.[46]

A year and a half into the war, the conservative Democratic political positions on slavery seemed clear: slavery was a regrettable "misfortune" in the nation, but one that existed protected by laws. The radical abolitionists deserved most of the blame for the Civil War because they had destabilized the nation by posing a threat to the southern slaveocracy. And, these conservative voices insisted, if the nation wished to abandon slavery there were constitutional routes available. It remained to be seen how Democrats across their party spectrum would respond once emancipation became federal law.

When outgoing congressman Clement Vallandigham spoke on January 14, 1863, two weeks after the Emancipation Proclamation, he had much to denounce. Vallandigham broke with moderate Democrats in insisting that slavery was a fine system of labor for the southern states and "perfectly compatible with the dignity of free white labor in the same community." He saw outrageous hypocrisy in northern radicals stressing the "sin and barbarism of African slavery" while ignoring the ongoing damage that the war was doing to the United States. For Vallandigham, the political battle was absolute, and the enemies were northern fanatics who threatened to destroy the nation.[47]

Bishop John H. Hopkins plays a distinctive role in this narrative. He first published his thoughts on the *Bible View of Slavery* shortly after Lincoln's election. His words included an extended scriptural argument that the Bible did not prohibit slavery. The group of moderate Democrats who arranged to reprint the Bishop's revised pamphlet in April 1863 simply wanted a clear public statement providing spiritual cover to their political stance that it was fine to be indifferent to slavery as a moral issue.[48] They welcomed a bold statement that would help make the issue go away.[49]

That May, Chicago's Democratic mayor Francis Sherman delivered his inaugural address after a hotly contested election. Sherman had much to say about municipal matters, but he ended his remarks with nearly eight hundred words on "national affairs." He defended himself against charges of disloyalty and explained the Democratic critique against the administration on various constitutional points, insisting that the party's dissent represented ideological purity rather than treasonous talk. Four months after the Emancipation Proclamation, the careful Democrat did not utter the words "slavery" or "emancipation," or say anything that suggested that those issues were a part of national affairs.[50]

The following month, when Pennsylvania Democrats met in their state convention, they passed a series of resolutions on a host of topics, generally disagreeing with Republican practices while also insisting on the party's overall loyalty. One numbered resolution objected to the notion of *compensated* emancipation, because of its feared strain on the federal treasury. Another noted "the encroachments of the abolitionists" on national affairs, while another referred to the dangers of the "ultra abolitionists." Here again these political actors in mid-1863 steered clear of any commentary on the morality of slavery, or even the propriety of the Emancipation Proclamation.[51]

By 1864 the Emancipation Proclamation had been in place for a year, and Democrats had developed multiple responses. Emma Webb, unlike most of her antiwar contemporaries, reminded her audience of the physical horrors of all sorts of warfare. On slavery she also adopted a distinctive path. Claiming some personal experience witnessing the institution, Webb insisted that "slavery is the normal condition of the negro," and that emancipation would not only hurt them but threaten White working men. Once again, the crux of the

Copperhead argument turned on the unsettling implications of southern emancipation for northern White workers.[52]

Maryland's Senator Reverdy Johnson considered emancipation differently. The moderate border-state politician favored the proposed constitutional amendment ending slavery. He had concluded that the peculiar institution could only be ended by a constitutional amendment, and he supported such a move as a morally correct measure and as the only way to achieve a lasting peace.[53] On these last points Johnson's speech sounded a bit like Robert Dale Owen's message to Indiana Democrats a year earlier. Owen had also become increasingly antislavery in his own thoughts, but on that day he argued that the best path to peace would be a complete end to slavery for broader practical reasons.

By the middle of 1864 Democratic insiders had come to accept the Emancipation Proclamation for practical reasons, even while many continued to worry about freed Blacks entering their nearly all-White societies. Some, such as Owens and Johnson, had concluded that lasting peace and moral law depended on the permanent end of slavery across the United States. But there was still a presidential election to be contested, and here the political messages about emancipation were not so bold.

Even before he was nominated, George McClellan had worked hard to sculpt a political identity by reprinting various letters and speeches. His official message was that the war must be fought to preserve the Union, and not with emancipation as a goal. When the Democrats met in Chicago and nominated McClellan, they passed a platform that famously criticized the progress of the war and called for peace. But that platform spoke with equal clarity in saying nothing at all about slavery or emancipation. Most voters quickly understood that the candidate was not in the pocket of the Peace Democrats and would only pursue an honorable end to the conflict. But they also recognized that the Democratic Party was not the party of emancipation.

When Robert C. Winthrop, the one-time cotton Whig, spoke for McClellan's candidacy, he brought a message of patriotism and Union. Looking to the future, Winthrop explained that McClellan promised a just "restoration" of the Union, rather than some sort of radical "reconstruction." Abraham Lincoln, in contrast, had cast himself as "the great Liberator of the African race." The conservative Winthrop acknowledged that those were morally worthy goals, but they stood in the way of a rapid return to peace and Union.[54]

This was the ground on which the political battle would be fought. Some moderates—in both parties—who ultimately supported Lincoln agreed that lasting peace and Union required the end of slavery. Any negotiated peace that allowed the southern states to keep their slaves would just invite a new round of conflicts in the decades to come. Many appeals to Democratic voters turned on the argument that the Confederate states would fight harder and longer if emancipation was the price of peace. Better to elect a new president whose commitment was to victory and Union, and not to ending slavery.

With Abraham Lincoln's victory, and the military handwriting on the wall, enough Democrats in Congress agreed to support the 13th Amendment that it finally passed, sending the amendment to the states for ratification. It was hardly a moment of ideological transformation for the party, but it appeared to be a victory for political pragmatism.

Prior to 1860 the Democratic Party was the party whose powerful southern members supported the expansion of slavery into the territories, and that periodically acted to buttress the peculiar institution against antislavery threats. During the Civil War it is difficult to prove, but easy to imagine, what northern Democrats—both leaders and the rank and file—said about race in their private conversations. What assumptions did they make? What words did they use? It is a fair bet that modern readers would find the personal thoughts of most White northerners in 1860 pretty appalling, and perhaps those Democrats were the more appalling. It is also likely that in the nearly all-White swaths of the North, powerful racial prejudices existed and were rarely contemplated in daily life.

If we restrict ourselves to these public political messages from northern Democrats (as opposed to their private chats at their clubs and salons), the messages fall into clear patterns. Most had nothing to say about the morality of slavery as an institution and a human experience. Those who did mention the topic generally acknowledged the fundamental evils of slavery while quickly turning to practical matters. Some took a more extreme stand, defending slavery on economic or spiritual grounds. But true Democratic politicians preferred to focus on the practical terrain, while perhaps catering to the racial prejudices of the electorate.

In the first years of the war these Democrats focused on northern abolitionist extremists, rather than on southern enslaved people. They argued, again and again, that regardless of the moral failings of southern slaveholders, the true villains were those abolitionists. Some were willing to paint Lincoln as a moderate—perhaps even a conservative—under the sway of radicals in his own party. Later, as talk of emancipation grew, northern Democrats spoke more of the dangers of emancipation to their White constituents. Feeding on the rising talk of "miscegenation" and recalling the warnings from Henry Clay decades earlier, they embraced the political argument that the freeing of slaves in the South would be bad for the lives of White northern voters.

When it came to slavery and the legal status of African Americans, the ground shifted quite rapidly from 1860 to 1865, and then to 1872 and beyond. Conservative northern Democrats resisted change at each step along the way. In their political statements they declined to engage with discussions of morality and racial justice, except when they paid lip service to the central point that the system of slavery that had long existed was a moral evil inherited from previous generations. In the simplest terms, these conservatives resisted change. The Democrats saw themselves as a party of grand longevity that transcended the immediate issues concerning slavery or emancipation. Some felt personal loyalties to the southern states and their White residents, while others claimed a loyalty to a Constitution as it was, which respected the rights of individual states. Most, rather like Stephen Douglas, saw the slave issue as a political nuisance to be circumnavigated, as opposed to a grand moral dilemma that required equally grand national debate.

Northern Democrats were on the wrong side of history again and again. Some opposed the war that would save the Union, either at the outset of the conflict or years later. Others accepted the Civil War as patriotic War Democrats, but they objected to a whole series of measures pursued by Lincoln or passed by a Republican legislature to fight that war. They were constitutional conservatives in a moment of rapid change. Perhaps a few were really "disloyal" to the United States, but many more were like Chauncey Burr, feeling a passionate loyalty to what they saw as a "Union as it is, and a Constitution as it was."

The Civil War—which began as a war to defend the Union—eventually became a war for emancipation as well as Union. Here again the Democrats placed themselves on the wrong side of history. They were no doubt racist men and women, perhaps more so than their Republican opponents. Certainly an important slice of Democratic newspapers embraced racist tropes as part of their common language, infecting readers with a barrage of racial stereotypes and distortions. But as political partisans and ideological conservatives, the party leaders skirted large moral questions to resist the process of change on limited, practical, political terms.

Clement Vallandigham holds a particular place in our collective memory as the widely recognized voice for the fundamentally racist, passionately anti-Lincoln wing of the northern Democrats. It is perhaps significant, or at least metaphorical, that in June 1871—only days before he accidentally shot himself in the gut—Vallandigham was pitching his "New Departure" to Ohio Democrats. Five years after the war's end, the one-time Copperhead argued that the national Democratic Party should end its policy of resistance and embrace all the postwar constitutional amendments protecting the rights of freed people. And they should do whatever they could to convince southern freed men that these newly enfranchised voters should join the Democratic Party in the future. Whatever else he was, Clement Vallandigham could read the political landscape and come to a practical, perhaps politically viable decision, apparently undeterred by the irony and pathos of the moment.

NOTES

Introduction

1. Note that "casualties" refers to the dead, wounded, and missing.

2. Gallagher and Waugh, *The American War,* 118–25; Varon, *Armies of Deliverance,* 168–78, 210–15. I consider the conscription legislation and other events later in the text.

3. "Racist" and "racism" are words that are almost automatically "presentist," in that today's Americans would see nearly all Civil War–era Americans as more or less "racist." I use the term occasionally to describe individuals or publications that were particularly egregious in their language about race. Later in this volume I have more to say about what the northern Democrats thought about race.

4. *The Old Guard* (1863–65); George, "'Abraham Africanus I'"; Mott, *A History of American Magazines,* 544–46; Longdon and Lore, *The Conservative Press in Eighteenth and Nineteenth-Century America,* 73–79.

5. *The Old Guard* 1 (July 1863): 154.

6. *The Old Guard* 1 (August 1863): 214.

7. Fuller, *Oliver Morton and the Politics of the Civil War and Reconstruction,* 78–79; Dell, *Lincoln and the War Democrats,* 201 and *passim.*

8. Jane Standard to William Standard, February 12, 1863, in Roberts, *"This Infernal War,"* 71.

9. Knupfer, *Union as It Is,* esp. 211.

10. Bogue, *The Congressman's Civil War,* 65. Bogue concluded that Vallandigham shared that title with New York's Benjamin Wood.

11. *Congressional Globe,* House of Representatives, 37th Congress, 3rd Session, December 5, 1862, p. 15; December 4, 1862, p. 12; December 16, 1862, p. 80.

12. *Cadiz Democratic Sentinel,* September 18, 1861; *Democratic Press,* April 3, 1862; *Holmes County Farmer,* June 5, 1862.

13. *Democratic Press,* September 4, 1862; *Holmes County Farmer,* August 20, 1863.

14. *Muscatine Weekly Journal,* February 20, 27, 1863.

15. Williams, *Letter to A.B.J.* Williams published his twenty-five-page pamphlet with his initials and dated his letter March 1863. A.B.J. was Utica banker Alexander Bryan Johnson. His original pamphlet was A.B.J., *The Union as It Was and the Constitution as It Is* (N.p., 1862). I have not seen the Johnson pamphlet and have no idea who read either.

16. Hays, *The Constitution as It Is, the Union as It Was.* The historian Jennifer L. Weber notes that New Yorker Horatio Seymour coined the slogan for his gubernatorial campaign in late 1862. And she points out that "The Union as It Was, the Constitution as It

Is" became the rallying cry of conservative Democrats throughout the war. She also notes that wartime Peace Democrats, or "Copperheads," adopted the slogan. But it is perhaps worth noting that all conservative northern Democrats, including Seymour, were not really Peace Democrats and certainly not Copperheads. Weber, *Copperheads,* 60, 6.

17. Gallagher, *The Union War,* 42–44.

18. Needless to say, when dissent turned to outright treason or simply outrageous rhetoric, party regulars sometimes disavowed the worst offenders.

19. Varon, *Armies of Deliverance,* 9.

20. I have selected the individuals and episodes that comprise this assortment of case studies based on stories that interest me and that I hope will be of interest to readers. I have not attempted to be comprehensive, but I have tried to convey the ideological, geographic, and experiential diversity that collectively says something about wartime Democrats. Some will be familiar, at least to the experts. I hope others will be new.

21. The notes mention the sources for particular claims, but I have not attempted to produce comprehensive notes on the important scholarship on each topic.

22. The timeline only includes moments that figure prominently in this book.

23. I do not venture into those battles.

1. A Political Collapse

1. For a recent overview of the election of 1860 and the events that preceded it, see Holt, *The Election of 1860.* On conservative Democrats and the election, see Smith, *The Stormy Present,* 134–65. On the election and the significance of the Democrats' ties to the South, see Landis, *Northern Men with Southern Loyalties,* 236–43. A valuable, brief overview of these events can be found in Gallagher and Waugh, *The American War,* 5–20. On the complex historiography on realignment and the election of 1860, see Smith, "Beyond the Realignment Synthesis."

2. Baker, *Affairs of Party,* 145. Jean H. Baker offers a superb portrait of the northern Democrats and their thoughts. Baker's quote actually ends with "Unionism based on a white man's government." For an excellent analysis of these decades, see Howe, *What Hath God Wrought.* For recent essays that dissect politics in the period, see Adams, *A Companion to the Era of Andrew Jackson,* especially the essays by Thomas Coens, Sharon Ann Murphy, John M. Sacher, Nancy Morgan, and Frank Towers. For a historiographic overview that notes the interpretive limitations of the "second party system" framework, see Towers, "Party Politics and the Sectional Crisis."

3. For a recent treatment of the Democrats and Kansas, see Smith, *The Stormy Present,* 68–99. The standard biography of Stephen Douglas is Johannsen, *Stephen A. Douglas.* In 2006 Johannsen's students published a fine festschrift that, not surprisingly, includes multiple perspective on Douglas. See McDonough and Noe, *Politics and Culture of the Civil War Era,* particularly the contributions by John Hoffman, James L. Huston, and Willard Carl Klunder. On Douglas's thoughts on race, see Baker, *Affairs*

of Party, 177–96. For an excellent recent discussion, see Crofts, *Lincoln and the Politics of Slavery,* 50–51.

4. Medford, *Lincoln and Emancipation,* 14–16.

5. Political historians note that even while party identities and affiliations were in flux in mid-decade, partisan politics was already easing into a new "Civil War party system" with hardened party loyalties that emerged early in the war and remained for a decade after Appomattox. See Baum, *The Civil War Party System,* 8–17.

6. For Abraham Lincoln and slavery, see Foner, *The Fiery Trial.*

7. Barlow's correspondence is housed in the Samuel L. M. Barlow Papers at the Huntington Library, San Marino, California (hereafter HL).

8. See Holt, *Election of 1860,* 49 and *passim.*

9. Samuel Butterworth to Samuel Barlow, February 14, 1860, Barlow Papers, HL.

10. Lewis Baldwin Parsons to Samuel Barlow, February 22, 1860, Barlow Papers, HL.

11. William Montague Brown to Samuel Barlow, May 14, 1860, Barlow Papers, HL.

12. Horatio Seymour to Samuel Barlow, May 15, 1860, Barlow Papers, HL. Seymour would go on to be reelected governor.

13. Samuel Butterworth to Samuel Barlow, June 22, 1860, Barlow Papers, HL.

14. Smith, *The Stormy Present,* 147–55.

15. Jesse David Bright to Samuel Barlow, July 14, 19, 1860, Barlow Papers, HL.

16. Douglas Brown to Samuel Barlow, June 29, 1860, Barlow Papers, HL. See also June 29 (2nd letter), July 1, 3, 1860. Brown would go on to move to Georgia, where he would serve as Jefferson Davis's assistant secretary of state.

17. Samuel A. Bridges to Lewis S. Coryell, July 7, 1860, Lewis S. Coryell Papers, Historical Society of Pennsylvania, Philadelphia (hereafter HSP).

18. Baum, *The Civil War Party System,* 49–50.

19. Cowden, *"Heaven Will Frown on Such a Cause as This,"* 37.

20. John Slidell to Samuel Barlow, September 11, 1860, Barlow Papers, HL. A month later Slidell lost what faith he had had in the fusion ticket. See Slidell to Barlow, October 17, 1860, Barlow Papers, HL.

21. John Stuyker to Samuel Barlow, September 10, 1860, Barlow Papers, HL.

22. James Tophan Brady to Samuel Barlow, September 24, 1860, Barlow Papers, HL.

23. James Asheton Bayard to Samuel Barlow, October 4, 1860, Barlow Papers, HL. For the emergence of fusion tickets, especially in New York, New Jersey, and Pennsylvania, see Holt, *Election of 1860,* 152–53, 170–73, and Furniss, "States of the Union," 47–48, 54. On Bayard, see Cowden, *"Heaven Will Frown on Such a Cause as This,"* 67–93.

24. Spann, *Gotham at War,* 3–4.

25. James Buchanan to Lewis Coryell, September 26, 1860, Coryell Papers, HSP. On Buchanan's hostility to Douglas, see Holt, *Election of 1860,* 37–38 and *passim.*

26. Benjamin Penhallow Shillabar to Charles Graham Halpine, October 1, 1860, Charles Graham Halpine Papers, HL. Of course "rail splitter" refers to Abraham Lincoln.

27. Samuel A. Bridges to Lewis S. Coryell, October 18, 1860, Coryell Papers, HSP.

28. Henry Waller to Sarah B. Waller, September 28, October 7, 1860; Sarah B. Waller to Henry Waller, October 4, 14, 1860, Henry Waller Papers, HL. The couple were temporarily separated because they were in the process of moving to Chicago, and Sarah remained in Kentucky preparing their homestead for the move.

29. See Holt, *Election of 1860,* 152–53, 173, 194. Holt offers a brief explanation of the New Jersey voting on pages 173 and 230n17, and he refers the reader to the great political historian Walter Dean Burnham, *Presidential Ballots,* 933, for further details. On Pennsylvania, see also Pflug, "Pennsylvania Politics," 148.

30. Smith, *The Stormy Present,* 165.

31. Silbey, *A Respectable Minority,* 19.

32. For the southern secession debates, see Dew, *Apostles of Disunion.*

33. Henry Douglas Bacon to Samuel Barlow, November 2, 7, 1860, Barlow Papers, HL.

34. Furniss, "States of the Union," 27, citing Samuel Barlow to James Asheton Bayard, October 22, 1860, Barlow Papers, HL.

35. William Montague Browne to Samuel Barlow, November 18, 1860, Barlow Papers, HL.

36. William Montague Browne to Samuel Barlow, November 22, 1860, Barlow Papers, HL.

37. James Asheton Bayard to Samuel Barlow, November 29, 1860, Barlow Papers, HL. See Cowden, *"Heaven Will Frown on Such a Cause as This,"* 73–74.

38. *Sunday Dispatch,* December 16, 1860.

39. McPherson, *Battle Cry of Freedom,* 235, 246, and *passim.*

40. Samuel Barlow to George B. McClellan, December 6, 1860, quoted in McPherson, *Battle Cry of Freedom,* 247.

41. Judah P. Benjamin to Samuel Barlow, December 9, 1860, Barlow Papers, HL.

42. John B. Cochrane to Samuel Barlow, December 13, 1860, Barlow Papers, HL.

43. James Asheton Bayard to Samuel Barlow, December 18, 1860, Barlow Papers, HL.

44. See Freehling, *The Road to Disunion,* 470–75, and McPherson, *Battle Cry of Freedom,* 252–54.

45. William Montague Browne to Samuel Barlow, December 10, 1860, Barlow Papers, HL.

46. Henry Douglas Bacon to Samuel Barlow, January 12, 17, 1861, Barlow Papers, HL.

47. Judah P. Benjamin to Samuel Barlow, January 19, 1861, Barlow Papers, HL.

48. Henry Douglas Bacon to Samuel Barlow, February 27, 1861, Barlow Papers, HL.

49. Spann, *Gotham at War,* 5–6.

50. William Edward Dorsheimer to Isaac Sherman, December 29, 1860, Isaac Sherman Papers, HL.

51. John L. Smith Diary, January 5, 1861, HSP. As is discussed later, this is almost certainly not his actual name.

52. Shankman, *The Pennsylvania Antiwar Movement,* 47. Shankman's notes list several Pennsylvania newspapers but do not identify this quotation.

53. *Sunday Dispatch,* January 20, 27, 1861; Shankman, *The Pennsylvania Antislavery Movement,* 47.

54. Gallman, *Mastering Wartime,* 85–87; *North American,* February 19–23, 1861. Gallman cites the *Public Ledger,* February 21, 22, 23, 25, 1861, and George, "Philadelphians Greet Their President-Elect."

55. Gallman, *Mastering Wartime,* 86; *North American,* February 18, 23, 25, 1861.

56. Spann, *Gotham at War,* 2, quoting *New York Freeman's Journal,* October 6, 1860.

57. Crofts, *Lincoln and the Politics of Slavery,* 9. All of that which follows comes directly from Crofts's marvelous book on the amendment.

58. The fundamental point that hugely important constitutional amendments have generally been the product of much internal debate and compromise should not come as a surprise. For a study of the three postwar amendments, the 13th, 14th, and 15th, see Foner, *The Second Founding.*

59. Thomas Corwin to Abraham Lincoln, January 16, 1861, Abraham Lincoln Papers, Library of Congress, Washington, D.C., quoted in Crofts, *Lincoln and the Politics of Slavery,* 40.

60. For vote totals, see Crofts, *Lincoln and the Politics of Slavery,* 217.

61. Crofts, *Lincoln and the Politics of Slavery,* 11.

62. See Gallagher, *The Union War.*

63. Crofts, *Lincoln and the Politics of Slavery,* 101, quoting *Congressional Globe,* House of Representatives, 36th Congress, 2nd Session, January 14, 1861, p. 374.

64. Crofts, *Lincoln and the Politics of Slavery,* 4, 288n6.

65. Crofts, *Lincoln and the Politics of Slavery,* 6; Abraham Lincoln, First Inaugural Address.

2. Stumbling into War

1. Daly, *Diary of a Union Lady,* 12.

2. *Daily Journal,* April 18, 1861.

3. Neely, "The Civil War and the Two-Party System," 88.

4. Baum, *The Civil War Party System,* 58.

5. Robert Underwood Johnson and Clarence Clough Buel, eds., *Battles and Leaders of the Civil War,* 4 vols. (New York: Century, 1887), 1:85, quoted in Holzer, *Lincoln and the Power of the Press,* 301.

6. *Delaware Gazette,* April 19, 1861; *Burlington Free Press,* April 19, 1861; *Bellows Falls Times,* April 19, 1861; Holzer, *Lincoln and the Power of the Press,* 301.

7. Strong, *The Diary of George Templeton Strong,* 3:187; Holzer, *Lincoln and the Power of the Press,* 301–3; Neely, "The Civil War and the Two-Party System," 88; Spann,

Gotham at War, 14–15. The phrase "No Party Now" became a rallying cry for the North's Union Leagues as they did battle with the Democratic Party.

8. *North American,* April 15, 1861 (two stories); *Sunday Dispatch,* April 14, 1861.

9. *North American,* April 16, 1861.

10. *North American,* April 16, 1861. The newspapers included similar accounts of other men who were accosted around the intersection of Third and Chestnut. The name *Palmetto Flag* signaled to all a connection with South Carolina.

11. Katherine Brinley Wharton Diary, April 15, 1861, Katherine Johnstone Brinley Wharton Papers, HSP.

12. Fisher, *A Philadelphia Perspective,* 84–85.

13. John L. Smith Diary, April 16, 17, 1861.

14. Wister and Wister, "Sarah Butler Wister's Civil War Diary," 274–76. The manuscript of the Wister Diary is in the Wister and Butler Family Papers, HSP.

15. *New York Herald,* April 16, 1861.

16. *Cleveland Morning Leader,* April 16, 1861.

17. *Burlington Free Press,* April 19, 1861.

18. *New York Herald,* April 15, 1861; *National Republican,* April 15, 1861; *Chicago Tribune,* April 15, 1861; *Daily Ohio Statesman,* April 15, 1861; *Hillsdale Standard,* April 16, 1861. Each of these newspapers, and no doubt dozens of others, ran short versions of the story about the Baltimore man with a secessionist cockade.

19. *Daily Journal,* April 18, 1861.

20. White, *Abraham Lincoln and Treason in the Civil War,* 11–15 and *passim;* McPherson, *Battle Cry of Freedom,* 287.

21. S. M. Felton to Alexander Henry, April 22, 1861; W. Thomas to Henry, April 30, 1861; William H. Cranston? to Henry, May 16, 1861, Alexander Henry Papers, HSP.

22. Harris, *Lincoln and the Border States.*

23. White, *Abraham Lincoln and Treason in the Civil War,* 15–20; McPherson, *Battle Cry of Freedom,* 287–88; Harris, *Lincoln and the Border States,* 59–64, 60, 61 (quotations). See also Harris, *Two against Lincoln,* 32–34. Note that although Lincoln conferred with Bates and Johnson before making his decision, their most important written statements postdate Lincoln's response to Taney.

24. Jeffrey, "'They Cannot Expect,'" 12.

25. The scholarship on civil liberties during the Civil War is vast. See Blair, *With Malice toward Some,* and Jeffrey, "'They Cannot Expect.'"

26. James Asheton Bayard to Samuel Barlow, August 4, 1861, Barlow Papers, HL.

27. Leonard, *Lincoln's Forgotten Ally,* 113–57; Harris, *Lincoln and the Border States,* 8–92; Lee, "Unionism, Emancipation, and the Origins of Kentucky's Confederate Identity"; Lewis, *For Slavery and Union;* Astor, *Rebels on the Border,* 77–84.

28. *Letter from the Hon. Joseph Holt,* 12.

29. Leonard, *Lincoln's Forgotten Ally,* 144.

30. These letters are housed in a small collection, Joseph Holt Papers, boxes 3–5, HL. The letters are arranged alphabetically by author. The bulk of Holt's papers are housed in the Library of Congress.

31. Ellen Wallace Diary, January 6, 10, April 19, 1861, transcript, Ellen Wallace and Annie Starling Diaries (hereafter Ellen Wallace Diary), Kentucky Historical Society (hereafter KHS).

32. Henry Haviland to Susan Scrogin, April 25, 1861, Susan Scrogin and Henry Haviland Letters, KHS. For concerns about the potential economic cost of secession, see Lewis, *For Slavery and Union,* 60–61.

33. Harris, *Lincoln and the Border States,* 90–93.

34. Ellen Wallace Diary, July 28, 1861.

35. J.T. Barlow to Lucy Barlow, Barlow Family U.S. Civil War Collection, KHS; Harris, *Lincoln and the Border States,* 93–98.

36. Burlingame, *Abraham Lincoln: A Life,* 2:230; Abraham Lincoln, "Annual Message to Congress," December 3, 1861, in Lincoln, *Collected Works,* 5:36–53.

37. Ellen Wallace Diary, December 15, 1861.

38. Phillips, *The Rivers Ran Backwards,* 142.

39. Weigley, *Philadelphia,* 389, 392; Smith, *The Stormy Present,* 122–23; McPherson and Hogue, *Ordeal by Fire,* 114–16.

40. Forney, *Eulogy upon the Hon. Stephen A. Douglas.*

41. *Sunday Dispatch,* June 9, 1861.

42. Bailey, *The Weeping Time;* Fisher, *A Philadelphia Perspective,* 32n5. On Kemble, see Clinton, *Fanny Kemble's Civil Wars.*

43. Fisher, *A Philadelphia Perspective,* 45.

44. Fisher, *A Philadelphia Perspective,* 68–69.

45. Wister and Wister, "Sarah Butler Wister's Civil War Diary."

46. Wister and Wister, "Sarah Butler Wister's Civil War Diary," 289.

47. Wister and Wister, "Sarah Butler Wister's Civil War Diary," 298–99. Winans, a member of Maryland's House of Delegates, was arrested and released several times for his open support of the Confederacy, most notably in mid-May. Although he was arrested under Lincoln's suspension of the writ of habeas corpus, Winans was released on signing a parole.

48. Wister and Wister, "Sarah Butler Wister's Civil War Diary," 304, 318–19.

49. Simon Cameron to William Millward, August 15, 1861, in *War of the Rebellion,* ser. 2, 2:505 (hereafter *OR*).

50. Elizabeth Ingersoll Fisher Diary, August 20, 1861, HSP; Fisher, *A Philadelphia Perspective,* 108.

51. Emma Biddle to Charles Biddle, August 20, 1861, Biddle Family Papers, HSP.

52. Wister and Wister, "Sarah Butler Wister's Civil War Diary," 322.

53. Wister and Wister, "Sarah Butler Wister's Civil War Diary," 322–27.

54. Pierce Butler to General George Cadwalader, September 4, 12, 30, 1861, George Cadwalader Papers, HSP.

55. Charles Henry Fisher to Abraham Lincoln, September 12, 1861; Fisher to General Simon Cameron, September 13, 16, 1861; Cameron to Fisher, September 14, 1861; Cameron to Lieutenant Colonel Martin Burke, copy of order, September 14, 1861; Fisher to William D. Kelly, September 16, 1861, telegram; Fisher and George Cadwalader to Kelly, September 16, 1861, Charles Henry Fisher Letters, Society Collection, HSP.

56. Charles Henry Fisher to Simon Cameron, September 18, 1861, in *OR,* ser. 2, 2:505–6. The husband Fisher refers to is Sarah's husband, wealthy doctor Owen Jones Wister. Fisher's reference to "our party" might have been intended to remind Cameron that he had been a Democrat for quite some time.

57. *OR,* ser. 2, 2:505.

58. For a brief overview of the Butler case, see Blair, *With Malice toward Some,* 48–49.

3. The Opposition's War

1. This language borrows from the subtitle used by Allan Nevins in *Ordeal of the Union* (1947–71), his multivolume history of the Civil War era.

2. Rawley, *The Politics of Union,* 31.

3. Baker, "A Loyal Opposition," 139n1.

4. McPherson and Hogue, *Ordeal by Fire,* 285–87.

5. Bogue, *The Earnest Men,* 47.

6. Cowden, *"Heaven Will Frown on Such a Cause as This,"* 83.

7. Henry Douglas Bacon to Samuel Barlow, January 21, 28, 1862; Jesse Bright to Barlow, July 14, 19, 1860, Barlow Papers, HL; Bogue, *The Earnest Men,* 278 and *passim.* Bacon quoted from a letter Bright had written to Jefferson Davis, introducing an arms dealer to the president of the Confederacy. Congress had learned of the text of that incriminating letter.

8. Bogue, *The Earnest Men,* 278–85; Engle, *Gathering to Save a Nation,* 122. Stark served until the end of 1862, when the Oregon legislature convened and replaced him with powerful Democrat Benjamin F. Harding for the third session. Bogue, *The Earnest Men,* 44; Engle, *Gathering to Save a Nation,* 122.

9. McPherson and Hogue, *Ordeal by Fire,* 295; Varon, *Armies of Deliverance,* 103–5. Allan G. Bogue's count of senators for the second session of the 37th Congress included thirty-one Republicans, eleven Democrats, five Border Unionists, and one Northern Unionist. Bogue, "Bloc and Party in the United States Senate," 223.

10. Baum, *The Civil War Party System,* 9; Bogue, "Bloc and Party in the United States Senate." See also Bogue, *The Earnest Men.*

11. James Buchanan to Lewis S. Coryell, September 18, 1861, Coryell Papers, HSP.

12. Benjamin Stark to Samuel Barlow, March 27, 1862, Barlow Papers, HL.

13. Bogue, *The Earnest Men,* 285. Bogue cites Stark's March 27, 1862, letter to Barlow.

14. Henry Douglas Bacon to Abraham Lincoln, December 10, 1861. A copy of this letter is in the Barlow Papers, HL. The original is in the Abraham Lincoln Papers, Library of Congress.

15. New York's Horatio Seymour shared a similar vision of his conservative "Republican friends" whose ideological roots were with the old Whig Party. See Furniss, "To Save the Union 'in Behalf of Conservative Men,'" 67 and *passim.*

16. Biddle, *The Alliance with the Negro.* For a discussion of this pamphlet, see Smith, *The Stormy Present,* 199–200.

17. Benjamin Mifflin to Charles Biddle, August 6, 1860; Craig Biddle to Charles Biddle, September 1, 1861, Biddle Family Papers, HSP; *Sunday Express,* August 18, 1861.

18. For a detailed study of congressional life before the war, see Shelden, *Washington Brotherhood.*

19. Charles Biddle to Emma Biddle, February 9, [n.d.], Biddle Family Papers, HSP.

20. Charles Biddle to Emma Biddle, miscellaneous letters, box 32, folders 3–12, Biddle Family Papers, HSP. The Biddles commonly failed to note the years in their letters. Usually the year can be gleaned from context.

21. Charles Biddle to Emma Biddle, February 9, [1863], Biddle Family Papers, HSP.

22. Charles Biddle to Emma Biddle, December 10, [1861?], Biddle Family Papers, HSP.

23. Charles Biddle to Emma Biddle, January 23, [1863?], Biddle Family Papers, HSP.

24. Biddle, *The Alliance with the Negro,* 1, 4, 6, 8.

25. Charles Biddle to Charles Stillé, March 28, 1863, Biddle Family Papers, HSP.

26. These letters (at least forty) are in the Biddle Family Papers, box 38, folders 2–4, HSP.

27. John Belle Robinson to Charles Biddle, March 24, 1862, Biddle Family Papers, HSP.

28. Joseph Reed Ingersoll to Charles Biddle, March 20, 1862, Biddle Family Papers, HSP.

29. Sears, *George B. McClellan,* 44–67 and *passim.*

30. Sears, *George B. McClellan,* 63–45; Henry Douglas Bacon to Samuel Barlow, July 3, 1860, April 25, 1861, Barlow Papers, HL; Refuse, *McClellan's War,* 81–82.

31. Sears, *George B. McClellan,* 56, 58, 104; Refuse, *McClellan's War,* 71–75 and *passim.*

32. This book includes few military details and nothing remotely original about the war's military history. In addition to Sears's biography, I have turned to Gallagher et al., *The American Civil War,* 43–45.

33. George B. McClellan to Samuel Barlow, November 8, 1861, in McClellan, *The Civil War Papers of George B. McClellan,* 128. See also Varon, *Armies of Deliverance,* 55.

34. James Asheton Bayard to Samuel Barlow, December 6, 1861, Barlow Papers, HL.

35. Henry Douglas Bacon to Samuel Barlow, April 7, 1862, Barlow Papers, HL.

36. Sears, *George B. McClellan,* 27–35.

37. Emma Biddle to Charles Biddle, May 29, July 7, 1862, Biddle Family Papers, HSP.

38. John D. Stiles to Lewis S. Coryell, July 22, 1862, Coryell Papers, HSP.

39. John L. Smith Diary, September 1, 1862.

40. *New York World,* August 7, 1862, quoted in Sears, *George B. McClellan,* 230. Stanton had been secretary of war since January 1862.

41. George B. McClellan to Abraham Lincoln, July 7, 1862, in McClellan, *The Civil War Papers of George B. McClellan,* 344–45.

42. Sears, *George B. McClellan,* 227–29.

43. Varon, *Armies of Deliverance,* 93.

44. *Emancipation and Its Results.* For a discussion of this speech, see Escott, *The Worst Passions of Human Nature,* 47–48.

45. Kurtz, "The Union as It Was," 105–6; Kurtz, *Excommunicated from the Union,* 99–106; Ural, "'Ye Sons of Green Erin Assemble'"; Samito, *Becoming American under Fire,* 128 and *passim.*

46. *New York World,* October 18, 1862, quoted in Wood, *Black Scare,* 20, 27.

47. McPherson and Hogue, *Ordeal by Fire,* 273; Rawley, *The Politics of Union,* 54–56. On conscription, see Gallman, *The North Fights the Civil War,* 6–73.

48. For useful overviews of Wisconsin's Democrats, see Klement, *Wisconsin in the Civil War;* Larson, *Wisconsin and the Civil War;* and Klement, "Copperheads and Copperheadism in Wisconsin." On Catholic immigrants and conscription, see Kurtz, *Excommunicated from the Union,* 116, and Ural, "'Ye Sons of Green Erin Assemble,'" 121. On the political positions of German immigrants, see Engle, "Yankee Dutchmen."

49. Klement, *Wisconsin in the Civil War,* 34–36.

50. Ryan et al., *Address to the People of the Democracy of Wisconsin.*

51. Carpenter, *Mat. H. Carpenter's Review of Mr. Ryan's Address.* Thanks to Ronald Paul Larson for sharing this pamphlet with me.

52. Klement, *Copperheads in the Middle West,* 99, citing the Milwaukee *Daily News,* July 2, 1863.

53. Boyle, *Senators of the United States,* 52, citing Thompson, *Matthew Hale Carpenter.*

54. Larson, *Wisconsin and the Civil War,* 70–71.

55. T. J. Barnett to Samuel Barlow, September 19, 1862, Barlow Papers, HL.

56. Varon, *Armies of Deliverance,* 157–58.

57. Ural, "'Ye Sons of Green Erin Assemble.'"

58. Escott, *The Worst Passions of Human Nature,* 50, citing the *Cincinnati Enquirer,* April 18, May 1, 1862.

59. Horatio Seymour to Samuel Barlow, September 18, 1862, Barlow Papers, HL.

60. Samuel Butterworth to Samuel Barlow, September 23, 1862, Barlow Papers, HL.

61. William Steel to Frank Ruff, Esq., September 26, 1862, William Alexander Steel Letterbooks, HL.

62. Flyer, September 26, 1862, Barlow Papers, HL.

63. George William Clinton to Isaac Sherman, September 22, 1862, Isaac Sherman Papers, HL.

64. On New York and Seymour's election, see Furniss, "States of the Union," 171–84; Furniss, "To Save the Union 'in Behalf of Conservative Men'"; and Harris, *Two against Lincoln,* 124–36.

65. Ingersoll, *A Letter to a Friend in a Slave State,* 2, 27, 55, 58.

66. Thayer, *A Reply to Mr. Charles Ingersoll's "Letter to a Friend in a Slave State."*

67. Fisher, *A Philadelphia Perspective,* 144–45.

68. Elizabeth Ingersoll Fisher Diary, April 29, 1862, HSP.

69. Dusinberre, *Civil War Issues in Philadelphia,* 142–43.

70. *Germantown Telegraph,* August 27, 1862.

71. *Germantown Telegraph,* September 3, 1862, reprinting a long column from the Philadelphia *Press.*

72. Fisher, *A Philadelphia Perspective,* 159–64.

73. Anna Mercer LaRoche Francis Journal, September 1, 1862, Rare Book and Manuscript Library, Columbia University, New York.

74. Shankman, *The Pennsylvania Antiwar Movement,* 93; Dusinberre, *Civil War Issues in Philadelphia,* 143.

75. T. J. Barnett to Samuel Barlow, October 6, 1862, Barlow Papers, HL.

76. McPherson and Hogue, *Ordeal by Fire,* 319–21; Harris, *Two against Lincoln,* 131; Waugh, *Reelecting Lincoln,* 11; Phillips, *The Rivers Ran Backward,* 221–26.

77. William Steel to John [Devining], October 18, November 6, 1862, Steel Letterbooks, HL.

78. George McClellan to Samuel Barlow, October 17, 1862, Barlow Papers, HL.

79. Henry Joseph Gardner to Samuel Barlow, November 10, 1862, Barlow Papers, HL. Gardner was the one-time nativist governor of Massachusetts.

80. David Hartley Armstrong to Samuel Barlow, November 10, 1862, Barlow Papers, HL.

81. Neely, *The Union Divided,* 42–45.

82. Harris, *Two against Lincoln,* 131. Massachusetts governor John A. Andrew (and many other political insiders) shared this Republican perspective, blaming the election returns on military failures. Baum, *The Civil War Party System,* 69.

83. Neely, *Lincoln and the Democrats,* 45–61, 49, 51 (quotations).

84. Furniss, "To Save the Union 'in Behalf of Conservative Men.'"

85. Neely, *Lincoln and the Democrats,* 53–59. Neely relies on the research of historian Joel Silbey for voter turnout data.

86. Daly, *Diary of a Union Lady,* 195.

87. Vallandigham, *The Great Civil War in America;* some excerpts taken from Clement Vallandigham, "The War and Its Conduct," January 14, 1863, Teaching American History, http://teachingamericanhistory.org/library/document/on-the-war-and-its-conduct/. See Varon, *Armies of Deliverance,* 230–31, and Cowden, *"Heaven Will Frown on Such a Cause as This,"* 1, 167–73.

88. *Letter from the Right Rev. John H. Hopkins;* Levy, "Bishop Hopkins and the Dilemma of Slavery"; Stout, *Upon the Altar of the Nation,* 283.

89. For a handful of newspapers that commented on the bishop's 1861 pamphlet, see *Sunday Dispatch,* February 17, 1861; *Bellows Falls Times,* May 17, 1861; *Athens Post,* March 1, 1861; *Hancock Jeffersonian,* April 19, 1861; *Yorkville Enquirer,* March 7, 1861; *Holmes County Farmer.,* March 7, 1861; *Daily Dispatch,* February 16, 1861; *Vermont Phœnix,* April 4, 1861.

90. See Gallman, *Defining Duty in the Civil War,* 9–10; Friedel, *Union Pamphlets of the Civil War;* Friedel, "The Loyal Publication Society"; and Neely, *Lincoln and the Triumph of the Nation,* 280–81.

91. *Society for the Diffusion of Political Knowledge. No. 1.* This sixteen-page pamphlet, the first published by the SDPK, includes the society's constitution and texts of various addresses. Friedel, "The Loyal Publication Society," 360; Taylor, *"The Most Complete Political Machine Ever Known,"* 98–101; Bernstein, *The New York City Draft Riots,* 148–49.

92. Turpie, *Speech of Mr. Turpie.* For the emergence of "no party" rhetoric in the North, see Smith, *No Party Now.*

93. John H. Hopkins to Peter McCall, January 16; February 12, 1863, Peter McCall Papers, Cadwalader Family Papers, HSP.

94. Charles Mason to Peter McCall, May 19, 1863, McCall Papers, HSP.

95. Charles Mason to Peter McCall, May–July 1863, McCall Papers, HSP.

96. Hopkins, *Bible View of Slavery* (Philadelphia); Wainwright, "The Loyal Opposition in Civil War Philadelphia," 304–5.

97. Hopkins, *Bible View of Slavery* (New York).

98. Levy, "Bishop Hopkins and the Dilemma of Slavery," 66–67.

99. Charles Mason to Peter McCall, August 31, 1863, McCall Papers, HSP.

100. We hear about Woodward's campaign in chapter 6.

101. Fisher, *A Philadelphia Perspective,* 209.

102. *Protest of the Bishop and Clergy of the Diocese of.* This is a three-page pamphlet. The signatures were presumably local clergy, although they are not identified by their titles or positions. Wainwright, "The Loyal Opposition in Civil War Pennsylvania," 305. See also Shankman, *The Pennsylvania Antiwar Movement,* 127–28.

103. *Philadelphia Age,* October 9, 1863; Hopkins, *A Scriptural, Ecclesiastical, and Historical View of Slavery.* Bishop Hopkins corresponded with Peter McCall about this latest pamphlet. See Hopkins to McCall, November–December 1863, McCall Papers, HSP. The *Philadelphia Age* ran a positive review of the new Hopkins pamphlet on May 5, 1864.

104. Hopkins, *The Life of the Late Right Reverend John Henry Hopkins;* Wikipedia, entry on John Henry Hopkins.

105. The anecdotal evidence certainly indicates that the major pamphlets circulated widely, although it is safe to assume that they were read most extensively in middle-class and upper-class homes. For observations about the general circulation of wartime publications, see Gallman, *Defining Duty in the Civil War,* 1–26.

106. Samuel Evans to Andrew Evans, February 8, 15, 1863, in Engs and Brooks, *Their Patriotic Duty,* 95, 102.

107. White, *Emancipation, the Union Army, and the Reelection of Abraham Lincoln,* 38–97; Orr, "An Army Divided." Thanks to Timothy Orr for sharing a copy of his unpublished paper.

4. Politics Is Personal/Politics Is Local

1. This is a huge topic. For some further thoughts about wartime women in public (although generally discussing Republican women), see Gallman, *America's Joan of Arc,* and on women in public discourse, see Gallman, *Defining Duty in the Civil War,* esp. 188–222. See also Silber, *Daughters of the Union.*

2. Fisher, *A Philadelphia Perspective,* 75.

3. See chapter 3 for more on Elizabeth Fisher's thoughts about her brothers.

4. Elizabeth Ingersoll Fisher Diary, April 29, 1862; January 24, 1863, HSP.

5. See chapter 3.

6. Biddle Family Papers, HSP.

7. Wister and Wister, "Sarah Butler Wister's Civil War Diary," 284.

8. Anna Mercer LaRoche Francis Journal, February 28; March 15, 25; May 17, 1863.

9. Anna Mercer LaRoche Francis Journal, May 19, 27, 28, 1864.

10. The couple would go on to have two children, but both died in infancy.

11. Note that in these later entries the diarist was named "Anna LaRoche Francis."

12. This discussion comes from Mujic, "'We Are Setting the Terms Now.'" The original correspondence is in the Newberry Library, Chicago. Mujic relied on the microfilmed collection at the Wisconsin Historical Society, Madison.

13. Mujic, "'We Are Setting the Terms Now,'" 107.

14. Mujic, "'We Are Setting the Terms Now,'" 117–19, quoting Gideon Allen to Annie Cox, February 10, 1863; Cox to Allen, February 1, 1863, Allen Papers, Newberry Library.

15. Mujic, "'We Are Setting the Terms Now,'" 127, quoting Gideon Allen to Annie Cox, December 30, 1863; January 4, 1864, Allen Papers, Newberry Library.

16. Mujic, "'We Are Setting the Terms Now,'" 114.

17. Susan Scrogin to Henry Haviland, December 1860, Susan Scrogin and Henry Haviland Letters, KHS. Note that we have already met this Kentucky couple in chapter 2.

18. Susan Scrogin to Henry Haviland, January 24, 1861; Haviland to Scrogin, April 25, 1861, Susan Scrogin and Henry Haviland Letters, KHS.

19. Susan Scrogin to Henry Haviland, June 5, 1861, Susan Scrogin and Henry Haviland Letters, KHS.

20. Henry Haviland to Susan Scrogin, July 10, 1861, Susan Scrogin and Henry Haviland Letters, KHS.

21. Susan Scrogin to Henry Haviland, December 7, 1861, Susan Scrogin and Henry Haviland Letters, KHS.

22. Harris, *Lincoln and the Border States,* 159–223; Phillips, *The Rivers Ran Backward,* 186–90, 211–35, and *passim.*

23. Wesley, *The Politics of Faith during the Civil War,* 66–67.

24. For a scholarly assessment of Wallace's diary as well as the journals of other Kentucky women, see Marshall, "A 'Sister's War.'"

25. Ellen Wallace Diary, December 15, 1861, September 29, 1862, and *passim.* Wallace also appears in chapter 2. See also Phillips, *The Rivers Ran Backward,* 235.

26. For background on the Wallers (in addition to HL's fine finding aid for the Waller Papers), see Bowman, *In the Precipice,* 328, 68, and *passim,* and Gallman, "'What Is the Case of "Willie Waller" at Maysville, Kentucky?'"

27. U.S. Census of 1860.

28. Henry Waller to Sarah Waller, September 28, October 7, 1860; Sarah Waller to Henry Waller, October 4, 14, 1860, Waller Papers, HL.

29. Henry Waller to Sarah Waller, October 8, 19, 12, 1861, Waller Papers, HL. While both Henry and Sarah wrote about the practical issues surrounding slavery and emancipation, neither commented on the institution's morality.

30. Sarah Waller to Henry Waller, January 3, 6, 8, 1863, Waller Papers, HL.

31. Lizzie McDowell to Henry Waller, March 16, 29, 1862; George W. Cullen to Henry Waller, March 31, 1862, Waller Papers, HL. Halleck's orders were enclosed with General Cullen's letter.

32. Sarah Waller to "Mother," July 1863; Sarah Waller to Henry Waller, January 7, June 31, August 15, 1864; Sarah Waller, miscellaneous letters, 1863, Camp Douglas folder, Waller Papers, HL. For Sarah Waller's wartime work at Camp Douglas, see Underwood, *Report of Proceedings Incidental to the Erection and Dedication of the Confederate Monument,* 213–14.

33. The scholarship on northern women and the Civil War is vast. A good starting point is Silber, *Daughters of the Union.* The scholarship on the Midwest during the war, and particularly the experiences of farming women, is emerging. See the essays in Aley and Anderson, *Union Heartland.*

34. See McPherson, *For Cause and Comrades.*

35. Gallman, *Defining Duty in the Civil War,* 7–9.

36. In this book I am not attempting any systematic analysis of the political beliefs of Union soldiers although their voting behavior is discussed in chapter 8.

37. Roberts, *"This Infernal War."* Note that the reader first met this couple in the introduction.

38. Roberts, *"This Infernal War,"* 6–8.

39. In addition to commentary on slavery and emancipation, both Jane and William's letters are liberally peppered with the "N word," used as both description and metaphor.

40. Jane Standard to William Standard, September 28, 1862; William to Jane and children, December 12, 1862; William to Jane, January 22, February 1, 9, 1863, in Roberts, *"This Infernal War,"* 19–20, 46–47, 60, 66, 71.

41. William Standard to Jane Standard, February 9, 1863; Jane to William, February 1, 12, March 1, 1863, in Roberts, *"This Infernal War,"* 72, 62, 73, 83.

42. William Standard to Jane Standard, [September 20, 1863], in Roberts, *"This Infernal War,"* 153.

43. William Standard to Jane Standard, January 28, February 9, 1864, in Roberts, *"This Infernal War,* 166, 170–71. For the experiences of white officers in the United States Colored Troops, see Glatthaar, *Forged in Battle.*

44. William Standard to Jane Standard, March 2, 1864, in Roberts, *"This Infernal War,"* 172.

45. William Standard to Jane Standard, April 11, 25, 1864, in Roberts, *"This Infernal War,"* 183, 189.

46. Blair, *With Malice toward Some,* 172; Donald, *Lincoln,* 419–20.

47. Neely, *The Union Divided,* 57–61.

48. See chapter 3.

49. Blair, *With Malice toward Some,* 178; General Ambrose Burnside, "General Orders No. 38," Department of the Ohio, April 13, 1863, in *OR,* ser. 1, 23:237.

50. Blair, *With Malice toward Some,* 177–78; Varon, *Armies of Deliverance,* 230–34.

51. The focus here is on Illinois, and especially Chicago. Immediately to the east, other stories had unfolded in Indiana a few months before, illustrating the larger point that the particular circumstances in individual states and communities mattered, as did their relationship with federal authorities. In the spring of 1863 Burnside ordered General Milo S. Hascall to command the military in Indiana. Hascall took to the task with enthusiasm, issuing his own General Orders no. 9 as an adjunct to Burnside's no. 38. Hascall shut down a series of Democratic newspapers and arrested editors, particularly in the northern part of the state. Indiana's Democratic editors and state congressmen fired back with angry editorials, which proved ineffectual. Although Republican governor Oliver Morton was no fan of his Democratic critics, he disliked federal usurpation of civil affairs more. He complained to Lincoln. Quite a bit. By late May Hascall had toned down his suppression of Democratic dissent. Days later Burnside shut down the *Chicago Times.* This interesting story is nicely told in Towne, "Killing the Serpent Speedily."

52. Historical Reports of State Acting Assistant Provost Marshals General and District Provost Marshals, 1865, M1163, reel 1, Illinois (hereafter Historical Reports), 88–89, National Archives, Washington, D.C. For more on this collection, see chapter 5, note 12, below.

53. Tenney, "To Suppress or Not to Suppress," 249, citing *OR,* ser. 1, vol. 23, part 1, 12.

54. Karamanski, *Rally 'Round the Flag,* 188–93; Tenney, "To Suppress or Not to Suppress," 251–53; *OR,* ser. 1, vol. 23, part 2, 381 (Burnside quotation). See also Blair, *With Malice toward Some,* 62.

55. Tenney, "To Suppress or Not to Suppress," 254–59; Karamanski, *Rally 'Round the Flag,* 192–98.

56. "Mayors of Chicago"; Karamanski, *Rally 'Round the Flag,* 91–92; Sherman, *Quest for a Star,* 2, 9, 29.

57. *Chicago Tribune,* April 20, 21, 1863.

58. *Burlington Weekly Hawk-Eye,* April 25, 1863. Christopher Dell reported that Sherman won by 550 of about 29,000 votes. Dell, *Lincoln and the War Democrats,* 252.

59. *Ottawa Free Trader,* April 25, 1863.

60. *Chicago Tribune,* April 22, 1863.

61. "Mayor Francis Cornwall Sherman Inaugural Address," 1–3; *Chicago Tribune,* May 6, 1863.

62. Francis T. Sherman (son) to Francis C. Sherman (father), February 18, 1863, in Sherman, *Quest for a Star,* 30–31.

63. Francis T. Sherman to Frederick Tuttle, February 18, 1863, in Sherman, *Quest for a Star,* 31–32; *Chicago Tribune,* February 23, 1863. Editor C. Knight Aldrich dates this letter as February 18 (the same day Sherman wrote to his father); the *Tribune* dates it as February 14.

64. Francis T. Sherman (son) to Francis C. Sherman (father) and to parents, excerpts, various dates, in Sherman, *Quest for a Star,* 33–37.

65. See Taylor, *The Divided Family in Civil War America.*

66. For a longer treatment of these events, see Gallman, "'What Is the Case of "Willie Waller" at Maysville, Kentucky?'"

67. Harrison Blanton to Montgomery Blair, June 8, 1863, Lincoln Papers, Library of Congress.

68. Montgomery Blair to Abraham Lincoln, June 11, 1863, Lincoln Papers, Library of Congress.

69. This is really three separate messages. The first, from Abraham Lincoln to Ambrose Burnside, June 26, 1863, appears in Lincoln, *Collected Works,* 6:296. The other two messages appear in an editorial note accompanying this telegram in the *Collected Works.*

70. Again, for a much more detailed version of this story, see Gallman, "'What Is the Case of "Willie Waller" at Maysville, Kentucky?'"

71. Of course the differences are immense, beginning with the fact that Waller was caught recruiting for the enemy whereas Butler's chief offense was that he spoke fondly of the Confederate cause.

72. Form signed by Captain Matthew Jouett, April 12, 1864, Jonathan Davis Hale Papers, HL. On race in wartime Kentucky, see Astor, "The Crouching Lion's Fate," and Crane, "The Demise of Slavery on the Border." On conflicts over passes in Kentucky, see Oakes, *Freedom National,* 487.

73. Solomon Long to Jonathan Davis Hale, April 4, 1861, Hale Papers, HL.

74. On the election and secession, see Frisby, "The Vortex of Secession," and McKenzie, "'An Unconditional, Straight-Out Union Man.'"

75. For the classic study of conflict in eastern Tennessee, see Paludan, *Victims.* For guerrilla warfare in Tennessee, placed within a national context, see Sutherland, *Savage Conflict.*

76. Hale's background comes from the materials in the Hale Papers, HL.

77. See Sutherland, *Savage Conflict*, 157–60 and *passim.*

78. Sutherland, *Savage Conflict*, 82–83, 228–30. See also McKnight, "'Time by the Forelock.'"

79. A memo by General George H. Thomas, dated May 2, 1863, explains Pheroba's situation and requests that she be allowed to purchase supplies for subsistence. Hale Papers, HL.

80. Pheroba Hale to Jonathan Hale, December 20, 1862; Jonathan Hale to Pheroba Hale, December 21, 1862, Hale Papers, HL. Given the timing of these two letters it is possible that Jonathan was responding to an earlier letter expressing similar sentiments.

81. Pheroba Hale to Jonathan Hale, January 14, 1863, Hale Papers, HL.

82. Jonathan Hale to Pheroba Hale, January 27, 1863, Hale Papers, HL.

83. Jonathan Hale to Pheroba Hale, March 26, 1863, Hale Papers, HL.

84. Jonathan Hale to Pheroba Hale, June 28, July 5, 1863, Hale Papers, HL.

85. Pheroba Hale to Jonathan Hale, August 7, 1863, Hale Papers, HL.

86. Jonathan Hale to Pheroba Hale, August 8, 1863, Hale Papers, HL.

87. Undated manuscript, box 6, folder JDH 145, Hale Papers, HL. This passage is undated but appears to have been written in the 1890s.

88. See Sutherland, *Savage Conflict*, 157–60.

89. Hale's papers at the Huntington Library are thick with accounts of his efforts against Champ Ferguson and other guerillas. Those same papers include multiple postwar reports by Union officers attesting to his value to the cause and calling on the federal government to reward him for his patriotic service. In addition to the work by Daniel Sutherland, see also McKnight, "'Time by the Forelock.'"

90. Pheroba Hale to Jonathan Hale, May 27, August 10, September 18, November 27, 1864, Hale Papers, HL.

91. Pheroba Hale to Jonathan Hale, February 20, June 15, 30, 1865, Hale Papers, HL.

92. For a much more extensive analysis of Daly and her diary, see Gallman, "Maria Lydig Daly."

93. Daly, *Diary of a Union Lady*, 198–99, 213.

5. Politics in the Streets

1. These are overlapping categories of publications. Sermons and speeches often reappeared as published pamphlets or in the columns of newspapers.

2. The level of engagement in this printed discourse varied by race, class, and ethnicity. Literacy rates were high across the entire population, but different groups encountered different publications, either directly or indirectly. For some thoughts on these topics, see Gallman, *Defining Duty in the Civil*, 1–26 and *passim.*

3. I have written about public fisticuffs over war matters in Gallman, *Mastering Wartime.*

4. This argument seems obvious on its face, but it is not clear that the Union's overall approach to manpower really did produce a "poor man's fight." But in political terms the popular convictions were more important than the empirical realities.

5. The scholarship on the Civil War draft is substantial. The best two books are still Geary, *We Need Men*, and Murdock, *One Million Men*. For home-front complaints about the unfair treatment of Democrats, see Phillips, *The River Runs Backward*, 275. For regional complaints about unfair treatment, see Etcheson, *A Generation at War*, 105.

6. For a general discussion of German Americans and partisan politics during the war, see Engle, "Yankee Dutchmen," esp. 22.

7. Larsen, "Draft Riot in Wisconsin, 1862," 421–27; *Milwaukee Pilot*, November 12, 1862.

8. "Civil War: Draft Riots (1862)," Wisconsin Historical Society, https://www.wisconsinhistory.org/Records/Article/CS6448.

9. Geary, *We Need Men*; Murdock, *One Million Men*. The removal of the commutation fee resulted in elevated prices for substitutes.

10. Gallman, *The North Fights the Civil War*, 62–71; Gallman, *Defining Duty in the Civil War*, 6–9.

11. John Milton Hay to Charles Graham Halpine, August 14, 1863, Halpine Papers, HL.

12. Historical Reports. These reports are in five reels of microfilm, duplicated onto five CDs. Nearly every state is represented, for a total of roughly 175 district reports. The following discussion comes from a reading of all five thousand pages of these reports, but in some cases the handwriting or reproductions made the reports unintelligible, and in many cases I skimmed long reports for those sections where the most useful material would likely appear. In short, this analysis is neither a systematic "sampling" of the reports nor does it represent a complete reading of every word. But it does reflect a fairly close reading of the entire body of reports.

13. For the most part the evidence in this section comes from those postwar reports. Contemporary newspapers and scholarly studies are full of accounts of small-scale draft resistance and disorder, both real and exaggerated. For a treasure drove of such episodes, including the riots in New York City, see Weber, *Copperheads*, esp. 102–13.

14. An entire unit in a "Historical Methods" class could be devoted to the accuracy of these reports. The marshals wrote immediately after the war, so their memories were fresh and the war was over. They had massive records to consult. Their reports on purely empirical things, such as where events occurred or how many people were injured, are probably most trustworthy. Their comments about the ethnic identity of individuals or communities could reflect confusion or bias. Their opinions about *why* civilians resisted are merely their informed opinions.

15. Historical Reports, reel 4, p. 769.

16. Historical Reports, reel 3, p. 213.

17. Historical Reports, reel 5, p. 258.

18. Historical Reports, reel 5, p. 636.

19. Historical Reports, reel 5, pp. 720, 775.

20. Historical Reports, reel 3, p. 1003. On other occasions Irish Catholic priests helped to calm potential draft rioters. See Wesley, *The Politics of Faith during the Civil War,* 41.

21. Historical Reports, reel 4, pp. 861–62, 1110–11, 1143 (quotation).

22. Historical Reports, reel 5, pp. 127–28.

23. Historical Reports, reel 5, p. 62.

24. Historical Reports, reel 1, pp. 1–4.

25. Historical Reports, reel 5, pp. 530–31.

26. Historical Reports, reel 2, pp. 225–26.

27. Historical Reports, reel 3, p. 492.

28. Historical Reports, reel 4, p. 669.

29. Historical Reports, reel 4, p. 1014.

30. Historical Reports, reel 5, p. 639.

31. Historical Reports, reel 5, pp. 623–24.

32. On naturalization laws, see Samito, *Becoming American under Fire,* 38.

33. Historical Reports, reel 2, pp. 817–18.

34. Historical Reports, reel 3, pp. 488–90.

35. Historical Reports, reel 4, p. 1144.

36. Historical Reports, reel 5, p. 233.

37. Historical Reports, reel 4, p. 991.

38. Historical Reports, reel 2, pp. 714–15.

39. Historical Reports, reel 5, pp. 1153–54, 1130.

40. Historical Reports, reel 5, pp. 644–45.

41. Historical Reports, reel 1, p. 88–89. The *Times* would be temporarily shut down for its actions. See chapter 4.

42. Historical Reports, reel 1, pp. 23–25.

43. Historical Reports, reel 1, pp. 626–28.

44. Historical Reports, reel 2, pp. 75–76, 162, 179–83, 201. Note that while we think of "deserters" as men in uniform who ran from the ranks, in these reports men who were drafted and then ran before serving at all classified as deserters.

45. Historical Reports, reel 1, p. 855.

46. Historical Reports, reel 1, pp. 946–55. See also Phillips, *The Rivers Ran Backward,* 275.

47. Historical Reports, reel 1, pp. 1028–34.

48. Historical Reports, reel 1, pp. 1053–54.

49. Historical Reports, reel 2, p. 624.

50. Historical Reports, reel 4, pp. 1110–51.

51. Historical Reports, reel 5, pp. 221–22. See also Sandow, *Deserter Country.*

52. Historical Reports, reel 2, pp. 915–16.

53. Among the vast literature on the New York City draft riots, two full-length monographs stand out: Bernstein, *The New York City Draft Riots*, and Cook, *The Armies of the Streets*. The best single-volume history of New York during the Civil War is Spann, *Gotham at War*.

54. "The Irish in New York City," Ancestry.com, https://www.ancestry.com/contextux/historicalinsights/irish-new-york-city.

55. Spann, *Gotham at War*, 93–97; Kurtz, "The Union as It Was," 106–9.

56. Varon, *Armies of Deliverance*, 243; Spann, *Gotham at War*, 96–97, citing *Weekly Caucasian*, June 27, 1863; Historical Reports, reel 3, pp. 743–69.

57. Spann, *Gotham at War*, 97, citing the *New York Tribune*, July 6, 1863; Harris, *Two against Lincoln*, 155.

58. Spann, *Gotham at War*, 96, citing the New York *Daily News*, July 11, 1863; Holzer, *Lincoln and the Power of the Press*, 441.

59. Historical Reports, New York, reel 3.

60. Spann, *Gotham at War*, 98–103. Spann estimates that 120–150 people perished in the riots. The police superintendent put that figure at 1,155.

61. Gallman, "Preserving the Peace."

62. Harris, *Two against Lincoln*, 155; Holzer, *Lincoln and the Power of the Press*, 441.

63. Spann, *Gotham at War*, 102.

64. Historical Reports, reel 3, p. 769.

65. Wood, *Black Scare*, 23–28, quoting the Albany *Atlas and Argus*, February 28, 1863, and New York *Daily News*, March 19, 1864.

66. Varon, *Armies of Deliverance*, 275.

67. Daly, *Diary of a Union Lady*, 248, 251; Keating, "Perspectives on Irish American Loyalty and Patriotism"; Ural, "'Ye Sons of Green Erin Assemble,'" 121–25; Stout, *Upon the Altar of the Nation*, 246–47.

68. Escott, *The Worst Passions of Human Nature*, 73–74.

69. Gallman, "Preserving the Peace"; Schneider, "Detroit and the Problem of Disorder"; Escott, *The Worst Passions of Human Nature*, 74–75; Coleman and Spence, "The Charleston Riot, March 28 1864"; Lane, *Policing the City*, 133–34; Weber, *Copperheads*, 112.

70. For the classic works debunking the secret societies as myth, see Klement, *The Copperheads in the Middle West*, and Klement, *Dark Lanterns*. Other works that generally agree with Klement include Shankman, *The Pennsylvania Antiwar Movement;* Sandow, *Deserter Country*; and Sandow, "Damnable Treason or Party Organs." For a modern study that gives more credence to these secret societies as a challenge to the Union war effort, see Weber's *Copperheads*. For a regional study that finds diverse secret societies in the Middle Border, see Phillips, *The Rivers Ran Backward*, 268–69. For an important, as of yet unpublished, analysis of the northern hysteria about secret societies, see Ruehlen, "The Specter of Subversion." For an excellent historiographic discussion of the

work of Klement, Weber, and Joel Silbey (and others), see Rodgers, "Copperheads or a Respectable Minority."

71. For background on Bickley and the Knights, see Lause, *A Secret Society History of the Civil War*; Klement, *Dark Lanterns*, 7–12; and Weber, *Copperheads*, 25.

72. *Congressional Globe*, House of Representatives, 36th Congress, 2nd Session, 1859–61, pp. 571–72, as discussed and cited by Ruehlen, "The Specter of Subversion," 71.

73. *Boston Herald*, April 12, 1861; *Newark Daily Advertiser*, April 8, 1861; *Philadelphia Inquirer*, May 8, 1861. These and similar stories are discussed in Ruehlen, "The Specter of Subversion."

74. Ruehlen, "The Specter of Subversion."

75. Historical Reports, reel 1, pp. 22–34; *OR*, ser. 1, vol. L, part 2, 938–41. The Knights of the Golden Circle had the longest, as well as the most notorious, reputation in the North. Robinson submitted his report before the end of the war, although it became a part of Fry's postwar documents.

76. Historical Reports, reel 1, pp. 1047–48.

77. Historical Reports, reel 2, pp. 179–83.

78. Historical Reports, reel 2, p. 226.

79. Historical Reports, reel 4, p. 1148.

80. Historical Reports, reel 1, pp. 929, 1180; reel 4, p. 681. Indiana saw considerable disorder surrounding the draft and much talk of secret societies (some of which is discussed below). Etcheson, *A Generation at War*, 108–13.

81. For a detailed analysis of secret societies, and rumors of secret societies, in Berks County, Pennsylvania, see Ruehlen, "The Specter of Subversion."

82. Phillips, *The Rivers Ran Backward*, 275; Historical Reports, reel 4, p. 642.

83. For Sandow's broader study, see Sandow, *Deserter Country*. Most of the discussion that follows comes from his superb discussion of secret societies in two Pennsylvania counties in Sandow, "Damnable Treason or Party Organs."

84. Sandow, "Damnable Treason or Party Organs," citing Richard I. Dodge to James B. Fry, November 1, 1864, in *OR*, ser. 1, vol. 43, part 2, 525. See also Weber, *Copperheads*, 195.

85. Sandow, "Damnable Treason or Party Organs," 58, citing the *Clearfield Republican*, February 8, 1865.

86. Historical Report, reel 5, p. 221.

87. Sandow, "Damnable Treason," 58; Blair, *With Malice toward Some*, 214; Klement, *Dark Lanterns*, 136–50.

88. Klement, *Dark Lanterns*, 91–135; Weber, *Copperheads*, 128–29 and *passim*.

89. *Plymouth Democrat*, August 25, 1864. This story soon appeared in newspapers all over the North.

90. *Indianapolis Daily Sentinel*, August 22, 1864, quoted in the *Plymouth Democrat*, September 1, 1864.

91. *Marshall County Republican*, August 25, 1864, citing the *Cincinnati Gazette*.

92. Klement, *Dark Lanterns*, 91–135. For much more on Dodd, see Weber, *Copperheads*, 148–49 and *passim,* and Etcheson, *A Generation at War,* 115–16.

93. Blair, *With Malice toward Some*, 40, 49.

94. Sandow, "Damnable Treason or Party Organs," 51.

6. An Organized War, a Disorganized Party?

1. See Neely, "The Civil War and the Two-Party System," 92.

2. For some discussion of these citizen-soldiers as part of public discourse, see Gallman, *Defining Duty in the Civil War,* 164–67.

3. Jeffrey, "'They Cannot Expect.'"

4. On republican ideology and disloyalty, see Rodgers, "Copperheads or a Respectable Minority."

5. Taylor, *"The Most Complete Political Machine Ever Known,"* Philadelphia membership numbers on page 71; Lawson, *Patriot Fires,* 98–128 and *passim.* Francis Lieber's pamphlet of the same name made the phrase into Union League discourse. Lieber, *No Party Now; But All for Our Country.*

6. Other Democrats, like Lincoln's secretary of war, Edwin Stanton, shifted to the Republican Party.

7. Phillips, *The Rivers Ran Backward,* 270, quoting the *Centralia* (Ill.) *Sentinel.* This language appears in the July 16, 1863, issue.

8. The best detailed treatment of the War Democrats is Dell, *Lincoln and the War Democrats.* Dell is more comfortable speaking in terms of categories of Democrats than I might be.

9. Fuller, *Oliver Morton and the Politics of the Civil War and Reconstruction,* 78–79; Dell, *Lincoln and the War Democrats*, 201 and *passim.*

10. William Henry Wadsworth to Samuel Barlow, February 3, 1863, Barlow Papers, HL

11. James Wall to Henry Hurlbert, n.d. 1863, Barlow Papers, HL.

12. T. J. Barnett to Samuel Barlow, May 15, 1863 (two letters), Barlow Papers, HL.

13. T. J. Barnett to Samuel Barlow, June 6, July 10, 1863, Barlow Papers, HL.

14. For a discussion of these issues, see Neely, *Lincoln and the Democrats*, esp. 74–84.

15. *New York World*, February 19, 1863, quoted in Neely, *Lincoln and the Democrats*, 73.

16. *North American*, January 20, 29, 1863; Fisher, *A Philadelphia Perspective*, 183; George W. Fahnestock Diary, January 31, 1863, HSP; Charles Biddle to Emma Biddle, February 7, [1863], Biddle Family Papers, HSP; Wainwright, "The Loyal Opposition in Civil War Philadelphia," 299–300.

17. Anna Mercer LaRoche Francis Journal, February 29, 1863. See chapter 4.

18. *Philadelphia Age,* February 25, 1863.

19. *Philadelphia Age,* March 26, 28, 1863.

20. *Press* (Philadelphia), May 9, 1863; Gallman, *Mastering Wartime,* 183.

21. Fisher, *A Philadelphia Perspective*, 191–92.

22. *Press* (Philadelphia), May 11, 1863; *North American*, May 11, 1863; *Philadelphia Age,* May 11, 1863; Anna Mercer LaRoche Francis Journal, May 10, 1863.

23. The local press gave substantial coverage to the Vallandigham trial. See *Press* (Philadelphia), May 11, 1863, and *Philadelphia Age,* May 11, 12 (quotation), 21, 1863.

24. *North American*, June 2, 1863; *Philadelphia Age*, June 2, 9, 1863; *Press* (Philadelphia), June 2, 3, 1863; Fisher, *A Philadelphia Perspective*, 192–93.

25. Ingersoll, *A Convention of the People*. See *Philadelphia Age,* April 23, 1863.

26. Neely, *The Fate of Liberty,* 65–67.

27. *Rutland Weekly Herald*, May 14, 1863, quoting the *New York Herald.*

28. *Daily Intelligencer*, May 18, 1863; *Cleveland Morning Leader*, May 18, 1863.

29. Abraham Lincoln to Erastus Corning and Others, June 6, 1863, in Lincoln, *Collected Works*, 6:262–69; Blair, *With Malice toward Some,* 178–79; Neely, *The Fate of Liberty*, 67–68; Foner, *The Fiery Trial,* 263–64; Varon, *Armies of Deliverance,* 230–32.

30. *Philadelphia Age,* May 14, 1863.

31. *New York Herald,* May 14, 1863, quoted in Neely, *Lincoln and the Democrats*, 90–92.

32. Neely, *Lincoln and the Democrats*, 92, quoting Sunset Cox to Manton Marble, June 14, 1863, Marble Papers, Library of Congress. See also Furniss, "States of the Union," 78.

33. Weber, "The Political Culture of the North," 98, quoting William D. Dillon, ed., "The Civil War Letters of Enos Barret Lewis, 101st Ohio Volunteer Infantry," *Northwest Historical Quarterly* 57 (1985): 90.

34. Furniss, "States of the Union," 15; Varon, *Armies of Deliverance*, 233–34.

35. William Tecumseh Sherman to Charles Anderson, August 1863, Richard Clough Anderson Papers, HL.

36. Thomas McArthur Anderson to Charles Anderson, November 7, 1863, Anderson Papers, HL.

37. Andrew Evans to Samuel Evans, April 5, 1863; Samuel Evans to Andrew Evans, April 19, 26, 1863, in Engs and Brooks, *Their Patriotic Duty,* 123, 130, 132.

38. Andrew Evans to Samuel Evans, June 11, 27, 1863, in Engs and Brooks, *Their Patriotic Duty,* 157, 162.

39. *M'Arthur Democrat*, March 5, 1863

40. *Dayton Daily Empire*, September 8, 1863.

41. *Gallipolis Journal*, September 10, 1863. The paper quoted the *Ohio Statesman* without noting a date.

42. Warshauer, *Connecticut in the American Civil War,* 55, 107–13; Cowden, *"Heaven Will Frown on Such a Cause as This,"* 25–65; Neely, *Lincoln and the Democrats*, 88–89.

43. Harris, *Lincoln and the Border States,* 232–34; Lewis, *For Slavery and Union,* 125.

44. T. J. Barnett to Samuel Barlow, July 6, 1863, Barlow Papers, HL.

45. For McClellan's time as a private citizen prior to his nomination in 1863, see Sears, *George B. McClellan*, 344–70, and George B. McClellan to Elizabeth B. McClellan, December 6, 1863, in McClellan, *The Civil War Papers of George B. McClellan,* 562–63.

46. Emma Biddle to Charles Biddle, December 8, 17, 1862, Biddle Family Papers, HSP.

47. John L. Smith Diary, January 9, 1863.

48. *Philadelphia Age,* June 30, July 13, 1863; Sears, *George B. McClellan,* 354.

49. Daly, *Diary of a Union Lady,* 212.

50. T. J. Barnett to Samuel Barlow, May 15, 1863, Barlow Papers, HL; Sears, *George B. McClellan,* 346.

51. William Bradford Reed to Samuel Barlow, May 25, 1863, Barlow Papers, HL; Shankman, "William B. Reed and the Civil War."

52. George McClellan to Charles C. Fulton, May 28, 1863; McClellan to Samuel S. Cox, June 8, 1863; McClellan to Thurlow Weed, June 13, 1863, in McClellan, *The Civil War Papers of George B. McClellan,* 548–49; Sears, *George B. McClellan,* 355.

53. *Philadelphia Age,* June 19, 1863. The paper ran almost daily comments praising Woodward's candidacy.

54. C. L. Ward to George W. Woodward, June 15, 1863; Woodward to Charles Biddle, undated note that follows above letter in file, Biddle Family Papers, HSP. Biddle's files include many letters from Woodward about political details.

55. George W. Woodward to Charles Biddle, June 29, 1863; Biddle to Woodward, July 7, 1863, Biddle Family Papers, HSP.

56. James Buchanan to Ellis Lewis, August 28, 1863, Ellis Lewis Papers, HSP.

57. Charles Biddle to George McClellan, draft, September 2, 1863, Biddle Family Papers, HSP.

58. See Unknown to Charles Biddle, September 24, 1863, Biddle Family Papers, HSP.

59. George McClellan to Samuel Barlow, September 25, 1863, Barlow Papers, HL, in McClellan, *The Civil War Papers of George McClellan,* 558. In a note to this letter Sears quotes Barlow to McClellan, September 26, 1863, McClellan Papers, Library of Congress.

60. David H. Williams to Samuel Barlow, September 29, 1863, Barlow Papers, HL.

61. Charles Biddle to George W. Woodward, draft, September 30, 1863, Biddle Family Papers, HSP.

62. Charles Biddle to General Andrew Porter, October 2, 1863, Biddle Family Papers, HSP.

63. *Soldiers Read!* This letter from McClellan to Biddle appears in many published forms.

64. Shankman, *The Pennsylvania Antiwar Movement,* 134–36.

65. Sears, *George B. McClellan,* 357–58. Sears does not seem to document these discussions with his normal alacrity.

66. *Speech of Hon. George W. Woodward.*

67. *Speech of Hon. George W. Woodward,* 14 (quotation).

68. Shankman, *The Pennsylvania Antiwar Movement,* 129–30.

69. *The Old Guard* 1 (September 1863): 217–29.

70. *Speech of Hon. George W. Woodward*, 3.

71. *Press* (Philadelphia), September 17, 1863.

72. *Press* (Philadelphia), October 13, 1863.

73. *Press* (Philadelphia), October 14, 1863.

74. *Philadelphia Age*, October 14, 1863.

75. *Raftsman's Journal* (Clearfield, Penn.), October 21, 1863, reprinted from the *Harrisburg Telegraph*, October 15, 1863.

76. *Sunbury American*, October 17, 1863.

77. *Chicago Tribune*, October 13, 1863.

78. *Sun* (New York), October 13, 1863; *Dayton Daily Empire*, October 13, 1863; *Daily Green Mountain Freeman.*, October 13, 1863; *Indiana State Sentinel*, October 19, 1863; *Daily Journal*, October 19, 1863; *Urbana Union*, October 21, 1863; *Daily National Republican*, October 14, 1863.

79. *Cleveland Morning Leader*, October 19, 1863.

80. *Western Reserve Chronicle* (Warren, Ohio), October 14, 1863.

81. *Chicago Tribune*, October 16, 1863. The *Hillsdale Standard* ran the same editorial on October 20, 1863. Neither paper noted where it originated.

82. *Delaware State Journal and Statesman*, October 16, 1863.

83. *Daily Intelligencer*, October 20, 1863. See also the *Caledonian*, October 16, 1863, for similar sentiments.

84. Scholars discussing wartime politics routinely link Vallandigham, Seymour, and Woodward as a trio of Copperhead candidates.

85. Stout, *Upon the Altar of the Nation*, 270–72; Gallagher and Waugh, *The American War*, 132.

86. See Gallman, *Defining Duty in the Civil War*, 132–35. On northern ministers (and priests) and political discourse, see Wesley, *The Politics of Faith during the Civil War*.

87. For a discussion of Union as a driving ideological force, see Gallagher, *The Union War*.

88. Andreasen, "Lincoln's Religious Critics."

89. Timothy L. Wesley makes this point about the suppression of speech at multiple points in *The Politics of Faith during the Civil War*. See also Blair, *With Malice toward Some*, 59–63.

90. Scott, "William S. Plumer's Defense of an Apolitical Pulpit."

91. Holm, *A Kingdom Divided*, 101–23; Wesley, *The Politics of Faith during the Civil War*, 66–8.

92. Stout, *Upon the Altar of the Nation*, 388.

93. Holm, *A Kingdom Divided*, 119–22. On McPheeters, see also Phillips, *The Rivers Ran Backward*, 178, and Stout, *Upon the Altar of the Nation*, 388. On Lincoln's January 2, 1863, letter, also see Wesley, *The Politics of Faith during the Civil War*, 70.

94. Holm, *A Kingdom Divided*, 123.

95. See Phillips, *The Rivers Ran Backwards*, 178–79.

96. Phillips, *The Rivers Ran Backwards*, 179–80.

97. The historian Harry S. Stout writes that "most Northern Protestant pulpits and publications espoused Republican views." He later notes that "clerical Democratic dissenters spoke at their own risk." Stout, *Upon the Altar of the Nation,* 283–84.

98. Wesley, *The Politics of Faith during the Civil War*, 43–92, 73 (quotation). See also Andreasen, "Lincoln's Religious Critics."

99. Andreasen, "Civil War Church Trials"; Wesley, *The Politics of Faith during the Civil War*, 77.

100. Wesley, *The Politics of Faith during the Civil War*, 48.

101. *The Old Guard* 1 (October–December 1863): 249.

102. Van Dyke, *The Spirituality and Independence of the Church.*

103. Stout, *Upon the Altar of the Nation*, 284, 388–89. Stout describes the sermon on pages 388–89 and the abolitionist mob on page 284, with no specific reference.

104. Croly and Wakeman, *Miscegenation*; Neely, *Lincoln and the Democrats*, 108–9; Lemire, *"Miscegenation,"* 115–18.

7. Bracing for an Electoral Clash

1. Levine, "Draft Evasion in the North during the Civil War."

2. Wood, *Black Scare,* 42–43, 63; *Chicago Times,* May 5, 1864, quoting from the *Philadelphia Age,* May 5, 1864; *The Old Guard* 2 (April 1864): 93; Weber, *Copperheads,* 160 and *passim.*

3. Wood, *Black Scare*, 50; Escott, *The Worst Passions of Human Nature,* 153. On racism in the Democratic press, also see Neely, *Lincoln and the Democrats,* 105–7.

4. On the military events, see Varon, *Armies of Deliverance,* 331–39 and *passim,* and Gallagher et al., *The American Civil War,* 185–200.

5. Bordewich, *Congress at War,* 286.

6. Waugh, *Reelecting Lincoln,* 86–88.

7. See Gallman, *The North Fights the Civil War.*

8. *Harper's Weekly,* November 21, 1863; Gallman, *Defining Duty in the Civil War,* 119–21.

9. These were small photographs capable of being mass-produced inexpensively.

10. For thoughts on the commodification of fame, see Gallman, *America's Joan of Arc.* For the changing cultural universe during the Civil War era, see Gallman, *Defining Duty in the Civil War.*

11. See Gallman, *America's Joan of Arc.*

12. For a few of the many stories on their travels, see *Daily Evening Bulletin*, June 24, 1859; *New York Herald,* January 10, 31, 1860; and *Milwaukee Daily Sentinel,* April 28, 1860. For a short discussion of Webb's wartime lecturing career, see Venet, *Neither Ballots nor Bullets,* 128–30.

13. Curry, *Nineteenth-Century American Women Theatre Managers,* 94.

14. The Library of Congress has one *carte de visite* in the Brady-Handy Photograph Collection, Prints and Photographs Division. The National Portrait Gallery in Washington, D.C., has an image of Emma and Ada Webb in its Frederick Hill Meserve Collection. Both images are also in their online digital collections. If the sisters' presence in newspaper announcements and the modest array of photographs is any indication, they had developed a modest level of fame by 1863.

15. *New York Herald,* March 4, 1864. Virginia's *Alexandria Gazette* published the *Herald*'s short notice on March 5, 1864; the *Daily Ohio Statesman* ran it on March 8, 1864. The *Chicago Tribune* ran the same notice on March 8, 1864.

16. *Cleveland Morning Herald,* March 4, 1864.

17. *Daily Ohio Statesman,* March 6, 1864.

18. *Ohio Statesman,* March 9, 1864, quoting the *New York News,* March 5, 1864. The reporter for the *News* seemed to be using direct quotations from the speech. Various other newspapers covered the lecture in some detail or reprinted accounts of the event. One of the most detailed accounts appeared in the *Liberator,* April 15, 1864.

19. *Boston Daily Advertiser,* March 8, 1864, quoting the *New York Tribune.*

20. *Daily National Republican,* March 9, 1864.

21. *Rutland Weekly Herald,* March 10, 1864, paraphrasing the *New York Herald.*

22. *Cleveland Morning Leader,* May 5, 1864. This story, and its use of the word "copperheady," was actually discussing a later talk by Webb on the same themes.

23. *Chicago Tribune,* March 15, 1864.

24. *Ripley Bee,* April 14, 1864; *Aegis and Intelligencer,* April 29, 1864. Both papers, and many others, reprinted the April 1 letter. The *Bee* reprinted it from the *New York Express.*

25. *Cleveland Morning Leader,* May 5, 1864, quoting from a recent issue of the *Troy* (N.Y.) *Times.*

26. *Cleveland Morning Leader,* August 30, 1864.

27. On the history of antiwar literature, which largely emerged after the Civil War, see Wachtell, *War No More.*

28. For the best overview, see Thompson, "Sanitary Fairs in the Civil War." On Philadelphia's fair, see Gallman, "Voluntarism in Wartime." On the fair movement and nationalism, see Lawson, *Patriotic Fires,* 14–39.

29. The idea of presenting beloved commanders with presents had some history in the Union Army. In the fall of 1863 Democratic supporters of George McClellan engaged in a fundraising effort, called the "McClellan Testimonial," where volunteers made donations toward purchasing an item—probably a sword—for their deposed leader. It was a controversial idea that fizzled with time. Orr, "Protesting the McClellan Testimonial"; Orr, "An Army Divided."

30. Thompson, "Sanitary Fairs in the Civil War," 59; *Daily Evening Bulletin,* May 9, 1864.

31. *Daily Evening Bulletin*, May 20, 1864, quoting the *New York Post*, April 25, 1864.

32. *Daily Cleveland Herald*, April 25, 1864; *Lowell Daily Citizen and News*, April 26, 1864. Both stories ran extended quotations from an undated issue of the *New York Herald.*

33. *Lowell Daily Citizen and News*, April 26, 1864, quoting various newspapers.

34. Strong, *The Diary of George Templeton Strong,* 4:432.

35. *Daily Evening Bulletin,* May 9, 1864, quoting several New York newspapers.

36. *Daily Cleveland Herald,* April 26, 1864, quoting the *New York Herald.*

37. *Daily Cleveland Herald,* April 26, 1864; *Daily Evening Bulletin,* May 9, 20, 1864. Both newspapers cite the *New York Tribune* and unnamed New York papers.

38. Gallman, *Defining Duty in the Civil War*, 233–34.

39. Harris, *Two against Lincoln.*

40. Vorenberg, *Final Freedom,* 75.

41. *Speech of Hon. Reverdy Johnson, of Maryland.* In addition of the text itself, see Vorenberg, *Final Freedom*, esp. 96–98, and Harris, *Two against Lincoln*, 71–73 and *passim.*

42. Harris, *Two against Lincoln*, 71; Vorenberg, *Final Freedom*, 96–97; *New York Herald*, April 7, 1864; *Chicago Tribune*, April 10, 11 ("stiff" conservative), 1864.

43. Holzer, *Lincoln and the Power of the Press,* 488–89. On Marble, see McJimsey, *Genteel Partisan*. For a description of this episode that stresses New York politics, see Neely, *The Union Divided,* 111–17.

44. Holzer, *Lincoln and the Power of the Press*, 489–91; McJimsey, *Genteel Partisan*, 52–53.

45. Holzer, *Lincoln and the Power of the Press*, 492–93; Welles, *The Civil War Diary of Gideon Welles,* 415–16.

46. *Daily Intelligencer*, May 25, 1864.

47. *Cleveland Morning Leader,* May 25, 1864.

48. *Chicago Tribune*, May 27, 1864. The *Cleveland Morning Leader* reprinted the *Tribune*'s brief mockery on May 31, 1864.

49. *Der Westbote,* June 2, 1864; *Bedford Gazette*, June 10, 1864.

50. On the letter and responses, see Holzer, *Lincoln and the Power of the Press*, 492–94.

51. Marble, *Freedom of the Press Wantonly Violated.*

52. For an excellent treatment of both speeches, see Varon, *Armies of Deliverance,* 300–302.

53. McPherson and Hogue, *Ordeal by Fire*, 425–26; Varon, *Armies of Deliverance*, 306–12.

54. McPherson and Hogue, *Ordeal by Fire*, 439–40; Varon, *Armies of Deliverance*, 342–45, 344 (quotation).

55. Abraham Lincoln, "Memorandum Concerning His Probable Failure of Re-Election," August 23, 1864, in Lincoln, *Collected Works*, 7:514.

56. I am thinking specifically of the peculiar circumstances that led the president to ask his cabinet members to sign this document without reading it. Since the memo did

not become public until after the election, Lincoln's intentions need not occupy us here. I offered my own thoughts in Gallman, "The Election of 1864."

57. Henry Stebbins to Samuel Barlow, January 23, 1864, Barlow Papers, HL.

58. Hay, *Lincoln and the Civil War in the Diaries and Letters of John Hay*, 143–44. See also Waugh, *Reelecting Lincoln,* 130.

59. David Hunter to Charles Graham Halpine, March 10, 1864, Halpine Papers, HL.

60. Samuel Sullivan Cox to Samuel Barlow, March 10, 1864, Barlow Papers, HL.

61. Waugh, *Reelecting Lincoln*, 145.

62. Sears, *George B. McClellan,* 352–60.

63. Henry Stebbins to Samuel Barlow, January 20, 1864, Barlow Papers, HL.

64. James Harrison to Samuel Barlow, April 6, 1864, Barlow Papers, HL.

65. Clement Hoffman to "Mother," April 16, 1864, Clement Hoffman Letters, Harrisburg Civil War Round Table Collection, US Army Military History Institute, Carlisle, Penna. Thanks to Jonathan White for sharing this source with me.

66. Montgomery Blair to Samuel Barlow, May 1, 1864, Barlow Papers, HL. These quotations come from two letters that appear to have been mailed together on May 1. Blair might have written the first portion of the letter on April 28. Thanks to Jonathan White for sharing his transcriptions of these letters.

67. Joseph McKibben to Samuel Barlow, October 1, 1864, Barlow Papers, HL.

68. *Press* (Philadelphia), August 11, 1864.

69. James Steel to William Steel, June 11, 1864, Steel Letterbooks, HL.

70. Fernando Wood to Samuel Barlow, June 15, 1864, Barlow Papers, HL.

71. Augustus Belmont to Samuel Barlow, telegram, June 15, 1864, Barlow Papers, HL.

72. Waugh, *Reelecting Lincoln,* 207–8.

73. John V. L. Pruyn to Samuel Barlow, June 18, 1864, Barlow Papers, HL.

74. A. Banning Norton to Samuel Barlow, June 22, 1864, Barlow Papers, HL.

75. David H. Williams to Samuel Barlow, June 23, July 2, 1864, Barlow Papers, HL.

76. Sears, *George B. McClellan*, 363.

77. George B. McClellan to Manton Marble, June 25, [1864], in McClellan, *The Civil War Papers of George B. McClellan,* 479–80; Waugh, *Reelecting Lincoln*, 207–8; Sears, *George B. McClellan*, 369.

78. Anne G. Wright to Samuel Barlow, July 12, 1864, Barlow Papers, HL.

79. Sears, *George B. McClellan*, 364–65; George B. McClellan to Francis P. Blair, July 22, 1864, in McLellan, *The Civil War Papers of George B. McClellan*, 583–85.

80. Durbin Ward to Samuel Sullivan Cox, August 2, 1864, Samuel Sullivan Cox Papers, Brown University. See also Lindsey, "The Presidential Campaign of 1864 as Viewed by a Federal Army Colonel."

81. Charles D. Robinson to Abraham Lincoln, August 7, 1864, in Lincoln, *Collected Works,* 7:501–2. This letter appears in a footnote to the drafts of Lincoln's response.

82. Sears, *George B. McClellan*, 372.

83. Thomas Marshall Key to Samuel Barlow, August 24, 1864, Barlow Papers, HL.

84. Sears, *George B. McClellan*, 372, quoting August Belmont to Samuel Barlow, August 29, 1864.

85. Silbey, *A Respectable Minority*, 117.

86. Sears, *George B. McClellan*, 363.

87. Brooks, "Two War-Time Conventions."

88. Brooks, "Two War-Time Conventions," 733.

89. Sears, *George B. McClellan*, 373.

90. Silbey, *A Respectable Minority*, 123–32.

91. Brooks, "Two War-Time Conventions," 732–53; Noah Brooks to John Nicolay, August 29, September 2, 1864, in Brooks, *Lincoln Observed*, 132–137; Waugh, *Reelecting Lincoln*, 276–94. Brooks's contemporary account and his letters to Nicolay are not always identical.

92. Theodore Romeyn to Samuel Barlow, August 31, 1864, Barlow Papers, HL.

93. Daniel Devlin to Samuel Barlow, September 1, 1864, Barlow Papers, HL.

94. James Buchanan to Lewis S. Coryell, September 6, 1864, Coryell Papers, HSP.

95. Sears, *George B. McClellan*, 374–78.

96. Andrew Morris to Samuel Barlow, September 2, 1864, Barlow Papers, HL.

97. William Cassidy to Samuel Barlow, September 5, 1864, Barlow Papers, HL.

98. William B. Reed to Samuel Barlow, September 1, 4, 1864, Barlow Papers, HL.

99. George McClellan to Democratic National Committee, September 4, 8, 1864, in McClellan, *The Civil War Papers of George B. McClellan*, 590–97; Silbey, *A Respectable Minority*, 134–36; Waugh, *Reelecting Lincoln*, 298–302.

8. 1864

1. On the Atlanta campaign, see Hess, *The Civil War in the West*, esp. 213–32. For an older but still superb treatment of the election of 1864, see Silbey, *A Respectable Minority*, 118–57.

2. Varon, *Armies of Deliverance*, 357–62.

3. Phillips, *The Rivers Ran Backward*, 261–62, quoting from Johanna L. Underwood Diary, Western Kentucky University, Bowling Green.

4. Phillips, *The Rivers Ran Backward*, 282.

5. For just two examples, separated by half a century, see Rawley, *Turning Points of the Civil War*, 169–205, and Redd, "The Election of 1864."

6. Perhaps the most important concern in the months before the election centered on the soldiers' vote: which soldiers would be allowed to vote, and who would they support? On this crucial topic, see White, *Emancipation, the Union Army, and the Reelection of Abraham Lincoln*.

7. J. Henry Liebenau to George McClellan, October 8, 1864, in McClellan, *The Civil War Papers of George B. McClellan*, 612n1; Sears, *George B. McClellan*, 380–81.

8. Daly, *Diary of a Union Lady*, 307.

9. Charles Mason to George McClellan, October 3, 1864; McClellan to Samuel Barlow, [October 4, 1864], in McClellan, *The Civil War Papers of George McClellan*, 608–10.

10. Sears, *George B. McClellan*, 379–80.

11. See Manton Marble to George McClellan, September 12, 1864; McClellan to Marble, September 17, [1864]; McClellan to Samuel Barlow, in McClellan, *The Civil War Papers of George B. McClellan*, 599–601, 601n1.

12. George McClellan to Samuel Barlow, September 23, [1864]; McClellan to Henry M. Naglee, September 23, [1864], in McClellan, *The Civil War Papers of George B. McClellan*, 600–603.

13. George McClellan to Allan Pinkerton, October 20, [1864], in McClellan, *The Civil War Paper of George B. McClellan*, 614–15.

14. *New York Herald*, September 11, 1864, cited in Waugh, *Reelecting Lincoln*, 302.

15. John W. Wall to George McClellan, September 1, 1864, in McClellan, *The Civil War Papers of George B. McClellan*, 592; Sears cites the original in the Library of Congress. McClellan sent this letter to Samuel Barlow in a September 6, 1864, letter. This quote is in a note to that letter. McClellan to Barlow, September 6, 1864, in McClellan, *The Civil War Papers of George B. McClellan*, 592.

16. Samuel Barlow to George McClellan, September 12, 1864; McClellan to Barlow, September 13, 1864, in McClellan, *The Civil War Papers of George B. McClellan*, 598, 598n1. The letter from Barlow is quoted in a note to the letter of the 13th.

17. William Reed to Samuel Barlow, September 13, 1864, Barlow Papers, HL.

18. George McClellan to Samuel Barlow, September 23, 1864, in McClellan, *The Civil War Paper of George B. McClellan*, 602–3.

19. Henry Myer Phillips to Samuel Barlow, September 30, 1864, Barlow Papers, HL.

20. Furniss, "States of the Union," 298–99, 302–4. See also Harris, *Two against Lincoln*, 115–68.

21. For a discussion of the local fundraising for the event, see Douglas Taylor to Samuel Barlow, September 13, 1864, Barlow Papers, HL.

22. George McClellan to Robert C. Winthrop, March 25, [1863]; January 1, 1864, in McClellan, *The Civil War Papers of George B. McClellan*, 543, 564.

23. *Speech of Hon. Robert C. Winthrop*. On Winthrop, see Smith, *No Party Now*, 127–29.

24. William Endicott to Robert C. Winthrop, September 21, 1864, Winthrop Papers, Massachusetts Historical Society, Boston.

25. George McClellan to Robert C. Winthrop, September 20, 1864, Winthrop Papers, Massachusetts Historical Society.

26. *National Intelligencer*, September 22, 1864, quoting the *New York World*.

27. *Ohio Statesman*, September 24, 1864, quoting the *Chicago Times*, September 19, 1864; *Manitowoc Pilot*, September 23, 1864.

28. See Neely, *Lincoln and the Democrats*, 15, 20, and *passim;* Altschuler and Blumin, *Rude Republic*, 163–64 and *passim;* and Neely, *The Union Divided*, 63–64.

29. *Daily Register*, September 22, 1864.

30. *Columbia Democrat and Bloomsburg General Advertiser*, September 24, 1864. The paper made a similar point on October 1, 1864.

31. *Daily Press*, September 22, 1864.

32. *Cleveland Morning Leader*, September 21, 1864.

33. *Burlington Weekly Hawk-Eye*, October 1, 1864. The paper reprinted the *New York Herald* article.

34. *New York World*, October 20, 1864, cited in Waugh, *Reelecting Lincoln*, 322.

35. George McClellan to Robert C. Winthrop, October 22, [1864], in McClellan, *The Civil War Papers of George B. McClellan*, 615–16.

36. McGerr, *The Decline of Popular Politics*, 69–70.

37. Neely, *Lincoln and the Democrats*, 111.

38. The New London speech and its accompanying documents, pamphlet no. 23, is reprinted in Friedel, *Union Pamphlets of the Civil War*, 1076–1108; Waugh, *Reelecting Lincoln*, 322; Taylor, *"The Most Complete Political Machine Ever Known,"* 208.

39. *Speech of Hon. Robert C. Winthrop;* Friedel, *Union Pamphlets of the Civil War*, 1076–1108.

40. Wood, *Black Scare*, 71–73, citing the *New York World*, September 23, 26, 27, 28; New York *Weekly Day Book*, October 1, 8, 1864; and Albany *Atlas and Argus*, October 1, 1864.

41. *Ohio Statesman*, September 28, 1864.

42. *Daily Register*. September 29, 1864.

43. *Wilmington Gazette*, September 20, 1864.

44. Wood, *Black Scare*, 62–65 and *passim.*

45. William A. Blair makes this point in *With Malice toward Some,* 10. See also Neely, *Lincoln and the Democrats*, 107–8.

46. Warshauer, *Connecticut in the American Civil War*, 163.

47. *North Branch Democrat*, August 12, 1864; *Clearfield Republican*, November 2, 1864.

48. *Campaign Songs.*

49. *Copperhead Minstrel.* On the second edition, see Neely, *The Boundaries of American Political Culture in the Civil War Era*, 123.

50. For a discussion of antebellum minstrel traditions and racial stereotypes in popular culture, see Baker, *Affairs of Party*, 212–43.

51. Neely, *Lincoln and the Democrats*, 130–32.

52. On antebellum and wartime political culture, particularly in urban settings, see McGerr, *The Decline of Popular Politics*; Altschuler and Blumin, *Rude Republic*; Neely, *The Union Divided*; Henkin, *City Reading*; and Gallman, *Defining Duty in the Civil War*.

53. This section includes a diversity of printed sources aimed at "workers" or "workingmen." Collectively they illustrate how both Republicans and Democrats tried to explain their partisan positions to broad swaths of White male voters. But those terms are imprecise. Some seemed aimed at literate, unskilled urban workers, while others

probably targeted the sort of skilled artisans who had marched in Philadelphia in February 1861. Some editors may have included farm laborers in their target audience. Definitions are unclear, although in nearly all that follows there is a presumption that the readers (those "workers") would care about personal economic matters as well as the best route to a lasting peace.

54. Varon, *Armies of Deliverance*, 273–74.

55. Baum, *The Civil War Party System,* 85–87, 100; Ural, "'Ye Sons of Green Erin Assemble,'" 126.

56. Montgomery, *Beyond Equality,* 101–2.

57. *Address of the Workingmen's United Political Association*; *Columbia Democrat and Bloomsburg General Advertiser*, August 20, 1864. The printed pamphlet dates the speech as July 4, but the complete copy from the *Columbia Democrat* dates it as August 4, which makes more sense in context.

58. *To Working Men*. This broadside appears in eight institutions in WorldCat as well as the New York Public Library. None hint at a place of publication. For a pamphlet aimed at Philadelphia workingmen making the same argument that the Democrats were of the aristocracy and aligned with the southern slaveocracy, see *Proofs for Workingmen*.

59. *Democrats Who Love the Union.*

60. *A Traitor's Peace!* Of course this broadside appeared before the Democrats had selected their candidate.

61. *The Workingman*. The text refers to Conness as "Conners."

62. *Union County Star and Lewisburg Chronicle*, November 1, 1864.

63. *Rutland Weekly Herald*, November 3, 1864.

64. *Victory Union Peace.*

65. *Clearfield Republican*, August 24, 1864.

66. *Ashland Union*, September 28, 1864.

67. *Dayton Daily Empire*, October 8, 1864.

68. *Joliet Signal*, October 4, 1864; *Grand Haven News*, October 19, 1864. This short squib appears to be the sort of item borrowed from other papers.

69. *Aegis and Intelligencer*, October 21, 1864, reprinted from the *New Haven Register*.

70. Baum, *The Civil War Party System*, 94–95 (quoting the *Boston Pilot*); Kurtz, "The Union as It Was," 109–10; Kurtz, *Excommunicated from the Union,* 122–23.

71. Montgomery, *Beyond Equality*, 109–112, 109 (1st quotation), 112 (2nd quotation, from *Fincher's Trades Review,* August 20, 1864).

72. White, *Emancipation, the Union Army, and the Reelection of Abraham Lincoln.*

73. Silbey, *A Respectable Minority*, 149, 150, 162. Silbey relied on the foundational research of Walter Dean Burnham.

74. Rawley, *The Politics of Union,* 161; Silbey, *A Respectable Minority*, 149, 155; Varon, *Armies of Deliverance*, 372–53.

75. White, *Emancipation, the Union Army, and the Reelection of Abraham Lincoln,* 1–9 and *passim*; Varon, *Armies of Deliverance*, 373–74. In Indiana, where absentee ballots

were not allowed and only a handful of regiments were furloughed to return home and vote, Republicans managed to reelect Governor Morton and support Lincoln by about twenty thousand votes. Etcheson, *A Generation at War,* 120. Timothy Orr notes that soldiers from New York, Connecticut, and Minnesota were allowed to vote secretly, with their ballots returned to their home districts to be lumped in with all other ballots. Thus, insofar as intimidation inhibited Democratic absentee balloting, these votes might have yielded different results. He concludes that the overall soldier vote was likely closer. Orr, "An Army Divided."

76. As discussed earlier, John L. Smith's diaries and his letters from the Union Army are housed together in the Historical Society of Pennsylvania. In truth the letters and the diaries are not written by the same person, and the letters were from John Smith. I devoted many hours to trying to identify the diarist, and I had help. I still do not know his name, so it seems fair to call this anonymous figure "John Smith."

77. The "n-word" appears thirty-three times in Smith's wartime diary, mostly in 1863 and 1864.

78. John L. Smith Diary, January 9, February 23, March 6, 1863, and *passim.* Once he became a part of the Saturday Evening Club, he seems to have attended almost every week, noting the host and some of the men he saw but never commenting on the event itself.

79. John L. Smith Diary, November 9, 1864.

80. John L. Smith Diary, January 3, April 15, 1865, and *passim.*

81. Katherine Brinley Wharton Diary, January 23, April 10, May 12, 1861; September 5, 1862.

82. Katherine Brinley Wharton Diary, November 10, 1862; January 7, April 12, June 21, 1863.

83. Katherine Brinley Wharton Diary, July 19, October 11, November 8, 1864; May 4, 1865. There is a gap in the diary as the family relocated.

84. Ellen Wallace Diary, September–November 1864, November 8, 11, 1864 (quotations).

85. Andrew Evans to Samuel Evans, August 16, October 18, 1863; Samuel Evans to Andrew Evans, August 23, 1863, in Engs and Brooks, *Their Patriotic Duty,* 183–86.

86. Samuel Evans to Andrew Evans, September 1, 26, 1864; Andrew Evans to Samuel Evans, September 4, October 23, 1864, in Engs and Brooks, *Their Patriotic Duty*, 285, 287, 289, 302–4.

87. Mary Evans to Samuel Evans, October 7, 1863; Jane Evans to Samuel Evans, September 11, 1864; Samuel Evans to Andrew Evans, September 24, 1864, in Engs and Brooks, *Their Patriotic Duty*, 201, 287–90, 292.

88. Samuel Evans to Jane Evans, October 15, 1864, in Engs and Brooks, *Their Patriotic Duty*, 299–301.

89. Jane Standard to William Standard, March 31, October 6, 1864, in Roberts, *"This Infernal War,"* 178, 222.

90. William Standard to Jane Standard, August 21, September 11, 1864, in Roberts, *"This Infernal War,"* 214, 216.

91. William Standard to Jane Standard, September 24, 1864, in Roberts, *"This Infernal War,"* 219.

92. William Steel to James Steel, June 11, 1864, Steel Letterbooks, HL. This letter is also discussed in chapter 7.

93. William Steel to "my dear mother," June 27, 1864, Steel Letterbooks, HL.

94. Anna Mercer LaRoche Francis Journal, November 1, 1864.

95. Daly, *Diary of a Union Lady,* 306, 310.

96. William Henry Wadsworth to Samuel Barlow, October 10, 1864, Barlow Papers, HL.

97. Samuel Butterworth to Samuel Barlow, October 22, 1864, Barlow Papers, HL.

98. John Thomas Doyle to Samuel Barlow, October 31, 1864, Barlow Papers, HL.

99. Samuel Asheton Bayard to Samuel Barlow, October 29, 1863, Barlow Papers, HL.

100. James Harrison to Samuel Barlow, October 30, 1864, Barlow Papers, HL.

101. Henry Douglas Bacon to Samuel Barlow, November 18, 1864, Barlow Papers, HL.

102. Dale Baum argued that in Massachusetts the "Union" designation probably had a negligible impact on Democratic voting. State voters who voted Democrat in 1860 generally remained with the party in 1864. Baum did suggest that some voters who abstained in 1860 or who voted for the Constitutional Union Party in 1860 may have gravitated toward Republicans in 1864, perhaps responding to the "Union" rhetoric. Baum, *The Civil War Party System*, 70–71.

103. These platforms are available in many places. I used the wonderful Teaching American History website, https://teachingamericanhistory.org/library/document/the-1864-republican-party-platform/.

104. Randall, *Lincoln the President*, 211. Thanks to Tom Pegram for pointing out this quotation.

105. It is at least worth considering that the much-examined soldiers' vote included a younger subset of the overall White male population, and most had no political recollection of a moment when the Republicans had not existed.

106. Rodgers, "Copperheads or a Respectable Minority," 132.

107. Washington McLean to Samuel Barlow, December 4, 1864, Barlow Papers, HL.

9. Peace and an Uncertain Future

1. Buchanan, *Mr. Buchanan's Administration on the Eve of the Administration*, iv–v and *passim.*

2. Vorenberg, *Final Freedom,* 174.

3. Varon, *Armies of Deliverance,* 392–95, 393, 395 (quotations); Vorenberg, *Final Freedom*, 197–210; Summers, *The Ordeal of the Reunion,* 7–8.

4. Placed in the context of Lincoln's other writings about emancipation and Reconstruction, it is certainly possible to imagine a more optimistic future implied in his Second Inaugural. Thanks to Vernon Burton for discussions on this point.

5. Varon, *Armies of Deliverance*, 396–99; White, *Lincoln's Greatest Speech.*

6. Ellen Wallace Diary, March 4, 1865.

7. *Historical Statistics of the U.S. Colonial Times to 1970,* 1083. The data from *Historical Statistics* combines Republicans and Union Party members in one column: House, 42 Democrats, 149 Unionists; Senate, 10 Democrats, 42 Unionists.

8. On these days see Varon, *Appomattox.*

9. Ellen Wallace Diary, April 11, 1865.

10. Varon, *Appomattox*, 215–16.

11. James Asheton Bayard to Samuel Barlow, April 19, 1865, Barlow Papers, HL.

12. *The Old Guard* 3 (May 1, 1865): 240.

13. Much has been written about the aftermath of the assassination, including Turner, *Beware the People Weeping*, and Hodes, *Mourning Lincoln.*

14. *Public Ledger*, April 17, 1865; Gallman, *Mastering Wartime* 189.

15. Gallman, *Mastering Wartime*, 189, citing Isaac Hacker Diary, HSP.

16. Hodes, *Mourning Lincoln*, 83–84.

17. Hodes, *Mourning Lincoln*, 83–85.

18. Hodes, *Mourning Lincoln*, 85–86. Hodes quotes Dall and the Chicagoan.

19. Hodes, *Mourning Lincoln*, 87–91.

20. Turner, *Beware the People Weeping*, 81–82.

21. Hodes, *Mourning Lincoln*, 83.

22. Edward Waln Diary, April 23, 1865, HSP.

23. Katherine Brinley Wharton Diary, May 4, 1865, Wharton Papers, HSP; Gallman, *Mastering Wartime*, 111–12.

24. Daly, *Diary of a Union Lady*, 353–55.

25. *Chicago Tribune*, May 3, 1865. This story covers the New York speech, although the *Tribune* identified the wrong brother at the rostrum. Sidney George Fisher's diary, cited below, includes the same details.

26. Fisher, *A Philadelphia Perspective,* 254–55.

27. *New York Herald*, April 28, 1865; *Cleveland Morning Leader*, April 28, 1865; Fisher, *A Philadelphia Perspective*, 255–59.

28. See citations above to the *New York Herald*, *Chicago Tribune*, and *Cleveland Morning Herald.*

29. *Clearfield Republican*, May 3, 1865.

30. What follows are my general thoughts after a career of reading. Some useful broad studies of Reconstruction that consider northern politics include Foner, *Reconstruction*; Richardson, *West after Appomattox*; Summers, *The Ordeal of the Reunion*; and Foner, *The Second Founding.*

31. Summers, *The Ordeal of the Reunion,* 62–64; Donald, Baker, and Holt, *The Civil War and Reconstruction,* 528–29.

32. Summers, *The Ordeal of the Reunion,* 141–51.

33. Summers, *The Ordeal of the Reunion,* 300–302; Cowden, *"Heaven Will Frown on Such a Cause as This,"* 192–94.

34. *Philadelphia Telegraph,* June 17, 1871, quoting George William Curtis in *Harper's Weekly.*

35. *Stark County Democrat,* June 22, 1871.

36. *A History of the Life and Trials of Thomas McGehean.*

37. Summers, *The Ordeal of the Reunion,* 306–16.

Conclusion

1. For a valuable survey of how historians have used labels, and some important observations about the contested meaning of "disloyalty," see Rodgers, "Copperheads or a Respectable Minority."

2. The reader might expect a long citation here listing all the books I think handled these topics poorly. Sorry.

3. Weber, "The Political Culture of the North," 94. Weber cites her own previous work, *Copperheads,* 17–20.

4. For detailed biographies of six key Peace Democrats, including a chapter on Seymour, see Cowden, *"Heaven Will Frown on Such a Cause as This."*

5. For a good short collection of wartime writings, including both Whitman and a taste of soldiers' writings, see Masur, *". . . The Real War Will Never Get in the Books."*

6. *Ohio Statesman,* March 6, 1864, quoting the *New York News,* March 5, 1864.

7. In her study of Putnam County, Indiana, Nicole Etcheson notes that "Copperhead sentiment rose with victory and fell with defeat." Etcheson, *A Generation at War,* 105.

8. For a detailed analysis of the meaning of treason in legal and public discourse, see Blair, *With Malice toward Some.*

9. This discussion touches on a rich scholarship on the meanings of "duty," "loyalty," and "patriotism" during the Civil War (and during wartime in general). These discussions often build on the core observation that patriotic individuals might feel that the dictates of "duty" as they understand those requirements (legally, morally, etc.) might run counter to a national cause. Or, in other contexts, an individual's actions might be driven by multiple "loyalties" to different ideas, individuals, or institutions. For a discussion of the latter point in a Confederate context, see Gallagher, *Becoming Confederates.* For a collection of essays with an excellent introduction on these subjects, see Sandow, *Contested Loyalty.*

10. Weber's *Copperheads* is a treasure-trove of accounts of such plans, including Dodd's.

11. Putnam County, Indiana, saw lots of wartime conflict, some violent, and Copperheads maintained an active presence throughout the conflict. The historian of the county's war concludes that the Copperheads "may have skirted the line between loyalty and treason," but it is unclear if they ever really crossed that line. Etcheson, *A Generation at War*, 100.

12. Blair, *With Malice toward Some*; Holzer, *Lincoln and the Power of the Press.*

13. For the best analysis, see Neely, *The Fate of Liberty.*

14. Blair, *With Malice toward Some*, 59 and *passim.* See also Holzer, *Lincoln and the Power of the Press*, 353–58.

15. We should not exaggerate. While quite a few newspapers faced attacks, the overall violence directed at Copperheads pales in comparison to political violence in other places and times, including the antebellum attacks on abolitionists.

16. Vallandigham, *The Great Civil War in America.* See chapter 3.

17. *The Old Guard* 1 (August 1863): 214. See also the introduction.

18. At the end of 1863 *The Old Guard* combined three months into one edition. On a few occasions publication glitches kept the journal from running the planned portrait.

19. On Olds, see Andreasen, "Lincoln's Religious Critics," 200–203.

20. *The Old Guard* 1 (February 1863): 43–45. See also chapter 5.

21. *The Old Guard* 1 (April 1863): 96.

22. *The Old Guard* 2 (February 1864): 37–39

23. *The Old Guard* 2 (March 1864): 56–58.

24. *The Old Guard* 1 (September 1863): 217–29.

25. *The Old Guard* 2 (July 1864): 162.

26. *The Old Guard* 1 (June 1863): 140–41.

27. *The Old Guard* 1 (October–December 1863): 287–88.

28. *The Old Guard* 2 (June 1864): 144.

29. *The Old Guard* 2 (February 1864): 43–44.

30. Cowden's *"Heaven Will Frown on Such a Cause as This"* profiles Thomas Hart Seymour, James Asheton Bayard, Clement Laird Vallandigham, and Alexander Long, all major Copperheads profiled in *The Old Guard.*

31. For an extended discussion of the idea of "white supremacy," see Neely, *Lincoln and the Democrats*, 96–107. Even if Democrats had endorsed the ideas we associate with the term, the phrase itself was not in wide wartime usage, nor were the politics of race central to the official Democratic message.

32. Again, the term "racist" really speaks more to our modern sensibilities, but here it suggests opinions and language that were quite extreme for the historic moment.

33. Baker, *Affairs of Party*, 214–43.

34. Jean H. Baker draws these links between racist popular culture and Democratic political discourse; see Baker, *Affairs of Party*, 249–58.

35. Maizlish, "Race and Politics in the Northern Democracy."

36. Schwalm, "'Overrun with Free Negroes.'"

37. Gallagher, *The Union War*, 94–100 and *passim*.

38. Gallman, *Defining Duty in the Civil War*, 25, 223–24.

39. Neely, *Lincoln and the Democrats*, 99–105, 102 (quotation).

40. Neely, *Lincoln and the Democrats*, 100–101. Neely notes that Jean H. Baker incorrectly describes Van Evrie as a Democratic pamphleteer. He may well have supported the party, but the party did not claim him. Baker, *Affairs of Party*, 178–79. For more on Van Evrie, see Escott, *The Worst Passions of Human Nature*, 81–82.

41. Baker, *Affairs of Party*, 177–90. Baker notes that "Douglas wished to replace moral judgments on good and evil with what he considered effective policy." Baker, *Affairs of Party*, 192.

42. Leonard, *Slaves, Slaveholders, and a Kentucky Community's Struggle toward Freedom*.

43. Biddle, *The Alliance with the Negro*.

44. Ingersoll, *A Letter to a Friend in a Slave State*, 27.

45. *Emancipation and Its Results*; Gallagher, *The Union War*, 42.

46. Ryan et al., *Address to the People of the Democracy of Wisconsin*.

47. Vallandigham, *The Great Civil War in America*. See chapter 3.

48. Hopkins, *Bible View of Slavery* (Philadelphia).

49. Hopkins, *Bible View of Slavery* (New York). See chapter 3.

50. "Mayor Francis Cornwall Sherman Inaugural Address," 1–3. See chapter 4.

51. *Speech of Hon. George W. Woodward*.

52. *Ohio Statesman*, March 9, 1864, quoting the *New York News*, March 5, 1864.

53. *Speech of Hon. Reverdy Johnson, of Maryland*.

54. *Speech of Hon. Robert C. Winthrop*. See chapter 8.

BIBLIOGRAPHY

Primary Sources

Manuscript Collections

Brown University, Providence, R.I.
  Samuel Sullivan Cox Papers (microfilm)

Columbia University, Rare Book and Manuscript Library, New York
  Anna Mercer LaRoche Francis Journal

Harrisburg Civil War Round Table Collection, U.S. Army Military History Institute, Carlisle, Penn.
  Clement Hoffman Letters (courtesy of Jonathan White)

Historical Society of Pennsylvania, Philadelphia
  Biddle Family Papers
  Lewis S. Coryell Papers
  George W. Fahnestock Diary
  Charles Henry Fisher Letters, Society Collection
  Elizabeth Ingersoll Fisher Diary (in Sidney George Fisher Collection)
  George Cadwalader Papers
  Isaac Hacker Diary
  Alexander Henry Papers
  Ellis Lewis Papers.
  Peter McCall Papers, Cadwalader Family Papers
  John L. Smith Diary
  Edward Waln Diary
  Katherine Johnstone Brinley Wharton Papers
  Sarah Butler Wister Diary, Wister and Butler Family Papers

Huntington Library, San Marino, Calif.
  Richard Clough Anderson Papers
  Samuel L. M. Barlow Papers
  Jonathan Davis Hale Papers
  Charles Graham Halpine Papers

Joseph Holt Papers
Isaac Sherman Papers
William Alexanders Steel Letterbooks
Henry Waller Papers

Kentucky Historical Society, Frankfort
Barlow Family U.S. Civil War Collection
Susan Scrogin and Henry Haviland Letters
Ellen Wallace and Annie Starling Diaries

Library of Congress, Washington, D.C.
Abraham Lincoln Papers

Massachusetts Historical Society, Boston
Winthrop Papers (digital collection)

National Archives, Washington, D.C.
Historical Reports of State Acting Assistant Provost Marshals General and District Provost Marshals, 1865, M1163

Newspapers and Journals

Aegis and Intelligencer (Bel Air, Md.)
Alexandria (Va.) *Gazette*
Ashland Union (Ashland County, Ohio)
Athens (Tenn.) *Post*
Bedford (Penn.) *Gazette*
Bellows Falls (Vt) *Times*
Boston Daily Advertiser
Boston Herald
Burlington (Iowa) *Weekly Hawk-Eye*
Burlington (Vt.) *Free Press*
Cadiz (Ohio) *Democratic Sentinel*
Caledonian (St. Johnsbury, Vt.).
Chicago Tribune
Clearfield (Penn.) *Republican*
Cleveland Morning Herald
Cleveland Morning Leader
Columbia (Penn.) *Democrat and Bloomsburg General Advertiser*
Daily Cleveland Herald
Daily Dispatch (Richmond, Va.)

Daily Evening Bulletin (San Francisco)
Daily Journal (Evansville, Ind.)
Daily Green Mountain Freeman (Montpelier, Vt.)
Daily Intelligencer (Wheeling, W.V.)
Daily National Republican (D.C.)
Daily Ohio Statesman (Columbus)
Daily Press (Portland, Maine)
Daily Register (Wheeling, W.Va.)
Dayton (Ohio) *Daily Empire*
Delaware (Ohio) *Gazette*
Delaware State Journal and Statesman (Wilmington)
Democratic Press (Eaton, Ohio)
Der Westbote (Columbus, Ohio)
Gallipolis (Ohio) *Journal*
Germantown (Penn.) *Telegraph*
Grand Haven (Mich.) *News*
Hancock (Ohio) *Jeffersonian*
Harper's Weekly
Harrisburg (Penn.) *Telegraph*
Hillsdale (Mich.) *Standard*
Holmes County Farmer (Millersburg, Ohio)
Indiana State Sentinel (Indianapolis)
Joliet (Ill.) *Signal*
Liberator (Boston)
Lowell (Mass.) *Daily Citizen and News*
Manitowoc (Wisc.) *Pilot*
Marshall County Republican (Plymouth, Ind.)
M'Arthur Democrat (Vinton County, Ohio)
Milwaukee Daily Sentinel
Milwaukee Pilot
Muscatine (Iowa) *Weekly Journal*
National Intelligencer (Washington, D.C.)
National Republican (Washington, D.C.)
Newark Daily Advertiser
New York Freeman's Journal
New York Herald
New York Times
North American (Philadelphia)
North Branch Democrat (Tunkhannock, Penn.)
Ohio Statesman (Columbus)
The Old Guard (New York)

Ottawa (Ill.) *Free Trader*
Philadelphia Age
Philadelphia Inquirer
Philadelphia Telegraph
Plymouth (Ind.) *Democrat*
Press (Philadelphia)
Public Ledger (Philadelphia)
Ripley (Ohio) *Bee*
Rutland (Vt.) *Weekly Herald*
Stark County Democrat (Canton, Ohio)
Sun (New York)
Sunbury (Penn.) *American*
Sunday Dispatch (Philadelphia)
Sunday Express (Philadelphia)
Union County Star and Lewisburg (Penn.) *Chronicle*
Urbana (Ohio) *Union*
Vermont Phœnix (Brattleboro)
Western Reserve Chronicle (Warren, Ohio)
Wilmington (Del.) *Gazette*
Yorkville (S.C.) *Enquirer*

Published Primary Sources

Documents

Congressional Globe. House of Representatives. Washington, D.C.

Democrat and Republican Party Platforms. 1864. Teaching American History. https://teachingamericanhistory.org/library/document/the-1864-republican-party-platform/.

Historical Statistics of the U.S. Colonial Times to 1970. Vol. 2. Washington, D.C.: U.S. Bureau of the Census, 1975.

"Mayor Francis Cornwall Sherman Inaugural Address." May 4, 1863. In Chicago Common Council. *Journal of the Proceedings,* May 4, 1863, 1–3. https://www.chipublib.org/mayor-francis-cornwall-sherman-inaugural-address-186/.

U.S. Census of 1860.

The War of the Rebellion: A Compilation of the Official Records of the Union and Confederate Armies. Washington, D.C.: Government Printing Office, 1880–1901.

Pamphlets, Lectures, and Broadsides

Address of the Workingmen's United Political Association of the City and County of New York to the Workingmen of the United States. New York, 1864.

Biddle, Charles J. *The Alliance with the Negro: Speech of Hon. Charles J. Biddle, of Pennsylvania; Delivered in the House of Representatives of the United States, March 6, 1862.* Washington, D.C., 1862.

Brooks, Noah. "Two War-Time Conventions." *Century,* March 1895, 732–37.

Buchanan, James. *Mr. Buchanan's Administration on the Eve of the Administration.* New York, 1866.

Campaign Songs. N.p., [1864].

Carpenter, Matthew H. *Mat. H. Carpenter's Review of Mr. Ryan's Address.* Milwaukee, 1862.

Copperhead Minstrel: A Choice Collection of Democratic Poems and Songs for the Use of Political Clubs and the Social Circle. New York, 1863.

Croly, David G., and George Wakeman. *Miscegenation: The Theory of the Blending of the Races, Applied to the American White Man and Negro.* New York, 1864.

Democrats Who Love the Union. Philadelphia, 1864.

Emancipation and Its Results—Is Ohio to Be Africanized? Speech of Hon. S. S. Cox, of Ohio. Delivered in the House of Representatives, June 6, 1862. Washington, D.C., 1862.

Forney, John W. *Eulogy upon the Hon. Stephen A. Douglas: Delivered at the Smithsonian Institute, Washington, July 3, 1861.* Philadelphia, 1861.

Friedel, Frank, ed. *Union Pamphlets of the Civil War, 1861–1865.* 2 vols. Cambridge, Mass.: Harvard University Press, 1967.

Hays, William S. *The Constitution as It Is, the Union as It Was.* Louisville, Ky., 1863.

A History of the Life and Trials of Thomas McGehean. Cincinnati, 1874.

Hopkins, John H. *Bible View of Slavery.* New York, [1863?].

———. *Bible View of Slavery.* Philadelphia, 1863.

———. *The Life of the Late Right Reverend John Henry Hopkins, First Bishop of Vermont, by One of His Sons.* New York, 1873.

———. *A Scriptural, Ecclesiastical, and Historical View of Slavery, from the Days of the Patriarch Abraham, to the Nineteenth Century: Addressed to the Right Rev. Alonzo Potter.* New York, [1864].

Ingersoll, Charles. *A Convention of the People: [Speech of Hon. Charles Ingersoll at a] Meeting of the Democratic Association of the 15th Ward.* Philadelphia, April 23, 1863.

———. *A Letter to a Friend in a Slave State. By a Citizen of Pennsylvania.* Philadelphia, 1862.

———. *Party Conservatism: Meeting of the Democratic Club, Manayunk, Philadelphia, June 10, 1863.* Philadelphia, 1863.

Letter from the Hon. Joseph Holt upon the Policy of the General Government, the Pending Revolution, Its Objects, Its Probable Results If Successful, and the Duty of Kentucky in the Crisis. Louisville, Ky., 1861.

Letter from the Right Rev. John H. Hopkins, D.D., Ll. D. Bishop of Vermont, on the Bible View of Slavery. New York, 1861.

Lieber, Francis. *No Party Now; But All for Our Country.* New York, 1863.

Marble, Manton. *Freedom of the Press Wantonly Violated: Letter of Mr. Marble to President Lincoln, Reappearance of the Journal of Commerce, Opinions of the Press on This Outrage.* New York, 1864.

Proofs for Workingmen of the Monarchic and Aristocratic Designs of the Southern Conspirators and Their Northern Allies. Philadelphia, 1864.

Protest of the Bishop and Clergy of the Diocese of Pennsylvania against Bishop Hopkins' Letter on African Slavery. Philadelphia, 1863.

Ryan, E. G., et al. *Address to the People of the Democracy of Wisconsin, Adopted in the State Convention at Milwaukee, September 3d, 1862.* Milwaukee, 1862.

Society for the Diffusion of Political Knowledge. No. 1. New York, 1863.

Soldiers Read! Philadelphia, October 12, 1863.

Speech of Hon. George W. Woodward, Delivered at the Great Union Meeting in Independence Square, Philadelphia, December 13th, 1860: The Democratic Platform, Adopted by the State Convention at Harrisburg, on the 17th June, 1863. Philadelphia, 1863.

Speech of Hon. Reverdy Johnson, of Maryland: In Support of the Resolution to Amend the Constitution of the United States, April 5, 1864. Washington, D.C., 1864.

Speech of Hon. Robert C. Winthrop, at the Great Ratification Meeting in Union Square, New York, September 17, 1864. New York, 1864.

Thayer, M. Russell. *A Reply to Mr. Charles Ingersoll's "Letter to a Friend in a Slave State."* Philadelphia, 1862.

A Traitor's Peace! A Democratic Workingman. [New York, 1863].

To Working Men. N.p., 1864.

Turpie, David. *Speech of Mr. Turpie Delivered in the Senate of the United States, February 7, 1863.* New York, 1863.

Underwood, John Cox. *Report of Proceedings Incidental to the Erection and Dedication of the Confederate Monument: Reception and Entertainment of Renowned Southern Generals Luncheon and Banquet Given Them at Cincinnati.* Chicago, 1896.

Vallandigham, Clement Laird. *The Great Civil War in America.* Washington, D.C., 1863.

Van Dyke, Henry J. *The Spirituality and Independence of the Church: A Speech Delivered in the Synod of New York, October 18th, 1864.* New York, 1864.

Victory Union Peace. N.p., [1864?].

Williams, John E. *Letter to A.B.J., Author of the Pamphlet Entitled "The Union as It Was and the Constitution as It Is."* New York, 1863.

The Workingman. New York, October 22, 1864.

Personal Papers

Brooks, Noah. *Lincoln Observed: Civil War Dispatches of Noah Brooks.* Edited by Michael Burlingame. Baltimore: Johns Hopkins University Press, 1998.

Daly, Maria Lydig. *Diary of a Union Lady, 1861–1865.* Edited by Harold Earl Hammond. 1962. Reprint, Lincoln: University of Nebraska Press, 2000.

Engs, Robert F., and Corey M. Brooks, eds. *Their Patriotic Duty: The Civil War Letters of the Evans Family of Brown County, Ohio.* New York: Fordham University Press, 2007.

Fisher, Sidney George. *A Philadelphia Perspective: The Civil War Diary of Sidney George Fisher.* Edited by Jonathan W. White. 1967. Reprint, New York: Fordham University Press, 2007.

Hay, John. *Lincoln and the Civil War in the Diaries and Letters of John Hay.* Edited by Tyler Dennett. 1939. Reprint, New York: Da Capo, 1988.

Lincoln, Abraham. *Collected Works of Abraham Lincoln.* 8 vols. Edited by Roy Basler. New Brunswick, N.J.: Rutgers University Press, 1953.

Masur, Louis P., ed. *". . . The Real War Will Never Get in the Books": Selections from Writers during the Civil War.* New York: Oxford University Press, 1995.

Roberts, Timothy Mason, ed. *"This Infernal War": The Civil War Letters of William and Jane Standard.* Kent, Ohio: Kent State University Press, 2017.

McClellan, George B. *The Civil War Papers of George B. McClellan: Selected Correspondence, 1860–1865.* Edited by Stephen W. Sears. New York: Da Capo, 1992.

Sherman, Francis T. *Quest for a Star: The Civil War Letters and Diaries of Colonel Francis T. Sherman of the 88th Illinois.* Edited by C. Knight Aldrich. Knoxville: University of Tennessee Press, 1999.

Strong, George Templeton. *The Diary of George Templeton Strong.* Edited by Allen Nevins and Milton Halsey Thomas. 4 vols. New York: Macmillan, 1952.

Welles, Gideon. *The Civil War Diary of Gideon Welles: Lincoln's Secretary of the Navy.* Edited by William E. Gienapp and Erica L. Gienapp. Urbana: University of Illinois Press, 2014.

Wister, Fanny Kemble, and Sarah Butler Wister. "Sarah Butler Wister's Civil War Diary." *Pennsylvania Magazine of History and Biography* 102 (July 1978): 271–323.

Secondary Sources

Adams, Sean Patrick, ed. *A Companion to the Era of Andrew Jackson.* Oxford: Blackwell, 2013.

Aley, Ginette, and J. L. Anderson, eds. *Union Heartland: The Midwestern Home Front during the Civil War.* Carbondale: Southern Illinois University Press, 2013.

Altschuler, Glenn C., and Stuart M. Blumin. *Rude Republic: Americans and Their Politics in the Nineteenth Century.* Princeton, N.J.: Princeton University Press, 2000.

Andreasen, Byron C. "Civil War Church Trials: Repressing Dissent on the Northern Home Front." In *An Uncommon Time: The Civil War and the Northern Home Front,* edited by Paul A. Cimbala and Randall M. Miller, 214–42. New York: Fordham University Press, 2001.

———. "Lincoln's Religious Critics: Copperhead Christian Reactions and the War." In *Politics and Culture of the Civil War Era: Essays in Honor of Robert W. Johannsen,* edited by Daniel McDonough and Kenneth W. Noe, 199–219. Selinsgrove, Penn.: Susquehanna University Press, 2006.

Astor, Aaron. "The Crouching Lion's Fate: Slavery and Conservative Unionism in Kentucky." *Register of the Kentucky Historical Society* 113 (Autumn 2012): 293–326.

———. *Rebels on the Border: Civil War, Emancipation, and the Reconstruction of Kentucky and Missouri.* Baton Rouge: Louisiana State University Press, 2012.

Bailey, Anne C. *The Weeping Time: Memory and the Largest Slave Auction in American History.* New York: Cambridge University Press, 2017.

Baker, Jean H. *Affairs of Party: The Political Culture of Northern Democrats in the Mid-Nineteenth Century.* 1983. Reprint, New York: Fordham University Press, 1998.

———. "A Loyal Opposition: Northern Democrats in the 37th Congress." *Civil War History* 25 (June 1979): 139–55.

Baum, Dale. *The Civil War Party System: The Case of Massachusetts, 1848–1876.* Chapel Hill: University of North Carolina Press, 1984.

Bernstein, Iver. *The New York City Draft Riots: Their Significance for American Society and Politics in the Age of the Civil War.* New York: Oxford University Press, 1990.

Blair, William A. *With Malice toward Some: Treason and Loyalty in the Civil War Era.* Chapel Hill: University of North Carolina Press, 2014.

Bogue, Allan G. "Bloc and Party in the United States Senate, 1861–1863." *Civil War History* 13 (September 1967): 221–41.

———. *The Congressman's Civil War.* New York: Cambridge University Press, 1989.

———. *The Earnest Men: Republicans of the Civil War Senate.* Ithaca, N.Y.: Cornell University Press, 1981.

Bordewich, Fergus M. *Congress at War: How Republican Reformers Fought the Civil War, Defied Lincoln, Ended Slavery, and Remade America.* New York: Knopf, 2020.

Bowman, Shearer Davis. *In the Precipice: Americans North and South during the Secession Crisis.* Chapel Hill: University of North Carolina Press, 2010.

Boyle, Diane B. *Senators of the United States: A Historical Bibliography: A Compilation of Works by and about Members of the United States Senate, 1789–1995.* Washington, D.C.: Government Printing Office, 1995.

Burlingame, Michael. *Abraham Lincoln: A Life.* 2 vols. Baltimore: Johns Hopkins University Press, 2008.

Burnham, Walter Dean. *Presidential Ballots, 1836–1892.* Baltimore: Johns Hopkins University Press, 1955.

Clinton, Catherine. *Fanny Kemble's Civil Wars.* New York: Simon and Schuster, 2000.

Coleman, Charles H., and Paul H. Spence. "The Charleston Riot, March 28 1864." *Journal of the Illinois State Historical Society* 33 (March 1940): 7–56.

Cook, Adrian. *The Armies of the Streets: The New York City Draft Riots of 1863.* Lexington: University Press of Kentucky, 1982.

Cowden, Joanna D. *"Heaven Will Frown on Such a Cause as This": Six Democrats Who Opposed Lincoln's War.* Lanham, Md.: University Press of America, 2001.

Crane, J. Michael, Jr. "The Demise of Slavery on the Border: Federal Policy and the Union Army in Henderson, Kentucky." *Register of the Kentucky Historical Society* 113 (Autumn 2015): 601–40.

Crofts, Daniel W. *Lincoln and the Politics of Slavery: The Other Thirteenth Amendment and the Struggle to Save the Union.* Chapel Hill: University of North Carolina Press, 2016.

Curry, Jane Kathleen. *Nineteenth-Century American Women Theatre Managers.* Westport, Conn.: Praeger, 1994.

Dell, Christopher. *Lincoln and the War Democrats: The Grand Erosion of Conservative Tradition.* Cranbury, N.J.: Farleigh Dickinson University Press, 1975.

Dew, Charles B. *Apostles of Disunion: Southern Secession Commissioners and the Causes of the Civil War.* Charlottesville: University of Virginia Press, 2002.

Dollar, Kent T., Larry H. Whiteaker, and W. Calvin Dickinson, eds. *Sister States, Enemy States: The Civil War in Kentucky and Tennessee.* Lexington: University Press of Kentucky, 2009.

Donald, David Herbert. *Lincoln.* New York: Simon and Schuster, 1995.

Donald, David Herbert, Jean Harvey Baker, and Michael F. Holt. *The Civil War and Reconstruction.* New York: Norton, 2001.

Dusinberre, William. *Civil War Issues in Philadelphia, 1856–1865.* Philadelphia: University of Pennsylvania Press, 1965.

Engle, Stephen D. *Gathering to Save a Nation: Lincoln and the Union's War Governors.* Chapel Hill: University of North Carolina Press, 2016.

———. "Yankee Dutchmen: Germans, the Union, and the Construction of a Wartime Identity." In *Civil War Citizens: Race, Ethnicity, and Identity in America's Bloodiest Conflict,* edited by Susannah J. Ural, 11–56. New York: New York University Press, 2010.

Escott, Paul D. *The Worst Passions of Human Nature: White Supremacy in the Civil War North.* Charlottesville: University of Virginia Press, 2020.

Etcheson, Nicole. *A Generation at War: The Civil War Era in a Northern Community.* Lawrence: University Press of Kansas, 2011.

Foner, Eric. *The Fiery Trial: Abraham Lincoln and American Slavery.* New York: Norton, 2011.

———. *Reconstruction: America's Unfinished Revolution, 1863–1877.* New York: HarperCollins, 1989.

———. *The Second Founding: How the Civil War and Reconstruction Remade the Constitution.* New York: Norton, 2019.

Freehling, William W. *The Road to Disunion,* vol. 2, *Secessionists Triumphant.* New York: Oxford University Press, 2007.

Friedel, Frank. "The Loyal Publication Society: A Pro-Union Propaganda Agency." *Mississippi Valley Historical Review* 26, no. 3 (December 1939): 359–76.

Frisby, Derek W. "The Vortex of Secession: West Tennesseans and the Rush to War." In *Sister States, Enemy States: The Civil War in Kentucky and Tennessee,* edited by Kent T. Dollar, Larry H. Whiteaker, and W. Calvin Dickinson, 46–71. Lexington: University Press of Kentucky, 2009.

Fuller, A. James. *Oliver Morton and the Politics of the Civil War and Reconstruction.* Kent, Ohio: Kent State University Press, 2017.

Furniss, Jack. "States of the Union: The Rise and Fall of the Political Center in the Civil War North." Ph.D. dissertation, University of Virginia, 2018.

———. "To Save the Union 'in Behalf of Conservative Men': Horatio Seymour and the Democratic Vision for War." In *New Perspectives on the Union War,* edited by Gary W. Gallagher and Elizabeth R. Varon, 147–202. New York: Fordham University Press, 2019.

Gallagher, Gary W. *Becoming Confederates: Paths to a New National Loyalty.* Athens: University of Georgia Press, 2012.

———. *The Union War.* Cambridge, Mass.: Harvard University Press, 2011.

Gallagher, Gary W., and Elizabeth R. Varon, eds. *New Perspectives on the Union War.* New York: Fordham University Press, 2019.

Gallagher, Gary W., and Joan Waugh. *The American War: A History of the Civil War Era.* 2nd edition. State College, Penn.: Flip Learning, 2019.

Gallagher, Gary W., et al. *The American Civil War: The Mighty Scourge of War.* Oxford: Osprey, 2003.

Gallman, J. Matthew. *America's Joan of Arc: The Life of Anna Dickinson.* New York: Oxford University Press, 2006.

———. *Defining Duty in the Civil War: Personal Choice, Popular Culture, and the Union Home Front.* Chapel Hill: University of North Carolina Press, 2015.

———. "The Election of 1864: Revisiting That 'Blind Memo.'" Lecture presented at "Ending a Mighty Conflict: The Civil War in 1864–1865 and Beyond," Huntington Library, San Marino, California, September 2015.

———. "Maria Lydig Daly: *Diary of a Union Lady, 1861–1865.*" In *So Stirring a Time: Civil War Witnesses and Their Books,* edited by Gary Gallagher and Stephen Cushman. Baton Rouge: Louisiana State University Press, forthcoming

———. *Mastering Wartime: A Social History of Philadelphia during the Civil War.* New York: Cambridge University Press, 1990.

———. *The North Fights the Civil War: The Home Front.* Chicago: Ivan Dee, 1994.

———. "Preserving the Peace: Order and Disorder in Civil War Philadelphia." *Pennsylvania History* 55 (October 1988): 201–15.

———. "Voluntarism in Wartime: Philadelphia's Great Central Fair." In *Toward a Social History of the American Civil War,* edited by Maris Vinovskis, 93–116. New York: Cambridge University Press, 1990.

———. "'What Is the Case of "Willie Waller" at Maysville, Kentucky?': The Strange Tale of a Kentucky Rebel." *Register of the Kentucky Historical Society* 17 (Winter 2019): 1–37.

Geary, James W. *We Need Men: The Union Draft in the Civil War.* DeKalb: Northern Illinois University Press. 1991.

George, Joseph, Jr. "'Abraham Africanus I': President Lincoln through the Eyes of a Copperhead Editor." *Civil War History* 14 (September 1968): 226–39.

———. "Philadelphians Greet Their President-Elect." *Pennsylvania History* 29 (October 1962): 381–90.

Glatthaar, Joseph T. *Forged in Battle: The Civil War Alliance of Black Soldiers and White Officers.* New York: Free Press, 1990.

Harris, William C. *Lincoln and the Border States: Preserving the Union.* Lawrence: University Press of Kansas, 2011.

———. *Two against Lincoln: Reverdy Johnson and Horatio Seymour, Champions of the Loyal Opposition.* Lawrence: University Press of Kansas, 2017.

Henkin, David M. *City Reading: Written Words and Public Spaces in Antebellum New York.* New York: Columbia University Press, 1998.

Hess, Earl. *The Civil War in the West: Victory and Defeat from the Appalachians to the Mississippi.* Chapel Hill: University of North Carolina Press, 2012.

Hodes, Martha. *Mourning Lincoln.* New Haven, Conn.: Yale University Press, 2015.

Holm, April E. *A Kingdom Divided: Evangelicals, Loyalty, and Sectionalism in the Civil War Era.* Baton Rouge: Louisiana State University Press, 2017.

Holt, Michael F. *The Election of 1860: "A Campaign Fraught with Consequences."* Lawrence: University Press of Kansas, 2017.

Holzer, Harold. *Lincoln and the Power of the Press.* New York: Simon and Schuster, 2014.

Howe, Daniel Walker. *What Hath God Wrought: The Transformation of America, 1815–1848.* New York: Oxford University Press, 2007.

Jeffrey, Julie Roy. "'They Cannot Expect . . . That a Loyal People Will Tolerate the Utterance of Such Sentiments': The Campaign against Treasonous Speech during the Civil War." *Civil War History* 65 (March 2019): 7–42.

Johannsen, Robert W. *Stephen A. Douglas.* New York: Oxford University Press, 1973.

Karamanski, Theodore. *Rally 'Round the Flag: Chicago and the Civil War.* Chicago: Nelson-Hall, 1993.

Keating, Ryan W. "Perspectives on Irish American Loyalty and Patriotism in the Wake of the New York City Draft Riots." In *Contested Loyalty: Debates over Patriotism in the Civil War North,* edited by Robert M. Sandow, 239–67. New York: Fordham University Press, 2018.

Klement, Frank. "Copperheads and Copperheadism in Wisconsin: Democratic Opposition to the Lincoln Administration." *Wisconsin Magazine of History* 42, no. 3 (Spring 1959): 182–88.

———. *Copperheads in the Middle West.* Chicago: University of Chicago Press, 1960.

———. *Dark Lanterns: Secret Political Societies, Conspiracies, and Treason Trials in the Civil War.* Baton Rouge: Louisiana State University Press, 1984.

———. *Wisconsin in the Civil War: The Home Front and the Battle Front, 1861–1865.* Madison: State Historical Society of Wisconsin, 1997.

Knupfer, Peter B. *Union as It Is: Constitutional Unionism and Sectional Compromise, 1787–1861.* Chapel Hill: University of North Carolina Press, 1991.

Kurtz, William B. *Excommunicated from the Union: How the Civil War Created a Separate Catholic America.* New York: Fordham University Press, 2016.

———. "The Union as It Was: Northern Catholics' Conservative Unionism." In *New Perspectives on the Union War,* edited by Gary W. Gallagher and Elizabeth R. Varon, 91–113. New York: Fordham University Press, 2019.

Landis, Michael Todd. *Northern Men with Southern Loyalties: The Democratic Party and the Sectional Crisis.* Ithaca, N.Y.: Cornell University Press, 2014.

Lane, Roger. *Policing the City, 1822–1885.* New York: Cambridge University Press. 1967.

Larsen, Lawrence H. "Draft Riot in Wisconsin, 1862." *Civil War History* 7, no. 4 (December 1961): 421–27.

Larson, Ronald Paul. *Wisconsin and the Civil War.* Charleston, S.C.: History Press, 2017.

Lause, Mark A. *A Secret Society History of the Civil War.* Urbana: University of Illinois Press, 2012.

Lawson, Melinda. *Patriotic Fires: Forging a New American Nationalism in the Civil War North.* Lawrence: University Press of Kansas, 2002.

Lee, Jacob F. "Unionism, Emancipation, and the Origins of Kentucky's Confederate Identity." *Register of the Kentucky Historical Association* 111 (Spring 2013): 199–233.

Lemire, Elise. *"Miscegenation": Making Race in America.* Philadelphia: University of Pennsylvania Press, 2001.

Leonard, Elizabeth D. *Lincoln's Forgotten Ally: Judge Advocate General Joseph Holt of Kentucky.* Chapel Hill: University of North Carolina Press, 2011.

———. *Slaves, Slaveholders, and a Kentucky Community's Struggle toward Freedom.* Lexington: University Press of Kentucky, 2019.

Levine, Peter. "Draft Evasion in the North during the Civil War, 1863–1865." *Journal of American History* 67 (March 1981): 816–34.

Levy, Ronald. "Bishop Hopkins and the Dilemma of Slavery." *Pennsylvania Magazine of History and Biography* 91 (January 1967): 56–71.

Lewis, Patrick A. *For Slavery and Union: Benjamin Buckner and Kentucky Loyalties in the Civil War.* Lexington: University Press of Kentucky, 2015.

Lindsey, David. "The Presidential Campaign of 1864 as Viewed by a Federal Army Colonel." *Georgia Historical Quarterly* 39, no. 2 (June 1955): 187–92.

Longdon, William Henry, and Ronald Lora, eds. *The Conservative Press in Eighteenth- and Nineteenth-Century America.* Westport, Conn.: Greenwood, 1999.

Maizlish, Stephen E. "Race and Politics in the Northern Democracy, 1854–1860." In *New Perspectives on Race and Slavery in America: Essays in Honor of Kenneth M. Stampp,* edited by Robert H. Abzug and Stephen E. Maizlish, 79–90. Lexington: University Press of Kentucky, 1986.

Marshall, Anne. "A 'Sister's War': Kentucky Women and Their Civil War Diaries." *Register of the Kentucky Historical Society* 110 (Summer–Autumn 2012): 481–502.

"Mayors of Chicago." Chicago Public Library. https://www.chipublib.org/mayor-francis-cornwall-sherman-biography/.

McDonough, Daniel, and Kenneth W. Noe, eds. *Politics and Culture of the Civil War Era: Essays in Honor of Robert W. Johannsen.* Selingsgrove, Penn.: Susquehanna University Press, 2006.

McGerr, Michael E. *The Decline of Popular Politics: The American North, 1865–1928.* New York: Oxford University Press, 1986.

McJimsey, George T. *Genteel Partisan: Manton Marble, 1834–1917.* Ames: Iowa State University Press, 1971.

McKenzie, Robert Tracy. "'An Unconditional, Straight-Out Union Man': Parson Brownlow and the Secession Crisis in East Tennessee." In *Sister States, Enemy States: The Civil War in Kentucky and Tennessee,* edited by Kent T. Dollar, Larry H. Whiteaker, and W. Calvin Dickinson, 72–96. Lexington: University Press of Kentucky, 2009.

McKnight, Brian D. "'Time by the Forelock': Champ Ferguson and the Borderland Style of Warfare." In *Sister States, Enemy States: The Civil War in Kentucky and Tennessee,* edited by Kent T. Dollar, Larry H. Whiteaker, and W. Calvin Dickinson, 140–67. Lexington: University Press of Kentucky, 2009.

McPherson, James M. *Battle Cry of Freedom: The Civil War Era.* New York: Oxford University Press, 1988.

———. *For Cause and Comrades: Why Men Fought in the Civil War.* New York: Oxford University Press, 1997.

McPherson, James M., and James Hogue. *Ordeal by Fire: The Civil War and Reconstruction.* 4th edition. New York: McGraw Hill, 2010.

Medord, Edna Greene. *Lincoln and Emancipation.* Carbondale: Southern Illinois University Press, 2015.

Montgomery, David. *Beyond Equality: Labor and the Radical Republicans, 1862–1872.* New York: Vintage, 1967.

Mott, Frank Luther. *A History of American Magazines, 1850–1865.* Cambridge, Mass.: Harvard University Press, 1938.

Mujic, Julie A. "'We Are Setting the Terms Now': Loyalty Rhetoric in Courtship." In *Contested Loyalty: Debates over Patriotism in the Civil War North,* edited by Robert M. Sandow, 107–36. New York: Fordham University Press, 2018.

Murdock, Eugene C. *One Million Men: The Civil War Draft in the North.* Madison: State Historical Society of Wisconsin, 1971.

Neely, Mark E., Jr. *The Boundaries of American Political Culture in the Civil War Era.* Chapel Hill: University of North Carolina Press, 2005.

———. "The Civil War and the Two-Party System." In *"We Cannot Escape History": Lincoln and the Last Best Hope of Earth,* edited by James M. McPherson, 86–104. Urbana: University of Illinois Press, 1995.

———. *The Fate of Liberty: Abraham Lincoln and Civil Liberties.* New York: Oxford University Press, 1991.

———. *Lincoln and the Democrats: The Politics of Opposition in the Civil War.* New York: Cambridge University Press, 2017.

———. *Lincoln and the Triumph of the Nation: Constitutional Conflict in the American Civil War.* Chapel Hill: University of North Carolina Press 2011.

———. *The Union Divided: Party Conflict in the Civil War North.* Cambridge, Mass.: Harvard University Press, 2002.

Nevins, Allan. *Ordeal of the Union.* 8 vols. New York: Scribners, 1947–71.

Oakes, James. *Freedom National: The Destruction of Slavery in the United States, 1861–1865.* New York: Norton, 2013.

Orr, Timothy. "An Army Divided: Party Politics Inside the Army of the Potomac." Lecture presented at the Civil War Institute, Gettysburg College, June 2019.

———. "Protesting the McClellan Testimonial: Photographing the 119th Pennsylvania, Part 3." Tales from the Army of the Potomac. May 22, 2019. http://talesfromaop.blogspot.com/2019/05/protesting-mcclellan-testimonial.html.

Paludan, Phillip Shaw. *Victims: A True Story of the Civil War.* Knoxville: University of Tennessee Press, 1981.

Pflug, Oliver L. "Pennsylvania Politics, 1854–1860." Master's thesis, University of Montana, 2002.

Phillips, Christopher. *The Rivers Ran Backward: The Civil War and the Remaking of the American Middle Border.* New York: Oxford University Press, 2016.

Randall, James G. *Lincoln the President,* vol. 2, *Springfield to Gettysburg.* New York: Da Capo, 1946.

Rawley, James A. *The Politics of Union: Northern Politics during the Civil War.* Lincoln: University of Nebraska Press, 1980.

———. *Turning Points of the Civil War.* Lincoln: University of Nebraska Press, 1966.

Redd, Rea Andrew. "The Election of 1864." In *Turning Points of the American Civil War,* edited by Chris Mackowski and Kristopher D. White, 211–29. Carbondale: Southern Illinois University Press, 2018.

Refuse, Ethan. *McClellan's War.* Bloomington: Indiana University Press, 2005.

Richardson, Heather Cox. *West after Appomattox: The Reconstruction of America after the Civil War.* New Haven, Conn.: Yale University Press, 2007.

Rodgers, Thomas E. "Copperheads or a Respectable Minority: Current Approaches to the Study of Civil War-Era Democrats." *Indiana Magazine of History* 31 (June 2013): 114–46.

Ruehlen, Christopher Ronald. "The Specter of Subversion: Fears, Perceptions, and Reactions to Dissent in the Civil War North." Ph.D. dissertation, University of Florida, 2014.

Samito, Christian G. *Becoming American under Fire: Irish Americans, African Americans, and the Politics of Citizenship during the Civil War Era.* Ithaca, N.Y.: Cornell University Press, 2009.

Sandow, Robert M., ed. *Contested Loyalty: Debates over Patriotism in the Civil War North.* New York: Fordham University Press, 2018.

———. "Damnable Treason or Party Organs: Democratic Secret Societies in Pennsylvania." In *This Distracted and Anarchical People,* edited by Andrew L. Slap and Michael Thomas Smith, 42–59. New York: Fordham University Press, 2013.

———. *Deserter Country: Civil War Opposition in the Pennsylvania Appalachians.* New York: Fordham University Press, 2009.

Schneider, John C. "Detroit and the Problem of Disorder: The Riot of 1863." *Michigan History* 38 (Spring 1974): 4–24.

Schwalm, Leslie A. "'Overrun with Free Negroes': Emancipation and Wartime Migration in the Upper Midwest." *Civil War History* 50 (June 2004): 145–74.

Scott, Sean A. "William S. Plumer's Defense of an Apolitical Pulpit." In *Contested Loyalty: Debates over Patriotism in the Civil War North,* edited by Robert M. Sandow, 168–97. New York: Fordham University Press, 2018.

Sears, Stephen W. *George B. McClellan: The Young Napoleon.* 1988. Reprint, New York: Da Capo, 1998.

Shankman, Arnold M. *The Pennsylvania Antiwar Movement, 1861–1865.* Rutherford, N.J.: Fairleigh Dickinson University Press, 1980.

———. "William B. Reed and the Civil War." *Pennsylvania History* 39 (October 1972): 455–69.

Shelden, Rachel A. *Washington Brotherhood: Politics, Social Life, and the Coming of the Civil War.* Chapel Hill: University of North Carolina Press, 2013.

Silber, Nina. *Daughters of the Union: Northern Women Fight the Civil War.* Cambridge, Mass.: Harvard University Press, 2005.

Silbey, Joel H. *A Respectable Minority: The Democratic Party in the Civil War Era, 1860–1868.* New York: Norton, 1977.

Smith, Adam I. P. "Beyond the Realignment Synthesis: The 1860 Election Reconsidered." In *America at the Ballot Box: Elections and Political History,* edited by D. Davies and J. Zelizer, 59–74. Philadelphia: University of Pennsylvania Press, 2015.

———. *No Party Now: Politics in the Civil War North.* New York: Oxford University Press, 2006.

———. *The Stormy Present: Conservativism and the Problem of Slavery in Northern Politics, 1846–1865.* Chapel Hill: University of North Carolina Press, 2017.

Spann, Edward K. *Gotham at War: New York City, 1860–1865.* Wilmington, Del.: Scholarly Resources, 2002.

Stout, Harry S. *Upon the Altar of the Nation: A Moral History of the Civil War.* New York: Viking, 2006.

Summers, Mark Wahlgren. *The Ordeal of the Reunion: A New History of Reconstruction.* Chapel Hill: University of North Carolina Press, 2014.

Sutherland, Daniel. *Savage Conflict: The Decisive Role of Guerrillas in the American Civil War.* Chapel Hill: University of North Carolina Press, 2009.

Taylor, Amy Murrell. *The Divided Family in Civil War America.* Chapel Hill: University of North Carolina Press, 2005.

Taylor, Paul. *"The Most Complete Political Machine Ever Known": The North's Union Leagues in the American Civil War.* Kent, Ohio: Kent State University Press, 2019.

Tenney, Craig D. "To Suppress or Not to Suppress: Abraham Lincoln and the Chicago Times." *Civil War History* 27 (September 1981): 248–59.

Thompson, E. Bruce. *Matthew Hale Carpenter: Webster of the West.* Madison: State Historical Society of Wisconsin, 1954.

Thompson, William Y. "Sanitary Fairs in the Civil War." *Civil War History* 4 (1958): 51–67.

Towers, Frank. "Party Politics and the Sectional Crisis: A Twenty-Year Renaissance in the Study of Antebellum Political History." In *The Routledge History of Nineteenth-Century America,* edited by Jonathan Daniel Wells, 109–30. New York: Routledge, 2017.

Towne, Stephen E. "Killing the Serpent Speedily: Governor Morton, General Hascall, and the Suppression of the Democratic Press in Indiana, 1863." *Civil War History* 52 (April 2006): 41–65.

Turner, Thomas Reed. *Beware the People Weeping: Public Opinion and the Assassination of Abraham Lincoln.* Baton Rouge: Louisiana State University Press, 1982.

Ural, Susannah J. "'Ye Sons of Green Erin Assemble': Northern Irish American Catholics and the Union War Effort, 1861–1865." In *Civil War Citizens: Race, Ethnicity, and Identity in America's Bloodiest Conflict,* edited by Susannah J. Ural, 99–132. New York: New York University Press, 2010.

Varon, Elizabeth R. *Appomattox: Victory, Defeat, and Freedom at the End of the Civil War.* New York: Oxford University Press, 2013.

———. *Armies of Deliverance: A New History of the Civil War.* New York: Oxford University Press, 2019.

Venet, Wendy Hamand. *Neither Ballots nor Bullets: Women Abolitionists and the Civil War.* Charlottesville: University Press of Virginia, 1991.

Vorenberg, Michael. *Final Freedom: The Civil War, the Abolition of Slavery, and the Thirteenth Amendment.* New York: Cambridge University Press, 2001.

Wachtell, Cynthia. *War No More: The Anti-War Impulse in American Literature, 1861–1914.* Baton Rouge: Louisiana State University Press, 2010.

Wainwright, Nicholas B. "The Loyal Opposition in Civil War Philadelphia." *Pennsylvania Magazine of History and Biography* 88, no. 3 (July 1964): 294–315.

Warshauer, Matthew. *Connecticut in the American Civil War: Slavery, Sacrifice, and Survival.* Middletown, Conn.: Wesleyan University Press, 2011.

Waugh, John C. *Reelecting Lincoln: The Battle for the 1864 Presidency.* New York: Da Capo, 1997.

Weber, Jennifer L. *Copperheads: The Rise and Fall of Lincoln's Opponents in the North.* New York: Oxford University Press, 2001.

———. "The Political Culture of the North: Party Politics of Nation." In *The War Worth Fighting: Abraham Lincoln's Presidency and Civil War America,* edited by Stephen D. Engle, 91–109. Gainesville: University Press of Florida, 2015.

Weigley, Russell F., ed. *Philadelphia: A 300-Year History.* New York: Norton, 1982.

Wesley, Timothy L. *The Politics of Faith during the Civil War.* Baton Rouge: Louisiana State University Press, 2013.

White, Jonathan W. *Abraham Lincoln and Treason in the Civil War: The Trials of John Merryman.* Baton Rouge: Louisiana State University Press, 2011.

———. *Emancipation, the Union Army, and the Reelection of Abraham Lincoln.* Baton Rouge: Louisiana State University Press, 2014.

White, Ronald C., Jr. *Lincoln's Greatest Speech: The Second Inaugural.* New York: Simon and Schuster, 2006.

Wood, Forrest G. *Black Scare.* Los Angeles: University of California Press, 1968.

INDEX

RECENT BOOKS IN THE SERIES

A Nation Divided: Studies in the Civil War Era

My Work among the Freedmen: The Civil War and Reconstruction Letters of Harriet M. Buss
EDITED BY JONATHAN W. WHITE AND LYDIA J. DAVIS

Colossal Ambitions: Confederate Planning for a Post–Civil War World
ADRIAN BRETTLE

Newest Born of Nations: European Nationalist Movements and the Making of the Confederacy
ANN L. TUCKER

The Worst Passions of Human Nature: White Supremacy in the Civil War North
PAUL D. ESCOTT

Preserving the White Man's Republic: Jacksonian Democracy, Race, and the Transformation of American Conservatism
JOSHUA A. LYNN

American Abolitionism: Its Direct Political Impact from Colonial Times into Reconstruction
STANLEY HARROLD

A Strife of Tongues: The Compromise of 1850 and the Ideological Foundations of the American Civil War
STEPHEN E. MAIZLISH

The First Republican Army: The Army of Virginia and the Radicalization of the Civil War
JOHN H. MATSUI

War upon Our Border: Two Ohio Valley Communities Navigate the Civil War
STEPHEN I. ROCKENBACH

Gold and Freedom: The Political Economy of Reconstruction
NICOLAS BARREYRE, TRANSLATED BY ARTHUR GOLDHAMMER

Daydreams and Nightmares: A Virginia Family Faces Secession and War
BRENT TARTER

Intimate Reconstructions: Children in Postemancipation Virginia
CATHERINE A. JONES

Lincoln's Dilemma: Blair, Sumner, and the Republican Struggle over Racism and Equality in the Civil War Era
PAUL D. ESCOTT

Slavery and War in the Americas: Race, Citizenship, and State Building in the United States and Brazil, 1861–1870
VITOR IZECKSOHN

Marching Masters: Slavery, Race, and the Confederate Army during the Civil War
COLIN EDWARD WOODWARD

Confederate Visions: Nationalism, Symbolism, and the Imagined South in the Civil War
IAN BINNINGTON

Frederick Douglass: A Life in Documents
L. DIANE BARNES, EDITOR

Reconstructing the Campus: Higher Education and the American Civil War
MICHAEL DAVID COHEN

Worth a Dozen Men: Women and Nursing in the Civil War South
LIBRA R. HILDE